POVERTY AND SOCIAL EXCLUSION IN THE UK

Volume 2 – The dimensions of disadvantage

Edited by Glen Bramley and Nick Bailey

First published in Great Britain in 2018 by

Policy Press
University of Bristol
1-9 Old Park Hill
Bristol
BS2 8BB
UK
t: +44 (0)117 954 5940
pp-info@bristol.ac.uk
www.policypress.co.uk

North America office:
Policy Press
c/o The University of Chicago Press
1427 East 60th Street
Chicago, IL 60637, USA
t: +1 773 702 7700
f: +1 773-702-9756
sales@press.uchicago.edu
www.press.uchicago.edu

© Policy Press 2018

British Library Cataloguing in Publication Data
A catalogue record for this book is available from the British Library

Library of Congress Cataloging-in-Publication Data
A catalog record for this book has been requested

978-1-4473-3422-4 hardback
978-1-4473-3427-9 paperback
978-1-4473-3426-2 ePdf
978-1-4473-3428-6 ePub
978-1-4473-3429-3 Mobi

The rights of Glen Bramley and Nick Bailey to be identified as editors of this work has been asserted by them in accordance with the Copyright, Designs and Patents Act 1988.

Cover design by Hayes Design
Front cover image: Timm Sonnenschein/Report digital
Printed and bound in Great Britain by CPI Group (UK) Ltd, Croydon, CR0 4YY
Policy Press uses environmentally responsible print partners

Contents

List of tables and figures   iv
Glossary   viii
Notes on contributors   xii
Acknowledgements   xv

Introduction   1
Nick Bailey and Glen Bramley

Part 1: Resources   25

one   Fifty years of poverty in the UK   27
Joanna Mack

two   Living standards in the UK   57
Demi Patsios, Marco Pomati and Paddy Hillyard

three   Severe poverty and destitution   91
Glen Bramley, Suzanne Fitzpatrick and Filip Sosenko

four   Poverty, local services and austerity   113
Glen Bramley and Kirsten Besemer

Part 2: Participation   135

five   Social participation and social support   137
Lisa Wilson, Eldin Fahmy and Nick Bailey

six   Employment, poverty and social exclusion   159
Nick Bailey

seven   Poverty, social exclusion and civic engagement   179
Eldin Fahmy

Part 3: Quality of life   201

eight   Poverty and health: thirty years of progress?   203
Lucy Prior and David Manley

nine   Housing and the living environment   225
Glen Bramley

ten   Poverty and social harm: challenging discourses of risk,   245
resilience and choice
Simon Pemberton, Christina Pantazis and Paddy Hillyard

eleven   Financial inclusion, financial stress and debt   267
Glen Bramley and Kirsten Besemer

twelve   The poverty of well-being   289
Mike Tomlinson and Lisa Wilson

Part 4: Bringing it together   309

thirteen   The multidimensional analysis of social exclusion   311
Nick Bailey, Eldin Fahmy and Jonathan Bradshaw

fourteen   Conclusions and emerging themes   343
Glen Bramley and Nick Bailey

Index   363

List of tables and figures

*All tables and figures in this book are based on the PSE–UK survey
and are therefore for 2012 unless otherwise indicated.*

Tables

0.1	Public attitudes to and proportions lacking adult and household necessities, UK 2012	7
0.2	Public attitudes to and proportions of children lacking child necessities	9
0.3	Deprivation by age group	12
0.4	Classification on the PSE-UK poverty measure by age group	13
0.5	Subjective poverty and living standards measures	14
1.1	Attitudes to necessities for adults, Britain: 1983, 1990, 1999, 2012	32
1.2	Attitudes to child necessities, Britain: 1999 and 2012	34
1.3	Percentages unable to participate in activities seen as necessities: UK, 2012	38
1.4	The factors which are important in preventing non-participation in activities	39
1.5	Percentages unable to afford necessities, 1983, 1990, 1999, 2012	43
1.6	Households going without: 1999 and 2012	44
2.1	UK-LS framework of domains, dimensions and indicators	63
2.2	Median dimension scores in 'what we have' domain by household type	66
2.3	Relationships between objective and subjective dimension scores on 'what we have' domain	68
2.4	Zapf's typology of welfare positions	69
2.5	'What we have' domain scores (objective and subjective) by poverty measures	75
2.6	Proportion of bottom decile on 'what we have' domain (objective and subjective) identified as poor	76
A2.1	Brand's (2007) dimensions in different models of objective multidimensional individual welfare	86
3.1	Problems/issues experienced in last 12 months by destitute service users in three main demographic sub-groups	103
4.1	Effects of neighbourhood deprivation on local service usage constraints	124
4.2	Overlap between social exclusion, economic deprivation and other domains of deprivation (percent of households experiencing both of each pair of deprivations, as proportion of households experiencing either)	126

List of tables and figures

5.1	The prevalence of common social activities in the UK, 2012 (%)	146
6.1	Characteristics of those in exclusionary employment	166
6.2	Percentage reporting other aspects of exclusion by exclusionary employment status	169
7.1	Indicators of political participation, civic engagement and political efficacy in the 2012 PSE-UK survey	184
7.2	PSE poverty and political engagement in the UK (%)	188
7.3	The probability of political disengagement by poverty status: PSE, subjective, deprivation and income poverty (relative risk ratios: ref=poor)	189
7.4	Poverty, political action and perceptions of civic efficacy in the UK: PSE, subjective, deprivation and income poverty measures (relative risk ratios: ref=poor)	191
7.5	The determinants of civic and political action in the UK (logistic regression odds ratios)	194
9.1	Proportion of households experiencing housing deprivations which are counted within general material deprivation index	228
9.2	Proportion of households experiencing other housing-related problems in 1999 and 2012	229
10.1	Percent of adults experiencing physical harms in the previous 12 months	252
10.2	Percent of adults experiencing financial harms in the previous 12 months	254
10.3	Percent of adults expressing that they are fairly or very worried about possibility of experiencing financial harms	255
10.4	Percent of adults reporting misrecognition in the previous 12 months	258
10.5	Percent of adults reporting going without social participation because they cannot afford activity	261
11.1	Key financial exclusion measures over time and by poverty status (percent within each year/poverty group)	273
11.2	Lenders used for borrowing to meet day-to-day needs, 1999 and 2012 and by poverty indicator (percent of households within each year/poverty group)	274
12.1	Satisfaction with life by income poverty, deprivation and combined income and deprivation poverty	296
12.2	PSE poverty and low satisfaction	297
12.3	PSE poverty and dissatisfaction	298
12.4	Subjective poverty and satisfaction	299
12.5	Low satisfaction rates for key social variables	301
12.6	Binary logistic regression results for factors associated with low satisfaction with life	302
13.1	Social exclusion domains and indicators, UK	316
13.2	Social exclusion in Britain, 1999 and 2012	318

13.3	The prevalence of social exclusion by B-SEM domain and selected respondent characteristics	324
13.4	Social exclusion factor scores by selected respondent characteristics	326
13.5	Relationships between domains of social exclusion, relative risk ratios	329
13.6	Relationships between dimensions of exclusion, factor score correlations	330
13.7	Levels of exclusion on domains by poverty status	331
13.8	Levels of exclusion on dimensions by poverty status	332
A13.1	Sub-domain scores and indicators for factor analysis	340

Figures

0.1	The Bristol Social Exclusion Matrix (B-SEM)	16
1.1	Relative income poverty using 60% median and 50% mean incomes, before and after housing costs: 1961-2015/16, Britain	40
1.2	Rise in absolute and relative deprivation: adults, Britain	46
2.1	Welfare typologies for 'what we have' domain by household type	70
2.2	Housing and local area conditions by economic resources, selected household types and gender	72
2.3	Participation in social activities by housing and local area conditions (objective), selected household types and gender	73
2.4	Objective dimension scores in 'what we have' domain (bottom versus top deciles) by household type	77
3.1	Severe poverty timelines 1996-2012, based on UK Household Longitudinal Surveys and Family Resource Survey (FRS) (working age only)	96
3.2	Household types of destitute service users compared with severe poverty group and UK households	100
3.3	Estimated annual destitution rates by local authority district (% of households)	102
3.4	Sources of financial support for destitute service users in past month by main sub-groups	105
4.1	Proportion of people thinking different local services are 'essential' in 1990, 1999 and 2011	115
4.2	Change in usage of services of general interest, Great Britain, 1999-2012 (percentage point changes in usage rates)	116
4.3	Usage of children's services, 1999 and 2012	118
4.4	Usage rate by income quartile for selected services, 2012	119
5.1	Social contact, communications and constraints (logistic regression models)	143

5.2	Low participation in social activities (one or none out of eight) (logistic regression models)	147
5.3	Low support and low satisfaction with personal relationships (logistic regression models)	151
6.1	Health and well-being by level of exclusionary employment	170
6.2	Social networks and social participation by level of exclusionary employment	172
6.3	Housing and neighbourhood environment by level of exclusionary employment	174
6.4	Relationships between exclusionary employment and other forms of exclusion	175
8.1	Percentage of adults with bad general health and LLTI by poverty definition	206
8.2	Predicted probability of being in bad health (by log income and deprivation index)	208
8.3	Percentage of adults with bad health and LLTI by history of poverty	209
8.4	Percentage of adults with poor mental states and reporting a chronic mental health condition by poverty definition	213
8.5	Predicted mental health score (by log income and deprivation index)	214
8.6	Percentage of adults with poor mental states by social resources	218
9.1	Changes in poverty risk and affordability problems, and PSE poverty by household type, 1999-2012	227
9.2	Selected housing needs incidence by time period, GB 1991-2011	230
9.3	Core housing needs by broad household type and tenure, UK 2012	232
9.4	Core and wider fuel poverty impact by severity of poverty or financial pressure	237
9.5	Neighbourhood problem scores by urban, rural, individual and area poverty levels	239
11.1	Households with arrears/'behind' by type of bill/payment, 1999 and 2012 (percent)	276
11.2	Households with arrears/'behind' by type of bill/payment and degree of poverty (percent)	277
11.3	Indicators of financial pressure by poverty, financial exclusion, household type and tenure	278
11.4	What households cut back on 'often' by poverty and financial pressure status (percent)	280
12.1	Average satisfaction with life scores by number of deprivation items lacking (all individuals)	297
12.2	Overall life satisfaction by income quintiles	299

Glossary

After Housing Costs (AHC) poverty – a relative low-income poverty measure, defined as below 60 per cent of median equivalised net household income after deduction of housing costs (mortgage or rent, maintenance, insurance, property tax).

At-risk-of-poverty (AROP) – an alternative name for the relative low-income poverty measures.

Austerity – the policy of significant real cuts in public expenditure on services and welfare adopted after 2010 by UK and certain other governments, in order to attempt to reduce public sector deficits (along with, or in place of, the alternative strategy of raising taxes).

Basic bank accounts – simple bank accounts which enable customers to deposit money, receive payments, and make payments via a debit card or direct debit, without overdraft or credit facilities and with no charges.

Before Housing Costs (BHC) poverty – a relative low-income poverty measure, defined as below 60 per cent of median equivalised net household income before deduction of housing costs.

Deprivation – a poverty measure based on whether people lack a number of items (goods, services, activities) which they would like to have or do, because they cannot afford them. The items are termed 'necessities' because a majority of people in the UK agree that everyone should have access to these and no one should have to go without.

Equivalised income – household income adjusted to take account of the size and composition of the household, so that incomes are comparable across different household types.

Exclusionary employment – the situation for people who are in paid work but suffering forms exclusion which arise from their employment: where pay and conditions are such that individuals remain in poverty, or they are in low quality work, or have low security.

Financial exclusion – a general concept to describe the process by which social groups and individuals are excluded from access to financial services, including loans, bank accounts and insurance.

Financial inclusion – policies and practices which enable all members of society to obtain access to financial services, including non-exploitative forms of lending; the opposite of financial exclusion.

Financial stress – households reporting subjective indicators of financial pressure, including reporting that: it is 'a constant struggle' to keep up with bills or that they are not keeping up; that they could not meet a major expense of £500; they cannot spend money on self; or that their income is a lot below the amount they consider they need to avoid poverty.

Financialisation – a general process by which financial institutions, markets and services become more embedded in different aspects of social, institutional as well as economic life, including more extensive use of credit and debt.

Fuel poverty – households who are poor because of, or have their poverty exacerbated by, a relatively high level of energy costs required to maintain a standard temperature regime in their home, given its energy-efficiency characteristics.

Housing affordability – this problem arises when housing costs represent an excessive burden on incomes, and may be measured by various ratios including housing costs to income, residual income after housing costs against a standard related to household composition, AHC poverty (see entry above), or subjective indicators of payment problems.

Informal borrowing – household use of pawnbrokers, cash converters, moneylenders, payday loans, unlicensed lenders, friends or family as a source of borrowing to meet day-to-day needs.

Logistic regression (model) – a statistical technique for separating out the associations between multiple variables (independent variables) and a single 'outcome' (dependent) variable which has just two categories (e.g. poor/not poor). In these models, the regression coefficient (B) reports the strength of the relationship between each independent variable and the dependent variable, after the effects of the other independent variables has been removed.

Low income poverty – a household is judged to be in low income poverty where its equivalised income is below a particular threshold. Thresholds may be set by an explicit calculation of the minimum income needed to achieve a given standard of living or, more commonly, by selecting a (more or less arbitrary) level in relation to the average or median income for a society as a whole. In the UK, for example, the most commonly used low-income poverty measure is 60% of median household income.

National Statistics Socio-Economic Classification (NS-SEC) – the official UK classification of individuals' socio-economic status based on their occupation, widely used for publication of statistics data including that from the Census 2011. (Details provided in: Rose, D., Pevalin, D.J., and O'Reilly, K. (2005) *The NS-SEC: Origins, development and use*, London: Palgrave.)

Poverty – the situation that arises where an individual has insufficient resources to achieve a minimum standard of living or consumption. Absolute poverty focuses on the ability to sustain life in a biological sense notably through minimum standards of diet, clothing or shelter. Relative poverty focuses on the ability to sustain life as a social being and a member of a society with social norms and expectations.

Precarity – a term which highlights insecurity and uncertainty as issues for social welfare. It is associated in particular with insecurity in the labour market, and the rise of temporary and 'flexible' forms of work. It draws attention to both the material and the psychological impacts for individual welfare.

Pro-poor services – services used relatively more by lower income or poorer groups (pro-rich being the opposite case).

Problem debt – being behind or in arrears on regular payment commitments, including mortgage/rent, council tax, fuel or phone bills, bank loans, HP, credit card or other loans.

PSE poverty – a measure of poverty that judges individuals as poor where they are both deprived and on a low income.

Residualisation – a process whereby social rented housing has become increasingly a tenure occupied by poorer and more disadvantaged households, and perceived as such by the wider public.

Service constraint – where households report a service to be inadequate, unavailable or unaffordable, regardless of whether they use it or not.

Service exclusion – households not using 3 or more out of 25 general or demographically relevant local public and private services, because they are unavailable, inadequate, or unaffordable.

Service of general interest (SGI) – services provided by local government, other public bodies, or a regulated private sector which are universally available to all within a geographical area.

Social exclusion – a term for individual welfare that generally refers to a broader or more multidimensional set of conditions than poverty. People can be excluded in multiple ways, not just through a lack of resources but also by discrimination or stigmatisation. Exclusion can be judged not just by living standards or consumption, but by the ability to participate in society or enjoy a decent quality of life.

Social housing – rented housing provided at subsidised or sub-market rent levels on a secure, regulated basis by local authorities or (mainly) non-profit housing associations, to households selected on a basis of need.

Social support – the capacity of our social networks of family and friends to provide emotional, material or practical assistance. It can be measured in terms of the specific support that has been provided or in terms of our beliefs about how much support we could access if we needed to.

Subjective poverty – measures where the individual is asked to judge for themselves whether they are in poverty or not. These contrast with the more widely used objective-measures, which are based on information about incomes or deprivations.

Well-being – a term that focuses on an individual's subjective assessment of their welfare. Often closely related to 'happiness', it draws attention to individual perceptions and experiences in contrast to objective measures such as those provided by income or deprivation.

Notes on contributors

Glen Bramley is Professor of Urban Studies based in the Institute for Social Policy, Housing and Equalities Research at Heriot-Watt University in Edinburgh. His recent research has focused on planning for new housing, housing affordability, social sustainability and aspects of poverty, including destitution, homelessness, access to services and the costs of poverty. He has published several books and numerous journal articles. From 2006 to 2010 he was on the Board of the National Housing and Planning Advice Unit, and from 2010 to 2014 part of the PSE-UK (Poverty and Social Exclusion UK Survey 2012) research team.

Nick Bailey is Professor of Urban Studies based in the School of Social and Political Sciences at the University of Glasgow. He has published in the fields of housing and urban policy, as well as in poverty, and has advised national and local government on the analysis of poverty and social exclusion. In addition to his involvement in the PSE-UK research team, he has more recently played a leading role in the development of research using administrative data, through both the Urban Big Data Centre at Glasgow, and the Administrative Data Research Centre for Scotland.

Kirsten Besemer is a Postdoctoral Research Fellow in the School of Criminology and Criminal Justice at Griffith University, Australia, working on research into vulnerable families. She contributed to the PSE work on local services and financial exclusion.

Jonathan Bradshaw, CBE FBA, is Emeritus Professor of Social Policy at the University of York. He was a PI (Principal Investigator) on the PSE project responsible for the child poverty analysis. His research is focused on child poverty, child benefits and comparative social policy and he is a Trustee of the Child Poverty Action Group and a Fellow of the British Academy.

Eldin Fahmy is a Senior Lecturer in the School of Policy Studies at Bristol University and Head of the Centre for the Study of Poverty and Social Justice. His current research focuses on poverty and social exclusion in the UK and understanding the social impacts of UK climate-change policies.

Suzanne Fitzpatrick is Professor of Housing and Social Policy and directs the Institute for Social Policy, Housing and Equalities Research at Heriot-Watt University in Edinburgh. She specialises in research on homelessness and housing exclusion, and much of her work has an international comparative dimension.

Paddy Hillyard is Professor Emeritus of Sociology at Queen's University, Belfast. His main research interest is in social order and control in modern welfare states focusing on a number of substantive areas: 'crime', social harm, political violence, poverty and inequality.

Joanna Mack is Honorary Senior Research Fellow at the Open and Bristol universities and co-author (with Stewart Lansley) of *Breadline Britain – The rise of mass poverty* (2015). She was Principal Investigator of the 1983 *Breadline Britain* survey, which pioneered measuring poverty using publicly determined needs.

David Manley is Reader in Quantitative Geography at the University of Bristol. His main interests relate to the spatial expression of inequality and the impacts that such contexts can have on individual life courses. He is an editor of three volumes on neighbourhood effects published by Springer.

Christina Pantazis is Reader in Zemiology in the Centre for the Study of Poverty and Social Justice in the School for Policy Studies at the University of Bristol. Her research interests include poverty, social exclusion and inequalities, and crime, social harm, and criminalisation.

Demi Patsios is a Senior Research Fellow in the School for Policy Studies at the University of Bristol. He has maintained a primary interest in the effects of an ageing population on policy development and on the capacity of the health and welfare systems to respond to these needs.

Simon Pemberton is Birmingham Fellow and Co-Head of the Department of Social Policy and Social Work in the University of Birmingham. His current research focuses on social harm caused by states as well as social structures, particularly inequality.

Marco Pomati is a Lecturer in the School of Social Sciences at Cardiff University. His recent research focuses on the measurement of poverty and the impact of poverty on parents.

Lucy Prior is a PhD student on the Advanced Quantitative Methods pathway at the University of Bristol. Lucy's research focuses on place and health relationships over the lifecourse, with particular interest in the investigation of biologically plausible pathways.

Filip Sosenko is a Research Fellow at the Institute for Social Policy, Housing and Equalities Research at Heriot-Watt University in Edinburgh. His main research interests lie in the areas of complex needs, destitution, and food poverty.

Mike Tomlinson is Emeritus Professor of Social Policy at Queen's University Belfast. His main research interests lie in the causes and consequences of economic and social marginalisation for communities, families and children. He focuses particularly on Northern Ireland and has published articles on child poverty, suicide, austerity, and the measurement of well-being.

Lisa Wilson is currently working as an Economist in the Belfast office of the Nevin Economic Research Institute. Her key research interests are in the areas of poverty, inequality, and well-being, with particular interest in labour-market-related issues.

Acknowledgements

This book is one key output from *The Poverty and Social Exclusion* research project, funded by the Economic and Social Research Council between 2010 and 2014 (ESRC Grant RES-060-25-0052). This is the largest ever study of poverty conducted in the UK and the authors gratefully acknowledge this crucial support from ESRC for the study. We are also indebted to Jo Goddard, Paul Meller, Bruce Jackson and Mary Hickman who looked after the project from ESRC over its life.

The study also received funding from the Scottish Government, to pay for an increased sample size in rural areas of Scotland for the PSE main survey and the additional analyses of these data. We are grateful for this support and also for the strong input of interest from Scottish Government colleagues, particularly Paul Tyrer, including through the organisation of a special seminar in Edinburgh in 2014.

The PSE-UK research was a major collaboration between the University of Bristol, Heriot-Watt University, the Open University, Queen's University Belfast, the University of Glasgow and the University of York, working with the National Centre for Social Research and the Northern Ireland Statistics and Research Agency. The authors acknowledge the support of all of these institutions in carrying out this work. Particular thanks are due to Professor David Gordon (Principal Investigator), for carrying the whole project forward to fruition, and other colleagues in the core team at Bristol University for undertaking core analyses and data management and to Nikki Hicks (Project Administrator) for managing demanding programmes of Partners and Advisory Group meetings. In addition to authors of this volume we acknowledge the contribution of colleagues at these institutions, including Pauline Heslop, Prof Ruth Levitas, Esther Dermott, Sarah Payne, Eileen Sutton, Shailen Nandy, Karen Bell, Saffren Karsten (Bristol), Mark Livingston, Maria Gannon (Glasgow), David Watkins (Heriot-Watt), Prof Mary Daly (Oxford), Grace Kelly Ronan Smyth, Kirsty McLaughlin (Queens), and Gill Main (York).

The PSE website, www.poverty.ac.uk, was developed at the Open University by a team led by Joanna Mack and assisted by Stewart Lansley, Gabi Kent and Sasah Laurel Jagroo, Pete Mitton, Tammy Alexander, Jamie Danields, Jennifer Nockles, Glen Darby, Hong Yu and Sharon Telfer.

The 'Necessities of Life' and 'Living Standards' surveys were carried out by the National Centre for Social Research (NatCen) in Britain.

We particularly acknowledge the inputs of Emma Drever, Jo Maher, and colleagues Tracy Anderson, Clare Tait, Colin Setchfield, Kevin Pickering, Andrew Shaw, Eleanor Taylor, Liz Clery, Kirby Swales and Kevin Palmer, as well as Dermot Donnelly at NISRA and the dozens of interviewers who conducted the survey and the thousands of individuals and households who participated in what was often quite a demanding interview. Assistance with access and linkage to FRS data was facilitated by Julie Sullivan, Vekaria Rupesh and David Evans and the Department for Work and Pensions, and Gemma Thomas and Steven Dunstan at the Office for National Statistics. Thanks are also due to Beverley Parker and Steve Yates (Xited Ltd), Simon Hudson (Propeller Research) and Jackie Shelton (JHTS Translations).

The project benefitted from the wisdom and advice of its Advisory Groups and we are appreciative of this input from the members of the UK Advisory Group: Prof Danny Dorling, Dr Mike Harmer, Prof Stephen Jenkins, Prof Jane Lewis, Nuala Gormley, Sam Coope, Paul Tyrer, Jill Morton, Anne MacDonald, Tim Crosier, Peter Matejic, Rachel Concell, Jean Martin, Prof Monica McWilliams, Prof Robert Walker, Alison Garnham, Prof Ros Edwards, June Burrough, and Polly Toynbee.

And similarly from the International Advisory Group: Dr Aye Abe, Dr Petra Boehnke, Prof Julio Boltvinik, Prof Bjorn Hallerod, Dr Daniel He-chiun Liou, Prof Brian Nolan, Bryan Perry, Prof Veli-Matti Ritakallio, Pedro Sainz, Prof Peter Saunders, Dr Gemma Wright, Madio Fall, Melissa Wong, David McLennan.

Introduction

Nick Bailey and Glen Bramley

> In 2012, nearly three out of every ten people in Britain fell below the minimum living standard set by society as a whole, twice as many as did so in 1983. One-in-ten households lived in a damp home, a thirty-year high. The number of those who could not afford to heat their home adequately had trebled since the 1990s, rising from three to nine percent. The number of those who had skimped on meals from time to time over the previous year had doubled since 1983 – up from thirteen to twenty eight percent. (Lansley and Mack, 2015: p ix)

The Poverty and Social Exclusion UK (PSE-UK) Survey is the largest and most comprehensive survey of its kind ever carried out in the UK. Funded by the Economic and Social Research Council (ESRC),[1] the 2012 exercise was the latest in a succession of surveys which have been assessing poverty in the UK since the late 1960s. One key contribution of the study is to update the measure of relative poverty based on the number of people suffering different forms of deprivation. As it is based on a consensual or democratic approach, this measure carries a unique political legitimacy and moral imperative: we can show that a majority of the British public views these conditions as unacceptable. The PSE-UK approach provides a very direct, easily understood picture of what it means to be poor today: inadequate housing, a lack of heating, and insufficient food, as the quote above shows. And it can be used to assess change over time. As Lansley and Mack's overview of the evidence shows, poverty has actually risen at the same time as the country has become considerably richer.

The PSE-UK approach has been hugely influential nationally and internationally. These deprivation scales are used in the UK's official measures of child poverty[2] and in the EU's poverty reduction target for 2020, for example. However, they are much less widely reported or discussed than other poverty measures, notably those based on low income. The PSE-UK survey therefore assesses poverty on wide range of measures. Comparing results across these alternatives enables us to contribute important evidence to debates about the validity of different measures as well as improving our knowledge of how

1

the choice of measure shapes our understanding of the extent and incidence of poverty.

A third contribution of the PSE-UK study – and a major innovation of the 2012 survey – is that it provides a unique opportunity to look more broadly at disadvantage using the concept of 'social exclusion'. Although exclusion does not have a widely accepted definition, it is generally viewed as being inherently multidimensional: people can be excluded in different ways or in different aspects of their life. Building on a major review, Levitas et al (2007) developed the Bristol Social Exclusion Matrix (B-SEM) to try to capture the full range of these dimensions or 'domains'. They also showed that no existing survey in the UK at that time captured disadvantage on all of these domains, or even most of them. It was not possible, therefore, to examine how some aspects of exclusion were experienced along with others, or what forms exclusion took for different groups. The PSE-UK is the first to measure exclusion across all of the domains of the B-SEM and hence to support a truly multidimensional analysis. The chapters which follow start with a focus on a particular domain – for example, access to services or social participation – but they are all concerned with how disadvantage on one relates to disadvantage on others. As we stress in the concluding chapter to this volume, the evidence from reviewing a wide range of dimensions of social exclusion, and perspectives on these, strongly confirms the centrality of poverty in the experience of exclusion.

At its core, then, the PSE-UK study is a major survey of household living standards and social exclusion. In this and the companion volume (Dermott and Main, 2017), our focus is very much on this quantitative evidence. This volume approaches the data thematically, while the companion volume comprises chapters on different social groups or geographic locations. The purpose of this introduction is to set out the background to this work, summarising the history of the PSE and predecessor surveys, and the social and economic context in which the current work was conducted, before explaining how we define and measure both poverty and social exclusion. It also provides an initial look at some of the headline results in relation to poverty. It concludes by introducing the chapters which follow.

It is important to note, however, that the PSE-UK study built on a much broader foundation, including original focus group research exploring public perceptions of poverty and social exclusion (for details, see Fahmy, Pemberton and Sutton, 2012). Furthermore, the study also included two major strands of original qualitative research. Results of that work are discussed in a range of other publications, notably Pemberton, Sutton, Fahmy and Bell (2016) on the lived experiences of poorer individuals in a time of 'austerity' and Daly and Kelly (2015) on the role of family for poorer households.

The history of the PSE

The PSE-UK 2012 is the latest in a long line of surveys stretching back 50 years. In Chapter 1, Joanna Mack describes how the successive surveys evolved and shows how they can be used to trace changes in poverty over time. This introduction provides a brief summary of the development of the method. The approach begins with Peter Townsend's study, *Poverty in the UK*, published in 1979 but based on fieldwork in 1968/69 (Townsend, 1979). Townsend's approach was pioneering in looking at poverty in terms of deprivation rather than income: whether people were able to afford basic 'necessities of life'. While hugely influential, his approach did attract some criticism, notably around the means used to identify 'necessities' where Townsend's professional judgement played a significant role (Piachaud, 1987). In measurement terms, the selection of necessities probably has little impact on the results but, in political terms, it makes it easier to ignore the results since it can be suggested they represent just one person's view.

In the 1980s, therefore, Mack and Lansley added the important innovation of using public opinion to identify the necessities, giving the measure a democratic or consensual basis and hence an additional political force. Starting from focus group research, they drew up an initial list of items that were potential necessities. The list covered diverse aspects of social and personal life, including goods such as food, housing and clothing as well as social or leisure activities. A survey then established which of these items received majority support as 'necessities', as well as examining whether people were able to afford them or not. Major surveys were conducted using this approach in 1983 (Mack and Lansley, 1985) and 1990 (Gordon and Pantazis, 1997), and the results were used as the basis of two documentary series, both titled *Breadline Britain*.

In 1999, the survey evolved again as it began to expand to capture aspects of social exclusion in addition to poverty, becoming the *Poverty and Social Exclusion 1999 Survey (PSE 1999)* (Gordon et al, 2000; Pantazis et al, 2006). In addition to impoverishment, exclusion was viewed in terms of three dimensions: labour market exclusion, services exclusion and exclusion from social relations. That survey focused on Britain but was also used as the basis for a very similar exercise in Northern Ireland (Hillyard et al, 2003). The 1999 survey also introduced a separate list of children's necessities for the first time, to capture child poverty in more detail.

In 2012, the PSE was enhanced still further. First, as noted above, the survey implemented a much broader approach to capturing social exclusion. Second, it achieved full UK coverage. Significant boosts to the sample enabled detailed analysis of Northern Ireland and Scotland separately, as well as England and Wales. Third, the questionnaire was administered to all adults in each household in an attempt to capture intra-household variations in living standards – something which income-based measures of poverty conspicuously fail to do.

The context for the survey

The UK has been one of the most unequal of the developed nations since the sharp rises in inequality of the 1980s (Hills, 2015). Since then, the economic, social and political landscape has been through significant changes, although the fundamentals have remained the same. The 2012 survey took place while the effects of the crash of 2007/08 were still playing out. While the economy had grown steadily in the early 2000s, the global financial crisis of 2007 and the ensuing severe recession meant many of the gains were wiped out. Employment rates were slightly lower in 2012 than at the time of the previous PSE survey in 1999, while unemployment was higher, averaging 8.0 per cent across 2012 compared with 6.0 per cent in 1999 (ONS, 2017). Median household incomes in 2012 had fallen back to the level of about 2006 (Belfield et al, 2016) but, due to the unequal rates of growth, most households were barely any better off – a 'lost decade' (Lansley and Mack, 2015).

Income inequality had fallen slightly during the recession but remained at the high levels it had reached following the 1980s. The overall poverty rate also fell slightly between 1999 and 2012, at least using the standard relative low income measure – down from 24 to 21 per cent on the 'After Housing Costs' (AHC) measure.[3] The most visible change has been a huge shift in the risks of being poor. For older people (over pension age), poverty rates halved on the standard low income measure (from 28 to 13 per cent), thanks very largely to policies pursued by the New Labour government, notably means-tested income top-ups in the form of Pension Credit. Child poverty rates have also fallen, although by much less (from 33 to 27 per cent). By contrast, poverty rates for working-age adults without children have risen (from 15 to 19 per cent).

In terms of social policy, the period leading up to the 2012 survey can also be seen as one of expansion followed by contraction. During the New Labour period in office (1997-2010), public spending rose from 40 to 47 per cent of GDP (Lupton et al, 2013). Until the recession struck in 2008, however, this merely reversed the effect of reductions under the preceding governments. UK public spending in 2008 was unexceptional, either by comparison with earlier periods in our own history or by comparison with similar countries in Europe. Public services were a major beneficiary, notably health and education which both took a rising share of the total. Average outcomes improved in both cases and, for schools at least, the gap between richer and poorer also narrowed (Lupton et al, 2013). For lower income households, the value of public services represents a much larger share of their overall income (Bailey and McNulty, 2017) so this growth ought to have been particularly valuable for them.

Following the recession and the 2010 election of the Conservative-Liberal Democrat coalition, the government adopted a policy of swift reductions in public expenditure, largely eschewing the alternative option of tax rises. The pace of these cuts was among the fastest in the developed world according to the IMF (cited in Joyce and Sibieta, 2011). Some areas of expenditure have been relatively sheltered, notably health and schools as well as pensions, but the result is that the burden of cuts has fallen disproportionately on others, notably other local authority services and welfare payments for working-age groups. At the time of the 2012 survey, however, it should be noted that the process of implementing many of these cuts was only beginning and had not even reached its mid-point (Hastings et al, 2015). Many of the harshest effects of reduced entitlements and rising levels of sanctions would not be felt until after 2012 (Webster, 2016). The PSE-UK survey therefore provides a snapshot of living standards at a particularly important time but one where the full impact of the Government's efforts to roll back state welfare – at least, for those of working age – had yet to be felt.

Measuring poverty

One of the main aims of the PSE-UK survey is to update and refine core measures of poverty and deprivation. The starting point for this work is Townsend's definition of relative poverty:

> People are relatively deprived if they cannot obtain, at all or sufficiently, the conditions of life – that is, the diets,

amenities, standards and services – which allow them to play the roles, participate in the relationships and follow the customary behaviour which is expected of them by virtue of their membership of society. If they lack or are denied resources to obtain access to these conditions of life and so fulfil membership of society they may be said to be in poverty. (Townsend, 1993: p 36)

There are lengthy debates about the merits of different kinds of poverty measure. One of the great strengths of the PSE-UK survey is that it permits several different measures to be compared, showing how they vary in terms of levels of poverty identified but also relative risks of poverty for different groups. The consensual measure of deprivation is based on an assessment of public attitudes so we discuss first how these are captured before introducing the poverty measures from the main survey of living standards, including the consensual poverty measure itself.

Public attitudes to the 'necessities of life'

The PSE measure of deprivation is based on assessing whether people are able to afford the 'necessities of life'. Necessities are items or activities which a majority of the public believes everyone should be able to afford, and which no one should have to go without. An initial survey therefore collected data on public attitudes to necessities. This involved two linked exercises covering 2000 people across the UK (see the Appendix to this introduction for details). A long list of 76 potential necessities was drawn up on the basis of reviews of previous research and extensive focus group discussions (Fahmy et al, 2012). The survey revealed majority support for 25 adult items and 24 child items being regarded necessities (Table 0.1 and 0.2).

It is an important part of the PSE's claim to offer a *consensual* poverty measure that necessities do not just carry majority support but also have broadly similar levels of support across society (Pantazis et al, 2006). As with the previous survey in 1999, results in 2012 showed great consistency across a wide range of social divisions: 'Across gender, age, marital status, ethnicity, health, employment status, occupation, nature of work, education level, dependent children, housing tenure, and income level, there are very similar views on the relative importance of different items and activities' (Mack et al, 2013: p 12).[4] There is even a high degree of consensus across people with different political outlooks (see Figure 4 in Lansley and Mack, 2015, p 28).

Table 0.1: Public attitudes to and proportions lacking adult and household necessities, UK 2012*

	Item	% view as necessity[†]	% adults lack item[‡]
1	Heating to keep home adequately warm	95	7
2	Damp-free home	94	11
3	Two meals a day	91	2
4	Visit friends or family in hospital or other institutions	89	3
5	Replace or repair broken electrical goods	86	26
6	Fresh fruit and vegetables every day	82	6
7	Washing machine[†]	82	1
8	All recommended dental treatment	81	17
9	Celebrations on special occasions	80	3
10	Warm, waterproof coat	79	4
11	Attend weddings, funerals and other such occasions	78	3
12	Telephone at home (landline or mobile)[†]	76	2
13	Meat, fish or vegetarian equivalent every other day	76	4
14	Curtains or window blinds	70	1
15	Hobby or leisure activity	70	8
16	Household contents insurance	69	11
17	Enough money to keep your home in a decent state of decoration	69	19
18	Appropriate clothes for job interviews	68	8
19	Table and chairs at which all the family can eat	63	4
20	Taking part in sport or exercise activities or classes	55	10
21	To be able to pay unexpected costs of £500	55	0
22	Two pairs of all-weather shoes	54	7
23	Regular savings (of at least £20 a month) for rainy days	52	31
24	Television[§]	51	0
25	Regular payments to an occupational or private pension	50	27[¶]
26	Replace worn-out clothes with new not secondhand clothes	46	14
27	Presents for family or friends once a year	46	7
28	Friends or family around for meal or drink at least once a month	45	9
29	Car	43	9
30	Holiday away from home, not staying with relatives	42	24
31	Small amount of money to spend each week on yourself	42	18
32	Internet connection at home	39	5
33	Replace any worn-out furniture	39	32
34	Home computer	39	5
35	Mobile phone	39	1
36	Outfit to wear for social or family occasions such as parties, etc	37	8

(continued)

7

Table 0.1: Public attitudes to and proportions lacking adult and household necessities, UK 2012* (continued)

Item	% view as necessity[†]	% adults lack item[‡]
37 Roast joint or equivalent once a week	36	8
38 Hair done or cut regularly	35	12
39 Going out socially once a fortnight	34	17
40 Attend place of worship	29	2
41 Visit friends/family in other parts of country four times a year	26	21
42 Meal out once a month	25	20
43 Holidays abroad once a year	17	32
44 Drink out once a fortnight	17	14
45 Going to cinema, theatre or music event once a month	15	21
46 Dishwasher	10	14

Notes:

* All tables and figures in this book are based on PSE–UK-2012 survey unless otherwise indicated. Small differences between this table and Table 1.1 are due to slight differences in the inclusion or exclusion criteria for the samples used to produce the results.

[†] From omnibus survey. N=2111 on average. For calculation of percentages, 'don't know' (up to 3 per cent) included in negative category.

[§] Dropped from final deprivation scale.

[‡] From main survey. N=8478 on average. For calculation of percentages, 'don't know' included in not lacking category.

[¶] Dashed rule between items 25 and 26 represents the difference between majority and minority support.

An important task for the PSE-UK 2012 study is to update the list of necessities to reflect changes in social attitudes since the 1999 survey. This re-basing is what gives the measure its relative quality. Comparing attitudes in 2012 with previous versions of the survey from 1983, 1990 and 1999 (all for Britain only), we tend to see a gradual increase in the proportion of people viewing items as necessities, especially in the case of many consumer goods such as washing machines (Lansley and Mack. 2015). This reflects rising living standards and increasing ownership of items, as well as falling real costs for many manufactured goods.

Looking at the most recent period (1999 to 2012), however, people appear to have become somewhat less 'generous' in their views about the social minimum. While support for many consumer items has continued to rise, many of the social and leisure activities saw a drop in support. For example, two items that had majority support in 1999 fell below that level in 2012: a holiday away from home once a year not staying with family; and having family or friends round for a meal or a drink once a month. As Lansley and Mack (2015) discuss, a number

Table 0.2: Public attitudes to and proportions of children lacking child necessities

	Item	% view as necessity *	% children lack item†
1	Warm winter coat	97	1
2	Fresh fruit or veg at least once a day	95	3
3	New properly fitting shoes	93	4
4	Three meals a day	92	1
5	Garden or outdoor space to play in safely	92	5
6	Books at home suitable for their ages [2-17]	91	2
7	Child celebration or special occasions	91	1
8	Meat, fish or vegetarian equivalent at least once a day	90	3
9	Suitable place at home to study or do homework [5-17]	89	5
10	Child hobby or leisure activity [5-17]	88	6
11	Toddler/nursery/play group once a week for pre-school children [0-4]	86	4
12	Indoor games suitable for their age‡	80	1
13	Children's clubs or activities such as drama or football training [2-17]	74	8
14	Enough bedrooms for every child 10+ of diff. sex to have own room [10-17]	74	11
15	Some new not secondhand clothes	65	4
16	Computer and internet for homework [5-17]	65	6
17	Day trips with family once a month	59	19
18	Outdoor leisure equipment – roller skates, football, etc	58	6
19	At least 4 pairs of trousers, leggings, jeans or jogging bottoms	56	5
20	Going away on a school trip at least once a term [5-17]	55	7
21	Money to save [5-17]	54	32
22	Pocket money [5-17]	54	16
23	Construction toys (like Lego, Duplo etc)‡	53	4
24	Child holiday away from home for at least 1 week per year	52	25§
25	Child has friends round for tea or a snack once a fortnight [5-17]	49	7
26	Bicycle [5-17]	45	6
27	Clothes to fit in with friends [11-17]	31	9
28	Mobile phone for children [11-17]	26	3
29	MP3 player such as an iPod [11-17]	8	15
30	Designer or brand name trainers [11-17]	6	20

Notes:

* From omnibus survey. N=2100 on average. For calculation of percentage viewing item as a necessity, those responding 'don't know' (up to 3 per cent) were included in the negative category.

‡ Dropped from final deprivation scale.

† From main survey. Percentage of children of relevant age, as shown in brackets if not applicable to all. N=700 to 2440 depending on age range.

§ Dashed rule between items 24 and 25 represents the difference between majority and minority support.

of factors may be at work here. First, median incomes in 2011/12 were almost identical to those in 2001/2 in real terms, suggesting little or no impact from changes in living standards. Second, the recession and increased economic uncertainties may have reduced public expectations. And third, the relentless portrayal of those in poverty, especially those in receipt of (working-age) benefits, as 'undeserving' may have encouraged a less generous view of the 'minimum'.

Living standards and poverty measures

The PSE-UK survey provides access to a broad selection of poverty measures, of three main types. The first comprises **low-income poverty measures**, sometimes also referred as 'at-risk-of-poverty' (AROP) measures. These are widely reported because they are relatively transparent or objective in their construction, and can be easily used for comparisons over time or between countries. Net or disposable incomes are equivalised (that is, adjusted to allow for differences in household size and composition). The PSE-UK survey uses the scale devised for the PSE 1999 survey. Both surveys give slightly more weight to children, particularly young children and disabled children than conventional 'modified OECD Scales' (see Gordon et al, 2000, Appendix 4 for details). Households with incomes below a certain threshold are regarded as poor. The standard threshold used in official analyses is 60 per cent of the median – the nearest the UK has to an official poverty line. Low-income poverty may be assessed before or after housing costs have been taken into account (BHC or AHC). In the PSE-UK survey, 18 per cent were poor on the BHC measure but 25 per cent on the AHC measure. With the BHC measure, poverty rates were similar for children, working adults and pensioners but, with the AHC measure, they were lower for pensioners (19 per cent) and much higher for households containing children (33 per cent).

In spite of their popularity, low-income poverty measures come in for particular criticism. First, they are 'indirect' measures of poverty. They capture the resources which a household has, not the standard of living which it can achieve (Ringen, 1988) – hence the label 'at-risk-of-poverty'. Many factors can mean there is a poor fit between incomes and living standards, not least that incomes are measured at one moment in time whereas living standards are affected by the longer-term availability of resources. There are significant challenges in measuring income, particularly for those who are self-employed; there, recorded incomes can appear very low, even negative, even though the household does not lack access to goods or services (Brewer et al, 2009). Second, significant differences in the cost of living across the country may lead income measures to give a distorted picture of poverty as the same income goes further in lower-cost regions (Jin et al, 2011). Third, cash incomes are only one kind of resource. Savings may be another source, as can assets such as home ownership or the ownership of household goods. Income measures may take account of the income provided by interest on savings but they do not reflect the ability of a household to use savings to meet current expenditure needs. Fourth, resources may flow through support from family or friends in the form of gifts of cash or in-kind and these are not usually captured. Fifth, low-income measures mask intra-household inequalities because they assume that resources are shared equally by household members even though we know this is not the case.

A different criticism (which the UK government has made much of recently) is that, in periods of economic downturn (such as 2008-11), poverty may appear to fall on the low-income measure because the benchmark median income falls (DWP, 2015). This criticism is misplaced for two reasons. First, poverty will only fall in these circumstances if incomes for those at the bottom end of the distribution fall by less than the median. The fact that this occurred in the UK during the recession is a sign that the social security safety net was operating as intended, protecting the least fortunate households from the worst effects of the downturn. Second, the measure is arguably acting in the way a relative poverty measure should do: as society has become poorer as a whole, so the standard for being judged poor may also decline, with the result that poverty may not rise – and may even fall. As noted in the previous section, public attitudes towards the necessities also became less generous in this period, so the low-income standard is moving in the same direction as public opinion.

The principal alternative to indirect poverty measures based on low income are direct measures based on achieved living standards, our second type of measure. The PSE-UK **deprivation measure** is an example, with individuals regarded as poor if they are unable to afford a number of 'necessities'. While the initial list of necessities is identified using the consensual approach described above, a barrage of statistical checks is made to ensure that each item on the list works as expected, adding to the quality of the measure. These are tests for validity, reliability and additivity, described in detail in Gordon (2017). These checks lead to five of the 49 items being dropped (as indicated in Tables 0.1 and 0.2), resulting in a scale with 44 items. Questions on whole household items (for example, contents insurance) were answered by one adult with all household members assigned the same response. Questions on individual adult items were answered by each adult separately. For children, questions on the child items were answered by one adult from the household on behalf of all children, with children assigned the scores for items relevant to their age (as indicated in Table 0.2). For household or adult items, children were also assigned the average score for their household.

Having finalised the deprivation scale, the last stage is to identify the threshold which best distinguishes deprived from non-deprived groups. This is done by looking at how average household incomes fall as deprivation rises to provide an 'objectively defined' cut-off point. The threshold is set at the point which maximises the difference in incomes between the groups and minimises the difference within the groups (Gordon, 2017). In 2012, the threshold for being regarded as deprived was to be lacking three or more items.[5] Table 0.3 shows levels of deprivation in the population as a whole, and for three major age groups. In 2012, 34 per cent lacked three or more of the necessities, with deprivation higher among working-age adults (39 per cent) and lower for pensioners (just 15 per cent).

In addition to the deprivation measure, there is also a **PSE poverty measure**, which combines deprivation and income information in a four-category measure. To be regarded as 'poor', respondents must be deprived (lacking three or more items) *and* have an income below the median for people lacking three items. People who are deprived but who have unusually high incomes are regarded as having recently 'risen' out of poverty: their income has risen but their living standard

Table 0.3: Deprivation by age group

Deprivations	All	0-17	18-64	65+
0	41%	37%	37%	60%
1	16%	17%	15%	16%
2	10%	12%	9%	9%
3	7%	9%	8%	4%
4	5%	5%	6%	3%
5	5%	5%	5%	2%
6	4%	4%	4%	2%
7	3%	2%	4%	1%
8	2%	1%	3%	1%
9	2%	2%	3%	1%
10+	5%	4%	7%	1%
All	100%	100%	100%	100%
N	10556	2323	6441	1792

has yet to catch up. Another group is regarded as being 'vulnerable' to poverty. This comprises people with incomes below the median but who were not deprived, who are regarded as 'vulnerable' to poverty. The assumption here is that incomes have only fallen relatively recently so the household continues to enjoy a better standard of living. The last group is the non-poor, covering everyone else. Again, details are provided in Gordon (2017). Table 0.4 shows the proportions in each group, again broken down by age. Just over one in five (22 per cent) are regarded as poor on this combined measure, with the highest rates now for children (27 per cent) and the lowest again for pensioners (10 per cent). In 1999, 26 per cent of adults were regarded as poor on the PSE poverty measure (Gordon et al, 2000).

Subjective poverty measures form the last category captured by the PSE-UK survey. In these cases, individuals are asked in various ways to identify whether they regard themselves as poor, defining the standard for poverty implicitly or explicitly in the process. These measures are used relatively little in public debates: they are seen as providing the least persuasive evidence since they rest entirely on individuals' subjective opinions. Nevertheless, they are not only an important indicator of perceptions, but also prove to be effective discriminators in practice. They are widely used to corroborate other kinds of measure and to enrich our understanding of poverty more generally.

The PSE-UK survey contains three subjective measures. Each adult is asked to say whether they 'could genuinely say [they] are poor now all the time, sometimes or never'. They are also asked to look back over their life and say how often they 'have lived in poverty by the standards of that time'. Lastly, one adult in each household is asked to say how much income is required 'to keep a household such as the one you live in, out of poverty', and then to say how far above or below that level their own household is. In addition, each adult is also asked more generally, how they would rate their standard of living.

Table 0.4: Classification on the PSE-UK poverty measure by age group

Poverty group	All	0-17	18-64	65+
Poor	22%	27%	24%	10%
Rising	1%	1%	1%	0%
Vulnerable	10%	13%	7%	14%
Not poor	67%	59%	68%	75%
All	100%	100%	100%	100%
N	11528	2489	7140	1899

Table 0.5 summarises responses on each of these four measures. The measure asking people to think about their poverty status across the whole of their life yields relatively similar responses by age: one in nine regard themselves as having been poor often or most of the time, with similar values for people who are currently working age or pensioners. The measures reflecting current poverty status show much more variation, with working-age adults consistently reporting higher rates of poverty and a lower standard of living than pensioners. Two in five working-age adults regard themselves as genuinely poor at least some of the time (39 per cent) and one in three has an income below the level required to keep them out of poverty (32 per cent). In every case, children appear to live in even poorer households: in households with children, one in two adult respondents (48 per cent) feels they are genuinely poor at least some of the time.

Table 0.5: Subjective poverty and living standards measures

Age	Can genuinely say they are poor sometimes or all the time	Over their life, has lived in poverty often or most of the time	Income is below the level needed to keep them out of poverty	Standard of living below average
*0-17**	*48%*	*13%*	*34%*	*19%*
18-64	39%	11%	32%	17%
65+	21%	9%	20%	8%
All	**38%**	**11%**	**30%**	**15%**
N	10990	10992	7387	10986

Note: *Children given value for household respondent.

Measuring social exclusion

The term 'social exclusion' has more recent origins than the term poverty, entering European social policy discussions from the late 1980s (Room, 1995) and taking off in UK policy debates from the 1990s, particularly with the election of the New Labour government (Levitas, 2006). There is some debate about whether exclusion really does provide a radically different focus than poverty. Indeed, it has been noted that, much of the time, the two terms are used as 'an inseparable dyad', suggesting they are being used to refer to the same set of problems (Levitas et al, 2007, p 20). Furthermore, some of the differences attributed to the term social exclusion appear to be more ones of 'custom and practice' than of deep conceptual divergence. For example, it is often claimed that social exclusion shifts attention from material resources to more multidimensional forms of disadvantage, and highlights the processes or dynamics of movement in and out of the excluded state (Room, 1995). Yet others argue there is little in the term that is not covered by Townsend's definition of relative poverty noted above (Burchardt et al, 2002) and that studies of poverty can focus on processes and dynamics just as easily (Jenkins and Rigg, 2001).

Within the UK, however, it does appear to be true that social exclusion has been used to identify a broader and more varied or multidimensional set of problems than the term 'poverty' is usually understood to refer to. Levitas et al (2007) conducted a major review of the use of the term for the UK government, listing a dozen definitions at one point. From this, they propose a synthesised working definition as follows:

> Social exclusion is a complex and multi-dimensional process. It involves the lack or denial of *resources*, rights, goods and services, and the inability to *participate* in the normal relationships and activities, available to the majority of people in a society, whether in economic, social, cultural or political arenas. It affects both the *quality of life* of individuals and the equity and cohesion of society as a whole. (Levitas et al 2007: p 9 – emphasis added)

They note that all definitions are developed with specific purposes in mind and that this one reflects their desire to facilitate the measurement of exclusion at the individual or household level. As a result, it does not highlight some of the structural causes or processes which feature in other definitions.

From this definition, Levitas et al (2007) recommend operationalising exclusion by identifying a number of domains under the three broader headings of resources, participation and quality of life (the Bristol Social Exclusion Matrix or B-SEM, see Figure 0.1).[6] This framework is not meant as a theory of exclusion. It does not make claims about the relative importance of different domains, for example, whether material or resource disadvantage is necessary for someone to be considered excluded or not. It is unclear whether exclusion on one domain tends to be associated with exclusion on many others or, conversely, whether they are distinct patterns or forms of exclusion: whether people could have similar 'levels' of exclusion arising from quite different circumstances and manifesting in different ways. Nor does the framework propose any means of identifying thresholds or levels at which exclusion begins or ends. Rather the framework is a description or heuristic device, which attempts to guide the design

Figure 0.1: The Bristol Social Exclusion Matrix (B-SEM)

Source: Levitas et al (2007)

of research instruments in order to support investigation of the phenomenon.

Reviewing previous attempts to measure exclusion, Levitas et al note that many of these have been based around the collation of a series of indicators from separate data sources. Examples include the Joseph Rowntree Foundation's (JRF) *Monitoring poverty and social exclusion* series of reports (most recently, Tinson et al, 2016). Valuable as these are for revealing differences between social groups or places and for tracking change over time and helping to hold policy makers to account, they cannot be used to explore the multidimensional nature of exclusion since they are not based on data at the individual level.

Some attempts have been made to operationalise measures of exclusion at the individual level using survey data: for example, Burchardt et al (2002) and Barnes (2005) using data from the British Household Panel Study and Pantazis et al (2006) using the PSE 1999 survey. Different definitions, domains and indicators are used in each case. More importantly, Levitas et al found that none of the existing UK surveys would permit measurement on anything like the range of domains identified in the B-SEM. The aim of the PSE–UK survey is to provide measures for each of these domains so that, for the first time in the UK, it is possible to look across all of them simultaneously and understand the relationships between them. It is the B-SEM which structures this book as a whole, with chapters each taking a focus on one or more of the domains.

Outline of the book

Apart from the introduction and conclusion, this volume contains thirteen substantive chapters divided into four sections. The structure follows that of the B-SEM, with chapters in the first three sections covering 'Resources', 'Participation' and 'Quality of life' respectively, while the fourth attempts to look across all of the domains simultaneously, providing a multidimensional analysis.

In the 'Resources' section, Mack starts in Chapter 1 with an overview of poverty studies in the UK. As well as tracing the development of the PSE-UK approach, she puts the results from the current survey in the context of those conducted on the same basis over the last 30 years to show how both views about necessities and actual levels of poverty have changed. In Chapter 2, going beyond the focus on poverty, Patsios, Hillyard and Pomati develop an innovative measure designed to capture living standards right across the spectrum. They take advantage of the breadth of the PSE-UK survey, drawing on questions on incomes and consumption, but also on health, social participation and community. Chapter 3 moves in the opposite direction, focusing attention on differences within the 'poor' group. Combining data from the PSE-UK with that from a number of other sources to capture more of the population not living in private households, Bramley, Fitzpatrick and Sosenko seek to identify those with the most severe levels of poverty and, indeed, those who are destitute. Lastly in the 'Resources' section, Chapter 4 by Bramley and Besemer looks at people's access to a wide range of public and private services.

The second section draws together chapters on the 'Participation' domains of the B-SEM. Chapter 5 by Wilson, Fahmy and Bailey looks at social networks and social participation. They examine social behaviours or levels of contact within networks of family and friends, and engagement in social activities. They also look at the affective side of participation through people's perceptions of social support and their satisfaction with social relationships. In Chapter 6, Bailey looks at the relationships between economic participation and social exclusion. While a lot of research has highlighted how in-work poverty has been rising in recent years, this chapter uses the PSE-UK survey to explore broader aspects of social exclusion for those in employment, looking at quality of employment and continuity or stability as well as material benefits or pay. The last 'Participation' contribution, Chapter 7 by Fahmy, looks at civic and political engagement, and how this relates to both poverty and wider dimensions of social exclusion.

In the third section, five contributions explore different facets of 'Quality of life'. Chapter 8 by Prior and Manley examines the PSE-UK data on physical and mental health, exploring relationships with poverty in particular. In Chapter 9, Bramley looks at variations in quality of housing and of the wider neighbourhood environment in which people live. Social harm is the focus of Chapter 10, by Pemberton, Pantazis and Hillyard. This shows how various harms that can arise in the home, the community or at work are not random but socially patterned, being exacerbated by poverty. Chapter 11 by Bramley and Besemer looks at financial exclusion. While there is clearly a resource dimension here, it is included in the quality of life section because it also emphasises the impacts of financial hardship through stress or worry. Lastly in this section, Tomlinson and Wilson in Chapter 12 look at some of the broadest indicators of quality of life – those where respondents are asked to assess their overall sense of well-being.

The final section of the book, 'Bringing it together', includes Chapter 13 by Bailey, Fahmy and Bradshaw. This explores different ways in which we might try to capture the multidimensional nature of social exclusion. No previous survey has permitted so many different aspects of exclusion to be captured. Rather than propose a single approach, this chapter examines different measures, and shows how our understanding of exclusion can change as a result. What remains constant, however, is the extent to which poverty is a central and defining feature of exclusion in the great majority of cases. Reflecting across all of the earlier chapters, the concluding chapter by Bramley and Bailey attempts to draw out some of the key findings which emerge across this body of work, and relates these to contemporary debates about society and policy.

Notes

[1] ESRC Large Grant RES-060-25-0052.

[2] Under the Child Poverty Act 2010, one of the last pieces of legislation passed by the Labour government, the measures were targets which the Government was required to achieve by 2020. The 2016 Welfare Reform

and Work Act removed their status as targets but requires the Government to continue to report on the same set of measures annually.

[3] Figures in this paragraph taken from the Institute for Fiscal Studies (IFS) spreadsheet on incomes and poverty, comparing 1999/2000 with 2012/13 on the 'After Housing Costs' measure.

[4] These data can be explored online via the PSE's website at www.poverty. ac.uk.

[5] In the 1999 survey, the threshold was lacking two or more items but the two figures cannot be compared directly: the earlier survey was using a much shorter list of necessities (Gordon et al, 2000); it covered Britain rather than the UK; and the threshold will depend on the nature of the items included in the list, that is, the balance between items which many people lack and those which only a few people lack.

[6] The original version of the B-SEM has ten domains (Levitas et al, 2006). During the development of the PSE-UK survey, this was extended to eleven.

References

Bailey, N. and McNulty, D. (2017) 'Inequality and poverty in Scotland', in K. Gibb, D. Maclennan, D. McNulty and M. Comerford (eds) *The Scottish economy: A living book*, London: Routledge, pp 194-214.

Barnes, M. (2005) *Social exclusion in Great Britain: An empirical investigation and comparison with the EU*, Aldershot: Ashgate.

Belfield, C., Cribb, J., Hood, A. and Joyce, R. (2016) *Living standards, poverty and inequality in the UK 2016*, London: Institute for Fiscal Studies.

Brewer, M., O'Dea, C., Paul, G. and Sibieta, L. (2009) 'The living standards of families with children reporting low incomes', *DWP Research Report 577*, London: DWP.

Burchardt, T., Le Grand, J. and Piachaud, D. (2002) 'Degrees of exclusion: developing a dynamic, multidimensional measure', in J. Hills, J. Le Grand and D. Piachaud (eds) *Understanding social exclusion*, Oxford: OUP, pp 30-43.

Daly, M. and Kelly, G. (2015) *Families and poverty: Everyday life on a low income,* Bristol: Policy Press.

Dermott, E. and Main, G. (2017) *Poverty and social exclusion in the UK: Vol. 1*, Bristol: Policy Press.

DWP (Department for Work and Pensions) (2015) *Households Below Average Incomes: An analysis of the income distribution 1994/95–2011/12*, London: DWP.

Fahmy, E., Pemberton, S. and Sutton, E. (2012) 'Public perceptions of poverty and social exclusion: final report on focus group findings', *PSE: UK Analysis Working Paper 3*, Bristol: PSE Project.

Gannon, M. and Bailey, N. (2014) 'Attitudes to the "necessities of life": would an independent Scotland set a different poverty standard to the rest of the UK?', *Social Policy and Society*, 13(3): 321-36.

Gordon, D. (2017) *Producing an 'objective' poverty line in eight easy steps: PSE 2012 Survey – adults and children*, Bristol: PSE Project.

Gordon, D. and Pantazis, C. (1997) *Breadline Britain in the 1990s*, Aldershot: Ashgate.

Gordon, D., Adelman, L., Ashworth, K., Bradshaw, J., Levitas, R., Middleton, S., Pantazis, C., Patsios, D., Payne, S., Townsend, P. and Williams, J. (2000) *Poverty and social exclusion in Britain*, York: Joseph Rowntree Foundation.

Hastings, A., Bailey, N., Besemer, K., Bramley, G., Gannon, M. and Watkins, D. (2015) *The cost of the cuts: The impact on local government and poorer communities*, York: Joseph Rowntree Foundation.

Hills, J. (2015) *Good times, bad times: The welfare myth of Them and Us*, Bristol: Policy Press.

Hillyard, P., Kelly, G., McLaughlin, E., Patsios, D. and Tomlinson, M. (2003) *Bare necessities: Poverty and social exclusion in Northern Ireland*, Belfast: Democratic Dialogue.

Jenkins, S. and Rigg, J. with Devicienti, F. (2001) *The dynamics of poverty in Britain*. Research Report No. 157. Report of Research carried out by the Institute for Economic and Social Research (ISER), University of Essex, on behalf of the Department of Work and Pensions, London: DWP, http://webarchive.nationalarchives.gov.uk/20130314011914/http://research.dwp.gov.uk/asd/asd5/rrep157.pdf

Jin, W., Joyce, R., Phillips, D. and Sibieta, L. (2011) 'Poverty and inequality in the UK 2011', *IFS Commentary C118*, London: Institute for Fiscal Studies.

Joyce, R. and Sibieta, L. (2011) 'Country case study – UK', in S. P. Jenkins, et al (eds) *The Great Recession and the distribution of household income*, Milan: Fondazione Rodolfo Debenedetti.

Kelly, G., Tomlinson, M., Daly, M., Hillyard, P., Nandy, S. and Patsios, D. (2012) 'The necessities of life in Northern Ireland', *PSE Working Paper – Analysis Series 1*. Bristol: PSE Project.

Lansley, S. and Mack, J. (2015) *Breadline Britain: The rise of mass poverty*, London: OneWorld.

Levin, H. M. (1996) 'Empowerment evaluation and Accelerated Schools', in D. Fetterman, S. Kaftarian and A. Wandersman (eds) *Empowerment evaluation: Knowledge and tools for self-assessment and accountability*, Thousand Oaks, CA: Sage, 49-64.

Levitas, R. (2006) 'The concept and measurement of social exclusion', in C. Pantazis, D. Gordon and R. Levitas (eds) *Poverty and social exclusion in Britain: The Millennium Survey*, Bristol: Policy Press, 123-62.

Levitas, R., Pantazis, C., Fahmy, E., Gordon, D., Lloyd, E. and Patsios, D. (2007) *The multi-dimensional analysis of social exclusion*, Bristol: University of Bristol.

Lupton, R., Hills, J., Stewart, K. and Vizard, P. (2013) 'Labour's social policy record: policy, spending and outcomes 1997-2010', *Social policy in a cold climate – Research report 1*, London: CASE, LSE.

Mack, J. and Lansley, S. (1985) *Poor Britain*, London: Allen and Unwin.

Mack, J., Lansley, S., Nandy, S. and Pantazis, C. (2013) 'Attitudes to the necessities in the PSE 2012 survey: are minimum standards becoming less generous?', *Working Paper, Analysis Series No. 4*, Bristol: PSE Project.

NatCen (2013) *NatCen Omnibus: Technical report*, London: NatCen.

NISRA (Northern Ireland Statistics and Research Agency) (2012) *Northern Ireland omnibus survey June 2012: Necessities of life module – codebook and technical summary* (revised October 2012), Belfast: NISRA.

NISRA (2013) *Northern Ireland faring badly*, http://www.poverty.ac.uk/pse-research/northern-ireland-faring-badly

ONS (Office for National Statistics) (2017) UK labour market: July 2017, https://www.ons.gov.uk/employmentandlabourmarket/peopleinwork/employmentandemployeetypes/bulletins/uklabourmarket/july2017. Accessed 18 August 2017.

Pantazis, C., Gordon, D. and Levitas, R. (2006) *Poverty and social exclusion in Britain: The Millennium Survey*, Bristol: Policy Press.

Pemberton, S., Fahmy, E., Sutton, E. and Bell, K. (2016) 'Endless pressure: life on a low income in austere times', *Social Policy & Administration*. DOI: 10.1111/spol.12233.

Piachaud, D. (1987) 'Problems in the definition and measurement of poverty', *Journal of Social Policy* 16(02): 147-64.

Ringen, S. (1988) 'Direct and indirect measures of poverty', *Journal of Social Policy*, 17(3): 351-65.

Room, G. (1995) *Beyond the threshold: The measurement and analysis of social exclusion*, Bristol: Policy Press.

Tinson, A., Ayrton, C., Barker, K., Born, T. B., Aldridge, H. and Kenway, P. (2016) *Monitoring poverty and social exclusion 2016,* York: Joseph Rowntree Foundation.

Townsend, P. (1979) *Poverty in the UK: A survey of household resources and living standards*, Harmondsworth: Allen Lane.

Townsend, P. (1993) *The international analysis of poverty*, London: Harvester Wheatsheaf.

Webster, D. (2016) *The DWP's JSA/ESA Sanctions Statistics Release*, 17 August 2016. Briefing. 31 August 2016, http://www.cpag.org.uk/david-webster

Appendix: PSE-UK survey methodology

This appendix provides brief methodological details on the two surveys, and references to further sources of information, all of which are available on the PSE-UK website – www.poverty.ac.uk.

Public attitudes survey

Data on public attitudes were collected through two closely related exercises, one for Britain and one for Northern Ireland. Results are for the combined UK dataset, weighted to reflect relative population sizes, unless otherwise stated. British data were collected through a standalone survey between May and August 2012, with 1,447 completed interviews – a 51 per cent response rate (NatCen, 2013). A 'sort card' exercise was used to collect data on attitudes to necessities, giving comparability with earlier British surveys. An adult was selected at random from the household and presented with two sets of cards – the first contained 46 items or activities appropriate to adults or to the household as a whole while the second comprised 30 items or activities appropriate to children. Respondents were asked to sort these cards to identify those they regarded as 'necessities': things which everyone 'should be able to afford and which they should not have to do without' (Mack et al, 2013).

Northern Irish data were collected through a module within the June 2012 Northern Irish Omnibus Survey. This covered a sample of 1,015 adults, this time assigned at random to one of two different methodologies for gathering opinions on necessities: a 'sort card' exercise and a computer-based questionnaire. The former gives comparability with the British survey conducted at the same time while the latter gives comparability with an earlier survey in Northern Ireland. Response from the two approaches differed with the computer-based exercise tending to produce higher levels of support for items (Kelly et al, 2012). For consistency, only the half of the sample comparable with the 'British' method is used here. This had 550 completed interviews with a 53 per cent response rate (NISRA, 2012). Weighting ensured that the number of responses in the combined dataset was representative of the UK as a whole.

A separate survey of attitudes was conducted in Scotland in 2011, using the 'sort card' design. This was used to explore differences between attitudes in Scotland and the rest of the UK in more detail. Due to the difference in timing, that data is not included here. See Gannon and Bailey (2014) for a comparison with UK results.

Main living standards survey

As with public attitudes, data on living standards were collected through two closely related exercises, covering Britain and Northern Ireland respectively (for details, see NatCen, 2013 and NISRA, 2012). Results quoted throughout the book are for the combined UK dataset, weighted to reflect relative population sizes, unless otherwise stated.

The two exercises had identical content apart from one additional module in the latter survey on the legacy of the Northern Irish 'Troubles'. Both were conducted as follow-ups to the *Family Resources Survey (FRS) 2010/11*, with the sample drawn from those who had given permission to be recontacted. Various groups were intentionally over-sampled, notably lower income households and those with members from minority ethnic groups, as well as those from Scotland as a whole, rural Scotland in particular, and Northern Ireland.

Fieldwork took place between March and December 2012, around 12 to 18 months after the initial FRS interview. The surveyors attempted to interview every adult in the household with one adult providing some information for the household as a whole and one adult (not necessarily the same) answering questions relating to children within it; children were not interviewed directly. The sample covered 5,193 households, containing 12,097 individuals (including children). Response rates were 59 per cent for households across the UK with 83 per cent of adults (7,511 individuals) giving full or partial interviews. Weights are used in all analyses to correct for sample structure and non-response.

Part 1:
Resources

ONE

Fifty years of poverty in the UK

Joanna Mack

Introduction

Over the last fifty years, poverty in the UK has been researched extensively. There has been much debate about definitions. Should it be relative or absolute? Should it be judged by income or living standards? Or should poverty be a wider concept, focusing on overall well-being? This chapter examines the development of these different approaches to poverty measurement and their relationship to different understandings of deprivation – and how these impact, or otherwise, on the political and policy process.

The chapter goes on to examine what different measures say about trends over time. Examining both income-based and deprivation-based measures, it will show that there has been a rise in relative poverty. This chapter argues that the processes that create poverty stem from those that create inequality – and that more attention needs to be given to these underlying social and economic inequalities if poverty is to be tackled.

The 'rediscovery' of poverty

Poverty research, with a long pedigree in Britain going back to the pioneering work of Booth and Rowntree at the end of the nineteenth century, was re-energised in the mid-1960s. By that time, there was growing concern that, despite the social and economic progress of the post-war years towards greater affluence and greater equality, the problems experienced by some groups, notably older people and sick and disabled people, showed no signs of diminishing. Faced with a lack of information about the living conditions of such groups, Brian Abel-Smith and Peter Townsend set about re-examining existing data from National Income and Expenditure surveys to identify the numbers, and characteristics, of those they described as having 'low levels of living'.

The result was the publication of *The poor and the poorest* (Abel–Smith and Townsend, 1965) and the start of the 'rediscovery' of poverty.

The poor and the poorest used a simple threshold – based on a percentage of what was then the National Assistance scale – as a measure of 'low living standards'. It did not, and did not set out to, re-conceptualise poverty. That was left to Abel–Smith and Townsend's next project – a detailed national survey of living standards and resources. Funded by the (now) Joseph Rowntree Foundation, this became the landmark 1968/69 'Poverty in the UK' survey.[1]

This was an ambitious undertaking. Four qualitative pilot studies were carried out of groups at risk of poverty to crystallise which issues in people's lives might be used as indicators of deprivation. The resultant questionnaire, over 40 pages long, included 60 indicators of living standards – ranging from diet and clothing to home amenities and recreation – as well as in-depth questions on household resources. It resulted in a mass of data to analyse in the days when computers were laboriously programmed using pre-defined holes on 'punch cards' and took all night to run.

The project was beset by delays and, in mid-1968, Abel–Smith left to become a senior advisor at the Department of Health and Social Security. Townsend's book, *Poverty in the UK*, eventually came out in 1979. It became an authoritative statement of the need to think about poverty in *relative* terms. In his much-quoted definition, Townsend saw people falling into poverty when:

> ... their resources are so seriously below those commanded by the average individual or family that they are, in effect, excluded from ordinary patterns, customs and activities. (Townsend, 1979: p 31)

To operationalise this norms-based approach, Townsend devised a 'deprivation index', based on twelve of the living standards indicators, and identified a 'poverty line' by using a statistical technique that related household incomes to the degree to which households lacked these items.

However, not doing or not having something that most others do or have does not in itself necessarily mean that people's lives are being diminished or limited. David Piachaud, one of Townsend's most influential critics, identified two key reasons for this (Piachaud, 1981). First, the lack of an item may have been out of choice. And second, the fact that something is commonly done or possessed does not on its own make it important. Conversely, just because something is not widespread or common within a particular society does not make it unimportant. This lies behind the argument, put forward most strongly by Amartya Sen, that a relativist view struggles to take adequate account of absolute conceptions of poverty. There was 'an irreducible absolutist core in the idea of poverty', argued Sen. 'If there is starvation and hunger, then – no matter what the relative picture looks like – there is clearly poverty' (Sen, 1983). Townsend rejected this criticism and disputed the tenability of the concept of absolute needs.

Yet, a problem remains with a definition of relative poverty based on norms derived from *what is commonly done*. If a society is in the depth of a famine where malnutrition is widespread, this approach, definitionally, would not identify those suffering as in poverty. This is clearly untenable. More generally, there is a problem in that basing your measure on what is average, or commonly done, in each country embeds into the concept of poverty an acceptance of deep international inequalities.

Townsend had aimed to exclude value judgements from the selection of indicators but in doing so failed to take account of, or relate to, any generally accepted view of 'need'. As Piachaud argued, it leaves the term 'poverty' devoid of any 'moral imperative that something should be done about it' (Piachaud, 1981). Or as Amartya Sen put it: 'material objects cannot be evaluated in this context without reference to how people view them' (Sen, 1981).

The concept of socially perceived necessities

The next development in this debate about poverty measurement came in 1983 with the *Breadline Britain* survey (sometimes known as the *Poor Britain* survey). The origins of this survey are quite different from the academic background of what had come before: it stemmed from a television series.

In the early 1980s, I was working as a producer/director at London Weekend Television (LWT), one of the companies that formed part of the ITV network, and was asked to make a series of four one-hour programmes for one of the network's 'adult education' slots. It was the first term of Margaret Thatcher's Conservative government, brought to power with a radical agenda to roll back the state and promote market forces. By the early 1980s, the UK was in the depths of recession, while unemployment was reaching record levels with more than a million having been unemployed for over a year. We decided that the focus should be on 'poverty'.

When this was mooted, there were some worried murmurs: was not the subject of 'poverty' too political? It was certainly not in the same category as the general run of 'adult education' programming which was more likely to look at English literature or Art or how to sail a boat. The senior executives at LWT stood by the decision, arguing that it was important to place the question of living standards firmly on the public agenda in a way that asked viewers to think about the kind of society they lived in and wanted to live in (Browne and Coueslant, 1984).

At that time, government statistics took those who fell below the Supplementary Benefit level – the amount paid to those who were not entitled to other benefits such as Unemployment Benefit – as a measure of poverty. But this was entirely arbitrary; the Supplementary Benefit rates were not based on any assessment of need but had simply stemmed from the 1945 Labour government's National Assistance rates. The Townsend survey had looked at people's actual living standards and the ways in which the poor missed out – but, by then, it was fifteen years out of date.

We decided to conduct a new survey.[2] Aware of Piachaud and Sen's criticisms, we felt that a new approach directly addressing the question of judgment and evaluation was needed. The survey organisation MORI was commissioned with the brief to establish 'whether there was a public consensus on what is an unacceptable standard of living' and if so 'who, if anyone, falls below that standard'. For television, this approach had the additional advantage that the understanding of poverty underlying the series would be widely shared by the audience.

Focus groups were held in different parts of the country to develop indicators of deprivation in tune with people's perceptions of what was necessary for living in Britain in the early 1980s. The final questionnaire asked about a wide range of items and activities, covering not just basic items but also consumer goods, leisure activities and social participation – and included a number of more discretionary items to ensure distinctions were being made. For each item and activity, the interviewees were asked (in face-to-face interviews) to distinguish between those they thought were 'necessary, and which all adults should be able to afford and which they should not have to go without' and those 'which may be desirable but are not necessary'. Items and activities classed as a necessity by 50 per cent or more of respondents were taken as part of a minimum standard.

The survey went on to ask people about their own living standard. For each of the items and activities, interviewees were asked whether they had them or not; and for those that they did not have, to distinguish between those they 'didn't have and didn't want' and those that they 'didn't have and couldn't afford'. In this way, the question of choice, which Piachaud had raised, was dealt with.

In this approach, poverty was defined in terms of 'an enforced lack of socially-perceived necessities' (Mack and Lansley, 1985, p 45). While maintaining Townsend's conception of poverty as deprivation stemming from a lack of command over resources, what counted as deprivation was determined not by average behaviours but by people's perceptions of need.

The *Breadline Britain* survey established, for the first time ever, that in Britain there was widespread agreement on what constitutes a minimum standard and that it was a standard that reflected contemporary ways of living. A majority saw the necessities of life as wide-ranging, including consumer goods and various social activities as well as more basic items such as food and heating. The survey also found very similar views on the relative importance of different items and activities across gender, occupation, income level, age and, notably, political preference (Mack and Lansley, 1985, pp 73-82). This consensus is important as, otherwise, the interests of minorities could be overlooked.

The *Breadline Britain* television series, setting out these minimum standards and the numbers falling below them, was broadcast in the summer of 1983, accompanied by a range of activities at a local level organised by the ITV regional company network. From the response from the viewing public and the press coverage (both extensive), the concept of necessities as determined by public opinion seemed to have been received favourably (Browne and Coueslant, 1984). The Conservative government dismissed the findings. In the House of Commons, Rhodes Boyson, the Social Security Minister, argued that the items in the list of necessities were such that '50 years ago, or even 25 years ago, people merely aspired to have such things' (Hansard, 1983a) while Margaret Thatcher asserted that 'people who are living in need are fully and properly provided for' (Hansard, 1983b). There was, however, a much more favourable reaction from the Labour Party, including the then newly elected MP Tony Blair who took a particular interest in the majoritarian basis of the measure, seeing it as having political leverage.[3]

Changing standards

In 1990, against a background of sharply rising inequality, a second series *Breadline Britain in the 1990s* was commissioned and a second survey undertaken. This survey confirmed that there was widespread agreement on a relatively based minimum standard of living and found that the percentage falling below this minimum standard had risen since 1983 (Frayman, 1991; Gordon and Pantazis, 1997).

In subsequent years, this approach has been widely adopted in poverty research. In the UK, it formed the basis of the 1999 Poverty and Social Exclusion (PSE-GB 1999) in Britain survey (Pantazis et al, 2006), the 2002/3 PSE survey in Northern Ireland (Hillyard et al, 2006) and the 2012 PSE survey in the UK (PSE-UK 2012). It has been used in studies in a large number of other countries, including Japan (Pantazis, 2014), South Africa (Wright, 2011), Benin (Nandy and Pomati, 2014) and Bangladesh (Ahmed, 2007). The European Union has also used the 'enforced lack of socially-perceived necessities' approach to measure deprivation in every country of the EU and is looking to include these indicators in its poverty targets (Gordon, 2011; Eurostat, 2012). These studies have confirmed the viability of the concept of socially perceived necessities.

In Britain, the 1983, 1990, 1999 and 2012 surveys, having used the same methods, enable trends in attitudes as to what should constitute a minimum standard to be tracked. Table 1.1 shows these trends for adults and Table 1.2 shows the trends in attitudes for children between 1999 (the first survey to ask in-depth questions relating to children) and 2012.

Table 1.1: Attitudes to necessities for adults, Britain: 1983, 1990, 1999, 2012

Items and activities	% thinking item to be a necessity			
	1983	1990	1999	2012
Heating to keep home adequately warm	97	97	95	96
Damp-free home	94	98	94	94
Two meals a day	64	90	91	91
Visit friends or family in hospital or other institutions			92	90
Replace or repair broken electrical goods			86	86
Fresh fruit and vegetables every day		88	87	83
Washing machine	67	73	77	82
All recommended dental work/treatment				82
Celebrations on special occasions	69	74	83	80
Warm, waterproof coat	87	91	87	79
Attend weddings, funerals and other such occasions			81	78
Telephone	43	56	72	77
Meat, fish (or vegetarian equivalent) every other day	63	77	81	76
Curtains or window blinds				71

(continued)

Table 1.1: Attitudes to necessities for adults, Britain: 1983, 1990, 1999, 2012 (continued)

Items and activities	% thinking item to be a necessity			
	1983	1990	1999	2012
Hobby or leisure activity	64	67	79	70
Enough money to keep your home in a decent state of decoration		88	80	69
Household contents insurance		92	83	69
Appropriate clothes for job interviews			70	69
A table, with chairs, at which all the family can eat				64
Taking part in sport/exercise activities or classes				56
To be able to pay an unexpected expense of £500				55
Two pairs of all-weather shoes	67	74	67	54
Regular savings (of at least £20 a month) for rainy days*		68	67	52
Television	51	58	58	51
Regular payments into an occupational or private pension				51
Replace worn-out clothes with new not secondhand clothes	64	65	50	46
Presents for family or friends once a year	58	69	58	46
Friends or family around for a meal or drink at least once a month	32	37	65	45
Car	22	26	36	44
A small amount of money to spend each week on yourself, not on your family			61	42
Holiday away from home, not staying with relatives	63	54	56	42
Internet connection at home			6	41
Home computer		5	11	40
Mobile phone			8	40
An outfit to wear for social or family occasions such as parties and weddings‡	48	54	51	38
Roast joint or equivalent once a week	67	64	58	36
Hair done or cut regularly				35
Going out socially once a fortnight	36	42	41	34
Attend place of worship			44	29
Visit friends or family in other parts of the country four times a year†			39	41	27
Meal out once a month			17	27	25
Holidays abroad once a year			17	20	18
Drink out once a fortnight			22	17
Going to the cinema, theatre or music event once a month				15
Dishwasher		4	7	10

Notes:

* £10/month in 1990 and 1999.

† Coach or train fares to visit family once a quarter in 1990 and 1999.

‡ In 1990 and 1983 this was phrased as 'A "best outfit" for special occasions'.

Items that are seen as a necessity by 50 per cent or more are classed as part of a minimum standard. For 2012, this is marked by the dashed line.

Table 1.2: Attitudes to child necessities, Britain: 1999 and 2012

Child items and activities	% thinking item to be a necessity	
	1999	2012
Warm winter coat	95%	97%
Fresh fruit or veg at least once a day	93%	96%
New properly fitting shoes	96%	93%
Three meals a day	91%	93%
Garden or outdoor space to play in safely*	68%	92%
Child celebration or special occasions	92%	91%
Books at home suitable for their ages†	90%	91%
Meat, fish or vegetarian equivalent at least once a day‡	76%	90%
Place to study	n/a	89%
Child hobby or leisure activity	88%	88%
Toddler group or nursery or play group at least once a week for pre-school aged children	89%	87%
Indoor games suitable for their ages (building blocks, board games, computer games, etc.)	n/a	81%
Enough bedrooms for every child aged 10+ of a different sex to have their own room	76%	74%
Clubs or activities such as drama or football training	n/a	74%
Computer and internet for homework	38%	66%
Some new not secondhand clothes	67%	65%
Day trips with family once a month	n/a	60%
Outdoor leisure equipment such as roller skates, skateboards, footballs etc	n/a	58%
At least 4 pairs of trousers, leggings, jeans or jogging bottoms	74%	57%
Going away on a school trip at least once a term	73%	55%
Money to save	n/a	55%
Pocket money	n/a	54%
Child holiday away from home for at least 1 week per year	63%	53%
Construction toys (like Lego, Duplo etc)	66%	53%
Child has friends round for tea or a snack once a fortnight	53%	49%
Bicycle	54%	45%
Clothes to fit in with friends	n/a	31%
Mobile phone	n/a	27%
MP3 player such as an iPod	n/a	8%
Designer/brand name trainers	n/a	6%

Notes:

* Garden in 1999.

† Books of their own in 1999.

‡ Twice a day in 1999.

Items that are seen as a necessity by 50 per cent or more are classed as part of a minimum standard. For 2012, this is marked by the dashed line.

As can be seen, people's perceptions of necessities are relative, moving with the times; as society changes, some items (particularly consumer goods) have become more important, others less. Overall, until 1999, rising living standards were reflected in changes to the minimum standard. In 2012, at a time when household incomes had become more constrained, this was halted with a decline for some items, in particular those related to leisure and social activities, with the result that a number of items dropped from above to below the 50 per cent threshold between 1999 and 2012 (Mack et al, 2013; Fahmy, 2014).

During this period, following extensive (and improved) qualitative development work, new items and activities were introduced into the surveys to ensure that the list reflected new consumer goods and changing priorities. So, for example, a computer, not asked about in 1983, was introduced as an item for adults in 1990 and for children in 1999 and has risen rapidly up the rankings; it is now seen as a necessity for children (Table 1.2). In 2012, other new items, which reflected concerns around financial insecurity and dental treatment that had arisen strongly from the focus groups (Fahmy et al, 2012), were tested and were seen to be necessities.

At the international level, the research introduced a mechanism whereby the minimum standards set for a society could be higher than prevailing standards. For example, a 2006 survey in South Africa by Oxford University's Centre of the Analysis of South African Social Policy found that eight out of 36 of the socially perceived necessities were *not* possessed by a majority of the population (Wright, 2011).

Over the last thirty years, these studies have had an impact. The material indicators of deprivation identified through these surveys have contributed to a number of official measures of poverty, including the 2010 Child Poverty Act in the UK and the poverty targets of the Irish government in 2007. The method is also being adopted by the governments of Mexico, the Solomon Islands, Tonga, Tuvalu, Uganda and New Zealand. UNICEF has used the EU's deprivation indicators for its Child Deprivation Index (Adamson, 2012).

Most particularly, the consensual nature of the method has played an important part in a wider acceptance of the relative view of poverty – that needs change over time. By the mid-2000s, the Conservative Party had backed the concept of relative poverty, explicitly rejecting the notion that poverty can only be seen in absolute terms (Cameron, 2006). This did not mean that the debate was closed, far from it. Instead the grounds were shifting from the denial that there was relative deprivation that had marked earlier Conservative pronouncements to disagreement about causations – and to proposals for alternative measures (discussed later) (Duncan Smith, 2006).

Wider views of deprivation

At the same time, there have been growing criticisms that this approach – based, as it is, on what households can purchase – incorporates too narrow a view of deprivation. The most substantial of these come from the perspective of the 'capabilities' approach developed over many years by Amartya Sen. From this perspective, Sen argues that poverty should be seen as the deprivation of a range of basic capabilities – the various 'functionings' that enable people to lead a life they choose and value (Sen, 2010; Sen, 2009, pp 231-65). The concept embraces a wide variety of factors – disability, discrimination, age, gender, environmental disadvantages, for example – which can limit people's ability to 'flourish' (Anand, 2016).

This leads to two main strands of criticism of using 'an enforced lack of necessities' as a measure of deprivation (Hick, 2012). The first is that linking the concept of necessities to items and activities that everyone should be able to afford, excludes many other aspects of life that are crucial to a person's well-being. The second is that, having identified these necessities, basing the concept of an 'enforced' lack on access to resources ignores other non-income constraints.

The first criticism is more a matter of how different aspects of deprivation are usefully categorised rather than a more fundamental disagreement about what might constitute multiple deprivation. One of the most difficult questions in this respect is how to handle those core aspects of our well-being that in some societies are left to private purchases but in others are publicly provided. In the UK, schooling and health services are (largely) free at the point of delivery, which means they are not included in measurements based on household and individual income. But it does not mean that they are unimportant to poverty. Clearly both are.

The 1983 *Breadline Britain* survey failed to include a sufficient coverage of services and was open to the criticism that, in J. K. Galbraith's iconic phrasing, by concentrating on access to 'private affluence' it had ignored 'public squalor' (Galbraith, 1958). In the 1990 survey, a set of questions on services was introduced mirroring the approach taken to 'necessities' – that is, people were asked about a range of services provided by public bodies and whether they were 'essential' or just 'desirable' and then about their use of these services and their adequacy (Gosschalk and Frayman, 1991) – an approach that was repeated in 1999 and 2012.

Analysis of the 2012 PSE-UK survey finds that those who are deprived (in that they cannot afford three or more necessities) are somewhat more likely than others to have experienced constraints in access to services but, overall, differences and constraints were relatively low for key publicly provided services, notably primary health care and school resources (Bramley and Besemer, 2016) (see also Chapter 4 in this volume). Universal services, such as those found in the UK, provide a crucial role in protecting those who are materially deprived.

In 1999, with social exclusion more prominent on political and policy agendas, the questionnaire expanded in other ways to include, for example, measures of social isolation and support and, taking account of the privatisation of many services, wider measures of service exclusion (Levitas, 2006, pp 123–60). Using a framework referred to as the 'Bristol Social Exclusion Matrix' (B-SEM) (Levitas et al, 2007), the PSE-UK 2012 survey furthered these developments with new measures to capture exclusion across a wider range of domains and to reflect underlying changes to society, such as changing labour market practices (see Chapter 6) and increasing concerns about the quality of life, particularly around the environment. These improvements mirror developments at an international level, where interest in well-being has joined with environmental concerns about growth (particularly the dangers posed by climate change) to promote a move away from the money metric measures that have dominated poverty reduction programmes in the past to wider measures of deprivation, such as the UN's Multidimensional Poverty Index or UNICEF's child well-being index (Bradshaw et al, 2006).

The second criticism – that linking 'enforced' to income ignores other constraints – also raises an important question. As Hick argues:

> It is incongruous, however, to argue that something is of serious concern if one is deprived of it because of a lack of resources but of little or no concern if as a result of other constraints. (Hick, 2012)

For a range of material goods, this has little bearing – for those who do not possess a good, the options are covered by 'not wanting' and 'can't afford'. But for social activities, this is not the case. A range of potential constraints – including disability, discrimination or time – may also be important, as may a lack of provision. In the 2012 PSE-UK survey, the question relating to participation in social activities was adapted so that, in addition to the options of 'do', 'don't do and don't want to do' and 'don't do and can't afford', a new option of 'don't do for any other reason' was introduced, along with a range of other reasons for which interviewees could identify all that applied.

Looking at the activities seen as necessities by a majority of people (see Table 1.3), non-monetary barriers on participation are, particularly for adults, significant and indeed more important for some activities than monetary constraints. For some – notably 'visiting family and friends in hospital or other institutions'– they are particularly striking. These non-monetary barriers affect all income groups, with similar levels of increased non-participation for each group.

Looking at those who do not participate in three or more activities (see Table 1.4), three constraints stand out as particularly important: lack of time due to paid work; lack of time due to child care; and poor health/disability. While the first of these is closely related to household resources (working more to earn enough), the others shift the focus to other factors – in particular, issues around gender and disability. Identifying these other constraints is important – and provides a baseline for future comparisons. Whether they should be incorporated into deprivation-based poverty measures, or not, is then a question of what provides most clarity. Incorporating too much in one measure can obscure rather than enlighten. Maintaining these wider conceptions of deprivation and non-monetary constraints as separate from a resource-based definition allows the interconnections to be

Table 1.3: Percentages unable to participate in activities seen as necessities: UK, 2012

	Do not do, cannot afford to do (%)	Do not do for another reason (%)
Activities seen as necessities for adults		
Taking part in sport/exercise activities or classes	11	12
A hobby or leisure activity	8	7
Celebrations on special occasions, such as Christmas	3	1
Attending weddings, funerals and other such occasions	3	4
Visiting friends or family in hospital or other institutions	3	20
Activities seen as necessities for children		
Celebrations on special occasions	2	0
A hobby or leisure activity	6	3
Going on a school trip at least once a term	7	9
Toddler group, nursery or play group once a week	4	10
Children's clubs or activities	9	8
Day trips with family once a month	21	5
A holiday away from home at least one week a year	26	2

Table 1.4: The factors which are important in preventing non-participation in activities*

	Percentage of those who do not participate in three or more activities mentioning the following factors[†]
Fear of burglary or vandalism	3
Fear of personal attack	4
Lack of time due to child care responsibilities	27
Lack of time during to other caring responsibilities	10
Lack of time due to paid work	29
Poor health/disability	22
No vehicle/poor public transport	14
No one to go out with	11
Problems with physical access	5
Feel unwelcome (eg due to disability, ethnicity, gender, age etc)	5

Notes:
* This includes all activities not just those seen as necessities and includes all reasons for non-participation.
[†] Respondents could identify more than one reason.

explored. With rising levels of economic inequality, it is particularly important to maintain the centrality to conceptions of poverty of resource-based measures.

Income-based measure of poverty

It is useful here to step back and examine income-based poverty measures, which have continued to dominate official measures of poverty as noted in the Introduction. They dominate, at least partly, because income data is already collected, making it easier to track trends or compare across countries.

Income-based measures all depend on identifying a threshold, below which people are classed as in poverty. Prior to 1985, the threshold was based on the Supplementary Benefit level but in 1988 this was changed and the first *explicitly relative* measure of income poverty was introduced, with the new 'Households Below Average Incomes' (HBAI) series. Initially, the government used a threshold of 50 per cent of *mean* incomes, which meant that the threshold reflected the whole income range, moving as incomes at the bottom or at the top rose or fell. During the 1990s, concerns grew that this made 'tackling poverty' too difficult, as rises in incomes of the poorest lifted the threshold. In 1999/2000, it was switched to using 60 per cent of *median* income (the mid-point). This meant that the threshold did not rise as the incomes of the poorest rose (as long as they remained below the median) but it also meant that increases to the incomes of the rich could be ignored.

When, in 1999, Tony Blair announced his ambitious promise to halve child poverty within twenty years, it was this 60 per cent of median income measure that was targeted. However, detaching the measure of poverty from the widening income inequality at the top has a significant implication for the degree of poverty measured.

Figure 1.1 shows the trends in relative income poverty using the 50 per cent mean and 60 per cent median measure for the whole population, both *before* and *after* housing costs (BHC and AHC). In the 1960s and 1970s, mean-based measures were significantly lower

Figure 1.1: Relative income poverty using 60% median and 50% mean incomes, before and after housing costs: 1961-2015/16, Britain

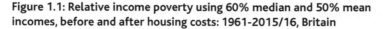

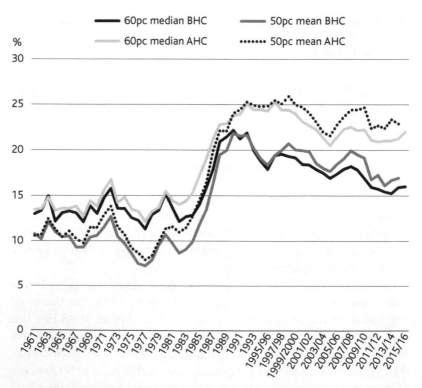

Note: BHC = before housing costs, AHC = after housing costs.

Source: Institute for Fiscal Studies, table Bn 19; Households Below Average Incomes, 1994/5 to 2015/16, table 3a

than those using the median. During the 1980s, as the rich pulled away from the rest of society, that gap closed and in the late 1990s, the paths crossed over. Since then, mean–based measures have been higher than the median-based ones. In addition, for both median- and mean-based measures, poverty has risen more sharply when based on income *after* rather than *before* housing costs. The 'official' relative income based on 60 per cent of median income before housing costs now produces the lowest level of poverty of all four measures (median and mean, before and after housing costs).

Nevertheless, whichever measure is taken, the trends are striking. There was a very sharp rise in income poverty during the 1980s, mirroring the sharp rise in income inequality during this decade (Atkinson, 2015). This stabilised at much higher rates during the 1990s and, with some fluctuations, ended up at the end of the decade at much the same levels. From the early 2000s, there was some reduction in income poverty, primarily as a result of a range of new means-tested benefits introduced by the Labour government and, with some fluctuations, it ended the decade lower than at the start. The reduction was greatest using 60 per cent of median income (BHC), the official measure, and, on this basis, it can be said that around 1 million children were taken out of 'poverty' during the Labour government years. It was, of course, this measure that was being targeted.

However, while this was clearly beneficial to the children concerned, the measure remains essentially arbitrary. Without external evidence as to what levels of income might be necessary to meet people's needs, there is little justification for saying that it has lifted people out of 'poverty'.

From the mid-1990s, an approach to measuring income-based poverty based on establishing the minimum income level necessary to meet people's needs was developed (Middleton et al, 1994; Bradshaw et al, 2008). This approach used focus groups to establish what people needed, unlike the PSE/*Breadline Britain* approach which uses a national survey. The focus groups, advised by experts where necessary on issues like nutrition, are charged with establishing, for a number of different family types, a minimum contemporary standard necessary to meet basic *needs* rather than *wants*. The budget necessary to achieve this standard is then calculated.[4] This requires a detailed list of *all* the sorts of items that are seen as necessary to be drawn up, unlike the PSE/*Breadline Britain* approach which works using a range of representative items. Since 2008, the Joseph Rowntree Foundation (JRF) has published a Minimum Income Standard (MIS) for different household types, updated annually.

This approach has the advantage, when looking at income poverty, of providing a clear basis for the choice of the threshold. It has highlighted the inadequacies of benefit levels and of using 60 per cent of median income as a threshold. Indeed, MIS as a percentage of median income (BHC) has grown for non-pensioner households from around 75 per cent in 2008/9 to between 85 and 90 per cent in 2012/13 (Hirsch, 2015, p 27). In addition, it has clear policy implications and, through the Living Wage Campaign, has had considerable impact.

But the relationship between income and deprivation is complex. Income is just one aspect of the financial resources households can draw on and households can have other demands on their incomes, notably debt repayments. Costs for some key aspects of living standards (notably housing and child care) can vary greatly depending on where you live and who you can draw on for support. In addition, deprivation and income operate on different timescales. Deprivation levels are affected by resources (as opposed to just income) *over time* while income measures are based on a snapshot of income at the current moment in time.

Deprivation trends

Indeed, while income-based measures have shown a decline in poverty, measures based on people's living standards have not. The PSE/*Breadline Britain* surveys allow trends to be tracked. Taking households who cannot afford three or more necessities – as defined at the time of each survey – there has been a sharp rise in multiply deprived households in Britain from 14 per cent in 1983 to 20 per cent in 1990, 22 per cent in 1999 and 30 per cent in 2012[5] (Lansley and Mack, 2015, p 54). Some critics argue that because the items seen as necessities change over time (reflecting changing standards) this invalidates comparisons over time, arguing that 'apples' are being compared to 'pears' (Snowdon, 2013). However, *all* comparisons of living standards over time require changes to the basket of goods included, precisely because society changes. The basket of goods making up the Consumer Price Index (CPI) is updated annually and hence real incomes (adjusted for inflation) – and, in turn, income-based poverty measures – are based on changing baskets. What matters is that, as is the case in the PSE/*Breadline Britain* research, the same methodology is used to determine the items included. On this basis, there has been a rise in overall *relative* deprivation across the last thirty years (Gordon, et al, 2013).

New items and activities, introduced to reflect changing lifestyles, have come to be seen as necessities, and increasing numbers have been unable to keep up with these higher standards. But the rise in deprivation since 1999 does not stem just from changes to the items seen as necessities. Table 1.5 looks at the items and activities seen as necessities in 1983 and in subsequent years (four items, marked with an asterisk, are included though they were no longer seen as a necessity in 2012). It shows the percentages for each year who cannot afford that item. Across this 30-year period, there were some improvements, in particular a decline in the percentages lacking key consumer goods. But for some necessities, levels of deprivation, which had shown some improvement in the 1990s, are now nearly as high, or higher, than in 1983; notably those relating to housing and heating, items which have been seen as a necessity by large majorities in all surveys.

Since 1999, the picture has deteriorated across the board. As can be seen from Table 1.6, for a majority of the items and activities seen as necessities in both 2012 and 1999 and for all those items seen as necessities in 1999 but not in 2012 (those below the dashed line in Table 1.6), the percentage who cannot afford them has risen and for only one item (a washing machine) has it fallen. Some of these rises,

Table 1.5: Percentages unable to afford necessities, 1983, 1990, 1999, 2012

	1983	1990	1999	2012
Household's items				
Can't afford adequate heating in home	5	3	3	9
Live in a damp home	6	2	7	10
Don't have enough bedrooms for children	10	7	3	9
Washing machine	6	4	2	1
Telephone	11	7	2	2
Television	(–)	1	(–)	(–)
Adults' items and activities				
Two meals a day	4	1	1	3
Meat, fish or vegetarian equivalent every other day	8	3	2	5
Warm, waterproof coat	7	4	4	4
Two-pairs of all-weather shoes	9	4	7	8
New, not secondhand clothes*	6	4	6	15
Celebrations on special occasions	4	4	2	4
Hobby or leisure activity	7	6	7	8
Presents for family and friends once a year*	5	5	4	7
Holiday away from home one week a year*	21	20	18	25
Roast joint/vegetarian equivalent once a week*	7	6	4	9

Notes:
* Not seen as a necessity in 2012 but seen as one in all previous years
(–) Too small to measure.

Table 1.6: Households going without: 1999 and 2012

Adult Items and activities	Percentage of households who cannot afford necessities: Great Britain		Percentage point change 1999 to 2012
	1999	2012	
	Lack, can't afford	Lack, can't afford	
Heating to keep home adequately warm	3	9	+6
Damp-free home	7	10	+3
Two meals a day	1	3	+2
Visit friends or family in hospital or other institutions*	3	3	0
Replace or repair broken electrical goods*	12	26	+14
Fresh fruit and vegetables every day	5	7	+2
Washing machine	2	1	−1
All recommended dental treatment*	n/a	17	n/a
Celebrations on special occasions	2	4	+2
Warm, waterproof coat	4	4	0
Attend weddings, funerals and other such occasions*	3	3	0
Telephone	2	2	0
Meat, fish or vegetarian equivalent every other day	2	5	+3
Enough bedrooms for every child aged 10+‡	3	9	+6
Curtains or window blinds	n/a	1	n/a
Hobby or leisure activity	7	8	+1
Enough money to keep your home in a decent state of decoration	15	20	+5
Household contents insurance	10	12	+2
Appropriate clothes for job interviews*	4	8	+4
Table and chairs at which all the family can eat	n/a	5	n/a
Taking part in sport/exercise activities or classes*	n/a	10	n/a
Two pairs of all-weather shoes	7	8	+1
Regular savings (of at least £20 a month) for rainy days§	27	33	+6
Television	0	0	0
Regular payments to an occupational or private pension†	n/a	30	n/a
Replace worn-out clothes with new not secondhand clothes	6	15	+9
Presents for family or friends once a year	4	7	+3

(continued)

Table 1.6: Households going without: 1999 and 2012 (continued)

Adult Items and activities	Percentage of households who cannot afford necessities: Great Britain		Percentage point change
	1999	2012	
	Lack, can't afford	Lack, can't afford	1999 to 2012
Friends or family around for a meal or drink at least once a month	6	11	+5
Holiday away from home, not staying with relatives	18	25	+7
An outfit to wear for social or family occasions such as parties and weddings*	4	8	+4

Notes:

Items are listed by the percentage thinking the item a necessity in 2012. Items below the dashed line were not seen a necessity in 2012 but were seen as one in 1999.

* These items and activities give percentage of adults not households.

† percentage of working age adults: taken as men aged 18-65, women aged 18-60.

‡ for households with children only, for children of different sex.

§ in 1999 this question was 'Regular savings (of at least £10 a month) for rainy days or retirement'.

n/a – not asked in 1999.

for example repairing or replacing broken electrical goods (which are increasingly manufactured in a way that makes them more difficult to repair), are particularly sharp. Similarly, levels of deprivation among children have risen since 1999, with the percentages going without because of their families' lack of money increasing for the majority of necessities (Lansley and Mack, 2015, p 45).

The overall impact is that, between 1999 and 2012, there has been a rise in both relative deprivation levels, using a changing standard, and absolute deprivation, using a fixed standard. This can be seen from Figure 1.2. This shows the cumulative counts for adults for: the percentages in 2012 unable to afford the items and activities *seen as necessities in 2012*; the percentages in 2012 unable to afford the items and activities *seen as necessities in 1999*[6]; and the percentages in 1999 unable to afford items and activities *seen as necessities in 1999*. When compared to the 1999 count, the 2012 count using the 1999 standard therefore shows changes in absolute (fixed–standard) deprivation, while the 2012 count using the 2012 standard shows changes in relative deprivation.

This rise in relative and absolute poverty since 1999 is a very different trend from that found using income measures (see Figure 1.1) – these

Figure 1.2: Rise in absolute and relative deprivation: adults, Britain

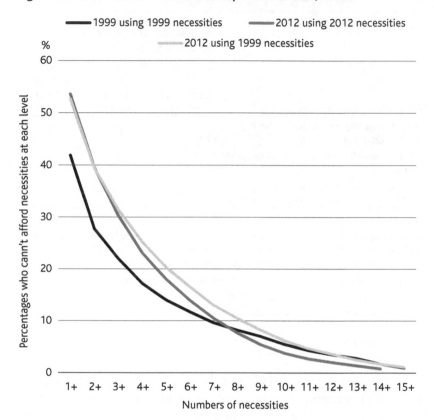

Source: Lansley and Mack (2015), p 56, 268

showed a decline in relative income poverty during this period for both before and after housing costs (though greater before housing costs). The difference is a result of a number of trends.

While the incomes of those at the bottom have risen compared to the median (hence the fall in relative income poverty), their incomes fell in real terms from 2008 as the recession and wider austerity began to bite, having been stagnating since 2004. The result was that in 2012/13, the incomes of those in the bottom quarter were no higher than in 2000 (IFS, 2016). Indeed, what's been happening is that the proceeds of growth have been increasingly skewed to the top 10 per cent and, in particular, the top 1 per cent. While overall measures of inequality such as the Gini coefficient (which is constructed in a way that means that it is more sensitive to changes in the middle, and less to changes in the extremes) showed a flattening of the rise in inequality from the 1990s, looking at the growth in incomes of different deciles shows the top pulling away from everyone (OECD, 2015; Atkinson, 2015).

At the same time, levels of debt among poorer households rose, partly because of declining incomes and partly because of the ease of credit. This had significant implications for the amount left to pay for everyday needs (Lansley and Mack, 2015, pp 58-60; see also Chapter 11). In addition, there have been differential changes in the cost of living with the prices of items brought by those on lower incomes rising faster than the CPI (Hirsch, 2013). This is particularly true for what had become private utilities, such as the energy companies (Hall, 2016).

There have also been fundamental changes in the nature of work that have led to greater insecurity in employment and great instability of incomes. It is marked by a rise in the use of 'self-employment' status by companies, short-term and zero-hours contracts, deteriorating holiday and sickness benefits, shorter and unpredictable hours and higher rates of job turnover (Standing, 2011; Bailey, 2016; see also Chapter 6). This has left people struggling to get by when in work, and unable to build up reserves for times out of work. Combined with increasingly inadequate levels of benefits and tougher conditionality tests for those excluded from the labour market, this has led to higher levels of deprivation and, in some cases, severe poverty and destitution (as described in Chapter 3).

The improvement in relative income poverty is misleading. It does not reflect the increased strains and stress on people's lives that stem from insecurity, indebtedness and the privatisation of risk and it hides the ways in which benefit changes have severely and adversely affected some groups. This underlines the value of using the PSE/ *Breadline Britain* measures of material and social deprivation based on consensually agreed minimum standards. By allowing both multiple aspects of deprivation and specific areas of deprivation to be examined, it offers a much fuller view of what really matters in people's lives.

A changing political backdrop

In 2010, the Conservative/Liberal Democrat Coalition government came to power determined on an aggressive programme of austerity, targeted largely on benefit cuts. Faced with the evidence of already high levels of deprivation and with their tax and benefit changes set to hit the poorest the hardest (Browne and Elming, 2015), they were keen to shift the debate to new measures based on subjective, rather than objective, indicators of people's well-being, and on lifestyles and behaviours rather than resources or living standards.

During the 2000s, there had been a growing interest in concepts like 'personal satisfaction' and 'happiness', notably from behavioural economics and 'positive' psychology (Layard, 2005) but also the sustainable development movement, and these had fallen on politically fertile ground. David Cameron had been an early advocate and soon after taking office set up a consultation on a National Well-being Index. In 2011, the Coalition government introduced new indicators of subjective well-being into government data collection (Tomlinson and Kelly, 2013; see also Chapter 12). But while such 'happiness' measures may tell us something about an individual's state of mind, for making *interpersonal* comparisons of well-being, they are both restrictive and misleading (Sen, 2009, pp 282-6). This is because people in adverse circumstances adapt to their situation, rating it by what they have come to expect. They 'come to terms' with it (Kelly, 2014).

The moves to undermine child poverty measurement caused greater controversy. Before the 2010 election, both the Conservatives and Liberal Democrats partners had signed up to the Child Poverty Act, one of the last acts of the Labour government, which had incorporated both income and deprivation indicators of poverty measurement. But on taking office there was a rapid retreat from these commitments.

In 2012, the Department of Work and Pensions put out a consultation document on child poverty measurement. Ignoring decades of academic research, it drew instead on proposals from the Centre for Social Justice (CSJ) – a think tank set up in 2004 under the auspices of Iain Duncan Smith. The CSJ had long argued that poverty was the result of behavioural problems and the government consultation document, directly echoing the CSJ's own proposals (Centre for Social Justice, 2012), proposed a shift to measuring worklessness, alcohol and drug abuse, family stability, parental skills and the like. Radically downplaying the role of income-based measures (misleadingly, using the limitations of these measures, discussed above, to deny the importance of income to people's lives) no mention was made of living standards or low pay. It was widely seen as a mishmash with one defining characteristic – it placed blame on individual behaviour not structural failure (Roberts and Stewart, 2015).

Those wishing to roll back the active state have long argued that the problem of poverty was the fault of the poor themselves, labelling them as 'skivers', 'lazy', 'profligate' and the like. With this consultation, and ministers' speeches, the rhetoric was being lifted to new levels by the Coalition government (Pantazis, 2016).

The consultation paper was condemned as possibly the worst document to have ever come out of the DWP, to have had no coherent concept of poverty, and to have completely muddled measures of poverty with possible causes and consequences of poverty, characteristics and associations (Bradshaw, 2013). In the end, this attempt to redefine poverty was put on the backburner for the duration of the Coalition – but not before it had achieved its primary aim of downplaying the importance of lack of income as a cause of poverty.

On winning the 2015 general election, the new Conservative government turned their attention back to this issue. With income-based child poverty projected to rise sharply, largely as a direct result of the next round of benefit cuts (Browne and Hood, 2016), in 2016 the Child Poverty Act and its targets were repealed. This was a blatant attempt to remove the question of rising poverty from political scrutiny, although, following an amendment in the House of Lords to retain a statutory duty on the government to publish the data for the indicators used to track child poverty, it will not, as explained in the concluding chapter, wholly succeed.

Conclusion: lessons learnt

Fifty years of poverty research has led to more sophisticated understandings of the different dimensions of deprivation and poverty. More reliable measures that capture and quantify the different ways in which an individual's experiences may be limited by a lack of household resources have been developed and tracked over time. The use of public opinion to establish minimum standards has helped establish agreement on the need to see poverty in *relative* terms, while at the same time enabling an approach which grounds poverty in concrete deprivations which can provide a basis for absolute, as well as relative, comparisons. This chapter has also argued that it is important to see measures of poverty based on deprivation stemming from a lack of resources alongside deprivations that stem from non-income constraints and lack of access to services.

The PSE/*Breadline Britain* research has shown the devastating effect that a lack of resources has on people's lives. It has uncovered rising levels of relative deprivation across this period, reflecting the widening of inequality. The PSE-UK 2012 research has also shown that levels of deprivation, both absolute and relative, have risen sharply in the twenty-first century while relative income poverty has remained static. This highlights the importance of looking directly at deprivation, rather than the proxy of income, in measuring poverty.

Yet, at a political level, the impact has been limited. The Conservative and Coalition governments have been more interested in trying to redefine poverty out of existence than acknowledging that there is a problem. Most particularly, there has been more effort to demonise the poor than address the underlying structural causes, an effort to which much of the popular media has enthusiastically contributed. While poverty research cannot be blamed for wider political trends, it is worth pausing to consider whether there needs to be a shift in emphasis.

Back in 1965, Richard Titmuss wrote a short essay on 'the rediscovery of poverty' (Titmuss, 1965). Noting that it was 'poverty', not 'inequality', that was being 'rediscovered', he warned of the dangers of programmes aimed at the poor 'as a definable class', namely that '*it risks stigmatising the poor by their personal characteristics and circumstances*'. He goes on to argue that:

> The political alternative to separate, deprecating programmes for the poor is to channel more resources to them through established, socially approved, 'normal' institutions. ... But what we are discussing then is something more fundamental: we are not defining poverty and devising separate laws for the poor, but embarking on a dialogue about inequality. (Titmuss, 1965)

It is, perhaps, this dialogue that needs to come more to the fore. And it is a good moment to be doing this. Poverty research, itself, is taking us there. The most fundamental conclusion of this research is that deprivation has risen as inequality has risen. Indeed, many are now arguing that it is impossible to tackle poverty without looking at the whole economic picture, including, perhaps most particularly, the increasing share taken by those at the top (Atkinson, 2015, p 25). Moreover, the research highlights an increasing overlap between the issues that many households face and the ones that push the poorest and most vulnerable households into poverty – whether it is rising housing costs and shortages, insecurity at work and low pay, stagnating incomes and rising prices, pressures on time, the additional costs of caring responsibilities, personal debt, coping with long-term illness and poor health, financial security in old age, and much else. In this context, a return to an emphasis on universalism – Titmuss's 'normal' institutions – aligns the interests of low, middle and even higher income groups.

There has been a rapid rise in interest, research and discussion around these issues and their interconnections. In particular, there is a growing critique of the failures of the current model of neo-liberal capitalism (Jacobs and Mazzucato, 2016) and the detrimental consequences it has had on people's lives (Pemberton, 2016; Cooper and Whyte, 2017; see also Chapter 11).

Poverty research needs to position itself firmly within these debates. It needs to see poverty not as a state but as a process, the poor not as a different group but as sharing the same vulnerabilities as all but the richest do. Poverty research, with its focus on what people need, plays a key part of this debate. It provides an alternative basis from that of the ideological mainstream – that of market forces, competition, profit maximisation – for a discussion about how resources (private and public) should be distributed. It could be said that it is a discussion about how to distribute the products of society to each according to their needs – and that idea goes back a lot further than fifty years.

Notes

[1] For details, including original documentation, see: http://www.poverty.ac.uk/townsend-archive.

[2] Stewart Lansley, who had worked on the National Institute of Economic and Social Research's study of low income households, was subsequently recruited to the LWT team.

[3] From private conversations with author.

[4] See the MIS project website, www.minimumincomestandards.org, for further details.

[5] For comparability across surveys, only those who can't afford a necessity are counted. If those who can't do activities for other reasons are included the percentages for 2012 rise from 30 to 35 per cent. Being able to afford an unexpected expense of £500 is excluded from this count as, though a seen as a necessity, it was asked about only on a 'yes'/'no' basis, if included the percentage rises for 30 to 33 per cent.

[6] That is, the 2012 count includes items and activities seen as necessities in 1999 even if they were no longer seen as necessities in 2012 (those below the dashed line in Table 1.6) and excludes those seen as necessities in 2012 not asked about in 1999. The 1999 count also included four items that were not asked about in 2012, namely visit to school, collecting children from school, a dictionary in the house, and carpets. As the percentages lacking these items in 1999 were small, the effect will be marginal.

References

Abel-Smith, B. and Townsend, P. (1965) *The poor and the poorest*, London: Bell.

Adamson, P. (2012) *Measuring child poverty in the world's rich countries; Report card 10*, Florence: UNICEF Innocenti Research Centre.

Ahmed, M. U. (2007) 'Consensual poverty in Britain, Sweden and Bangladesh', *Bangladesh e-Journal of Sociology*, 4(2), pp 56-77.

Anand, P. (2016) *Happiness explained*, Oxford: Oxford Univerity Press.

Atkinson, A. (2015) *Inequality*, Cambridge, Massachusetts: Harvard University Press.

Bailey, N. (2016) 'Exclusionary employment in Britain's broken labour market', *Critical Social Policy*, 36(1), pp 82-103.

Bradshaw, J. (2013) *Consultation on child poverty measurement*, http://www.poverty.ac.uk/pse-research/pse-uk/policy-response.

Bradshaw, J., Hoelscher, P. and Richardson, D. (2006) *Comparing child well-being in OECD countries: Concepts and methods*, Florence: UNICEF Innocenti Research Centre.

Bradshaw, J., Middleton, S., Davis, A., Oldfield, N., Smith, N., Cusworth, L. and Williams, J. (2008) *A Minimum Income Standard for Britain*, York: Joseph Rowntree Foundation.

Bramley, G. and Besemer, K. (2016) *Poverty and local services in the midst of austerity: A final report of the 2012 PSE study*, http://www.poverty.ac.uk/sites/default/files/attachments/PSE-Poverty-and-local-services-final-report-March-2016.pdf.

Browne, D. and Coueslant, P. (1984) *A report on the national backup initiative to the LWT series 'Breadline Britain'*, London: IBA.

Browne, J. and Elming, W. (2015) *The effect of the coalition's tax and benefit changes on household incomes and work incentives*, London: Institute for Fiscal Studies.

Browne, J. and Hood, A. (2016) *Living standards, poverty and inequality in the UK; 2015/16 to 2020-21*, London: Institute for Fiscal Studies.

Cameron, D. (2006) *Scarman lecture, 24 November*, http://conservative-speeches.sayit.mysociety.org/speech/599937.

Centre for Social Justice (2012) *Rethinking child poverty*, London: Centre for Social Justice.

Cooper, V. and Whyte, D. (2017) *The violence of austerity*, London: Pluto Press.

Duncan Smith, I. (2006) *State of the nation report: Economic dependency*, London: Social Policy Justice Group.

Eurostat (2012) *Measuring material deprivation in the EU*, Luxembourg: European Union.

Fahmy, E. (2014) 'Poverty in Britain, 1999 and 2012, some emerging findings', *Poverty and Social Justice*, 22(3), pp 181-91.

Fahmy, E., Pemberton, S. and Sutton, E. (2012) *Public perceptions of poverty and social exclusion: Final report of focus group findings*, http://www.poverty.ac.uk/sites/default/files/attachments/WP_Analysis_No3_Focus-groups_Fahmy-Pemberton-Sutton.pdf.

Frayman, H. (1991) *Breadline Britain in the 1990s*, London: LWT.

Galbraith, J. (1958) *The affluent society*, London: Penguin.

Gordon, D. (2011) *Europe 2020 poverty measurement*, http://www.poverty.ac.uk/pse-research/pse-uk/methods-development?page=1.

Gordon, D. and Pantazis, C. (1997) *Breadline Britain in the 1990s*, York: Ashgate.

Gordon, D. et al (2013) *The impoverishment of the UK: PSE-UK first report*, http://www.poverty.ac.uk/sites/default/files/attachments/The_Impoverishment_of_the_UK_PSE_UK_first_results_summary_report_March_28.pdf.

Gosschalk, B. and Frayman, H. (1991) *The changing nature of deprivation in Britain – the inner cities perspective*, Luxembourg, ESOMAR.

Hall, D. (2016) *Public ownership of the UK energy system – benefits costs and processes*, London: Public Services International Research Unit (PSIRU), University of Greenwich.

Hansard (1983a) *Report on proceedings in House of Commons 28 June 1983*, London: House of Commons.

Hansard (1983b) *Report on the proceedings in the House of Commons 20 December 1983*, London: House of Commons.

Hick, R. (2012) 'The capability approach: insights for a new poverty focus', *Journal of Social Policy*, Issue 2, pp 291-308.

Hillyard, P. et al (2006) *Bare necessities*, Belfast: Democratic Dialogue.

Hirsch, D. (2013) *A Minimum Income Standard for the UK in 2013*, York: Joseph Rowntree Foundation.

Hirsch, D. (2015) *A Minimum Income Standard for the UK in 2015*, York: Joseph Rowntree Foundation.

IFS (2016) *Relative income trends, Incomes (AHC) Bn 19-2016*, https://www.ifs.org.uk/tools_and_resources/incomes_in_uk.

Jacobs, M. and Mazzucato, M. (2016) *Rethinking capitalism*, Oxford: Wiley/Blackwell.

Kelly, G. (2014) 'Subjective well-being and the measurement of poverty' (PhD thesis), http://www.poverty.ac.uk/sites/default/files/attachments/GKelly_Subjective Well-being and the Measurement of Poverty_2014.pdf.

Lansley, S. and Mack, J. (2015) *Breadline Britain – the rise of mass poverty*, London: Oneworld.

Layard, R. (2005) *Happiness: Lessons from a new science*, London: Allen Lane.

Levitas, R. (2006) 'The concept and measurement of social exclusion', in C. Pantazis, D. Gordon and R. Levitas (eds) *Poverty and social exclusion in Britain*, Bristol: Policy Press.

Levitas, R. et al (2007) *The multi-dimensional analysis of social exclusion*, London: Department for Communities and Local Government.

Mack, J. and Lansley, S. (1985) *Poor Britain*, London: George Allen and Unwin.

Mack, J., Lansley, S., Nandy, S. and Pantazis, C. (2013) *Are minimum standards becoming less generous? Attitudes to necessities in the 2012 PSE UK survey*, http://www.poverty.ac.uk/pse-research/pse-uk/results-analysis.

Middleton, S., Ashworth, K. and Walker, R. (1994) *Family fortunes: Pressures on parents and children in the 1990s*, London: CPAG.

Nandy, S. and Pomati, M. (2014) 'Applying the consensual method of estimating poverty in a low income African setting', *Social Indicators Research*, Vol. 124, pp 693-726.

OECD (2015) *In it together – why less inequality benefits all*, Paris: OECD.

Pantazis, C. (2014) 'Comparative perspectives on poverty and inequality: Japan and the United Kingdom', *Social Policy and Society*, 13(1), pp 63-7.

Pantazis, C. (2016) 'Policies and discourses of poverty in a time of austerity', *Critical Social Policy*, 36(1), pp 3-20.

Pantazis, C., Gordon, D. and Levitas, R. (2006) *Poverty and social exclusion in Britain*, Bristol: Policy Press.

Payne, S. (2006) 'Mental health, poverty and social exclusion', in C. Pantazis, D. Gordon and R. Levitas (eds) *Poverty and social exclusion in Britain*, Bristol: Policy Press.

Pemberton, S. (2016) *Harmful societies*, Bristol: Policy Press.

Piachaud, D. (1981) 'Peter Townsend and the Holy Grail', *New Society*, Issue 10, September.

Roberts, N. and Stewart, K. (2015) 'Plans to axe child poverty measures contradict the vast majority of expert advice the government received', http://blogs.lse.ac.uk/politicsandpolicy/plans-to-axe-child-poverty-measures-have-no-support-among-experts/.

Sen, A. (1981) *Poverty and famines*, Oxford: Oxford University Press.

Sen, A. (1983) 'Poor relatively speaking', *Oxford Economic Papers*, 35(2), pp 153-69.

Sen, A. (2009) *The idea of justice*, London: Allen Lane.

Sen, A. (2010) 'On welfare: an interview with Joanna Mack for the Open University' [Interview] (August 2010).

Snowdon, C. (2013) 'Poverty, taxes and the cost of living', *Prospect*, pp 26-9.

Standing, G. (2011) *The precariat: The new dangerous class*, London: Bloomsbury.

Titmuss, R. (1965) 'Poverty versus inequality: diagnosis', *Nation*, Vol. 200, pp 130-33.

Tomlinson, M. and Kelly, G. (2013) 'Is everyone happy? The politics and measurement of national well-being', *Policy and Politics*, 41(2), pp 139-57.

Townsend, P. (1979) *Poverty in the United Kingdom*, London: Penguin.

Wright, G. (2011) 'Socially-perceived necessities in South Africa: patterns of possession', *Working Paper 10*, Oxford: CASASP.

TWO

Living standards in the UK

Demi Patsios, Marco Pomati and Paddy Hillyard

Introduction

Much research into poverty, deprivation and social exclusion is concerned with the living standards of individuals and households (Cribb, Hood and Joyce, 2015), how equally living standards are distributed, and how this has changed over time (Brewer and O'Dea, 2012). Yet there is little consensus on what constitutes 'living standards', or how they can be measured or utilised to inform policy making (Hobbs, Marrinan and Kenny, 2015). Instead, there has been an historic reliance on income-based measures of poverty. Although these measures are widely understood by policy makers, they are difficult to translate into real-life economic, material and social conditions of life (Barnes et al, 2012; Wood et al, 2012). Moreover, the focus on the lower end of the income spectrum serves to mask the experiences of the majority of the population who do not fall below the poverty threshold, including a minority just above this threshold who may in fact share many of the deprivations of those just below it. In addition, different measures of poverty identify slightly different groups of people. For example, there are discrepancies between low-income poverty and material deprivation measures (Nolan and Whelan, 1996; Perry, 2002; Bradshaw and Finch, 2003). Put simply, individuals and families with similar levels of 'resources' (for example, disposable income) may have very different experiences of or 'outcomes' from struggling financially, ranging from, for instance, not being able to go on annual holiday, facing accommodation difficulties, or specific problems in their local area.

Previous research into living standards has also tended to rely on objective measures of economic advantage and disadvantage in the UK, whereas more recently there has been an increase in the use of both objective and subjective measures (subjective poverty and financial security, for example). This rise in subjective assessments of poverty or life conditions resulted not only from an increase in the availability of data on these but also a clear sense that people's perceptions are needed in order to inform our understanding of the multidimensional nature of welfare (Veenhoven, 2002; Ravallion, 2012; OECD, 2013). The Stiglitz-Sen-Fitoussi report (2009) concluded that it is possible (and indeed crucial) to collect meaningful and reliable data on subjective as well as objective well-being.

This chapter presents an overview of a new conceptual framework and analytical tool for measuring living standards in the UK called the United Kingdom Living Standards (UK-LS) index. It begins with the rationale and a brief overview of the key literature informing our approach, followed by an operationalisation of living standards using an innovative set of objective and subjective indicators across eleven dimensions grouped within three overarching domains. After setting up the major elements of its architecture, we go on to present a framework for the multidimensional analysis of resources as a key measure of living standards. Four main sets of findings are presented: 1) an internal comparison of objective versus subjective indicators of resources; 2) a production of welfare typologies based on the comparison of objective with subjective assessments of resources; 3) some illustrative examples of the UK-LS, showing links between resources and outcomes; and 4) an external comparison of resources as found in UK-LS with common measures of poverty. The chapter concludes with a commentary on the extent to which an enhanced set of multidimensional indicators of living standards complements (but does not replace) current measures of poverty and social exclusion, and on how the UK-LS might inform policy and research into living standards in the UK.

Why a new conceptualisation of living standards?

The last three decades have witnessed major advances in the measurement of poverty. From Peter Townsend's (1979) pioneering work through the developments made by Mack and Lansley (1985) to the Poverty and Social Exclusion projects in 1999 and 2012, poverty measurement in the UK has moved from an indirect measure based solely on income to a more robust and scientific measure which combines income and deprivation. This body of scholarship has had a major influence on the measurement of poverty throughout the world (see Introduction and Chapter 1). Notwithstanding the profound impact of this work on policy and practice, this chapter contends that it is time to supplement a focus on the poor with a focus on the whole of the population through the construction of an additional tool which reflects the living standards across the spectrum.

There are several strong arguments for doing this. First, there is the theoretical argument that there can be no understanding of poverty in a society without studying the rich. Peter Townsend, throughout his work, emphasised that poverty was fundamentally a 'problem of riches' and that poverty could only be eradicated through profound changes in those structures of power and privilege which enhanced the resources of the rich to the detriment of the poor: 'The institutions which create or disadvantage the poor at the same time as they create or advantage the rich are institutions which have to be reconstructed' (Townsend, 1988: 59).

Second, there is now a considerable volume of work on the economic and social aspects of inequality (see for example: Hills, 2004; Wilkinson and Pickett, 2009; Dorling, 2010; Stiglitz, 2012; Piketty, 2014; Atkinson, 2015). These books focus on the distribution of resources throughout society, not simply on the poor. There is also increasing debate and research on new socio-economic groups such as the 'squeezed middle', 'millenials', and the 'precariat' as well as some important work being carried out on living standards for low- to middle-income households (Corlett, Finch and Whittaker, 2016).

The third argument is political and discursive. The strong academic focus on the poor has arguably made it easier for the current government (elected in 2015) to individualise the problem of poverty, to blame and stigmatise the poor. One need not look further than the government's research into 'troubled families' (Day et al, 2016). Unlike the concept of 'inequality', which explicitly focuses on the whole of society, the concept of 'poverty' refers to only one segment – the poor. However, much as we have attempted to talk about the 'problem of riches', as Lansley and Mack do in *Breadline Britain: The rise of mass poverty* (2015), for example, the concept of poverty is politically restricting and will always make it difficult to draw attention to the living standards of the better off and systems which advantage them.

What informed our conceptualisation of living standards?

The UK-LS conceptual framework and analytical tool draws on work in four key areas. First, it is heavily influenced by Townsend's (1979, 1988) position that understanding the 'conditions of life' and 'minimum necessities of life' requires expanding our focus beyond relative poverty and deprivation to include individual and groups not experiencing income poverty, material deprivation or social exclusion, that is, examining not just what some groups lack but what other groups 'have' or 'do'. As such, the UK-LS attempts to produce measures of multidimensional living standards across the spectrum of the population.

Second, it borrows partially from Sen's capability approach (Sen, 1987, 1993) by focusing on the positives (achieving a life that is valued), rather than solely on the negatives (a lack of materials resources which prevents people from achieving this) (Lister, 2004: 17). In general, concepts of 'well-being', 'quality of life' and 'social quality' involve a shift of perspective from negative to positive (Lister, 2004: 17).

Third, it draws heavily on a longstanding tradition of measuring different areas of material and social well-being from a range of international approaches: the Scandinavian 'objective' level of living approach (Johansson, 1973; Erikson and Uusitalo, 1987), the American 'subjective' well-being approach (Campbell, 1972, 1976; Diener and Suh, 1997), and German research on 'living conditions', which combines objective and subjective approaches (Glatzer and Zapf, 1984; Berger-Schmitt and Noll, 2000; Noll, 2002; Zapf, 2002; Perry, 2009, 2015).

Finally, it draws on recent attempts to measure national (societal) well-being across a number of life domains in the UK (ONS, 2015). This followed the important contribution of the Bristol Social Exclusion Matrix (B-SEM), which provided a multidimensional framework for analysis (Levitas et al, 2007). The UK-LS expands on B-SEM by distinguishing between 'resources' (means) and 'outcomes' (ends), and by assessing each using both 'objective' and 'subjective' measures.

The architecture of the UK-LS

Dimensions

Living standards can be measured across a variety of life dimensions or domains: income, housing, education, work, family and so on. According to Brand (2007), the 'commonality of dimensions is not, as one might expect, restricted to particular approaches (such as subjective well-being, micro or macro etc.), but appears indeed rather universal as far as the existing (culturally Western) frameworks are concerned' (p 143). Despite social and cultural differences in understandings of individual welfare, Brand argues that there are underlying commonalities between resources, outcomes and human needs across several conceptual frameworks.

Building on the work of Brand (2007), Table A2.1 in the Appendix to this chapter provides a summary of some of the key frameworks for measuring individual welfare noted above. Brand's original table was based on using sets of mutually exclusive welfare dimensions built from a critical review and synthesis of seven prominent frameworks for operationalising welfare measures. He grouped the seven into three broader perspectives by whether their focus was on outcomes, resources or human needs. We have added columns to show how two further existing UK frameworks – ONS' Measuring National Well-being model and the B-SEM – compare, as well as the UK-LS developed on the PSE-UK project. B-SEM and UK-LS have been added in a fourth group, 'welfare outcomes and resources' to reflect their more mixed approach.

As Table A2.1 shows, many of the frameworks share a common set of dimensions despite coming from different approaches (and countries and periods). Depending on the approach, similar dimensions (for example, social integration) may be assessed in terms of outcomes, resources or needs. This is explained by the theoretical perspective (ie. whether individual welfare is considered an outcome or resource, or means versus ends), social and cultural 'biases', and the different ways in which the dimensions have been operationalised, which in some instances reflected the availability of indicators (Brand, 2007). Moreover, there is an iterative process at play in terms of needs, resources and outcomes. According to Veit-Wilson (2004) 'meeting needs is a sequential process, a chain, in which a specified resource enables people to achieve a condition of life which is itself a resource to meet another need, and so on to the total life experience' (p 42).

Domains

Within the UK-LS, dimensions were grouped into three overarching domains by reviewing both B-SEM and ONS Measuring National Well-being measures. These domains are: 'what we have', 'what we do', and 'where we live'. The allocation of the 11 dimensions captured by the PSE-UK survey into these three domains is based on a supposition that how and where economic and social resources are deployed ('what we do' and 'where we live') play as important a role in one's objective living conditions and subjective experiences as does the actual (objective) level of resources ('what we have'). As can be seen in Table A2.1, the UK-LS 'what we have' and 'what we do' domains align closely with B-SEM 'resources'[1] and 'participation' domains (and themes), whereas there are slight variations in the UK-LS 'where we live' domain compared with the B-SEM 'quality of life' domain.[2] There are similarities between UK-LS and ONS Measuring National

Well-being domains, particularly in terms of the ONS domains 'what we do' and 'where we live'. The remaining ONS domains (with one exception)[3] align well with UK-LS 'what we have' domain.

Indicators

Lastly, we move to operationalise each dimension by identifying an appropriate set of indicators. Table 2.1 summarises the indicators from the PSE-UK 2012 survey used to measure individual living standards, across the 11 dimensions, and covering objective and subjective assessments. Each of the indicators was either developed by the research team for the purposes of the PSE-UK 2012 main survey or was available in Family Resources Survey 2010/11 (see the Introduction for explanation of the PSE-UK survey design).

Methodology

Sample size and weighting

Information on PSE-UK 2012 sample size (individuals and households) is covered in the Introduction. This chapter uses a slightly different set of weights to the Introduction, although we believe this has minimal impact on results.[4] The PSE-UK 2012 survey includes a combination of questions asked of each person 18+ in the household as well as those asked of the household reference person (HRP) on behalf of all members. The latter household-level information has been allocated to each adult in the household in order to derive individual-level estimates.

Indicator validation and inclusion/exclusion criteria

The indicators for each of the 11 dimensions of UK living standards identified in Table 2.1 were validated using a series of objective and subjective measures available in the PSE-UK 2012 survey. The three main validators used for all indicators were: subjective assessment of standard of living, PSE-equivalised household income (after housing costs) and social class using the National Statistics Socio-economic classification (NS-SEC). The indicators for 'what we do' were additionally validated using the GHQ-12 mental well-being scale, the ONS life satisfaction question, perceived social support and perceived obstacles to social activities.

All indicators showed the expected associations on at least two out of three main validators, with the exception of unpaid care (part of

Table 2.1: UK-LS framework of domains, dimensions and indicators

Domain/dimension	Objective indicators	Subjective indicators
(A) What we have		
1. Economic resources	• Income • Wealth (home ownership, savings, other assets)	• Subjective assessment of economic resources (subjective poverty)
2. Material goods	• Consumer durables (household goods) • Adult consumption (items and activities)	• Quality of household goods and adult consumption items
3. Personal and social resources	• Education and skills* • Financial and other help given to/received from friends and family*	• Impact on standard of living of receiving/giving financial and other types of assistance* • Perceived (potential) social support
4. Financial situation	• Finances (and debts)	• Financial difficulties (keeping up with bills) • Ability to pay unexpected expense • Spot purchases
5. Physical and mental health	• Physical health (longstanding illness) • Mental health (GHQ-12)	• Self-rated health • Extent to which health affects poverty • Time stress (crunch)
(B) What we do		
6. Social and political participation	• Participation in common social activities • Social and political engagement • Political participation	• Satisfaction with day-to-day activities • Satisfaction with feeling part of a community • Political efficacy
7. Paid and unpaid work	• Paid work • Unpaid work • Unpaid caring	• Quality of work (number of positive aspects of work) • Satisfaction with job
8. Social relations and integration	• Social networks (family and friends)	• Reasons for not seeing family/friends more often

(continued)

Table 2.1: UK-LS framework of domains, dimensions and indicators (continued)

Domain/dimension	Objective indicators	Subjective indicators
(C) *Where we live*		
9. Housing and accommodation	• General information (tenure, type of accommodation) • Problems with housing/ accommodation • Fuel poverty	• Satisfaction with housing • State of repair of home • Level of warmth in accommodation (comfort)
10. Local area/Neighbourhood	• Problems in local area • Crime and personal safety	• Satisfaction with local area • Perceptions of crime/safety
11. Local services	• Public and private services (available and suitable)	• Concern about losing public service

Note: * items excluded from final scores.

unpaid work) and social contact (social relations and integration). Omitting unpaid care would mean excluding an important activity while omitting social contact would mean leaving out a crucial part of social participation. These two were retained. However, a small number of personal and social resources dimension indicators were dropped due to either high levels of missing responses (for example, education) or the inability to allocate benefit unit level information to adults in the household (for example, giving/receiving help and its impact on standard of living). Indicators constructed from questions only asked of a subset of adults were also dropped (for example, services for older people).

Dimension and domain scoring

The analyses in this chapter use both dimension and domain scores. Dimension scores were created by summing together the relevant individual indicators, separately for objective and subjective aspects giving 22 dimension scores for each individual. If indicators were not binary, they were first standardised[5] so that each variable contributed broadly equally to the dimension score. Dimension scores were then further standardised[6] to ensure comparability when analysed separately. Domain scores were calculated by summing up the standardised dimension scores for the objective and subjective dimension scores within each, resulting in six domain scores for each individual.

Key findings from the UK-LS framework

Objective versus subjective indicators of 'what we have'

Table 2.2 shows median objective and subjective dimension scores within the 'what we have' domain, broken down by household type; shaded cells denote figures above the group median, i.e. relatively high living standards. For the objective economic resources dimension, income and wealth indicators are shown separately rather than the dimension score because of the important differences these reveal.

Table 2.2 reveals the higher levels of resources enjoyed by pensioner couples and couples without children, particularly in terms of economic resources, material goods, and financial situation. These groups were above the median on both objective and subjective ratings on all three dimensions while on a fourth (personal and social resources), both groups were above median on the subjective measure. Single pensioners also reported higher scores on wealth and financial

Table 2.2: Median dimension scores in 'what we have' domain by household type

	1. Economic resources		2. Material goods	3. Personal and social resources	4. Financial situation	5. Physical and mental health
Objective	Income	Wealth				
Pensioner couple	−0.2	0.8	0.3	−	0.7	0.2
Single pensioner	−0.3	0.5	−0.3	−	0.4	0.1
Couple with children	−0.3	−0.4	0.1	−	0.0	0.5
Single parent	−0.4	−0.7	−0.5	−	−0.5	0.3
Couple without children	0.1	0.0	0.5	−	0.4	0.3
Single without children	−0.3	−0.4	−0.2	−	−0.1	0.0
Other household type	−0.2	−0.3	0.3	−	0.3	0.4
All	*−0.2*	*−0.1*	*0.2*	*−*	*0.2*	*0.3*
Subjective						
Pensioner couple	0.5		0.5	0.5	0.7	0.2
Single pensioner	0.3		−0.1	0.0	0.4	0.0
Couple with children	0.2		−0.2	0.0	−0.5	0.2
Single parent	−0.4		−0.4	−0.6	−0.8	0.2
Couple without children	0.4		0.3	0.4	0.3	0.2
Single without children	−0.2		−0.5	−0.7	−0.4	0.0
Other household type	0.2		0.2	0.7	−0.1	0.4
All	*0.2*		*0.0*	*0.3*	*0.0*	*0.2*

Note: Grey shading – value above median, i.e. higher standard of living.

situation, both objectively and subjectively measured, but reported lower scores on material goods. In contrast, working-age singles (with and without children) report lower objective and subjective scores on every dimension.

We can assess the relationships between objective and subjective dimension scores directly (Table 2.3). Within each dimension, there is generally a clear positive relationship between objective and subjective scores. (On average, Spearman's rank correlations[7] (r_s) range from 0.4 to 0.7.) Another feature of Table 2.3 is that it reveals the relatively weak relationships between income and the various subjective dimension scores. The subjective scores tend to correlate less highly with income than with some of the other objective scores. The correlation between the overall objective and subjective domain scores (r_s=0.8) is substantially higher than the one between income and overall subjective domain score (r_s=0.5).

Table 2.3 models each of the subjective dimension scores using the objective scores, first excluding income (Model 1) and then including income (Model 2). Including income adds nothing to the predictive power of the model as the last two columns on Table 2.3 show. Without income, these objective scores explain 50 per cent of the variation in respondents' subjective assessments of their economic resources and financial situation. The same objective scores also explain 35 per cent of variation in the subjective assessments of material goods, and 58 per cent for physical and mental health. Only the personal and social resources dimension shows a poorer fit (this is most likely because there is no objective dimension score). Income does not explain any additional variation in any of the subjective dimensions (that is, the adjusted R squared remains the same). This shows the added value of objective non-income indicators in understanding the multidimensional personal welfare (see Veenhoven, 2002; Ravallion, 2012; OECD, 2013). In short, by relying solely on income as our main measure of welfare, we are potentially missing a great deal, not least in relation to subjective views about welfare.

Another way to corroborate these findings is to look at the proportion of variance in the subjective dimensions accounted for by income and then check how much additional variation is explained by objective indicators (in other words the opposite strategy to the one in Models 1 and 2 above). Findings (not provided here) show that income explains 21 per cent of the variation in the subjective assessment of one's income and wealth, yet adding the objective indicators can explain a further 30 per cent of variation, leading to an overall adjusted R squared of 51. Similarly, we moved from explaining 16 per cent of an individual's subjective assessment of their financial situation when using income only to explaining 50 per cent when using objective indicators. Overall, these findings confirm the results from Table 2.3 and the importance of the objective indicators in explaining subjective assessment of one's resources beyond income.

Table 2.3: Relationships between objective and subjective dimension scores on 'what we have' domain

	Objective						Adjusted R squared	
	Correlation (r_s)							
		1. Economic resources						
Subjective	Overall domain	Income	Wealth	2. Material goods	4. Financial situation	5. Physical and mental health	Model 1	Model 2
Overall domain	0.8	0.5	0.5	0.7	0.7	0.5	0.66	0.66
1. Economic resources	0.7	0.5	0.4	0.6	0.6	0.3	0.51	0.51
2. Material goods	0.6	0.4	0.3	0.6	0.5	0.3	0.35	0.35
3. Personal and social resources	0.3	0.1	0.1	0.2	0.3	0.2	0.11	0.11
4. Financial situation	0.7	0.4	0.6	0.6	0.7	0.3	0.50	0.50
5. Physical and mental health	0.5	0.2	0.2	0.3	0.3	0.7	0.58	0.58

Notes:

Model 1: with the set of four objective dimension scores as independent variables. Model 2: with the same scores plus income as independent variables.

Cells highlighted in grey show correlations of an objective dimension with its related subjective one.

Dimension 3: Personal and social resources objective scores excluded due to missing data and unit of measurement issues (see Methodology).

Welfare typologies and inequalities in living standards

Zapf (1984) has argued that we can draw on the relationship between objective and subjective assessments of welfare to produce a four-fold typology of welfare positions (Table 2.4). In two cases, objective and subjective assessments are in agreement while in the other two ('adaptation' and 'dissonance') they are opposed. According to Kohl and Wendt (2004), Zapf's approach 'draws our attention to the fact that subjective well-being does not simply "reflect" objective living conditions, but that seemingly inconsistent constellations of high satisfaction despite bad living conditions and dissatisfaction despite good living conditions are also possible' (p 312). They go on to state: 'It is then a matter of empirical analysis to explore how often these paradoxical constellations occur and by which intervening factors they can be explained' (Kohl and Wendt, 2004: 312).

Following the lead of Brand (2007), the median has been used to categorise people as 'high' or 'low' on their objective and subjective domain scores for 'what we have' and hence to allocate them to one of the four categories in Zapf's typology. Figure 2.1 shows how different household types are distributed across the four categories. The extent to which adaptive preferences (that is, the unconscious altering of preferences in light of the options available) plays an influential role in adults reporting an 'enforced lack of necessities', and is captured adequately by the PSE/*Breadline Britain* approach, has been addressed critically by other authors (Halleröd, 2006; Legard, Gray and Blake, 2008; McKay, 2004,[8] 2008, 2010; Hick, 2013). This contribution aims to expand on the debate by including different arrays of welfare typologies.

As discussed above, pensioner couples and couples without children enjoy high living standards on average. Pensioner couples are least likely to experience lower levels of well-being while lone parents most likely to be in this category – a gradient generally found in poverty

Table 2.4: Zapf's typology of welfare positions

Objective living conditions	Subjective well-being	
	High (good)	Low (bad)
High (good)	Higher well-being	Dissonance
Low (bad)	Adaptation	Lower well-being

Note: We have labelled the group in the bottom right corner 'lower well-being'. The original term used by Zapf was 'deprivation' but we wish to avoid confusion with the specific use of that term in this book.

Source: Zapf (1984), p. 25, English translation as cited in Berger-Schmitt & Noll, 2000: 11.

Figure 2.1: Welfare typologies for 'what we have' domain by household type

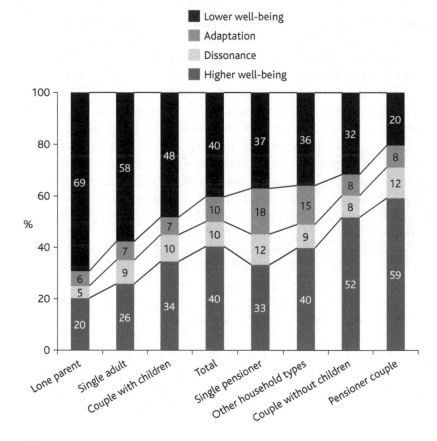

research. It is also interesting to note that pensioner couples appear to be equally likely to report adaptation (objective living conditions are low but subjective perceptions are high) as they are dissonance (objective living conditions are high and subjective perceptions are low). The adaptive preferences of older people have been covered extensively elsewhere (McKay, 2008; Hick, 2013). Dissonance amongst pensioners with respect to their living standards is not widely addressed in the literature, leaving us to speculate about the reasons. This might suggest, for example, that the set of objective resources and subjective outcomes used are not age neutral.

Considering the margins of error associated with these estimates, the overall pattern shown in this chart is of relatively similar levels of adaptation and dissonance across groups.[9] Some groups do seem slightly more likely to adapt (that is, single pensioners and other household types), whereas others (single adult and pensioner couples) seem slightly more likely to exhibit dissonance. Nevertheless, as shown in the literature (Pantazis, Gordon and Townsend, 2006; Hick, 2013), adaptation seems to be a relatively small phenomenon and is therefore unlikely to have much impact on the consensual poverty measure used in the PSE surveys. The chart also suggests that dissonance plays as small a role. Future work will look at how welfare typologies have changed over time in the UK.[10]

It should also be noted that Zapf's (1984) typology of welfare positions is not without its critics. For example, Veenhoven (2006) states that, although elegant, the distinctions between high and low have not proven very useful and do not explain much, mainly because the differences may be due more to the result of crude categorisations than experienced living standards. He argues further that the labelling gives rise to misunderstanding: 'The word objective suggests indisputable truth, whereas the term subjective is easily interpreted as a matter of arbitrary taste. This suggestion is false: the fact that income can be measured objectively does not mean that its value is beyond question' (p 75). The next section picks up on the issue of substance by moving beyond 'what we have' to look at the relationships with the domains of 'what we do' and 'where we live'.

Illustrating the potential use of UK-LS analytical tool: beyond 'what we have'

This section expands on one of the main themes in this chapter: that living standards dimensions are inextricably linked and that being clear about the relationships between resources and outcomes (or means versus ends) is necessary in order for the analytical tool to be useful in policy and research. To illustrate this, this section focuses on two relationships: the links between the economic resources dimension and the housing-and-accommodation and local area/neighbourhood dimensions; and the links between the latter dimensions and participation in common social activities, one of the indicators for the objective social and political participation dimension. Given the strong relationships between housing-and-accommodation and local area/neighbourhood dimension scores, we combine these two here, labelling the result 'housing and local area conditions'.

In both examples, the first step is to be clear about which are the resources (inputs) and which the outcomes (outputs) based on the architecture of UK-LS. In the first example, resources are defined in terms of the objective economic resources dimension score while the outcome is combined housing and local area score. The second example considers housing and local area conditions as a resource, with social participation the outcome. Both examples focus on single people without children, both working age and pensioners.

Figure 2.2 shows median scores for the 'housing and local area' combined dimension, both objective and subjective, by levels of economic resources, and household type and gender. The highest scores are reported by single pensioners with high economic resources and the lowest for working- age adults with lower economic resources. For most groups, subjective perceptions of housing and local area conditions are fairly consistent with objective living conditions. However, female single pensioners have lower subjective ratings than objective, as do single working-age adults with higher economic resources. This could be due to the fact that housing and local area characteristics covered in the PSE–UK survey focus mostly on negative characteristics; the absence of which are necessary but not sufficient in themselves to raise subjective scores for those who are higher up the spectrum of living standards. However, this does not explain the close match between objective and subjective ratings for single male pensioners.

Turning to the second question, we might want to know the extent to which housing and local area conditions are related to participation

Figure 2.2: Housing and local area conditions by economic resources, selected household types and gender

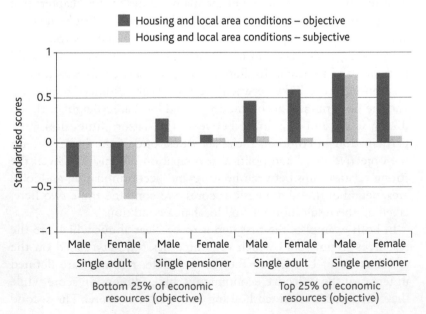

in social activities. For example, this could allow us to explore how adults with 'objectively' similar housing and local area conditions participate in (objective) and rate higher (subjective) hobby and leisure activities. Whereas in the previous example the key resource (or input) was economic (that is, income and wealth), in this example, the resource is housing and local area conditions (this is an example of the iterative switch described by Veit-Wilson (2004) from housing/ local area conditions as an outcome (or output) to an input).

As Figure 2.3 shows, there do appear to be inequalities in participation (both objective and subjective) between those living in different areas: those in the bottom 25 per cent of housing and local area conditions do less (social activity scores are on average negative) than those who are living in better areas (scores generally positive). Furthermore, in places with worse housing and local area conditions, there is a different pattern of association between objective and subjective scores for adults and pensioners. Comparing these groups suggests that both have low levels of participation, yet pensioners report slightly higher levels of satisfaction with participation. In contrast, those who live in better areas (right pane) are doing more (dark grey bars) and feel more satisfied with what they are doing (light grey bars). However, among those living in better areas, single adult females emerge as those with

Figure 2.3: Participation in social activities by housing and local area conditions (objective), selected household types and gender

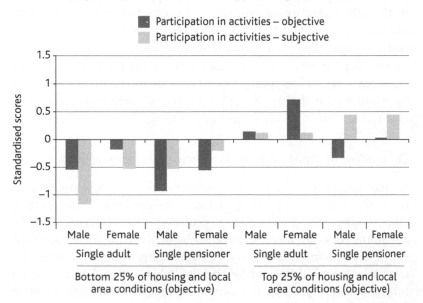

very high levels of participation, whereas single male pensioners have lower levels.

Of course, there are many other worked examples which could showcase the utility of the analytical tool but the selected ones feel relevant given the dual importance of place in poverty research (see De Boyser et al, 2009) and participation in customary activities (Townsend, 1979). And there are of course many other factors (dimensions and indicators) which could have been included in this example, but the object here is to show that there are ways in which UK-LS analytical tool can be used to inform policy and research.

Implications for policy

Despite variations in the impact of economic resources on living conditions and social participation, there is a clear message – neither objective living conditions nor subjective assessments of these living conditions should be used alone to determine living standards or alternatively levels of personal well-being. In practical policy terms, it is important therefore to take into account not only disposable income and other economic resources but also housing and neighbourhood quality (or deprivation) when assessing participation (or lack) in common social activities and how this might explain for example high or low subjective ratings of participation.

The two charts above give a glimpse of the complexity of living standards inequalities which the UK-LS approach opens up. Many of the differences found will most likely be better understood by theories and analyses that consider different patterns of socialisation and how these result in strong gender and life-course differences. Indeed, dealing with multidimensional inequalities in living standards questions whether inequalities in everyday life can be best summarised by resources. Furthermore, it calls for multidimensional theories of material and social disadvantage and advantage.

Comparison of 'what we have' domain with measures of poverty

As mentioned, one of the key rationales for the development of the living standards analytical tool was the possibility of expanding and complementing contemporary measures of poverty and social exclusion so as to include those individuals living in households above the low-income poverty or deprivation thresholds. Table 2.5 takes people with different levels on the 'what we have' domain score (objective and subjective), and shows the proportions identified as poor

Table 2.5: 'What we have' domain scores (objective and subjective) by poverty measures

	Low-income poverty	Deprivation	PSE poverty
Objective*			
Bottom 10%	67.5	95.3	80.6
Bottom 20%	56.2	89.1	71.0
Top 20%	9.1	1.1	0.3
Top 10%	8.1	0.8	0.3
Subjective			
Bottom 10%	64.6	93.9	78.9
Bottom 20%	53.9	85.8	66.6
Top 20%	8.7	3.1	2.2
Top 10%	9.0	0.9	0.8
Total	23.8	33.9	22.8

Note: * excludes PSE income (AHC – after housing costs).

using three of the PSE-UK indicators: low-income poverty; adult deprivation; and PSE poverty. Table 2.5 removes income from the objective domain score to avoid the duplication with the low-income and combined PSE poverty measures.

Table 2.5 suggests that there are some discrepancies between lower living standards and these common measures of poverty, with deprivation showing a closer match and low-income poverty showing less overlap. Only around two-thirds of those with the lowest objective and subjective domain scores (bottom 10 per cent) are identified as falling into low-income poverty, whereas the vast majority of these people are identified as materially deprived (around 95 per cent) and more than three-quarters as 'PSE poor'. When looking at the top 20 and 10 per cent, Table 2.5 also shows that, in order to capture 'better' living standards (that is, those farther up the 'resources' spectrum), additional indicators beyond low income and material deprivation should be considered, including those measured subjectively.

We then carried out further analyses to explore the relationships between poverty and poor living standards across various household types (Table 2.6). As Table 2.6 shows, there appears to be a strong but not altogether consistent pattern in terms of the household types which are identified as having low living standards (objectively and subjectively measured) when compared with common indicators of poverty. Material deprivation indicators and PSE poverty identify most lone parents and couples with children with low living standards (bottom decile) as poor, while this is not so much the case for single pensioners and couples with no children. Adults living in other

Table 2.6: Proportion of bottom decile on 'what we have' domain (objective and subjective) identified as poor

Household type	What we have – Objective*			What we have – Subjective		
	Low-income poverty	Depri-vation	PSE poverty	Low-income poverty	Depri-vation	PSE poverty
Pensioner couple	64	91	91	63	79	73
Single pensioner	58	84	70	43	81	61
Couple with children	83	99	93	66	98	84
Lone parent	69	97	86	65	99	85
Couple without children	50	99	64	48	86	67
Single adult	72	95	83	73	94	80
Other household type	45	80	56	43	81	45
Total	68	95	81	61	91	74

Notes: * excludes PSE income (AHC – after housing costs).

Grey shading = value above overall proportion, i.e. poorer households.

households also appear to show larger discrepancies depending on the poverty measure used.

To get a clearer sense about where the discrepancies between conventional measures of poverty and the UK-LS analytical tool arise, we can take a closer look at the bottom and top 10 per cent of adults according to their 'what we have' domain score, looking at the individual dimension scores by household type (see Figure 2.4).

Unsurprisingly, worse-off adults are much more likely to lack a number of key resources. Comparing the results from Table 2.6 and Figure 2.4 suggests that when considering deprivation and income jointly to identify 'the poor' (as in the PSE poverty measure), groups which have higher incomes and a better financial situation despite their relatively low living standards are not identified as poor. For example, pensioners have done remarkably well in the past 20 years with generally higher levels of income compared to most other adult groups. At the time of the PSE-UK 2012 survey, the proportion of pensioners in poverty was at the lowest level it had been for almost 30 years and they are now less likely to be in financial poverty than the majority of non-pensioners after housing costs (McKee, 2010). Although inequality within most of the top half of the pensioner income distribution has changed little, the poorest pensioners have fallen further behind middle-income pensioners (Cribb et al, 2013). Further analysis suggests that pensioner couples have relatively higher average income, something that appears in our index of economic resources (particularly wealth) and financial situation (see Figure 2.4).

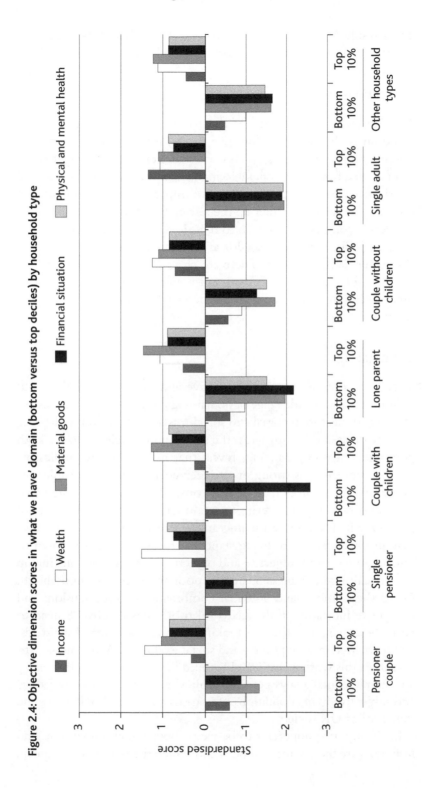

Figure 2.4: Objective dimension scores in 'what we have' domain (bottom versus top deciles) by household type

These results fit with a lot about what we already know about poverty, material deprivation and social exclusion in later life (McKee, 2010).

Implications for policy

This reiterates the validity of the joint deprivation and income approach outlined by Gordon et al (2000) for the purposes of anti-poverty policy; according to this, view policies should target those most in need of more disposable income and experiencing material deprivation. However, the external comparison also confirms that there are inequalities further up the resources spectrum. For example, pensioner couples (in both bottom and top deciles) are more likely to have higher (relative) wealth and financial situation scores but also lower levels of health. There are clear disparities in the levels of resources between the worse-off and better-off in society and these inequalities are even more pronounced when we look at specific resources.

Conclusion

This chapter argues that both objective and subjective measures and indicators across a wide range of domains and dimensions are necessary in order to measure material and social (dis)advantage and well-being of individuals and groups across the spectrum of society (that is, both poor and not poor). Findings reveal that many objective indicators of resources show as strong or stronger correlations with subjective indicators of resources than does income. The findings suggest that it is important in policy terms to retain tried and tested measures of poverty which combine income and material deprivation but also that an enhanced set of living standards measures could be used to inform policy. Both subjective and objective indicators are picking up on inequalities in living standards for poor and non-poor households. Given the number (and potential combinations) of dimensions and composite indicators in the analytical tool, users of UK-LS need to clear about what it is they are looking at in terms of living standards, and their overlap with poverty and social exclusion. A key message to take from this work is that UK-LS could be used as a complementary and supplemental analysis tool for policy and research into objective and subjective living conditions of persons and households across the spectrum of UK society.

In closing, it is important to be clear about which dimensions and indicators are the resources (inputs) and which the outcomes (outputs), and whether any throughputs (e.g. if we were to consider housing and local area conditions as both the outcome of economic resources and as inputs for participation in common social activities) need to be explored when carrying out analysis using UK-LS. Policy and research can then be linked to the specific resources needed to reduce inequalities – or lead to improvements – in overall personal well-being and living standards. Of course, all of this might sound sensible and logical to many people, as it likely fits with our general understanding of things, but to date it has been proven quite difficult to depict due to the lack of a bespoke survey on living standards. PSE-UK 2012 is such a dataset and offers new opportunities for informing policy and practice.

Finally, as we begin to understand inequalities multidimensionally, theories need to grapple with the idea that groups may be better in some respects (such as pensioners who emerge as having better levels of resources) but worse in other respects (such as health and social participation). We therefore need to question whether the existing theories that deal with poverty and social exclusion can provide theoretical guidance for future studies of multidimensional inequality in living standards.

Notes

[1] One notable difference between the UK-LS 'what we have' and B-SEM 'resources' domains is that 'Access to public and private services' has been allocated to the 'where we live' domain in UK-LS, whereas in B-SEM it is a 'theme' under the 'resources' domain.

[2] A key difference between UK-LS and B-SEM is that the 'health and well-being' sub-domain (and related measures/indicators) have been re-allocated to the 'personal and resources' and 'physical and mental health' dimensions in UK-LS.

[3] These domains are 'personal well-being', 'our relationships', 'health', 'personal finance', 'the economy', 'education and skills', and 'governance'. The ONS domain 'the natural environment' does not align with UK-LS domains.

[4] For the present analysis, data were re-weighted to population totals excluding adults in communal establishments (for example, residential care or nursing homes). The resulting weights are very similar to those used in other contributions in this volume, given the small percentage of adults living in communal establishments.

[5] Standardisation results in a score with an average of zero, where '+1' is one standard deviation above the mean score.

[6]   Standardisation was used so that the variability in the overall dimension indicator is not simply driven by differences in the level of measurement of the variables and/or by larger indicator sets (for example, consumer durables, participation in common social activities). There are nevertheless potential issues with the exchangeability and measurement invariance assumptions we make within the composite index: that not owning a car can be substituted by simply owning an extra item (for example, a second home) on a like-for-like basis across groups. Future analysis will have to be conducted using bespoke method that attempts to address these scoring issues.

[7]   We also checked these using Pearson's correlation and found no clear differences.

[8]   See Pantazis, Gordon and Townsend (2006) for a response to McKay's (2004) critique.

[9]   Sensitivity analysis using the 25th percentile (more in line with traditional measures of poverty) and 75th percentile (aligning with the 'better off' in society) were also carried out and results showed a similar overall pattern of welfare typologies.

[10] Using PSE-UK 2012 we were not able to determine the extent to which the UK is displaying a Swiss pattern of well-being and quality of life (sometime referred as the 'malaise Suisse', credited to Boltanski, 1966) has moved from a constellation of 'dissonance' towards 'well-being' and 'adaptation' over time. For further work in this area, see Suter, Iglesias and Moussa (2015).

References

Atkinson, A. B. (2015) *Inequality: What can be done?* Cambridge, MA: Harvard University Press.

Barnes, M., Brown, A., Morrell, G., Rahim, N., Ross, A., Sadro, F. and Tipping, S. (2012) *Multi-dimensional poverty: A research methodology to create poverty typologies*, London: NatCen/Demos.

Berger-Schmitt, R. and Noll, H.-H. (2000) 'Conceptual framework and structure of a European system of social indicators', *EuReporting Working Paper No. 9*, Mannheim: Centre for Survey Research and Methodology (ZUMA).

Boltanski, L. (1966) *Le bonheur suisse*, Paris: Minuit.

Bradshaw, J. and Finch, N. (2003) 'Overlaps in dimensions of poverty', *Journal of Social Policy*, 32(4): 513-25.

Brand, C. (2007) 'Breaking the GDP-cult: The potential of survey data for measuring and reporting individual welfare', Thesis submitted to the University of Manchester for the degree of Doctor of Philosophy in the Faculty of Humanities.

Brewer, M. and O'Dea, C. (2012) 'Measuring living standards with income and consumption: evidence from the UK', *ISER Working Paper Series*, London: ISER.

Campbell, A. (1972) 'Aspiration, satisfaction, and fulfilment', in A. Campbell and P. Converse, (eds) *The human meaning of social change*, New York: Russell Sage Foundation, pp 441-6.

Campbell, A., Converse, P. and Rodgers, W. (1976) *The quality of American life*, New York: Russell Sage Foundation.

Corlett, A., Finch, D. and Whittaker, M. (2016) *Living standards 2016: The experiences of low to middle income households in downturn and recovery*, London: Resolution Foundation.

Cribb, J., Hood, A. and Joyce, R. (2015) *Living standards: Recent trends and future challenges*, London: Institute for Fiscal Studies.

Day, L., Bryson, C., White, C., Purdon, S., Bewley, H., Kirchner Sala, L. and Portes, J. (2016) *National evaluation of the Troubled Families Programme final synthesis report*, London: Department for Communities and Local Government.

De Boyser, K., Dewilde, C., Dierckx, D. and Friedrichs, J. (eds) (2009) *Between the social and the spatial: Exploring the multiple dimensions of poverty and social exclusion*, Farnham: Ashgate Publishing.

Diener, E. and Suh, E. (1997) 'Measuring quality of life: economic, social and subjective indicators', *Social Indicators Research*, 40(1), pp 189-216.

Dorling, D. (2010) *Injustice: Why social inequality persists*, Bristol: Policy Press.

Erikson, R. and Uusitalo, H. (1987) *The Scandinavian approach to welfare research*, Swedish Institute for Social Research, Reprint Series No. 181, Stockholm: Almquist & Wiksell.

Glatzer, W. and Zapf, W. (1984), *Lebensqualität in der Bundesrepublik: Objektive Lebensbedingungen und subjektives Wohlbefinden* [Quality of life in the Federal Republic of Germany: Objective life situation and subjective well-being] Frankfurt: Campus.

Gordon, D., Adelman, L., Ashworth, K., Bradshaw, J., Levitas, R., Middleton, S., Pantazis, C., Patsios, D., Payne, S., Townsend, P. and Williams, J. (2000) *Poverty and social exclusion in Britain*, York: Joseph Rowntree Foundation.

Halleröd, B. (2006) 'Sour grapes: relative deprivation, adaptive preferences and the measurement of poverty', *Journal of Social Policy*, 35(3), 371-90.

Hobbs, A., Marrinan, S. and Kenny, C. (2015) 'Measuring living standards', *POSTnotes POST-PN-491*, London: Parliamentary Office of Science and Technology.

Hick, R. (2013) 'Poverty, preference or pensioners? Measuring material deprivation in the UK', *Fiscal Studies*, 34(1), 31-54.

Hills, J. (2004) *Inequality and the state*, Oxford: OUP.

Johansson, S. (1973) 'The level of living survey: A presentation', *Acta Sociologica*, 16(3), pp 211-19.

Kohl, J. and Wendt, C. (2004) 'Satisfaction with health care systems: A comparison of EU countries', in W. Glatzer, S. Von Below and M. Stoffregen (eds) *Challenges for quality of life in the contemporary world*, Vol. 24, Social Indicators Research Series, pp 311-31.

Lansley, S. and Mack, J. (2015) *Breadline Britain: The rise of mass poverty*, London: OneWorld.

Legard, R., Gray, M. and Blake, M. (2008) 'Cognitive testing: older people and the FRS material deprivation questions', *Working Paper No. 55*, London: Department for Work and Pensions.

Levitas, R., Pantazis, C., Fahmy, E., Gordon, D., Lloyd, E. and Patsios, D. (2007) *The multi-dimensional analysis of social exclusion*, London, Department for Communities and Local Government (DCLG).

Lister, R. (2004) *Poverty*, Cambridge: Polity Press.

Mack, J. and Lansley, S. (1985) *Poor Britain*, London: George Allen & Unwin.

McKay, S. (2004) 'Poverty or preference: what do "consensual deprivation indicators" really measure?', *Fiscal Studies*, 25, 201–23.

McKay, S. (2008) 'Measuring material deprivation among older people: Methodological study to revise the Family Resources Survey questions', *Working Paper No. 54*, London: Department for Work and Pensions.

McKay, S. (2010) 'Using the new Family Resources Survey question block to measure material deprivation among pensioners', *Working Paper No. 89*, London: Department for Work and Pensions.

McKee, S. (2010) *The forgotten age: Understanding poverty and social exclusion in later life, an interim report by the Older Age Working Group*, London: Centre for Social Justice.

Nolan, B. and Whelan, C. T. (1996) 'Measuring poverty using income and deprivation indicators: alternative approaches', *Journal of European Social Policy*, 6(3): 225-40.

Noll, H.-H. (2002) 'Towards a European system of social indicators: theoretical framework and system architecture', *Social Indicators Research*, 58(1/3), pp 47-84.

OECD (2013) *Guidelines on measuring subjective well-being*, Paris: OECD.

ONS (Office for National Statistics) (2015) *Statistical bulletin: Measuring national well-being: personal well-being in the UK, 2014 to 2015*, London: ONS.

Pantazis, C., Gordon, D. and Townsend, P. (2006), 'The necessities of life', in C. Pantazis, D. Gordon and R. Levitas (eds) *Poverty and social exclusion in Britain: The Millennium Survey*, Bristol: The Policy Press.

Perry, B. (2002) 'The mismatch between income measures and direct outcome measures of poverty', *Social Policy Journal of New Zealand*, 19: 101-27.

Perry, B. (2009) 'Non-income measures of material wellbeing and hardship: first results from the 2008 New Zealand Living Standards Survey, with international comparisons', *Working Paper 01/09*, Ministry of Social Development: Wellington.

Perry, B. (2015) *The material wellbeing of New Zealand households: Trends and relativities using non-income measures, with international comparisons*, Ministry of Social Development: Wellington.

Piketty, T. (2014) *Capital in the twenty-first century*, Cambridge, MA: Harvard University Press.

Ravallion, M. (2012) *Poor, or just feeling poor? On using subjective data in measuring poverty*, New York: World Bank.

Sen, A. K. (1987) *The standard of living: The Tanner Lectures on Human Values*, Cambridge: Cambridge University.

Sen, A. K. (1993) 'Capability and well-being', in M. C. Nussbaum and A. K. Sen (eds) *The quality of life*, Oxford: Clarendon Press, pp 30-53.

Stiglitz, J. E. (2012) *The price of inequality: How today's divided society endangers our future*, London: W. W. Norton & Company.

Stiglitz, J. E., Sen, A. and Fitoussi, J.-P. (2009) *Report by the Commission on the Measurement of Economic Performance and Social Progress*, Paris: INSEE/CMEPSP.

Suter, C., Iglesias, K. and Moussa, J. (2015) 'From dissonance to well-being and adaption? Quality of life in Switzerland over the past decades', in W. Glatzer et al (2015) *Global handbook of quality of life: Exploration of well-being of nations and continents*, New York: Springer: 685-714.

Townsend, P. (1979) *Poverty in the United Kingdom: A survey of household resources and standards of living*, Harmondsworth: Penguin.

Townsend, P. (1988) 'Combating poverty', in E. Hanna (ed) *Poverty in Ireland*, Social Study Conference Publications, Lurgan: Ronan Press.

Veenhoven, R. (2002) 'Why social policy needs subjective indicators', *Social Indicators Research*, 58(1): 33-46.

Veenhoven, R. (2006) 'The four qualities of life ordering concepts and measures of the good life', in M. McGillivray and M. Clark (eds) *Understanding human well-being*, Tokyo-New York-Paris: United Nations University Press, pp 74-100.

Veit–Wilson, J. (2004) 'Poverty, incomes and resources – concepts and measures', in N. Manning and N. Tikhonova (eds), *Poverty and social exclusion in the new Russia*, Ashgate: Aldershot, pp 37-62.

Wilkinson, R. G. and Pickett, K. (2009) *The spirit level: Why more equal societies almost always do better*, London: Allen Lane.

Wood, C., Salter, J., Morrell, G., Barnes, M., Paget, A. and O'Leary, D. (2012) *Poverty in perspective*, London: Demos.

Zapf, W. (1984) 'Individuelle Wohlfahrt: Lebensbedingungen und wahrgenommene Lebensqualität', in W. Glatzer and W. Zapf (eds) *Lebensqualität in der Bundesrepublik*, Frankfurt/Main: Campus, pp 13-26.

Zapf, W. (2002) *EuroModule: Towards a European welfare survey*, Berlin: Social Science Research Center Berlin (WZB).

Appendix

See Table A2.1 overleaf.

Table A2.1: Brand's (2007) dimensions in different models of objective multidimensional individual welfare

Generic categories	Welfare outcomes		Welfare resources (in terms of their empirical evidence)	
	NL Social & Cultural Planning Office	ONS Measuring National Well-being	Habich's 'Lebenslagen' Index	Hradil's Theoretical 'Soziale Lagen' model
Social integration	Social Participation (social isolation)	Our relationships – Satisfaction with family life, Satisfaction with social life, Potential social support	Social & Political participation	Social Relations Social Roles
Economic resources	Purchasing Power	Personal finance	Social situation of household Consumption	Money Poverty Risks Social Security
Housing	Housing	Where we live – Satisfaction with accommodation	Housing conditions	Housing Environment
Neighbourhood	Housing (neighbourhood quality)	Where we live – Neighbourhood attachment	—	Housing Environment (neighbourhood quality)
Physical health	Health	Health – Long-term illness/disability, Self-rated health	Health	Social Security (= access to health care)
Psychological health	Health (psychosomatic conditions)	Personal well-being – Satisfaction with lives overall, How worthwhile things they do are, Happiness yesterday, Anxiety yesterday Health – Depression/anxiety (GHQ)	SWB in separate index	'Negative conditions' (poor SWB)
Work and productive activity	*	What we do – Satisfaction with job, Volunteered	Elements of the social structure (employment)	Formal Power Working Conditions

Welfare resources (in terms of their empirical evidence)		Welfare outcomes and resources		Human needs	
Schwenk's empirical 'Soziale Lagen' model	Swedish Level of Living surveys (ULF system)	Bristol Social Exclusion Matrix (B-SEM)	PSE-UK 'Living Standards' (UK-LS)	Allardt's 'Having, Loving, Being' model	Max-Neef's basic human needs
Social Integration	Family & Social integration	Social resources	Social resources & Social relations and integration	Family attachment Friendship patterns	Affection Identity
Income	Economic resources	Material/ economic resources	Materials goods and services & Economic resources & Financial situation	Income	Subsistence
Housing Amenities & Space	Housing	Living environment	Housing and accommodation	Housing	Subsistence
(natural) Environment	Housing (neighbourhood quality)		Local area/ Neighbourhood	—	—
*	Health & access to health care	Health and well-being	Physical and mental health	Health	Subsistence
Anomie (or 'anomic' depression)	Health (psychosomatic conditions)		Physical and mental health	Alienation	Possibly Affection/ Identity
*	Employment & working conditions	Economic participation	Paid and unpaid work; quality of (paid) work	Employment Doing interesting things	Creation

(continued)

Poverty and social exclusion in the UK

Table A2.1: Brand's (2007) dimensions in different models of objective multidimensional individual welfare (continued)

| | Welfare outcomes | | Welfare resources (in terms of their empirical evidence) | |
Generic categories	NL Social & Cultural Planning Office	ONS Measuring National Well-being	Habich's 'Lebenslagen' Index	Hradil's Theoretical 'Soziale Lagen' model
Community	Social Participation	Governance – Voter turnout, Trust in government	Social & political participation	Democratic institutions Prestige
Personal safety	Housing (neighbourhood quality)	Where we live – Personal crime, Safe walking home after dark	—	Housing Environment (neighbourhood quality)
Education	*	Education and skills	Elements of the social structure (Education)	Education
Leisure	Leisure activities Sport activity holiday	What we do – Satisfaction with leisure time, Engaged in arts/cultural activity, Exercise	—	Leisure Conditions
Extra	Mobility	The economy The natural environment	—	Discrimination/ Privileges

Notes: * specific theoretical reasons for omission cited or implied.
SWB = subjective well-being.

Source: Brand (2007) Table 4.4.1.a (p.145), https://www.iser.essex.ac.uk/research/publications/513381. Author's permission to expand on original table granted to lead author in June 2016.

Welfare resources (in terms of their empirical evidence)		Welfare outcomes and resources		Human needs	
Schwenk's empirical 'Soziale Lagen' model	Swedish Level of Living surveys (ULF system)	Bristol Social Exclusion Matrix (B-SEM)	PSE-UK 'Living Standards' (UK-LS)	Allardt's 'Having, Loving, Being' model	Max-Neef's basic human needs
Participation	Political resources	Social participation Access to public and private services Political and civic participation	Social and political participation	Political resources Community attachment Personal prestige	Participation
—	Security of life & property	Crime, harm and criminalisation	Local area/ Neighbourhood – Crime and safety	Community attachment	Protection
Education	Education & Skills	Culture, education and skills	Personal resources – Education and skills	Education	Understanding
Leisure conditions	Recreation & culture		Social and political participation [Participation in common social activities]	Doing interesting things	Idleness
Discrimination Privileges	—	Exposure to bullying and harassment/ Discrimination	—	—	Freedom

THREE

Severe poverty and destitution

Glen Bramley, Suzanne Fitzpatrick and Filip Sosenko

Introduction

While most of this book is concerned with relative poverty and social disadvantage in the context of a mature post-industrial welfare state, this chapter focuses on the more extreme end of conventional poverty measures, 'severe poverty', and then steps beyond that to examine literal 'destitution'. There has been growing concern that such extreme manifestations have become more apparent in the UK since the late 2000s, for example with the rapid growth of food banks, with heightened awareness of the plight of some migrant groups, and with changes in the benefit system hard on the heels of a major recession. While traditionally such problems have been seen as associated with particular groups, such as single homeless people with complex needs or vulnerable migrant groups, there is a sense that they are spreading out to affect a wider spectrum of the UK population.

This chapter will combine evidence from the PSE-UK survey and other national surveys with evidence from a new study specially commissioned to investigate destitution in the UK. From the former, it will examine the picture on severe poverty, including trends over time and the demographic profile of who is affected. It will then put forward a robust definition of destitution which, like PSE-UK's definition of poverty, reflects public consensus views. It will report on an agency-based 'census' carried out in 10 local authority areas across the UK in 2015, and from this make national estimates of the scale of destitution nationwide. It will also present evidence on the socio-demographic profile of the destitute alongside the severely poor, on the background circumstances that underlie their plight, and on what sources of financial and in-kind support they rely upon. From all of this evidence, the authors argue that severe poverty has increased in the UK, and spread out from particular known vulnerable groups to a wider spectrum of UK households. The chapter discusses the proximate and underlying reasons for this spread, including a range of policy and administrative factors around the benefits and migration systems as well as underlying poverty (not least its geography) and the impacts of recession and austerity.

Definitions

Other chapters in this volume make use of the PSE-UK definition of poverty, which captures households experiencing a combination of low income and deprivation. Our definition of **severe poverty** is intended to capture households experiencing a combination of *very* low income, and *significant* material deprivation, and *subjectively acknowledged hardship* or *immediate financial difficulty*. It indicates a high risk of adverse consequences to health and well-being. The rationale for this approach is discussed in the following section.

In recent research we explored the definition of 'destitution', through literature, consultations and public opinion survey, in a process analogous to the PSE-UK's consensual approach to poverty (Fitzpatrick et al, 2015). The resulting consensus-based definition of **destitution** refers to **people who cannot afford to buy the absolute essentials that we all need to eat, stay warm and dry, and to keep clean**. Again, further details are provided later, in the context of an approach to measuring its incidence (see the Appendix).

Severe poverty

There has been growing concern in the UK about more extreme manifestations of poverty. Much media attention has been devoted to the prevalence of extreme hardship, and to the increased use of food banks in particular (Cooper and Dumpleton, 2013; Cooper et al, 2014; Sippitt and Ashworth-Hayes, 2015). At the same time, recent interventions by religious leaders, charities, politicians and researchers have made a connection between severe poverty or destitution and a range of developments including: immigration and asylum policy (Allsopp et al, 2014; Perry and Lukes, 2014); welfare reform and administration (Watts et al, 2014); homelessness policy and services for those with complex needs (Fitzpatrick et al, 2016); and exploitation and forced labour (de Lima et al, 2011; Lewis et al, 2013).

These concerns suggest that established assumptions about the 'welfare state', particularly about its comprehensiveness of coverage of groups and risks, might need to be questioned. Some might argue that over-emphasis on the main headline poverty definition might conceal gross disparities within the group identified as 'poor' as well as potential injustices. Others might stress the difference between 'potential risk' to health and well-being and a clear, direct and immediate risk.

However, there may also be a downside to focusing too much on the extremes of poverty, particularly if this were to lead to an undermining of the claims of those who are merely 'poor', in the sense that this term is generally used in the PSE-UK study. There has always been a strand of argument around the use of relative poverty definitions and the need for absolute benchmarks, and a focus on the extreme end may give fuel to those arguments. However, we would stress that our position remains committed to the PSE's consensual approach to poverty definition, while seeking to look at particular groups and issues within that broader frame.

Measuring severe poverty

Severe poverty is emerging as a focus for attention in mainstream and official poverty measurement but there is no standard, agreed definition. A natural temptation is to look at households in major national surveys like the Family Resources Survey (FRS) or the PSE-UK survey whose incomes are markedly below the conventional threshold of 60 per cent of median income. However, there has been growing realisation that, the further down you go into very low incomes, the more misleading are the survey data (Brewer et al, 2009). In other words, progressively more of the households recording these extremely low incomes turn out not to be poor on the basis of other evidence, for example material deprivations and other living standard indicators. Their low incomes may be due to measurement errors, the vagaries of self-employment declared incomes, their access to other assets or benefits in kind, or other factors. Therefore, any approach to measurement should not rely solely or largely on survey-based measures of income.

Material deprivation measures have become widely accepted, particularly consensually agreed sets as in the PSE and forerunner *Breadline Britain* studies (see Chapter 1). A combined low income–material deprivation measure is routinely reported in UK. In the most recent official report on child poverty measures (DWP, 2015, Chart 3), for example, combined low income (under 70 per cent of median BHC income) and material deprivation affected 13 per cent of children, while the combination with 'severe low income' (under 50 per cent BHC) affected 4 per cent, down slightly on the 6 per cent reported between 2004 and 2008. In some surveys (for example, UK longitudinal surveys), only a limited repertoire of deprivation items are used. These are deliberately pitched across the range from 'core necessities' which few go without and more marginal items which larger numbers of households lack, in some cases from choice. The more specialist PSE-UK survey tests a much larger range of items and enables us to choose a subset which can be claimed to be more core essentials (particularly food, clothing, housing).

The PSE-UK and predecessor studies have also found *subjective* poverty measures to be powerful predictors or discriminators when analysing related problems such as financial difficulties; for example, the indicator derived from the question: 'Do you think you could genuinely say you are poor now?' (Responses: all the time/sometimes/ never). There is a good case for including such a question as part of a composite indicator of severe poverty, partly because it is such a clear discriminator in terms of other outcomes, and partly because it would seem inappropriate to label or classify someone as 'severely poor' when they themselves do not regard themselves as 'poor'. Another kind of subjective measure would be household perceptions that they have difficulties in terms of financial payments, meeting bills, and incurring problem debt. On the other hand, many would question the use of subjective indicators on their own, without some confirmatory objective measures.

A further approach would be to use information on the persistence or duration of states, which enables one to distinguish transitional, recurrent and chronic poverty (Stephens et al, 2014). While such analyses may be informative and relevant for policy, it is not clear that they quite get at the idea of severity, although persistent chronic poverty may be a precondition for it (by eroding households' assets and resilience).

So there is generally a strong case for adopting a multi-criteria definition of severe poverty. This enables us to use income information without over-reliance upon this potentially flawed measure, possibly as well as selected material deprivation items, complemented by a subjective measure which confirms that what we are labelling as severe poverty is perceived as such by the people affected.

Severe poverty conceived in such a 'multi-criteria' fashion tends to require an in-depth household interview survey in order to identify households which simultaneously fulfil those multiple criteria. The longitudinal surveys permit the inclusion of criteria about persistence, although these are not intrinsically essential to the concept. However, all survey-based measures have the disadvantage of ignoring the population not in 'private households' (for example, rough sleepers, hostel dwellers, prisoners, long stay in-patients) as well as groups with very poor response to such surveys (for example, transients, 'sofa surfers'). This is a crucial difficulty when looking at extreme forms of poverty and disadvantage. This limitation of household surveys is one critical reason for drawing a distinction between 'severe poverty' and 'destitution': the latter is better estimated through other means as discussed below.

PSE-UK and other survey evidence

Given its particular advantages identified above, we used PSE-UK data to explore various severe poverty measures based on different versions of the three criteria: (a) low income (net equivalised AHC); (b) material deprivations; and (c) subjective poverty. We sought to test and validate these by relating each variant to a spectrum of indicators capturing the kinds of effects we would expect to be associated with severe poverty (for example, health being affected by low income; skimping on food; wearing secondhand/worn-out clothes; being embarrassed or made to feel small because of poverty; or reporting financial payment difficulties and problem debt).

The best versions of our severe poverty measure showed a very strong discrimination in terms of these indicators. For example, our preferred formulation (which had an overall incidence of 2.1 per cent) was associated with rates on these key confirmatory indicators between four and twenty times the average (for example, 'health affected by money', 33 per cent vs 1.7 per cent; 'worn-out clothes', 63 per cent vs 10 per cent; 'feel small', 64 per cent vs 16 per cent). This measure combined: (a) income below 40 per cent of median AHC; (b) two or more deprivations from a 'core essentials' set, and three or more overall; (c) subjectively feeling poor all the time, or having an income well below the self-defined poverty level of income, or having a living standard well below average.

For time series and persistence analyses, we can use the UK Household Longitudinal Study (UKHLS, known to respondents and the general public as 'Understanding Society') and its predecessor, the British Household Panel Survey (BHPS). With these surveys, we do not have the subjective poverty indicators so instead we use indicators of financial difficulty, while the more limited set of material deprivations are supplemented with some housing deprivations. A shorter time series is available from 2004-12 using the cross-sectional FRS, but only for working-age households. (Definitions are given in the Appendix.)

Figure 3.1 plots these time series, showing that severe poverty (like poverty generally) fell in the UK from the mid-1990s to the early 2000s. After slight fluctuation in the period 2003–07 there was a steep rise in 2008–10, which may be attributed primarily to the financial crisis and recession. Recently, severe poverty appears to have either plateaued or gone down and up again. Our interpretation here is that although the recession has gradually eased, welfare reforms and austerity cuts have been having increasing impacts, particularly from 2011 and again from 2013 (although this is off the end of these series).

This picture of recent increases in severe poverty is consistent with data on several phenomena associated with more extreme poverty and destitution. These include data on homelessness (Fitzpatrick et al, 2016), benefit sanctions (Watts et al, 2014), use of food banks (The Trussell Trust, 2015), and numbers of migrants who do not have recourse to public funds (Perry and Lukes, 2014); see also Bramley et al, 2016.

Further supporting evidence for this pattern can be found by comparing the results of the PSE surveys of 1999 and 2012. Comparison of the two shows substantial and significant increases in the incidence of a range of material deprivations which a large majority of people think are essentials in contemporary Britain. Examples would include the increases in people lacking the following items because they could not afford them: heating to keep a home adequately warm (3% to 9%); a damp-free home (7% to 10%); two meals a day (1%

Figure 3.1: Severe poverty timelines 1996-2012, based on UK Household Longitudinal Surveys and Family Resource Survey (FRS) (working age only)

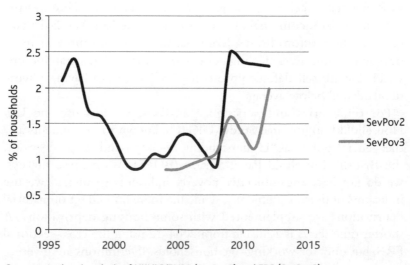

Sources: Authors' analysis of UKHLS/BHPS (SevPov2) and FRS (SevPov3)

to 3%); being able to replace/repair broken electrical goods (12% to 26%); fresh fruit/vegetables daily (5% to 7%); celebrations on special occasions (2% to 4%); meat/fish/vegetarian equivalent daily (2% to 5%); enough bedrooms for children (3% to 9% of children) (Lansley and Mack, 2015, Figure 6, p 42).

From the longitudinal studies, particularly BHPS, we can say that the persistence of severe poverty over two successive years is 20-30% on average. Severe poverty, like poverty generally, is more prevalent in social and private rental tenures, among lone-parent and single-adult households, and among younger adults.

Destitution

Measuring destitution

In seeking to first define and then measure 'destitution' in the contemporary UK, we carried out a literature review, engaged in consultation with 50 expert key informants, and then used an Omnibus Survey to test public opinion on the definition of destitution (Fitzpatrick et al, 2015). This process has strong parallels with that utilised in successive PSE studies. As no definition of destitution had been consistently employed before, we first developed a draft definition. In doing so, we found several areas of disagreement amongst experts, for example on duration and on the list of essentials.

It was therefore helpful to test our proposed definition with the general public through the Omnibus Survey of 2,000 adults. This showed strong support for the inclusion of six core essentials: shelter (96 per cent), food (89 per cent), heating (86 per cent), clothing (86 per cent), lighting (76 per cent), basic toiletries (75 per cent). No other items secured majority approval. There was also a clear steer on time parameters (for example, sleeping rough for one night, less than two meals on more than 2 days in a month). Also very significantly, majorities agreed that you were destitute if you were reliant on charity, forced labour, abusive relationships, friends or crime to meet your essential needs; there were more mixed (marginal) results on whether reliance on parents or payday loans were a marker of destitution. We also tested what income levels the public thought were required to avoid destitution, asking 'how much money to keep a household like yours out of destitution?'. The results matched fairly well to what the lowest income decile spend on these items and they correspond with 80 per cent of the 'Minimum Income Standard' (MIS) budget amounts for the same items.

From this extensive process, our **formal definition of destitution** is as follows:

People are **destitute** if, in the past month, they **lacked two or more** of following because they **could not afford them**:

Shelter (slept rough for one or more nights);

Food (fewer than two meals a day for two or more days);

Heating their home (have been unable to do this for five or more days);

Lighting their home (have been unable to do this for five or more days);

Clothing and footwear (appropriate for weather);

Basic toiletries (soap, shampoo, toothpaste, toothbrush).

People are also destitute if their income is so low that they are **unable to purchase these essentials for themselves** (based on a combination of what the poorest spend on these six essentials, 80 per cent of MIS for those items, and what public said they needed; for example: single, £70 per week; lone parent with one child, £90 per week; and couple without children, £100 per week).

By contrast with general or even severe poverty, destitution implies a crisis and an unsustainable position. Proximate causes ('routes in') are likely to involve disruptive events (this is discussed further in this chapter). It implies people are forced to rely on sources of material support which may not be 'acceptable', like charity or begging, and challenges our established assumptions about the nature of the welfare state (and of family/informal support structures). The element of crisis also provides a pointer to how we might measure and profile destitution, namely by surveying crisis services and their users.

Levels of destitution: local case studies and 'census surveys'

In light of the above insights, and working with the agreed definition, we chose to research the scale and profile of destitution in the UK in 2015 through in-depth case studies in ten local authority areas. In each area, we undertook a one-week 'census survey' of users of a representative set of voluntary sector services providing 'crisis' help, and followed this up with in-depth qualitative interviews. The ten areas were chosen from across UK to represent a range of contexts, informed by secondary data, with some bias towards areas with higher expected levels of destitution. In each area, we mapped all relevant crisis services, asking a random sample to participate (stratified by type and size of service to ensure they were representative). We undertook a one-week 'census' of service users using a self-completion questionnaire with assistance where necessary. A total of 2,009 forms were completed from 63 agencies in the ten areas, giving a response rate of 60 per cent of the estimated clients in the week. In reporting the quantitative results from the census survey, these have been reweighted to reflect our national annual estimate of numbers in different broad categories and types of area. (The use of secondary datasets to gain a national picture from the ten case study areas is discussed further in the Appendix).

Later, in-depth interviews were held with 80 destitute census respondents (selected to reflect the overall profile of those assessed as destitute). We do not report in detail on the findings from this part of the study, but suffice to say that there was strong reinforcement of findings from the census survey analysis, and a rich if distressing picture painted of the experiences of people in destitution today (see Fitzpatrick et al, 2016 for more detail).

Who is destitute?

Overall 57 per cent of voluntary sector crisis service users were 'destitute' according to our definition (and 43 per cent were not). The 57 per cent who were destitute comprised: 27 per cent who lacked at least two essentials; 7 per cent who had an income so low that they could not afford to buy at least two essentials for themselves; and 23 per cent who had both problems.

Figure 3.2 shows that single-person households predominate among the destitute population, whereas we found both severe and general poverty were concentrated among lone-parent and, to a lesser extent, couple families in the household-based survey (UKHLS, PSE). The lower incidence of destitution among families with children suggests that access to support mechanisms (family, benefits, social services) is greater for them, even though they are at higher risk of general poverty. Younger single men (under 35) were at greatest risk of destitution. The young are much more vulnerable to destitution, which is extremely rare among those post-retirement age (only 1.5 per cent of those aged over 65, compared with their roughly 16 per cent share of poverty). Few of the destitute population are currently in work (5 per cent), again in contrast with the general working-age poor, a majority of whom are now in work.

Figure 3.2: Household types of destitute service users compared with severe poverty group and UK households

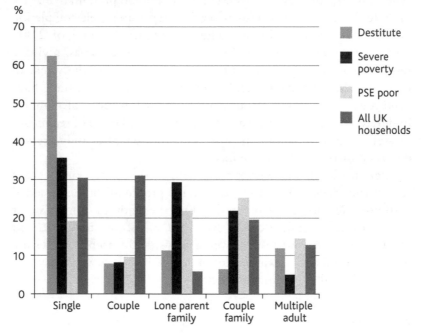

Sources: Destitution census survey; authors' analysis of UKHLS 2012

The analysis in Fitzpatrick et al (2016) suggests a broad three-way split of the people affected by destitution into: migrants (anyone born overseas), UK-born people with complex needs, and other UK groups. Despite most recent literature referring to destitution among migrants, particularly asylum seekers, we found that a majority of destitute are UK-born (79 per cent of annual estimate). Asylum seekers are particularly vulnerable to destitution, but they are a minority within a minority.

National and local estimates

No existing datasets measure destitution directly, but there is a range of sources which, taken together, enable us to investigate the national scale and geographic distribution of groups known to be at high risk of destitution, such as people in severe poverty, vulnerable migrants or people with complex needs. Combining the evidence on the distribution of these groups with our census survey results for the set of case study areas, we can make good estimates of national and local levels of destitution. By bringing in information on the frequency with which people made use of local services, we can make an estimate of the numbers destitute over the course of a year as well as providing estimates for numbers in a given week (see the Appendix). The data sources used and the way they were combined are described more fully in the Bramley et al, 2016.

Altogether about 24 indicators were combined into composite measures for the three sub-groups with high risk of destitution: migrants, UK-born with complex needs and other UK groups. These were expressed as a rate per 100 households. While these indices gave us a good measure of *relative* incidence by local authority, our census survey results for the ten case study areas gave us a direct estimate of the *absolute* number of destitute households in those areas. By combining these we could make a reasonable estimate of the national numbers.

The national (UK) total is around 185,000 households destitute in a typical week in early 2015. Over a whole year, we estimate the numbers of households affected by destitution in the UK at 670,000, containing *1,250,000 persons of whom 310,000 are children*. This is a relatively small fraction of the total population (2.5 per cent of all households), but still a huge number in absolute terms.

These are *conservative* estimates, based on a strict application of our definition and focused exclusively on those cases that come to the attention of voluntary sector crisis services in our case study areas, scaled up to national level. Destitute households which do not contact any crisis services, or which only contact statutory services, are not included. (From analysis of data on Local Welfare Assistance funds, the replacement of the former discretionary Social Fund, we know the latter group is likely to be substantial in number.) National numbers are clearly derived from both a local agency sampling process and grossing-up procedures dependent on the robustness of secondary data. We suggest in the technical report (Bramley et al, 2016) that the likely error margin would be of the order of 10-15 per cent.

The local indices when combined show an interesting geographical picture of destitution (Figure 3.3). We were also able to use multiple regression analysis to explore the relationships across Britain at local authority level between the estimated level of destitution and a range of socio-demographic variables. This found that, other things being equal, elevated rates of destitution were associated with several variables related to poverty, particularly concentrations of unemployment, low-income poverty and long-term sickness and disability (see Bramley et al, 2016). This statistical model does not prove causality but what can be said with certainty is that it summarises a geography of destitution

Figure 3.3: Estimated annual destitution rates by local authority district (% of households)

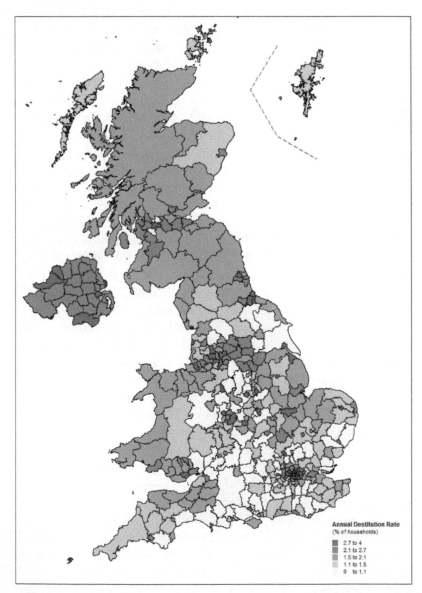

Annual Destitution Rate
(% of households)

■ 2.7 to 4
■ 2.1 to 2.7
▨ 1.5 to 2.1
░ 1.1 to 1.5
○ 0 to 1.1

Source: Authors' analysis of PSE, UKHLS and population census and other secondary data sources at local authority level

which matches very closely the geography of poverty in general, apart from some particularities related to the location of key migrant groups, including asylum seekers.

Routes into destitution

In the questionnaire given to service users in our case study areas, we asked respondents about a range of experiences over the previous 12 months that the existing literature and our key informant interviews suggested may contribute to destitution. As we would expect, there were differing experiences between our three main sub-groups (see Table 3.1).

Getting behind on bills was very common among UK-born service users, especially among those without complex needs, three-quarters of whom reported experiencing this in the last 12 months. Serious debt affected not quite so many respondents, but was still a significant phenomenon, reported by nearly two-fifths of the UK-other group. The role of the welfare benefits system as a route into destitution is quite striking with one in two reporting problems with benefit delays or benefit sanctions. Given that migrants are less likely than UK-born

Table 3.1: Problems/issues experienced in last 12 months by destitute service users in three main demographic sub-groups

Experienced in last 12 months	Migrant (%)	Complex need (%)	Other UK (%)	All destitute (%)
Getting behind on bills	31	56	73	57
Serious debt	23	27	43	33
Any financial problem	*36*	*57*	*75*	*60*
Benefit delays	25	45	42	40
Benefit sanctions	21	34	31	30
Any benefit problem	*36*	*57*	*53*	*51*
Serious health problems	24	32	29	29
Parents/family relationship breakdown	15	40	14	25
Divorce or separation	16	18	10	14
Domestic violence	9	18	4	11
Any relationship problem	*28*	*53*	*22*	*36*
Being evicted	13	26	16	19
Losing a job	20	13	16	16
Reduced hours or pay cut	7	3	8	6
Any job problem	*23*	*15*	*21*	*19*
Coming to the UK to live	16	1	1	4
None of these	11	7	7	8

Source: Destitution Census Survey, reweighted to give national annual picture.

respondents to be in receipt of benefits (as many lack eligibility), it is unsurprising that they less commonly reported such experiences.

As we would have expected (see also Fitzpatrick et al, 2013), relationship breakdown (with parents or family) and domestic violence were far more common among the complex needs cases than among the other two sub-groups. Perhaps surprisingly, however, serious health problems were reported almost as often by the UK-other group, and were also noted by one-quarter of migrants; such problems might have resulted from or compounded preceding severe poverty. While eviction was most frequently reported by UK-complex needs service users, it was also in evidence among the other two sub-groups. Negative work-related experiences, particularly losing a job, were most common among migrants, but even in this sub-group affected only a quarter overall; this may reflect the fact that many in our sample lacked the right to work in the UK. It is notable that only 16 per cent of destitute migrants had come to the UK to live in the past year, indicating that destitution does not affect only (or even mainly) 'new' migrants.

We do not report the qualitative interview evidence in detail, but it is particularly striking to note the concordance between the evidence from the census survey and the stories told by households in the follow-up interviews. Essentially, several interacting factors undermined the ability of those already on low incomes to meet essential needs, and usually this was not a one-off experience but repeated or sustained. Particularly common as main 'triggers' were:

- problem debt and arrears, especially with public authorities and utilities, rather than 'consumer credit';
- benefit issues: delays, levels and sanctions;
- additional expenditure associated with health;
- high living costs (housing and energy); and
- a range of specific issues for migrants.

The role of debt and arrears with public bodies or regulated utilities was a particularly striking finding, and specifically the problematic terms of repayment and the uncoordinated nature of debt recovery. This is discussed further in the light of PSE-UK evidence in Chapter 13, and echoes recent findings of Citizens Advice Scotland (2016).

Sources of support

The sources of both financial and in-kind support received by the three destitute sub-groups varied considerably, and revealed the particular vulnerability of the destitute migrants using voluntary sector crisis services (Figure 3.4). The benefits system remains most important as a source of financial support, but clearly in the case of destitute households it is failing to provide adequate support. If and when further cuts in benefit levels or eligibility are imposed, levels of destitution and severe poverty are likely to mount. Significantly, only just over half of migrant service users reported having received money from benefits (including Home Office support) in the past month, compared with more than three-quarters of the UK-born sub-groups. Migrants were also less likely than those who were UK-born to have received money from parents recently, although the levels of financial help from other relatives, friends, charities, and the Local Welfare Fund were more even across the sub-groups. Note the greater importance of friends than family as a source of financial help for all three sub-groups (contrast this with the situation of the broader poor group,

Figure 3.4: Sources of financial support for destitute service users in past month by main sub-groups

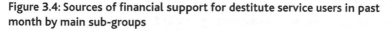

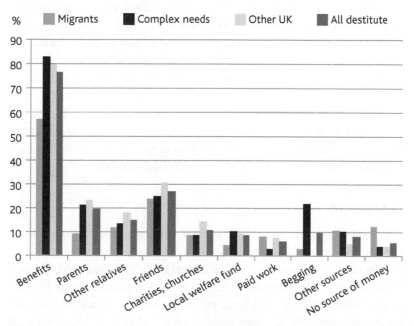

Source: Destitution census survey (Fitzpatrick et al, 2016)

who are able to and frequently do borrow from family, as shown in Chapter 13). Fewer than one in ten of any of the destitute sub-groups had received money from paid work in the past month. The other notable point is that 21 per cent of UK-complex needs service users reported having begged in the last month.

The data shows that destitute migrants were also less likely to report receipt of 'in-kind' support from most of these sources than UK-born service users, particularly again from parents, though note that around a third of all three sub-groups received in-kind help from a Local Welfare Fund. Both the Funds and charities appear to be a much more important source of in-kind than financial support, and were more prominent than family and friends.

Impacts of destitution on people's lives

The report by Fitzpatrick et al (2016) provides a rich picture of the impacts of destitution on the lives of eighty households in UK in 2015. While it is beyond the scope of this chapter to report this material in any detail, a number of findings are clear. Destitution was not a brief transitional experience, but more typically an extended episode preceded and followed by periods of poverty. Many people had to resort to quite radical economising, including strikingly widespread and persistent experience of going without food and other essentials such as heating or toiletries. People had been forced to seek assistance from charitable organisations but found it demeaning, shameful and humiliating to do so. Reliance on family and friends was tempered by the knowledge that they were frequently in situations almost as precarious, while many (including migrants) had no network to turn to. Many experienced mental and/or physical ill health, in some cases exacerbated by their material living conditions and often adding to their cost of living, while social isolation was also a very common experience, along with strained family relationships.

Conclusion

It is distressing, but arguably a sign of the times, that we should be writing a chapter about severe poverty and destitution in the context of a mature, sophisticated post-industrial welfare state like Britain. However, the evidence from PSE, other surveys, and a range of other sources makes it clear that these problems have been on the increase. From new research we have demonstrated that it is possible to get robust measures of the scale and profile of destitution in contemporary

Britain, by combining case study area census data on users of emergency services with a battery of secondary and administrative data. This picture can then be put together with the pattern of severe poverty within the household population from PSE and other major surveys.

The destitute population in contemporary Britain comprise three main groups, similar in numbers taken over a year: migrants (including asylum, EU and other sub-groups); UK-born people with complex needs; and, other UK-born people. The latter group may be seen as more newly emergent and growing in scale, with a clear link to benefit changes and administration, including sanctions. However, the evidence on routes into destitution underlines the range and complexity of issues, and the extent to which this is not a one-off experience, but rather an outcome from a prolonged period of poverty of varying severity, compounded by factors like debt/arrears, ill health, relationship breakdowns or job loss.

The people affected have generally shown considerable effort in coping strategies but have in the end reluctantly been forced to seek emergency assistance. While praising the personal kindness and consideration of voluntary sector helpers in food banks, drop-in centres and the like, they – like the British public as a whole – are clear that to have to seek charitable aid in these situations is unacceptable in twenty-first century Britain. Local welfare funds are playing quite a big role, but a very variable one across England thanks to 'localisation'. While there are many causal factors, it is striking the extent to which public policies and administration are implicated in many cases, whether in terms of groups of migrants prevented from working or subsisting on sub-destitution levels of income, the many people affected by unrealistic terms of debt recovery (and the uncoordinated nature of debt recovery procedures) from DWP, local authorities and utilities companies which leave them nothing to live on, or the widespread delays, sanctions and errors in benefit administration.

This study has shown that destitution is intrinsically linked to broader poverty, as is strikingly underlined by the geographical profile of destitution rates. Those experiencing destitution generally have long-term experience of poverty, driven by low income from work or benefits, the high cost of essentials and debts associated with paying for these essentials, poor health and in some cases addictions – factors which made them at risk of destitution. But destitute people have usually experienced some additional factors – specific income shocks associated with the benefit system (sanctions, delays, or errors), barriers posed by the immigration system (lack of access to the labour market, very limited or no benefit eligibility), lack of family support, and other adverse circumstances. If and when they recover from periods of destitution, many remain in poverty and vulnerable to finding themselves in that more extreme state again.

Poverty matters for many reasons. What this chapter has shown is that one important reason is that poverty exposes people and communities to a heightened risk of the extremes of hunger, cold, rooflessness, isolation, and mental and physical illness, by reducing their resilience to shocks. The risk of poverty becoming destitution has been increased by recent changes in welfare and other policies and their administration – there are more holes in the safety net. Policy makers should pay attention to the situation of people at the extremes: some have complex needs which warrant more intensive interventions, others are victims of systems which are not working effectively as well as a run of bad luck. This is not in any way to diminish the broader focus of policy concern that should be addressed to the wider problem of poverty in the UK which affects approaching a quarter of the entire population.

References

Allsopp, J., Sigona, N. and Phillimore, J. (2014) 'Poverty among refugees and asylum seekers in the UK', *Institute for Research into Superdiversity Working Paper Series*, 01/14, Birmingham: IRIS.

Bramley, G., Fitzpatrick, S. et al (2015) *Hard edges: Mapping severe and multiple disadvantage – England*, London: Lankelly Chase Foundation.

Bramley, G., Fitzpatrick, S. and Sosenko, F. (2016) *Destitution in the UK: Technical report*, Edinburgh: Heriot-Watt University.

Brewer, M., O'Dea, C., Paul, G. and Sibieta, L. (2009) 'The living standards of families with children reporting low incomes', *DWP Research Report 577*, London: DWP.

Citizens Advice Scotland (2016) *Living at the sharp end*, Citizens Advice Scotland.

Cooper, N. and Dumpleton, S. (2013) *Walking the breadline: The scandal of food poverty in 21st century Britain*, Manchester and Oxford: Church Action on Poverty and Oxfam.

Cooper, N., Purcell, S. and Jackson, R. (2014) *Below the breadline: The relentless rise of food poverty in Britain*, Manchester, Oxford and Salisbury: Church Action on Poverty, Oxfam and The Trussell Trust.

DWP (Department for Work and Pensions) (2015) *Households Below Average Income: an analysis of the income distribution 1994/95–2013/14*, London: DWP.

Fitzpatrick, S., Bramley, G., Blenkinsopp, J., Johnsen, S., Littlewood, M., Netto, G. I. and Watts, B. (2015) *Destitution in the UK: An interim report*, York: Joseph Rowntree Foundation.

Fitzpatrick, S., Bramley, G., Sosenko, F., Blenkinsopp, J., Johnsen, S., Littlewood, M., Netto, G. and Watts, B. (2016) *Destitution in the UK: Final report*, York: Joseph Rowntree Foundation.

Fitzpatrick, S., Pawson, H., Bramley, G., Wilcox, S. and Watts, B. (2016) *The homelessness monitor: England 2016*, London: Crisis.

Lansley, S. and Mack, J. (2015) *Breadline Britain – the rise of mass poverty*, London: Oneworld.

Lewis, H., Dwyer, P., Hodkinson, S. and Waite, L. (2013) *Precarious lives: Experiences of forced labour among refugees and asylum seekers in England*, Leeds: University of Leeds.

Lima, P. de, Arshad, R., Bell, A. and Braunholtz-Speight, T. (2011) *Community consultation on poverty and ethnicity in Scotland*, York: Joseph Rowntree Foundation.

Perry, J. and Lukes, S. (2014) *What shapes migrant destitution and what can be done about it?* Presented at the COMPAS Breakfast Briefing, Oxford.

Sippitt, A. and Ashworth-Hayes, S. (2015) *Food banks, zero hours contracts and falling wages: Are we worse off?* Full Fact blog, https://fullfact.org/economy/food-banks-zero-hours-contracts-and-falling-wages-are-we-worse/. Accessed 15 July 2017.

Standing, G. (2011) *The precariat: The new dangerous class*, London: Bloomsbury.

Stephens, M., Leishman, C., Bramley, G., Ferrari, E. and Rae, A. (2014) *Poverty and housing through the lifecourse*, York: Joseph Rowntree Foundation.

Trussell Trust, The (2015) 'Foodbank use tops one million for first time.' Press release. Briefing, Oxford.

Watts, B., Fitzpatrick, S., Bramley, G. and Watkins, D. (2014) *Welfare sanctions and conditionality in the UK*, York: Joseph Rowntree Foundation.

Appendix: Technical notes

Definitions of severe poverty

Understanding Society (UK Longitudinal 2009-) (SevPov2):
<40% median income AHC,
plus (deprived on more than one-third of adult OR child items OR one or more of four housing needs and unable to buy),

plus (any housing payment problem OR financial situation difficult OR expected to deteriorate) (prevalence 1.5%)

British Household Panel Survey 1996-2008: similar to Understanding Society

Family Resources Survey (FRS 2004-12) (SevPov3) is similar in principle: working-age households with:
income after housing cost below 40% of median,
plus 3 or more out of 7 adult deprivations,
plus 2 or more out of 6 household utility etc debts

Generating national estimates of destitution

In each case study area an initial mapping exercise produced a list of agencies/services which were classified by four main categories (advice/food/homelessness and complex needs/migrants) and by a broad size grouping. A sample of 6-8 of these services was then drawn, to achieve target numbers of 1-2 services in each category, with probability of selection being set at a higher level for 'large' services. Services were listed by category, size group, and then in alphabetical name order, and the sample was drawn using the appropriate sampling interval starting on a random number within this. From this sampling process, we know the probability of selection of each included service.

From the census returns and fieldwork we know the number of completed survey forms, and also the number or estimate of unique clients in scope that week. The ratio of these two numbers gives us a response rate for each agency/service. The combination of these two pieces of information gives us a weighting factor for each service agency, to get an estimate of the total number of service users in the case study area in the survey week.

Questions were included on how many times the same service had been used in the last year (banded), and also on the use of up to five other similar services. For the many respondents who did not complete this latter question (perhaps an example of 'survey fatigue'), we imputed values using a regression model from cases who did answer, expressed as a combined annual frequency. From these estimates of frequency of use of other services, we derive an annualisation factor (averaging 2.7, although differing markedly between types of service user.

A wide range of secondary data sources were used to generate predicted rates of incidence at local authority level across Great Britain (described in fuller detail in Bramley et al, 2016). These predictors relate to three broad groups. For destitute migrants, these comprise census data on selected recent migration numbers and countries of birth, Home Office supported asylum seeker numbers, historic demographic estimates of asylum and visa overstayers, and Citizens Advice caseloads. For complex needs cases, these draw on three major administrative datasets relating to homelessness, substance misuse and offending analysed in Bramley et al (2015), together with indicators on homelessness prevention and relief, reported shoplifting crime, and cases of child abuse and neglect. For the more general UK-other group the indices include synthetic predictions of severe poverty rates calibrated on PSE and UKHLS, DWP data on former Social Fund loans for living costs (2011) and Discretionary Housing Payments, as well as estimates of 2013 number of people on Job-Seeker's Allowance sanction and a general measure of numbers of working-age clients coming off benefits in this period, together with local homeless acceptance rates and CAB welfare benefit advice caseloads. Weighting of indicators is designed to adjust for different scales of measurement and give equal weighting except for some indicators deemed less robust (see Bramley et al, 2016).

In making our national estimate of the total numbers destitute, we 'anchor' the precise scaling of the predictive indices so that they give the 'right' predicted number for our case study areas taken as a group, that is, the number that we actually found in our census survey (grossed up and annualised). The final estimate used the three detailed indices for the three destitution groups (migrants, complex needs, other UK) and controlled to two groups of case study areas, those with relatively higher predicted destitution and those with relatively lower destitution. These indices (combined) also provide the basis for the map in Figure 3.3.

FOUR

Poverty, local services and austerity

Glen Bramley and Kirsten Besemer

Introduction

Good quality, accessible local services can provide significant benefits 'in kind' to households across the income spectrum and may help to compensate the poor for some material lacks as well as promoting a spirit and practice of common citizenship. Their presence and quality may provide a vital reassurance to people at particular life-stages or with particular needs (for example, for schools, or for health or social care). They may also play a 'gateway' role in terms of information, advice, mobility and access to wider opportunities (for example, libraries, Citizens Advice, post offices, transport), as well as significantly advancing quality of life and well-being (for example, parks, recreation, museums). Yet local services are under significant challenge from the austerity budgets of governments since 2010 and from market changes within the private sector, not to mention technological change.

The role of services in providing benefits in kind, sometimes termed a 'social wage', may have been understated in some broad theories of welfare state regimes, such as that associated with Esping-Andersen (1990). It has been claimed that such benefits represent an increasingly important part of the real income of poorer households (Sefton 1997, 2002; Bailey and McNulty 2017), and also that the nature of welfare regimes is more complex and diverse than suggested in Esping-Andersen's classic formulation once such services are taken into account (Esping-Anderson et al, 2002; Arts and Gelissen, 2002; Bambra 2005). Recent evidence on 'the cost of poverty' in the UK may also be interpreted as underlining the significance of public service spending being skewed towards poorer households in key sectors like health (Bramley et al, 2016). Local services also occupy a key role in theories about social justice and change at an urban and neighbourhood scale, as reflected in a later section within this chapter.

This chapter will assess the current state of local public and private services in 2012 and trends in usage and adequacy since 1999, as well as prospects for the near future. This will reveal a picture of improvements in some areas (especially for children and in public transport) and continuing strength in other areas (retail, core health services), but retreat in the field of general local public services in leisure, culture and information. It will go on to assess the distributional character of different services, in terms of whether usage tends to favour the poor or the rich, and how this has changed. Further modelling analysis looks at the extent to which service constraints in terms of availability, adequacy or affordability are experienced more by poorer households and neighbourhoods. After briefly reviewing other geographical differences between UK countries and between rural and urban areas, the chapter considers how far 'service exclusion' overlaps with other aspects of poverty and social exclusion. The conclusions will highlight a mixed, somewhat paradoxical picture of the role of services in tackling social exclusion, but will raise questions about the future nature and viability of universalist local public service provision under the UK's austerity programme.

Attitudes to services

Support for most local public services, in the sense of seeing them as being essential, remains very high and has in some cases increased since 1999 (Figure 4.1). This is despite serious cutbacks facing local public services in Britain, and also despite several decades of the promotion of ideas about privatisation or the use of a greater diversity of service providers, including the recently promoted notion of the 'Big Society'.

Some changes observed may be explained by technological and associated societal changes. For example, the rise of the internet and online forms of service access and communication may account for some decline in the proportion of adults regarding post offices as essential. This factor, together with the rising educational level of the population and perceived improved standards of schooling may account for the declining support for evening classes.

The services considered fall into three groups. First, considered essential by nearly everyone, come the NHS services of doctor, hospital and dentist (nothwithstanding evidence of difficulty accessing NHS dentistry reported later). Furthermore, separate social attitudes survey data on satisfaction and willingness to support greater public spending upholds the picture of strong support for health services (Besemer and Bramley, 2012, pp 10-13). Second, a significant group of services (including opticians, libraries, post offices and sports facilities) is considered essential by substantial majorities (over 80 per cent).

Figure 4.1: Proportion of people thinking different local services are 'essential' in 1990, 1999 and 2011

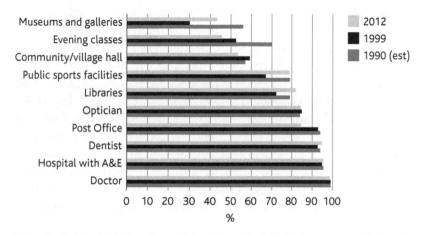

Notes: Derived from data from the 1999 Poverty and Social Exclusion survey and the 2011 omnibus survey. The 1990 *Breadline Britain* data is estimated from bar charts in a publication by Fisher and Bramley (2006) based on 1990 *Breadline Britain* data.

Source: PSE-UK 2012, PSE 1999 and *Breadline Britain* 1990 Surveys

Third, another group of services are closer to the margins between majority and minority support as 'essential'; this includes community halls, evening classes and museums (all three of which show a drop from 1990).

It is of interest to see whether there are differences in attitudes between different social or demographic groups: this may give some insight into differences and changes in the role of services in society and prospects for continuing political support. There is a strong relationship between attitudes to certain services (for example, post offices, libraries, community halls, evening classes) and older age. In some cases this reflects need, but in others it may be a generational or cohort effect associated with particular skills or practices. There is a surprising tendency for poorer groups to be less likely to rate services as 'essential', while typically it is middle-income groups who are most likely to support them. Some poorer groups may lack the time or other resources to utilise discretionary services. There are some relationships with political affiliation; Conservative supporters are less likely to regard some services as essential, for example. Perhaps more worrying is the significantly lower proportion of minority ethnic respondents seeing many services as essential, suggesting these services may not be culturally appropriate or easy to access.

Trends in usage and adequacy

In the main PSE-UK survey in 2012, households were asked about services which may exist in their area, whether they used these or not and whether they regarded them as adequate or not. For each service there were five possible responses: (1) Use – Adequate; (2) Use – Inadequate; (3) Don't Use – Unavailable or Inadequate; (4) Don't Use – Don't Want/Not Relevant; (5) Don't Use – Can't Afford. Figure 4.2 shows changes between 1999 and 2012 in the pattern of responses for 16 public and private 'services of general interest' to the population as a whole, for which data exist at both points. Services are ranked in descending order in terms of changes in the proportion responding 'Use – Adequate'; at the top of the figure are the services where there was the greatest increase in the proportion reporting that they used the

Figure 4.2: Change in usage of services of general interest, Great Britain, 1999-2012 (percentage point changes in usage rates)

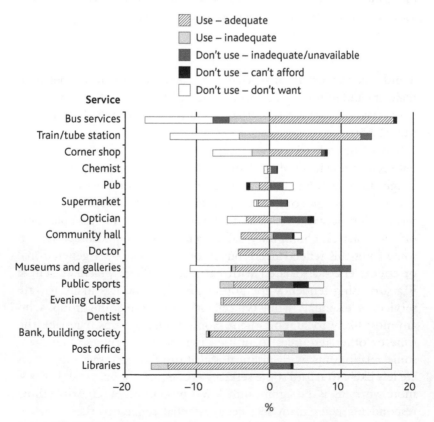

Source: PSE-UK 2012 and PSE 1999 surveys

service and found it adequate, while at the bottom are those showing the greatest decrease.

There has been a pronounced real rise in usage of three services where more people see them as relevant (that is, fewer say they don't want to use them) and fewer see them as inadequate: buses, trains and corner shops. The striking revival in public transport probably reflects a combination of congestion, fuel prices, service improvement/investment, declining car ownership among the young, and more generous concessionary fare schemes for older people and those with disabilities. The corner shops phenomenon probably reflects the shift of major supermarket chains into smaller local store formats.

For nearly all other general services there have been declines, of varying scale. These declines in some cases clearly reflect changes in technology and social practices regarding information, communication, leisure and finance, notably in respect of libraries but also post offices, evening classes and banks. It is also clear that constraints of inadequacy have increased quite a lot, including the effects of cuts in branch networks (post offices, banks). The cuts in local authority services (particularly since 2010 in England) would have been only just beginning to affect some of these services by 2012, with many authorities protecting frontline services in their earlier rounds of cuts (Hastings et al, 2013).

The decline in 'universal' local public services accentuates a trend apparent before 1999 and leads to a situation where these services are typically only used by minorities of the population. There may be a cycle of lessening support for such services, which then makes them more vulnerable to budget cuts in an extremely challenging budget context for local government (Hastings et al 2013, 2015). They are also vulnerable because: often, they are not services for which there is a statutory requirement; they are not in the high profile 'protected' categories like health, schools and (to some extent) social care; and/or their distributional profile suggests that they are used more by the better off (as confirmed below).

The story with services for children is rather different and generally more positive (Figure 4.3). Service usage has generally increased a lot and inadequacy/unavailability reduced, although this is still a significant factor for play and youth clubs. In this period, government did follow strategies of investing in early years provision, after-school clubs, parks and public realm (Social Exclusion Unit, 2001; Lupton et al, 2016), while school meals perhaps benefitted from celebrity media attention. For these services, one could perhaps discern a move *towards* universalism, at least among families (albeit this demographic segment is a minority of households).

Figure 4.3: Usage of children's services, 1999 and 2012

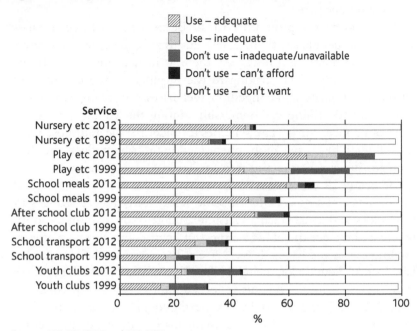

Source: PSE-UK 2012 and PSE 1000 surveys

The PSE surveys also asked parents about problems with school resources. Comparison with 1999 shows an increase in teacher shortage, but substantial reductions in most of the other resource problems, particularly large class sizes, access to computers or books, and building disrepair. This correlates with large increases in real public spending resources going into school education during this period. Resource problems are not strongly related to individual household poverty; in England (and for UK as a whole) poor families are slightly less likely to report these, although in Scotland and Northern Ireland they are still somewhat more likely to report such problems. Across the UK, school problems are less reported in the most deprived neighbourhoods.

Pupils experiencing difficulties (bullying, special needs, exclusion), however, showed relative stability over this period. Although the absolute numbers are relatively small, these difficulties, unlike resource problems, are strongly related to poverty, particularly in Scotland and Northern Ireland. They are also key early warning indicators of more serious 'multiple disadvantage' in later life that should be a target for early intervention activities (Bramley et al 2011, 2015).

For services targeted at older people or those with disabilities, which are largely rationed on a basis of needs with some means-testing, the broad picture is one of stability over this period (1999-2012). Typically around 10 per cent of the group use services, although meals-on-wheels are used by far fewer, appear to be in decline and widely seen as inadequate. Home care services saw some increase in usage and reduction in inadequacy, although affordability seems to feature rather more as an issue in this case. Special transport seemed to register an increase in reported inadequacy. A more widely used service for this group is chiropodists, used by two-fifths and mainly found adequate.

Who uses local services?

We are interested in the 'distributional' pattern of service usage and constraints across the socio-economic spectrum, and in particular in the extent to which the poor use services more or less, and whether they experience more constraints ('worse services'). We approach this both by employing relatively simple descriptive analyses and through multivariate modelling. Figure 4.4 illustrates the first approach, by showing the profile of usage rates for selected services (standardised for household composition) across income quartiles (equivalised, after housing cost) for a selection of universal services.[1] Public sports facilities are moderately 'pro-rich' in their distribution of usage, with people from the top quartile 42 per cent more likely to use this

Figure 4.4: Usage rate by income quartile for selected services, 2012

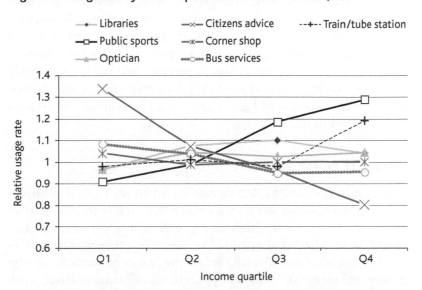

Note: Standardised for household composition; quartiles of net equivalent income AHC

service than those from the bottom quartile. Train/tube services are also used more by the better off, as are museums, evening classes, community halls and pubs (not shown). Libraries and opticians are used rather more by the middle groups. Corner shops are used a bit more by the lowest income group, while buses are used more by the lower half of the distribution and particularly the lowest quartile. The most strongly pro-poor service is Citizens Advice, reflecting its strengthening role in providing general debt and financial advice to households as well as helping those attempting to navigate the welfare benefits system (see also Chapter 11 on financial inclusion and debt), as well as other related problems such as homelessness. Out of 17 general services, 9 could be said to be pro-rich, 2 pro-poor and 6 neutral.

Similar analyses for children's services suggest a split between more pro-rich cases (nursery, play, after-school) and more pro-poor (school meals, youth clubs, school transport). Nursery use tends to rise slightly with income, perhaps because of its strong association with working parents. Services for older people or those with disabilities provide a picture broadly as expected, with mainly pro-poor distribution except in the case of chiropody.

While a number of the universal local public services in the leisure/ information/culture sector tend to be used more by the better off, there is a rather more encouraging finding that usage has become less unequal than it was in 1999. In a context of generally reducing usage, it may be the better-off groups, who have better access to alternative substitutes, who are ceasing to use the public services, although evidence on this is mixed (Hastings et al, 2015). Other services seeing a change in this direction (more pro-poor/less pro-rich) include trains, banks, most children's services, and home care. While on the whole this is a positive shift, it can carry with it the danger, especially in a context of budget cuts, of a retreat from universalism towards a 'residualised' service.

Who gets worse services?

The picture is somewhat less favourable when we look at *constraints* rather than at service usage. Constraint here refers to people who report a service to be inadequate, unavailable or unaffordable, regardless of whether they use it or not – in other words, it is an overlapping measure. Overall, across the range of services, poorer groups are more likely to report constraints in many cases, with relatively few cases where the poorer group reports significantly less constraints. Out of 28 services, using PSE poverty as the indicator of poverty, the score is 17 services where the poor group report constraints more often than the non-poor versus only 2 services where the poor report constraints less often; using social class, the score is 14:3, while using tenure (social rent) it is 15:3. Only with income does this pattern not appear. This suggests that the quality and access issues that are more important are less related to money and more to other factors such as location, language, culture and style of service. Services which appear to be less prone to this 'worse quality/access for poor' tendency include libraries, post offices, corner shops and school transport.

Some further insights can be gained from multivariate logistic regression models used to explain variation in service constraints. Looking at the results detailed in Bramley and Besemer (2016), a few patterns immediately jump out. Households containing people with sickness or disability generally have good access to services, but with some notable exceptions including doctors, corner shops and bus services. Also, households with low qualifications are much more likely to report constraints in accessing GP services. Female-headed households are somewhat more likely to report constraints on quite a lot of services. There is a more pronounced pattern of greater constraint affecting younger (under-25) households, particularly for healthcare related services. Older households are more likely to report constraints in four cases of services which they are perhaps more likely to want to use: post offices, chemists, corner shops and supermarkets. Non-white minority ethnic households are more likely to report problems with several services for children or for older people or people with disabilities.

Households on low income are generally more likely to report constraints across most services, except doctors, libraries and corner shops, confirming the simpler descriptive comparisons already reported. People in the worst 10 per cent of the most deprived neighbourhoods, and to some extent in the next 10 per cent, are more likely to report constraints in using a number of services, such as libraries, opticians and pubs. However, they are less likely to report constraints in quite a few cases, including museums, post offices, doctors, chemists, corner shops, supermarkets and bus services. Overall, this seems a more positive finding than might have been expected. However, for children's services, the second decile of neighbourhood deprivation seems to be particularly disadvantaged.

More negative, however, is the picture of experience for individually poor households, based on suffering multiple material deprivations.

This group are overwhelmingly more likely to report constraints in using nearly all services, when controlling for other factors.

Geographical aspects

Scotland appears to show lower levels of service constraint than England, whereas **Northern Ireland** shows higher levels of constraint for many services. For example, Scotland has higher usage of public sports facilities, museums and community halls, and less constraint on post offices, but more constraints on access to trains. Several children's services also appear to be 'worse' in Scotland than England in terms of usage or constraints, although these differences are marginal in terms of statistical significance.

Unsurprisingly, **rural areas** are associated with service constraints in nearly all services, and particularly in their use of public transport, shops, chemists and opticians, Citizens Advice, day centres and meals-on-wheels. In these cases, descriptive tables and multivariate models tell a similar story. More positively, services where rural and remote areas did not seem to be particularly disadvantaged included doctors, post offices, and most children's services. Chapter 10 by Bailey and Gannon in the companion volume (Dermott and Main, 2017) discusses the rural dimensions of poverty and exclusion, including services, while the situation of rural and remote areas in Scotland is discussed in greater depth in Bailey et al (2016).

Equally interesting, under the geographical heading, is the social and poverty profile of the **neighbourhood**. The classic literature on equity in urban services focuses mainly on geographical accessibility and on income/class divides (Davies, 1968; Harvey, 1973; Smith, 1977; Troy, 1982; Pinch, 1985). One strand in this literature argues that the middle classes and middle-class areas have diverse ways of influencing service provision in their favour (Le Grand, 1982; Goodin and Le Grand, 1987). Policy initiatives focused on regenerating deprived areas have also tended to argue that poor local services are part of the problem to be addressed, including problems with 'private' services like retailing and finance as well as public services (Robson, 1988; Social Exclusion Unit, 1998, 2001). Despite these concerns with spatial equity, public services are, at least in the UK and Europe, predominantly a mechanism for redistribution from general taxation to the general population as a whole and to lower income groups specifically (Sefton, 1997, 2002; Bailey and McNulty, forthcoming), and this is reflected in the picture of spatial distribution of public spending (Bramley and Evans, 2000).

Despite this, the conventional expectation from academic literature is that quality of services may be expected to be particularly low in poor neighbourhoods, for example, because of the lack of middle-class social capital or leadership to support or improve local service organisations (Wilson, 1987; Small et al, 2008) or as part of a wider process of 'territorial stigmatization' (Wacquant, 2008; Wacquant et al, 2014). However, this US-oriented literature may be misleading for the UK, given the type of welfare regime and the role played by key services within it (Esping-Andersen, 1990; Bambra, 2005). It may also ignore the fact that institutions providing services to poor neighbourhoods may be better resourced or better connected, or simply be providing more relevant services for poor households, than those available (or not) in more affluent areas (Pinkster, 2007; Small et al, 2008; Curley, 2010). These factors may lie behind some of the empirical results reported later in this chapter.

We test the impact of 'living in a poor area' on service constraint using logistic regression models, highlighting the effect of being in the 10 per cent most deprived or in the next 20 per cent of deprived neighbourhoods, after controlling for main socio-demographic features of households, including employment, low income and individual household deprivation. Table 4.1 presents the results of these models. The values show the estimated effect on the odds ratios of experiencing service constraints of living in the most-deprived and next-worst category of neighbourhoods; statistically significant effects (at 5 per cent level) are shown in bold. In the upper part of the table are impacts on 17 general services, while the blocks below show results for 6 services targeted at children and 5 services targeted at older people or people with disabilities.

Contrary to what much of the literature has previously identified, the results indicate that neighbourhood deprivation only affects a minority of general services, and not all of these impacts are in the direction of increasing constraints (worsening quality or access problems) in more deprived neighbourhoods. This only applies to libraries, opticians and pubs, in this set. For museums, corner shops and buses, it appears that constraints are *less* in deprived areas, underlining points made about urban structure and density in Bailey et al (2015) and Bramley and Besemer (2016). It is, however, true for rather more of the services targeted at families with children or at older people/people with disabilities that there is a significantly enhanced risk of constraint in poorer neighbourhoods, although in the former case this is more associated with the 'next 20 per cent' of neighbourhoods than with the 'worst 10 per cent'.

Table 4.1: Effects of neighbourhood deprivation on local service usage constraints

Service	Most deprived 10 per cent exp(B)*	Next most deprived 20 per cent exp(B)
General services		
Libraries	**1.78**	0.93
Public sports	1.06	1.03
Museums and galleries	**0.75**	**0.79**
Evening classes	1.20	1.19
Community hall	1.04	1.12
Doctor	0.79	1.09
Dentist	0.91	0.82
Optician	**1.62**	1.04
Post Office	0.77	1.06
Citizens Advice	1.02	1.07
Chemist	0.53	1.30
Corner shop	**0.71**	0.93
Supermarket	0.80	1.20
Bank, building society	1.02	1.17
Pub	**1.73**	**1.42**
Bus services	0.84	**0.79**
Train/tube service	0.88	1.14
Children's services		
Children's play	**3.18**	**1.94**
School meals	0.77	1.07
Youth clubs	1.28	**1.58**
After school club	0.57	1.21
School transport	0.82	0.87
Nursery	0.35	**2.33**
Services for older people or people with disabilities		
Home care	**2.51**	1.60
Meals on Wheels	1.09	1.19
Special transport	**2.05**	1.38
Day centres	**2.53**	**2.31**
Chiropodist	1.37	**1.62**

Notes:

Bold indicates effects significant at 5% level; values >1.00 indicate greater constraints/ inadequacies in more deprived neighbourhoods compared with the least deprived 70 per cent.

Table shows the impact on the odds of facing service constraints (* exponent of the regression coefficient, B) from logistic regression models with 15 other controls. Significance levels not adjusted for slight clustering in FRS/PSE sample. Control variables include demographics, country, urban-rural location, individual income and deprivation.

Services and wider social exclusion

This final section considers the relationship between local services and the wider spectrum of social exclusion and disadvantage which the PSE-UK survey is designed to measure, framed by the B-SEM (Levitas et al, 2007, as discussed in the Introduction). In this section, we use a set of simple categorical indicators of exclusion, one for each domain of exclusion. This deviates slightly from the original B-SEM, by splitting 'Living Environment' into 'Housing' and 'Area' deprivations, and by combining 'Education' and 'Cultural Participation' (neither of which are particularly well-measured in the PSE-UK). Chapter 13 provides a fuller discussion of the multiple dimensions of social exclusion.

Exclusion on the 'Services' domain is measured by taking households who are 'excluded' (that is, not using services because they are unavailable/inadequate or because they are unaffordable[2]) in three or more services out of 25. This includes child and elderly/disabled services where relevant, and those general services consensually (more than 50 per cent) agreed to be essential (this omits museums and evening classes). This affects 15.3 per cent of adults.

The main interest here focuses on the overlap (intersection) between service exclusion and the other ten domains of exclusion. Table 4.2 looks at this in terms of bilateral overlaps. The BSEM-based domains are listed down the left hand column.[3] The second and third columns show the degree of overlap between two particular domains, 'economic resources' and 'services', where overlap is defined as the number of households experiencing *both* deprivations divided by the number experiencing *either*. Economic deprivation is shown alongside services because it provides a useful contrast. It is closely related to our primary measures of income poverty, and as such we would expect it to be quite closely related to quite a lot of other domains of exclusion, as is in fact the case. So, for example, economic deprivation has quite strong overlaps with housing, with social activities[4] (both well above 30 per cent overlap), and moderately strong overlaps with employment, health and area (all more than 20 per cent). Economic deprivation is less strongly related to services, social activities/resources, or civic participation.

Service exclusion offers rather a strong contrast with this. Service exclusion shows limited overlap with any of the other domains, the highest in fact being economic and housing at around 15 per cent. Of all the domains compared, service exclusion actually shows the lowest overlap with other domains. For example, it is the only domain for which all overlaps are below 20%. Another way of illustrating this

Table 4.2: Overlap between social exclusion, economic deprivation and other domains of deprivation (percent of households experiencing both of each pair of deprivations, as proportion of households experiencing either)

Deprivation domain	Economic resources	Services
Economic	n/a	15.0
Services	15.0	n/a
Social	16.1	9.5
Activities	33.3	13.2
Employment	25.3	11.4
Civic	16.8	12.2
Education	17.9	12.9
Health	23.4	12.2
Area	21.0	13.5
Housing	36.8	14.4
Crime	19.1	10.1

Note: See chapter end note (3) for the definitional criteria used for each domain of exclusion.

rather striking finding is to look at the overlap between being deprived on a particular domain and experiencing multiple deprivation, in the sense of being deprived on a number of domains (between three and five). Again, service exclusion shows some of the lowest overlaps with multiple deprivation, second only to civic participation. Only 25 per cent of 'service excluded' households are multiply deprived on three or more domains, compared with 70 per cent of those deprived on social activities or 65 per cent of those deprived on the housing domain. It should also be pointed out that this finding is consistent with what Table 4.1 showed, particularly in respect of general/universal services: area deprivation did not often increase the risk of service constraint significantly.

How do we explain this lack of relationship to other domains of deprivation/exclusion, in the UK in 2012, and what inferences might be drawn about policy? This finding suggests that public services have succeeded, in some measure, in meeting their implicit goal of ensuring equal access across the socio-economic spectrum. It appears that they have, in some cases and to varying degrees, countered the phenomena referred to variously as the 'inverse care law', 'middle class capture', or 'territorial stigmatization'. This challenges the 'normal' expectation that poorer people will inevitably have worse access to valued resources, activities or environments. It can be related to the observation that services in kind have been an important and (until recently) growing part of the UK approach to welfare.

On reflection, perhaps this is what we should expect from a mature post-industrial, fully urbanised, welfare state, and clearly this situation would contrast strongly with what would be found in most developing countries, as well as in some developed countries with a different, more 'liberal' welfare regime (notably the USA). The favourable picture in relation to public services may be expected, after a decade or so of substantial increases in spending on such services (up to 2010). However, many of the services reviewed, particularly in the 'general' category, are privately provided by commercial enterprises, albeit subject to varying degrees of state regulation. Here, the findings perhaps reflect the relative sophistication and efficiency of the UK retail sector, for example, as well as the role of regulation in respect of some services.

Conclusion

The most 'universal' services in contemporary Britain are primary healthcare and convenience retail and financial services, underlining the mixture of public and private provision involved. These services have generally maintained their position in terms of high levels of usage and low levels of constraint or exclusion, although there has been a fall-off in adequacy/availability and/or affordability for some of these (dentists, opticians, banks). Widely used services include public transport, which has dramatically increased usage, and pubs, which are in decline.

Local authority-provided information, leisure and cultural services, although nominally 'universal', have seen falls in usage and are typically now used only by minorities of households. Taken together with the vulnerability of these services to local government spending cuts (Hastings et al, 2013, 2015), and notwithstanding generally strong public support for these services as 'essential' (documented more fully in Besemer and Bramley, 2012), there is a real risk of these services going into a spiral of decline, and thereby contributing to a significant retreat from universalism in local public services. While the benefits of additional investment in children's services and schools in the 2000s are apparent, these may not all be sustained under 'austerity'.

So far as public services are concerned, we can detect a net distributional shift with poorer households' usage increasing relative to richer households. Two factors are contributing to this: (a) a tendency for given services to become somewhat less pro-rich, or more pro-poor, over the period 1999-2012; (b) a reduction in provision of certain more pro-rich services as part of austerity. Partly contributing to this, particularly the first, is greater awareness within public authorities of equalities issues, and overt programmes to tackle these (notably in health and education).

However, it remains true that, when you look at constraints on usage, a majority of services still have significantly higher proportions of poor households reporting constraints. Thus, there is still further to go in countering the combination of factors that make it more difficult for poor people to use services. Cases where constraints facing the poor have been reduced since 1999 include bus services, childcare/nurseries, and play facilities, where service provision and usage have increased considerably. It is also clear that most school resource problems have reduced markedly over this period, except 'teacher shortage'. Remaining school resource problems are not more common for poor households, but individual pupil difficulties continue to be strongly related to poverty (and carry high risks for future life chances).

There are more similarities than differences between the UK countries in terms of service constraints. However, rural areas face significantly greater constraints in use or availability of a majority of general services, as well as some services for elderly/disabled clients (for example day centres and meals-on-wheels).

It is *not* the case, generally in the UK at the moment, that most services are worse in poor neighbourhoods, although there are some cases where this is true, particularly services more targeted on need for children, older people or those with disabilities. However, we found no cases of significantly better services in poor areas; in other words, there is no evidence here to support the argument that it is better to let poor people live together in neighbourhoods with other poor people, rather than live in mixed communities.

Service exclusion is, remarkably, little correlated or overlapping with other dimensions of social exclusion. We take this as positive evidence for a degree of success of policies for public provision or regulation which aim to give equal access regardless of who you are or where you are. It also clearly illustrates how recognition of the differing role of public services makes for a more diverse picture of national welfare regimes than in the simpler typologies, such as that of Esping-Andersen (1990). How sustainable this will be in the future, post-austerity, is less clear.

The emerging pattern of budget cuts in local government shows that the absolute and proportional scale of cuts in local government expenditure in England is greatest in the most deprived localities (Hastings et al, 2015; NAO, 2014). Since large concentrations of poorer people live in these areas, they are likely to suffer more in terms of a general worsening of services. However, in the way cuts have been applied across different services, there is some evidence of attempts to protect some more 'pro-poor' services, for example social care (Hastings et al, 2015). Services taking larger cuts can be characterised as both less 'essential' and more likely to be used or valued by middle class/higher income people (for example, cultural services). Nevertheless, services which are widely supported as essential and widely used and valued across the socio-economic spectrum, such as libraries, are taking substantial cuts as well. Another feature of the cuts is that services particularly used by young people seem to be taking a high level of cuts, perhaps partly because they are seen as 'non-statutory'. There is also a danger that more preventative services will lose out to core services, which focus on the casualties when things go wrong.

Notes

[1] Service usage rates are proportions reporting use of service (whether adequate or inadequate), standardised by calculating what they would be if each income quartile had the same household composition; the income quartiles are based on net equivalised household income after housing costs, using the PSE equivalisation scale to adjust for household composition.

[2] Note that this definition of the term 'service exclusion', which is consistent with how the term was used in the 1999 study and in relation to other domains, is narrower than the term 'service constraint' used elsewhere in this chapter.

[3] The definition of domains of social exclusion in Table 4.2 are:

'Services': Not using three or more out of 25 local services (consensually agreed to be essential) because unavailable or inadequate or cannot afford.

'Economic': PSE poor (3+ material deprivations and below income threshold) and either some indication of subjective poverty/hardship or some indication of financial pressure or problem debt.

'Social': Low social support score (would receive no support in some circumstances and limited support in others) and low levels of social contact (see relatives/friends less than once a month and not through choice).

'Activities': Adults do not do 4 or more from list of 15 social activities because can't afford or other reason, with at least one of 10 listed factors important.

'Employment': Currently unemployed or unemployed in recent past, on out of work benefits in FRS c.1 year previous, or workless household under 60 not student.

'Civic': Adult participates in 3 or less from 13 social group activities and 3 or less from 9 political activities (including voting) and scores low on 'efficacy' (1 or more out of 3 indicators), and does not volunteer much.

'Education': Adults with no qualifications, or family with 3 or more school resource problems, or household with child excluded from school, or speaks poor English.

'Health': Adults with poor mental health (GGQ>=4 or reporting specific mental illness), or self-reported poor/very poor health, or long term limiting illness/disability, or excluded from activities by health, or low score (<=4) on ONS well-being.

'Area': Household very dissatisfied with area or reporting 3 or more common neighbourhood problems out of 16.

'Housing': Having any of following housing need problems: affordability/ security (for example, forced move can't afford or eviction, mortgage/rent arrears); poor condition (poor repair, or damp or heating); health-related housing problem (for example, health move, housing affected health); crowding (families not enough bedrooms); or homeless in last 5 years.

'Crime': Adults with criminal record, been in prison, stopped and searched; or worried about home being broken into, or had home broken into, or physically attacked, or experienced domestic violence or sexual harm or need to ask partner's permission to work, shop, or visit friends or relatives.

[4] Deprivation on the social activities domain as defined here is relatively highly related to economic deprivation, in part because the questions used to identify non-participation in these activities explicitly have a clause about not being able to afford to participate.

References

Arts, W. and Gelissen, J. (2002) 'Three worlds of welfare capitalism or more? A state-of-the-art report', *Journal of European Social Policy*, 12, 137-60. DOI: 10.1177/0952872002012002114.

Bailey, N. and Gannon, M. (2017) 'Poverty and social exclusion in rural and urban locations', in E. Dermott and G. Main (eds) *Poverty and social exclusion in the UK: Vol. 1: The extent and nature of the problem*, Bristol: Policy Press.

Bailey, N. and McNulty, D. (2017) 'Inequality and poverty in Scotland', in K.Gibb, D. McLeanna, D. McNulty and M. Comerford (eds) *The Scottish Economy: a Living Book*, London: Taylor and Francis.

Bailey, N., Bramley, G., and Gannon, M. (2016) 'Poverty and social exclusion in urban and rural areas of Scotland', *PSE UK 2012 Working Paper*, http://www.poverty.ac.uk/sites/default/files/attachments/PSE-Report-Scotland-urban-rural-poverty-March-2016.pdf.

Bailey, N., Besemer, K., Bramley, G. and Livingston, M. (2015) 'How neighbourhood social mix shapes household resources through social networks and services', *Housing Studies*, 30(2), 295-314.

Bambra, C. (2005) 'Cash versus services: "Worlds of Welfare" and decommodification of cash benefits and health care services', *Journal of Social Policy*, 34(2), 195-213. DOI: http://dx.doi.org/10.1017/S0047279404008542.

Bashir, N., Batty, E., Cole, I., Crisp, R., Flint, J., Green, S., Hickman, P. and Robinson, D. (2011) 'Living through change in challenging neighbourhoods, thematic analysis', *JRF Programme Paper: Poverty and Place*, York: Joseph Rowntree Foundation.

Besemer, K. and Bramley, G. (2012) 'Local services under siege: attitudes to public services in a time of austerity', *PSE Analysis Working Paper Series*, http://www.poverty.ac.uk/working-papers-result-analysis-public-services-local-services-poverty-measurement-social-exclusion

Bramley, G. (1990) *Equalization grants and local expenditure needs: The price of equality*, Aldershot: Avebury.

Bramley, G. (1996) 'Who uses local public services? Need, demand and rationing in action' in G. Pola, G. France and R. Levaggi (eds) *Developments in local government finance: Theory and policy*, Cheltenham: Edward Elgar.

Bramley, G. (1997) 'Poverty and local public services', in D. Gordon and C. Pantazis (eds) *Breadline Britain in the 1990s*, Aldershot: Ashgate.

Bramley, G. and Besemer, K. (2016) 'Poverty and local services in the midst of austerity', *PSE Analysis Working Paper Series*, http://www.poverty.ac.uk/editorial/poverty-and-local-services-midst-austerity

Bramley, G. and Evans, M. (2000) 'Getting the smaller picture: small-area analysis of public expenditure incidence and deprivation in three English cities', *Fiscal Studies*, 21(2), 231-68.

Bramley, G., Watkins, D. and Karley, N. K. (2011) 'An outcome-based resource allocation model for local education services in Wales', *Environment & Planning C*, 29(5), 848-71.

Bramley, G., Hirsch, D., Littlewood, M. and Watkins, D. (2016) *Counting the cost of UK poverty*, York: Joseph Rowntree Foundation.

Bramley, G., Fitzpatrick, S., Edwards, J., Ford, D., Johnsen, S., Sosenko, F. and Watkins, D. (2015) *Hard edges: Mapping severe and multiple disadvantage in England*, London: Lankelly Chase Foundation.

Curley, A. (2010) 'Relocating the poor: social capital and neighbourhood resources', *Journal of Urban Affairs*, 32(1), 79-103.

Davies, B. (1968) *Social needs and resources in local services*, London: Michael Joseph.

Dermott, E. and Main, G. (2017) *Poverty and social exclusion in the UK: Vol 1: The extent and nature of the problem*, Bristol: Policy Press.

Duffy, B. (2000) 'Satisfaction and expectations: attitudes to public services in deprived areas', *CASEpaper 45*, Centre for the Analysis of Social Exclusion, London School of Economics.

Esping-Andersen, G. (1990) *The three worlds of welfare capitalism*, London and New York: John Wiley & Sons.

Esping-Andersen, G., with Gallie, D., Hemerijck, A. and Myles, J. (2002) *Why we need a new welfare state*, Oxford: Oxford University Press.

Forrest, R. and Kearns, A. (1999) *Joined-up places: Social cohesion and neighbourhood regeneration*, York: York Publishing Services.

Goodin, R. and Le Grand J. (1987) *Not only the poor: The middle classes and the welfare state*, London: Allen & Unwin.

Harvey, D. (1973) *Social justice and the city*, London: Edward Arnold.

Hastings, A., Bailey, N., Bramley, G., Gannon, M. and Watkins, D. (2015) *The cost of the cuts: The impact on local government and poorer communities*, York: Joseph Rowntree Foundation.

Hastings, A., Bailey, N., Besemer, K., Bramley, G., Gannon, M. and Watkins, D. (2013) 'Coping with the cuts? Local government and poorer communities', *JRF Programme Paper*, York: Joseph Rowntree Foundation.

Le Grand, J. (1982) *The strategy of equality: Redistribution and the social services*, London: George Allen & Unwin.

Levitas, R., Pantazis, C., Fahmy, E., Gordon, D., Lloyd, E. and Patsios, D. (2007) *The multi-dimensional analysis of social exclusion*, Bristol: University of Bristol.

Lupton, R., Burchardt, T., Hills, J., Stewart, K. and Vizard, P. (2016) *Social policy in a cold climate: Policies and their consequences since the crisis*, Bristol: Policy Press.

NAO (National Audit Office) (2014) *The impact of funding reductions on local authorities*, Local Government Report by the Comptroller and Auditor General, London: NAO.

Pinch, S. (1985) *Cities and services*, London: Routledge & Kegan Paul.

Pinkster, F. M. (2007) 'Localised social networks, socialisation and social mobility in a low income neighbourhood in the Netherlands', *Urban Studies*, 44(13), 2587-603.

Robson, B. (1988) *Those inner cities: Reconciling the social and economic aims of urban policy*, Oxford: Clarendon.

Sefton, T. (1997) *The changing distribution of the social wage*, London: STICERD, LSE.

Sefton, T. (2002) 'Recent changes in the distribution of the social wage', *Findings*. York: Joseph Rowntree Foundation, https://www.jrf.org.uk/report/recent-changes-distribution-social-wage.

Small, M., Jacobs, E. and Massengill, R. (2008) 'Why organizational ties matter for neighbourhood effects: resource access through childcare centres', *Social Forces*, 87(1), 387-414.

Smith, D. (1977) *Human geography: A welfare approach*, London: Edward Arnold.

Social Exclusion Unit (SEU) (1998) *Bringing Britain together: A national strategy for neighbourhood renewal*, London: SEU.

Social Exclusion Unit (SEU) (2001) *A new commitment to neighbourhood renewal: National strategy action plan*, London: Social Exclusion Unit.

Troy, P. (1982) *Equity in the city*, London: Harper Collins.

Wacquant, L. (2008) 'Relocating gentrification: the working class, science and the state in recent urban research', *International Journal of Urban and Regional Research*, 32(1), 198-205.

Wacquant, L., Slater, T. and Pereira, V., (2014) 'Territorial stigmatization in action', *Environment & Planning A*, 46, 1270-80.

Wilson, W. J. (1987) *The truly disadvantaged*, Chicago: University of Chicago Press.

Part 2: Participation

FIVE

Social participation and social support

Lisa Wilson, Eldin Fahmy and Nick Bailey

Introduction

The ability to maintain social relationships and networks, and to participate in widely enjoyed social activities, is as central to Townsend's conception of relative poverty as it is to definitions of social exclusion (Townsend, 1979; Levitas, 2006; Levitas et al, 2007). These relationships and activities matter because they form part of the 'customary norms' or expectations of us as members of our society. In this sense, they are an end in themselves. At the same time, social networks and activities can be a means to other ends. Our social networks can offer access to support when we need it, both emotional and practical. Supportive social contacts can in turn have important positive impacts on physical and mental health and on well-being. Social networks can provide access to information, particularly about employment opportunities, helping us to get on as well as get by. People living on low incomes can find these networks invaluable but they can equally find them to be a source of onerous demands on already stretched resources.

Many factors can act as barriers to social participation and lead to people becoming socially isolated or excluded. Low income is a key barrier to the maintenance of social networks and participation in social activities. The inability to afford to participate in a range of widely practised and valued social activities forms part of the core deprivation measure in the PSE-UK study for this reason. Other barriers include personal factors such as ill health and disability, or time pressures arising from paid work or unpaid caring responsibilities. The overall aim of this chapter is to explore how social contact and participation varies in relation to a wide range of factors, with a particular focus on poverty and material constraint in restricting participation. We exploit the wide range of measures of participation available within the PSE-UK survey, including measures of social contact with family and with friends, perceptions of social support, satisfaction with personal relationships, and participation in common social activities.

The importance of social connections

Household resources have a direct impact on social networks and activities. Indeed, in Townsend's (1993) conception of relative poverty, participation in customary social activities and the maintenance of social networks are seen as basic expectations of members of a society so that the inability to afford to do so is a marker or defining feature of poverty. At the same time, participation may have consequences for a household's material situation, as social networks are valued for both 'getting by' and 'getting ahead' (Briggs, 1998; Lister, 2004; Matthews and Besemer, 2014). These networks are a means to access material resources as well as emotional support which can help to ease the struggles of everyday life and assist in coping with crises: having family or a friend who can lend money to tide you over or having someone to turn to for support in an emergency. Social connections – who you know – remain valuable in getting a job and, of increasing importance in today's economy when starting your own business (Green et al, 2011; Green et al, 2012; Richez-Battesti and Lest 2013).

The support which social networks provide may be especially important for people experiencing poverty, with family tending to play a greater role than friends (Stack, 1974; Lin, 1999; Ridge, 2009). For example, compared with those on higher incomes, lower income households are much more reliant on family for childcare (Bradshaw and Wasoff, 2009), while low-income lone mothers have been shown to regularly rely on their social networks for housing and healthcare support (Heflin et al, 2011). One qualitative study found that gifts in cash or in kind make an important contribution to living standards for low-income households (Taylor and Brown, 2011). People also use social networks to help cope with or overcome some of the disadvantages associated with poverty, for example, using contacts to negotiate increased support from educational or health services or to assist them in finding a better job (McCabe et al, 2013). Low-income households which lack these networks may be in a particularly difficult position.

Social responsibilities or roles such as paid employment or unpaid caring can create constraints on time which inhibit participation while, at the same time, roles which are stressful or isolating may create a perceived need for more contact or support. Roles may also increase opportunities for participation indirectly through their influence on material resources or through the opportunities they provide to develop new social contacts. Paid work brings higher income in general but, with longer hours, it may reduce time for social participation (Kodz et al, 2003; Lee and Bhargava, 2004). Having responsibility for children tends to both reduce resources and constrain time for participation, but it may also create a need or desire for greater contact, particularly with family. Other caring responsibilities might have similar effects. Limiting health problems or disabilities may have both an indirect effect on participation through their impact on household resources (Gannon and Nolan, 2004) and separate direct effects, by inhibiting mobility or imposing other barriers to socialising.

In terms of sources of social support, there is some evidence that people experiencing poverty rely largely on others who are in a similar situation, indicating networks of reciprocity or solidarity (Cheshire, 2009; Livingston et al, 2010; Matthews and Besemer, 2015). However, using PSE-UK data, Bailey et al (2015) find that people living in more deprived neighbourhoods report that, on balance, they give somewhat less help than they receive. This implies that, while there may be important networks of reciprocity between those living in poorer communities, households in those communities also draw on wider networks which connect them to less deprived locations and, by implication, less deprived groups. More generally, Matthews and Besemer (2014) caution against overstating the scale of support which those living in poverty receive, pointing out that this is not enough to overcome broader socio-economic inequalities.

Moreover, research on reciprocity demonstrates that there are costs associated with maintaining social networks. As much as network membership may be a source of support, it can also be a source of stress and obligations perceived to be burdensome (Curley, 2010; Heflin et al, 2011; Howard, 2006). Offer (2012) argues that this 'burden of reciprocity' can lead to poorer people withdrawing from social networks, either to avoid obligations or the shame associated with dependence, or because they are excluded by others because of their inability to reciprocate. Indeed, qualitative evidence on poverty and shame, including that from the PSE-UK study, has shown the extent to which people withdraw from participation to avoid stigmatisation (for example, Pemberton et al, 2015; Chase and Walker, 2013). For all these reasons, lower income is consistently associated with smaller social networks and, thus, less access to support (Ajrouch et al, 2005; Bailey et al, 2015; Feldman and Steptoe, 2004).

The kinds of social activities in which one participates can have a fundamental impact on subsequent opportunities and life chances

(Matthews and Besemer, 2015). Egerton and Mullan (2008) found that being less affluent, less educated or female were all factors associated with greater involvement in informal social activities which are likely to have fewer benefits in terms of the opportunities that they may bring for 'getting ahead'. In contrast, the more affluent and the more educated are more likely to be involved in more formal organisations, including many that work to represent the particular interests of their members, such as political parties, or resident or community groups (Li et al, 2003; Matthews and Hastings, 2013).

Turning to wider aspects of social exclusion, many relationships with social participation might be explored. One is the complex and two-way relationship between social relations (networks, support, participation) and health and well-being. Poor health can obviously be a barrier to participation, as can some forms of disability, but reduced participation can also have negative impacts on health and well-being (Berkman and Glass, 2000; Cohen, 2004; Cohen et al, 2000; Lein and Sussman, 1983; Thoits, 2011). For instance, Barnett and Gotlib (1988) found that poor social connections (smaller social networks), fewer close relationships and lower perceived adequacy of social support were associated with both precipitating and exacerbating depressive symptoms. Numerous studies have documented a positive association between social participation and networks, and various measures of physical health, including lower rates of heart disease, cancer and infant mortality (Kawachi et al, 1997), and reduced adult mortality (Lochner et al, 2003).

Further to this, a substantial body of evidence shows that social ties, as well as participation in social activities and social support, have indirect effects on physical and mental health because they can prevent or modulate responses to harmful or stressful events (Cohen and Wills, 1985). For example, a longitudinal study of the consequences of involuntary job loss found that social support buffers the effects of the stress caused by unemployment on health (Gore, 1978). As Chapter 10 in this volume shows, low-income groups are more likely to suffer a wide range of harmful events, such as losing a job or being a victim of crime. The health benefits of social participation are particularly significant for people living on lower incomes (Kawachi and Berkman, 2001; Lee et al, 2008), so the potential loss is that much greater where lack of resources has eroded the capacity to sustain social networks and participation. Other studies have shown that social support also has an important positive influence on the quality of other social relationships, for example, in relation to the impact of maternal well-being and social assets (including the negative effects of persistent low income) on children's social, emotional and behavioural well-being (Treanor, 2016).

In analysing the PSE-UK data on social participation, this chapter therefore focuses on the following questions:

- In what ways does material constraint affect participation in common social activities? Which aspects of participation are most affected?
- How important are resource constraints in shaping participation, compared with other factors such as caring responsibilities or health? Does the shame associated with poverty result in lower participation?
- How do levels of social support vary with resources and with poverty in particular? To what extent are these differences explained by levels of social participation?
- What other factors influence one's sense of social support and how important are these relative to poverty?

Social networks and activities

Social networks

This section looks at the levels of contact people have with family and friends, the next at their participation in social activities. The PSE-UK 2012 survey contains four questions on the scale of social networks: how often people see or speak to relatives, and the number seen or spoken to at least monthly, with the same two questions relating to friends. Responses to the two questions about family are strongly correlated with each other, as are those about friends, but familial and friendship networks seem quite distinct. We therefore combine each pair and convert to binary measures identifying those with low contact; the same threshold[1] identifies 16 per cent in each case. Separately, respondents are asked whether they see family and friends as often as they want or not, regardless of how often they have contact. This allows us to identify those who feel their contact is constrained (57 per cent). If they do not see people as often as they want, respondents also indicate the factors that prevent them meeting up more often.

In addition to face-to-face or telephone contact, the PSE-UK survey asks about communication with family and friends by letter, text, email or social media. As we shall see, young adults are far more likely to use these media than older respondents, indicating very strongly that this is about *electronic* communications rather than letters. Answers to this question are not highly correlated with familial and friendship contact and are considered separately here. Respondents using these media less than once a month (22 per cent) are regarded as having low communications.

Taking each of the four forms of social contact – low social contact with family and with friends, low communications and constraints on contact – logistic regression is used to examine how each is affected by the range of potential constraints discussed above (Figure 5.1). Here we examine the independent effects of low income and deprivation on social contact, controlling for a range of covariates (that is, socio-demographic variables such as sex, age and ethnicity), and for other factors known to be potential constraining factors on social contact: household type (childcare), hours of paid work, long-term limiting illness or disability (LLTI), caring responsibilities, and experience of shame from poverty. The regression coefficients show the change in the predicted logged odds of having lower contact with family and friends, lower communications with friends and family and experiencing constraint as a result of a particular characteristic. A positive value for the regression coefficients indicates more exclusion, i.e. *lower* contact with family and with friends, *lower* (electronic) communications, and *greater* constraint. Taking the results for gender as an example, Figure 5.1 shows that women are less likely to have low levels of contact with family or friends, or low levels of electronic communications, but more likely to feel constraints on social contact than men.

Overall, Figure 5.1 confirms that social participation is influenced by a combination of factors which enable or restrict participation, such as material resources, and those which may indicate greater needs, notably caring roles as well as health. On the resource side, the models show that, as deprivation rises, the proportion of people reporting low contact or more constraint increases steadily. At lower levels of deprivation, people appear to maintain contacts with family more than with friends, as earlier work has shown. However, at very high levels of deprivation (lacking eight or more necessities), contact with family appears to be affected as much as contact with friends. Deprivation also results in lower use of electronic forms of communication and more constraints on social contact. On the latter, deprived respondents are particularly likely to mention cost or affordability problems, as well as health, transport, childcare and other caring responsibilities.

Using household income to measure command of resources, the picture is a little less clear. Contact with family is lower for those on the lowest incomes, but also for those on the highest; the results are very similar even if deprivation is excluded from the model. Moderate

Figure 5.1: Social contact, communications and constraints (logistic regression models)

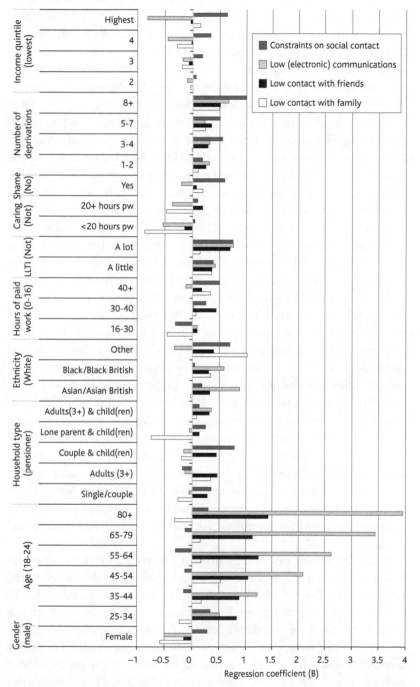

Notes: Nagelkerke *R* squared: 0.09, 0.05, 0.34 and 0.15 respectively. Number of unweighted cases: 7,538, 7,528, 7,531 and 7,531 respectively.

income appears to enable greater contact but, at higher incomes, other factors appear to come into play. It may be that these individuals feel less need to draw on family for support but it may also be that the demands of paid work impose additional barriers for many. It is striking, however, that perceptions of constraints on social contact are rather different. The highest income groups report much higher levels of constraint on social contact even though they have no less contact in practice than those on the lowest incomes. Looking in more detail at the reasons, it is clear that they face a very different set of barriers to those living on lower incomes. Of those in the highest income quintile, 29 per cent mention paid work as a barrier compared with just 11 per cent of those in the lowest income quintile. By contrast, lower income groups are much more likely to report constraints due to the cost or affordability of travel (26 per cent compared with 8 per cent), as well as transport problems (15 per cent compared with 4 per cent) and health-related problems (13 per cent compared with 2 per cent). Contact with friends varies little with income while the use of electronic communications rises significantly as income increases.

People with a LLTI have less contact with family and friends, as well as fewer communications, even after controlling for the effects of deprivation and income so this is not simply due to the impact of poor health on household resources. Contact with friends and communications fall further with increasing health restrictions, but contact with family does not – on the contrary, it is higher than for those with less limiting conditions. People with caring responsibilities, whether for children or others, appear to have closer connections to family and less contact with friends, reflecting their greater need for support but also the constraints on their time. Couples with children report lower contact with friends but no lower contact with family, while lone parents report more contact with family. All of these findings underline the importance of family as a source of practical and emotional support for groups where there are likely to be additional needs.

One area where our results do not clearly support the theories discussed above is in relation to the isolating effects of shame associated with poverty. People who report ever having experienced shame as a result of poverty do report lower contact with family and friends overall but, once we control for levels of deprivation, the relationship is not strong enough to appear statistically significant. There is a limitation with the question wording for current purposes since it refers to ever having felt shame due to poverty but, even if we restrict this group to those currently in poverty, the results do not change.

There are some other notable differences related to socio-demographic factors which may reflect a combination of resources as well as needs for support, but which may also reflect cultural differences. Women have more contact with family than men and make more use of electronic communications, but there is little difference in relation to contact with friends. Women also report more constraints. As we age, contact with family initially appears to fall before rising again as we enter retirement years but contact with friends falls progressively with age as does use of electronic communications.

Social activities

Another way of examining people's social participation is by looking at the range of common social activities in which they engage. The PSE-UK survey asks respondents whether they take part in 14 different activities with varying levels of frequency and, if not, whether this is due to not wanting to do so, not being able to afford to do so, or for any other reasons. The list of activities is shown in Table 5.1, and was drawn up on the basis of a review of previous studies as well as focus group discussions, as described in the Introduction. One activity (attending church, mosque, synagogue or other place of worship) is not viewed as desirable by a majority of respondents in the PSE-UK study (54 per cent said they did not want to do this) and the analysis therefore focuses on the remaining 13 activities.

The full list of 13 offers a broad focus by looking at participation in activities which the majority said they either did or wanted to do, and which can therefore be regarded as 'socially approved' activities. We count people as experiencing low participation if they participate in four or fewer activities (21 per cent). However, the public regarded five of these 13 as necessities, that is, activities which everyone should be able to do and no one should have to go without. Where people are unable to participate in these activities because of lack of money, they are counted as indicators of deprivation in the PSE-UK deprivation index. When looking at the factors which influence participation in these activities, there is a potential circularity due to the overlap with the PSE-UK's deprivation index. We therefore ran the same analyses using a measure of participation based on the remaining eight (non-necessity) activities to check that any relationship between deprivation and participation is not artificially inflated by this. Selecting a cut-off which identifies a similar proportion, low participation in this case identifies respondents reporting one or none of eight activities (22 per cent).

Table 5.1: The prevalence of common social activities in the UK, 2012 (%)

	Do	Do not want to do	Cannot afford to do	Do not do – other
Celebrations on special occasions, such as Christmas	84	3	3	1
Attending weddings, funerals and other such occasions	79	4	2	4
A hobby or leisure activity	64	13	7	6
Visit friends or family in hospital or other institutions	58	12	3	17
Friends/family round for meal or drink once a month	56	15	9	10
Holiday away from home for 1 week/year, not with family	54	9	22	5
A meal out once a month	54	13	18	5
Going out socially once a fortnight	49	18	16	8
Taking part in sport/exercise activities or classes	39	30	10	11
Holidays abroad once a year	38	17	29	6
Going out for a drink once a fortnight	37	31	13	8
Visit family/friends in other parts of country 4 times/year	37	20	19	13
Going to cinema/theatre/music event once a month	32	28	19	11
Attending place of worship	23	54	2	10

Note: **Bold** = PSE Necessity. Number of unweighted cases: 9,034.

Counting the number of activities in which people participate is a fairly crude measure of participation, as there is no assessment of the frequency with which different activities are undertaken, nor of the respondent's views about the quality of social interaction which occurs. Furthermore, social participation and interaction can occur as an integral part of many other activities, including during paid or voluntary work, or other civic or political activities, but we do not capture those aspects of socialising here. Despite this, the measure provides some guide to the range of socially approved activities undertaken.

Figure 5.2 shows regression models for low participation with the same set of independent variables as discussed for Figure 5.1 to capture a range of factors which may enable or constrain social participation, and which shape preferences and opportunities for engagement. The results are very similar whether we use the broader (13-item) or narrower (8-item) measure so we show only the latter here for simplicity. Model 1 excludes our measures of material resources

Figure 5.2: Low participation in social activities (one or none out of eight) (logistic regression models)

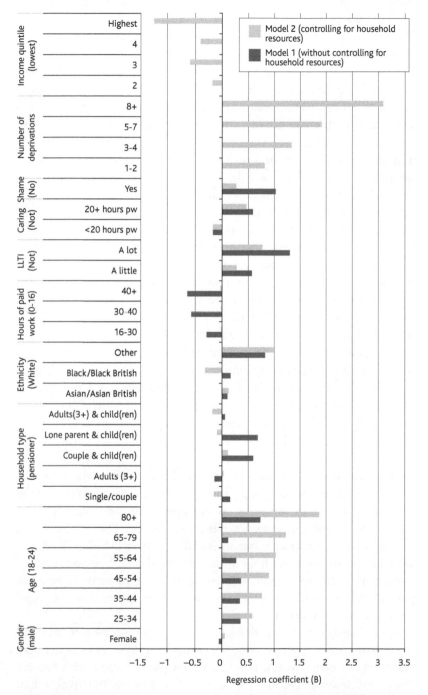

Notes: Nagelkerke *R* squared: 0.17 and 0.35 respectively. Number of unweighted cases: 7,539.

(income) and living standards (deprivation), whereas Model 2 includes these. (Again, a positive value on the regression coefficient represents *lower* participation.)

The results for Model 2 show the direct effect of resources on participation in common social activities. This appears greater than the effect of resources on social contact, with strong relationships with both deprivation and income measures. For example, of those reporting no deprivation, only 7 per cent are in the low activity group whereas two-thirds of those with eight or more deprivations are in this category; results are the same whichever activity measure is used. The effects appear continuous and progressive across the range of deprivation and income, and they are apparent after a range of other factors have been taken into account.

Comparing the two models allows us to examine the direct and indirect effects of other factors. In Model 1, for example, LLTI is associated with significantly greater risks of being in the low participation group but this could be due to two factors: the direct effects of health or disability on individual propensity to participate in particular activities, and indirect effects due to the impact of health or disability on resources. Model 2 shows the direct effect of health on its own (that is, after controlling for the effect of material resources). There remains a direct effect albeit reduced and more restricted to those with the most limiting long-term illnesses. For households with children, the picture is similar. Couples with children and lone parents both have lower participation in social activities (Model 1) but this is wholly accounted for by the negative impact on household material resources of raising children (Model 2). With other caring roles, resources appear to have less impact. Those caring 20 hours a week or more participate less, and this picture does not alter when we take account of resources, suggesting that constraints arise from the caring role itself. 'Lesser' caring roles do not appear to limit participation. The opposite pattern emerges with paid work. Those who work longer hours participate more in social activities (Model 1). When we take account of household resources (Model 2), however, rates of participation are no greater, suggesting it is the material benefits of paid work alone which matter for participation, rather than the social connections made through work.

Age is a major factor in engagement in many social activities and this is particularly apparent once we control for differences in material resources. In other words, falling rates of participation with age are not due to resource constraints, but occur despite the (relative) lack of constraints. Looking in more detail at the responses, it is clear that this is in part due to preferences altering with age, particularly for those 80 and over. This group identifies an average of 4.5 activities (out of 13) which they do not want to participate in, compared with 3.4 for those 65–79 and just 1.6 for those under 45. There is a particularly sharp drop off in relation to activities such as going to the cinema or similar, taking part in sport or exercise activities, going out for a drink or having a holiday (whether abroad or not). One of these – 'sport/exercise' – is a necessities item, suggesting that including this in the deprivation scale may introduce some age bias into the measure. However, older people are at most only marginally less likely to want to participate in the four activities which make up the rest of the necessities items: celebrating special occasions such as birthdays; attending weddings, funerals and so on; visiting friends or family in hospital or other institution; or hobby or leisure activity. These are also the most common activities, greatly reducing concerns about potential age biases.

Those not taking part in one or more activities are asked their reasons for this. The responses echo those given for not having more contact with family and friends, with lack of time due to paid work or childcare and problems related to health or disability mentioned most frequently. A small proportion of people (around one in twenty) say that the lack of people to go out with limits their participation. These people are more than twice as likely to report low contact with friends. So, while family may be more important as a route to support or resources, friends may have a slightly greater role when it comes to social activities. People with a LLTI are among those more likely to report not having people to go out with, but they are also particularly likely to report problems of physical access or of feeling unwelcome.

Social support and satisfaction

Having described in some detail participation behaviours, we turn now to the affective aspects of social relations – how people feel about their social networks. First, the PSE–UK survey asks a series of seven hypothetical questions to assess perceptions of social support. For example, people are asked to say how much support they think they would get if they were ill in bed and needed help at home, or if they needed advice about an important change in their life. Conceptually, these items may be thought of as capturing two distinct dimensions of support – emotional versus practical. In practice, they are all strongly correlated, suggesting they reflect a single underlying characteristic, social support; many other studies have obtained the same result (see

Thoits, 1995 for a review). We sum across all seven questions to produce a single, continuous variable and use this to create a binary measure to identify those with lower levels of support, using a cut-off which identifies those in the bottom 23 per cent of the distribution. The choice of cut-off does not have a significant impact on results and is selected to be broadly comparable to the low contact and low participation measures. Second, we look at responses to a single question on satisfaction with personal relationships (operationalised using a five-item Likert scale from 'Very satisfied' to 'Very dissatisfied'). We contrast those who were not satisfied with those who were, with 17 per cent in the former group, again giving broadly similar sample coverage to the dependent measures discussed above.

Figure 5.3 shows the logistic regression models for low support and low satisfaction, again using the same set of independent variables as previously discussed. There are some similarities between those reporting low support and those reporting low satisfaction, but some notable differences as well. Resources clearly shape perceptions of support and satisfaction but here, problems appear more confined to poorer groups. Social support and satisfaction with personal relationships both fall progressively as deprivation rises. However, with regard to income above the lowest income quintile, both appear quite similar across the other four quintiles (that is, there appears to be an income threshold effect for perceptions of support and relationship quality).

With age, there is a striking divergence in findings between social support and satisfaction with personal relationships for older adults. Across the age groups, perceptions of support are quite constant – none of these differences are statistically significant. Above the age of 55, however, people are much less likely to report themselves dissatisfied with their personal relationships. As previous results showed, older people do not have any more contact with family and, if anything, have less contact with friends – and they make only limited use of electronic communications. Despite this, satisfaction with social relationships appears to rise steadily as we age. There is a similar pattern with people from minority ethnic groups for whom satisfaction is much higher than sense of support.

Another notable finding is the extent to which lone parents feel they lack support and are dissatisfied with their relationships. They experience a combination of particularly acute pressures arising from their sole responsibility for childcare, combined with often limited household resources, although the problems for lone parents are still apparent even once we control for resource differences. Other parents

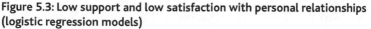

Figure 5.3: Low support and low satisfaction with personal relationships (logistic regression models)

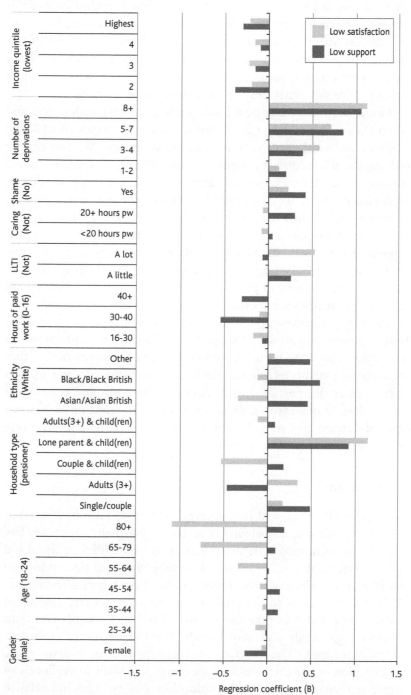

Notes: Nagelkerke *R* squared: 0.13 and 0.15 respectively. Number of unweighted cases: 7,134 and 7,164 respectively.

do not report the same kinds of problem. Those with a limiting long-term illness feel they have less support, although taking account of resource effects they are no different in this respect; they also feel more dissatisfied with their personal relationships. Working longer hours in paid employment is associated with greater support, whereas longer hours spent caring is associated with less. In both cases, however, there is no relationship with satisfaction with personal relationships.

Finally, we can look at how levels of social contact with family and with friends, (including via electronic communication) affect social support and satisfaction with personal relationships. We test this by adding the three contact measures (family, friends, communications) to our models for social support and relationship satisfaction (that is, retaining the same set of independent variables – results not shown). Contact with family and with friends both have a positive impact on sense of support and relationship satisfaction. Sense of support appears to be more affected by levels of contact with family than with friends, reinforcing the impression that family plays a more central role as a source of practical and emotional support. Family and friends appear equally important as influences on satisfaction, however. Interestingly, electronic communications do not appear to influence either perceptions of social support or relationship satisfaction. As such, they appear to be no substitute for personal interaction, either face-to-face or by telephone. Adding these factors to the models barely alters the relationships between deprivation and support or satisfaction. In other words, the main impact of deprivation on support and satisfaction appears to be a direct one, rather than an indirect one via its impact on social networks.

Conclusion

Townsend (1979) argued that poverty matters because it affects our ability to participate actively in our society. Nevertheless, relatively few studies have examined in detail the impact which insufficient command of material resources has on social participation and perceptions of social support. The main conclusion from our work is that Townsend's insight with regards to the relationship between poverty and social participation has stood the test of time. Limited resources constrain contact with family and with friends, and restrict use of electronic communications. They also reduce participation in a wide range of common social activities and are associated with lower levels of perceived social support and relationship quality. The importance of social networks and support for 'getting by' or dealing with the consequences of harmful events, not to mention their value in 'getting ahead', is now well documented in the literature. However, our findings reveal the existence of a mechanism which is likely to reinforce the harm caused by poverty and make it more difficult to escape: poverty increases the importance of, and likely need for, social networks and social support while simultaneously eroding them. The evidence of direct and indirect benefits of support for physical and mental health outcomes is further reason to be concerned about these findings.

The importance of contact with family in particular emerges clearly in this analysis. For those groups where there are likely to be additional needs for support as a result of caring roles or health problems, contact with family tends to be significantly higher – likely reflecting the importance of family as both the central source of financial resources and of practical and emotional support. Households in these circumstances who lack access to such family networks may face particularly serious disadvantages.

Beyond the impact of poverty, the analysis demonstrates that participation and perceptions of support are also sensitive to a range of other factors. The direct negative effects on participation of limiting health problems and disabilities accords with existing findings which have found that mobility barriers (such as lack of accessible transport) inhibit social participation. Furthermore, the indirect effects of limiting illness on social participation through its impact on command of material resources is an additional concern and highlights that people with limiting illnesses face a double barrier.

Ensuring people have sufficient material resources to avoid poverty is the best way of ensuring they can remain socially connected and supported. At the same time, policy needs to recognise the value of social relationships and networks for both coping with and escaping from poverty. Policies and institutions which enhance the ability to build and maintain positive relationships should be valued. Some recent developments in housing policy, notably the shift from social to private rental housing, and the growing constraints on welfare payments for housing (that is, Housing Benefit), undermine the ability of low-income households to maintain stable places of residence and build ties with their community. There is a significant challenge for researchers in exploring the impacts of these policies on social relations and community functioning, and hence on broader well-being.

Note

[1] The threshold is equivalent to seeing two or fewer family members or friends a few times a month.

References

Ajrouch K. J., Blandon A. Y. and Antonucci T. C. (2005) 'Social networks among men and women: the effects of age and socioeconomic status', *Journals of Gerontology B: psychological sciences and social sciences*, 60(6): S311-17.

Bailey, N., Besemer, K., Bramley, G. and Livingston, M. (2015) 'How neighbourhood social mix shapes access to resources from social networks and from services', *Housing Studies*, 30(2): 295-314.

Barnett, P. A. and Gotlib, I. H. (1988) 'Psychosocial functioning and depression: distinguishing among antecedents, concomitants and consequences', *Psychological Bulletin*, 104(1): 97-126.

Berkman, L. F. and Glass, T. (2000) 'Social integration, social networks, social support, and health', in L. F. Berkman, and I. Kawachi (eds) *Social epidemiology*, New York: Oxford University Press, pp 137-73.

Bradshaw, P. and Wasoff, F. (2009) *Growing up in Scotland: Multiple childcare provision and its effect on child outcomes*, Edinburgh: The Scottish Government.

Briggs, X. D. S. (1998) 'Brown kids in white suburbs: housing mobility and the many faces of social capital', *Housing Policy Debate*, 9(1): 177-221.

Chase, E. and Walker, R. (2013) 'The co-construction of shame in the context of poverty: beyond a threat to the social bond', *Sociology*, 47(4): 739-54.

Cheshire, P. (2009) 'Policies for mixed communities', *Intergenerational Regional Science Review*, 32(3): 343-75.

Cohen, S. (2004) 'Social relationships and health', *American Psychologist*, 59 (Special Issue): 676-84.

Cohen, S. and Wills, T. A. (1985) 'Stress, social support and the buffering hypothesis', *Psychological Bulletin*, 98(1): 310-57.

Cohen, S., Gottlieb, B. H. and Underwood, L. G. (2000) 'Social relationships and health', in S. Cohen, L. G. Underwood and B. H. Gottlieb (eds) *Social support measurement and intervention: A guide for health and social scientists*, New York: Oxford University Press.

Curley, A. M. (2010) 'Relocating the poor: Social capital and neighbourhood resources', *Journal of Urban Affairs*, 32(1): 79-103.

Egerton, M. and Mullan, K. (2008) 'Being a pretty good citizen: an analysis and monetary valuation of formal and informal voluntary work by gender and educational attainment', *British Journal of Sociology*, 59(1): 145-64.

Feldman, P. J. and Steptoe, A. (2004) 'How neighborhoods and physical functioning are related: the roles of neighborhood socioeconomic status, perceived neighborhood strain, and individual health risk factors', *Annals of Behavioral Medicine*, 27(2): 91-9.

Gannon, B. and Nolan, B. (2004) 'Disability and labour force participation in Ireland', *The Economic and Social Review*, 35(2): 135-55.

Gore, S. (1978) 'The effect of social support in moderating the health consequences of unemployment', *Journal of Health and Social Behaviour*, 19(2): 157-65.

Green, A. E., Li, Y., Owen, D. and de Hoyos, G. M. (2011) 'Inequalities in use of the internet for job search: similarities and contrasts by economic status in Great Britain', *Environment and Planning*, 44(10): 2344-58.

Green, A. E., de Hoyos, M., Li, Y. and Owen, D. (2012) *Job search study: Literature review and analysis of the Labour Force Survey*, London: Department for Work and Pensions.

Heflin, C., London, A. S. and Scott, E. K. (2011) 'Mitigating material hardship: the strategies low-income families employ to reduce the consequences of poverty', *Sociological Inquiry*, 81(2): 223-46.

Henley, J. R., Danziger, S. K. and Offer, S. (2005) 'The contribution of social support to the material well-being of low-income families', *Journal of Marriage and Family*, 67(1): 122-40.

Hetherington, E. M., Cox, M. and Cox, R. (1978) 'The aftermath of divorce', in J. H. Stevens and M. M. Matthews (eds) *Mother-child, father-child relations*, Washington, DC: National Association for the Education of Young Children, pp 110-55.

Howard, E. C. (2006) 'The informal social support, well-being and employment pathways of low-income mothers', in H. Yoshikawa, T. S. Weisner and E. D. Lowe (eds) *Making it work: Low-wage employment, family life and child development*, New York: Russell Sage Foundation, pp 256-72.

Kawachi, I., Kennedy, B. P., Lochner, K. and Prothrow-Stith, D. (1997) 'Social capital, income inequality, and mortality', *American Journal of Public Health*, 87(9): 1491-8.

Kodz, J., Davis, S., Lain, D., Strebler, M., Rick, J., Bates, P., Cummings, J., Meager, N., Anxo, D., Gineste, S., Trinczek, R. and Pamer, S. (2003) *Working long hours: A review of the evidence: Volume 1 – Main Report*, Employment Relations Research Series No. 16, Department of Trade and Industry: The Institute for Employment Studies.

Lee, Y. G. and Bhargava, V. (2004) 'Leisure time: do married and single individuals spend it differently?', *Family and Consumer Sciences*, 32(3): 254-74.

Lein, L. and Sussman, M. B. (1983) 'The ties that bind: men and women's social networks', *Marriage and Family Review*, Vol. 5, No. 4, New York: The Haworth Press.

Levitas, R. (2006) 'The concept and measurement of social exclusion', in C. Pantazis, D. Gordon and R. Levitas (eds) *Poverty and social exclusion in Britain: The Millennium Survey*, Bristol: Policy Press, pp 123-62.

Levitas, R., Pantazis, C., Fahmy, E., Gordon, D., Lloyd, E. and Patsios, D. (2007) *The multi-dimensional analysis of social exclusion*, Bristol: University of Bristol.

Li, Y., Savage, M. and Pickles, A. (2003) 'Social capital and social exclusion in England and Wales (1972-1999)', *British Journal of Sociology*, 54(4): 497-526.

Lin, N. (1999) 'Social networks and status attainment', *Annual Review of Sociology*, 25(1): 467-87.

Lister, R. (2004) *Poverty*, Cambridge: Polity Press.

Livingston, M., Bailey, N. and Kearns, A. (2010) 'Neighbourhood attachment in deprived areas: Evidence from the north of England', *Journal of Housing and the Built Environment*, 25(4): 409-27.

Lochner, K. A., Kawachi, I., Brennan, R. T. and Buka, S. L. (2003) 'Social capital and neighborhood mortality rates in Chicago', *Social Science & Medicine*, 56(8): 1797-805.

Matthews, P. and Besemer, K. (2015) *Poverty and social networks evidence review: A report from the Joseph Rowntree Foundation Anti-poverty Programme*, York: Joseph Rowntree Foundation.

Matthews, P. and Hastings, A. (2013) 'Middle-class political activism and middle-class advantage in relation to public services: a realist synthesis of the evidence base', *Social Policy and Administration*, 47(1): 72-92.

McCabe, A., Gilchrist, A., Harris, K., Afridi, A. and Kyprianou, P. (2013) *Making the links: Poverty, ethnicity and social networks*, York: Joseph Rowntree Foundation.

Offer, S. (2012) 'The burden of reciprocity: processes of exclusion and withdrawal from personal networks among low-income families', *Current Sociology*, 60(6): 788-805.

Pemberton, S., Fahmy. E., Sutton, E. and Bell, K. (2015) 'Navigating the stigmatised identities of poverty in austere times', *Critical Social Policy*, 36(1): 21-37.

Putnam, R. (2000) *Bowling alone: The collapse and revival of American community*, New York: Touchstone.

Richez-Battesti, N. and Lest, F. P. (2013) 'Social networks and entrepreneurship', in E. G. Carayannis (ed) *Encyclopedia of creativity, invention, innovation and entrepreneurship*, Dordrecht: Springer, pp 1693-700.

Ridge, T. (2009) 'Living with poverty: a review of the literature on children's and families' experiences of poverty', *DWP Research Report No 594*, HMSO: Norwich.

Stack, C. B. (1974) *All our kin: Strategies for survival in a black community*, New York: Harper and Row.

Taylor, S. and Brown, C. W. (2011) 'The contribution of gifts to the household economy of low-income families', *Social Policy and Society*, 10(2): 163-75.

Thoits, P. A. (1995) 'Stress, coping, and social support processes: Where are we? What next?', *Journal of Health & Social Behavior*, 36 (Extra issue): 53-79.

Thoits, P. A. (2011) 'Perceived social support and voluntary, mixed or pressured use of mental health services', *Society and Mental Health*, 1: 4-19.

Townsend, P. (1979) *Poverty in the UK: A survey of household resources and living standards*, Harmondsworth: Allen Lane.

Townsend, P. (1993) *The international analysis of poverty*, London: Harvester Wheatsheaf.

Treanor, M. (2016) 'Social assets, low income and child social, emotional and behavioural well-being', *Families, Relationships and Societies*, 5(2): 209-28.

SIX

Employment, poverty and social exclusion

Nick Bailey

Introduction

Paid work is, quite rightly, at the heart of many governments' responses to poverty and social exclusion. Most directly, paid work is a source of income which can reduce risks of poverty and raise living standards, both in the short and longer term, including in retirement. In addition, it is also seen as having a wider 'transformative potential' (Patrick, 2012). It can provide people with a social role and hence a source of identify and self-respect, as well as opening up opportunities for social contact, reducing risks of isolation. All of these can in turn have positive effects on health and well-being; for those suffering health problems, work can have a restorative potential (Waddell and Burton, 2006). As a result, some perspectives on social exclusion have come to equate employment with inclusion: to be in paid work is to be regarded as 'included' (Levitas, 1998).

Yet as many critics have observed, the benefits of employment have been growing more unequal in recent decades as the labour market has undergone a series of fundamental changes. These changes have been driven in part by technological developments which have reduced the value of some kinds of skills, while enhancing the value of others (Machin, 2011). At the same time, globalisation of the economy has meant increased competition for developed countries from lower-cost regions. However, the changes are also driven by conscious policy choices, notably in relation to labour markets and welfare.

Labour markets have been 'deregulated' to make it easier for businesses to determine the conditions under which they hire labour, while the balance between workers and employers has been further shifted by restrictions on trades unions (Dickens et al, 2003). The consequence has been the rise of 'flexible' forms of work involving variable and/or anti-social hours as well as widening inequality in rates of pay (Machin, 2011). The UK has some of the lowest levels of employment protection of any of the OECD countries (Venn, 2009).

Welfare systems have shifted from a safety-net function to become tools for 'activation' or for encouraging re-entry to employment for the unemployed and inactive (Gilbert and Besharov, 2011). Unemployment benefits have been reduced in value and hedged around with an increasing number of conditions or requirements, enforced through tough sanction regimes. Again the UK is regarded as operating a relatively harsh regime (Venn, 2012) – and that was before the most recent changes which further increased the maximum length of sanctions (Watts et al, 2014). Rising inequalities in wages have been the main driver of widening inequality in many developed countries, including the UK (Machin, 2011; OECD, 2011). They are also the reason why people in work now account for more than half of the working-age poor (DWP, 2017; Belfield et al, 2016).

Lone parents and people on long-term sickness benefits have come in for particular focus from governments seeking to reduce welfare expenditures and raise employment rates. Lone parents have been required to look for work once their youngest child turns five, rather than being allowed to remain a full-time parent until children reach eleven. For those with health problems, Incapacity Benefit has been reshaped into Employment Support Allowance with a tougher test for incapacity. Arguments can be made about the benefits of employment, including therapeutic effects for those with long-term health problems or role model effects for those with children. In both cases, however, there is an underlying assumption that the work itself is a means to inclusion, rather than de-humanising or demoralising.

Given this context, the aim of this chapter is to focus on those in employment and examine the variations in forms of exclusion within this group, rather than focusing on the contrast between those in and out of work. This chapter uses the PSE-UK data to look at the extent to which different groups appear to enjoy the inclusionary benefits of paid work. In particular, it seeks to build on an analysis presented in Bailey (2016), which constructed a measure of 'exclusionary employment'. This captures people who are in employment but who do not appear to be enjoying its inclusionary benefits. They may be working but have an income so low or so subject to fluctuation that they remain in poverty. Or their work may be of such low quality that it is unlikely to produce the health or social benefits that 'decent' jobs provide. Or, while they may be working at present, their security is so low that they are not likely to remain in that status for long. One in three people currently in employment in the UK falls into one or more of these groups.

In this chapter, the aim is to explore the nature of exclusionary employment further in two respects. First, it will examine in more detail the characteristics of people in exclusionary employment, exploring how the different aspects of employment exclusion overlap. Second, it takes a broader look at social exclusion, and examines the extent to which those who are excluded in employment are also excluded on a range of other domains. The PSE-UK survey captures exclusion on a wide range of domains, as discussed in the Introduction. Here we look at three which we might expect to have particularly close relationships with employment: health and well-being; social networks and participation; and housing and neighbourhood environment. The chapter therefore contributes towards the multidimensional understanding of exclusion which is the focus of Chapter 13.

The chapter begins by explaining how exclusionary employment is defined and measured. It then explores the individual risk factors associated with being in this state before going on to examine the relationship between this domain of exclusion and the other three noted above. The last section provides a concluding discussion.

Defining exclusionary employment

In some approaches to social exclusion, employment is treated as more or less synonymous with inclusion. This has been particularly true in some of the uses of the term in policy debates within Europe, as Levitas (1998) shows. One effect of this is to legitimise a wide range of actions to encourage those who are unemployed or inactive back into employment. It also has the effect of masking divisions or differences within the world of paid work, at exactly the same time that these differences are growing.

In response, a variety of concepts have been deployed to try to draw attention to these divisions, expanding the focus of policy beyond reducing unemployment or raising employment rates. The terms 'decent work' (ILO, 1999), 'fair work' (TUC, 2010) or 'good work' (Constable et al, 2009) all emphasise in various ways the importance of thinking about the quality of working lives. Other terms have focused on the negative side of the division, drawing attention directly to the more excluded groups. These run from Townsend's (1979) concept of 'employment deprivation' through to recent debates about 'precarious work' (Standing, 2011).

'Exclusionary employment' draws on the Bristol Social Exclusion Matrix (B–SEM) framework developed by Levitas et al (2006). This identifies multiple domains of exclusion under the three broad areas of resources, participation and quality of life. Exclusionary employment looks at the nature of employment in relation to each of these three areas. In relation to resources, exclusionary employment is paid work which has so few material benefits that people remain in poverty when in employment. In relation to participation, being in paid work is usually seen as a marker of inclusion on this basis with involuntary unemployment equated with exclusion. Exclusionary employment, however, occurs where paid work is highly insecure so that, while people may currently have a job, they have a high risk of this ending soon. In relation to quality of life, while employment is generally associated with better health, some employment may be harmful, through risks of physical injury but also through harm arising from the nature of the job role or the psychosocial environment. Exclusionary employment is low quality work.

These elements were used to construct a measure of exclusionary employment, that is, exclusion 'arising directly from an individual's labour market situation' (Bailey, 2016: 82). That paper argues that this is best captured by the following measures:

- **working poverty**, assessed for those in paid work as being in poverty on the PSE-UK combined deprivation and low income measure;
- **insecurity**, assessed through work history (six months or more unemployed in the last five years); or
- **low quality of employment**, based on a group of ten questions to capture satisfaction, control or flexibility for the worker, and physical conditions.[1]

There are of course many choices about exactly how we might identify exclusionary employment, and the full justification for the current measure is provided in Bailey (2016). First, on resources, the measure is not simply assessing low pay by reference to benchmarks such as the Living Wage but is a broader measure of the resource benefits of paid work which reflects hours of work and stability over time, as well as household composition or needs: are those in work able to escape poverty? Second, insecurity was measured by looking at recent work history rather than the respondents' subjective assessment of whether their current job was secure. The two have quite a weak relationship, in part because having a post which is insecure does not mean an individual faces high risk of becoming unemployed. While the measure used here is backward-looking, it is arguably a better guide to the prospects of remaining in employment in the near future. Third, the quality of employment measure included the three aspects of quality noted above. A fourth aspect of quality – job stress – might have been included as it is frequently identified in job quality measures. It was omitted here because the people who report this kind of problem tended to have much higher status jobs and had few other signs of being excluded. Our measure of low quality is one appropriate to lower status occupations.

Progression in the labour market

In addition to devising a measure for exclusionary employment, Bailey (2016) also looked at people's sense of progression in the labour market. This was an attempt to distinguish between people for whom exclusionary employment looked like a longer-lasting situation and those for whom it was likely to be more temporary. To assess progression, people were asked to compare their current job role with what they were doing five years earlier in terms of: level of skill, variety of tasks being undertaken, and level of responsibility. People were regarded as having made 'no progress' if they responded that their levels on these three aspects were, on average, the same or lower. Of course, it is recognised that some people do not wish to progress or move up in the labour market; they work to secure an income or other benefits, but their priorities lie elsewhere. Nevertheless, progression as we have defined it ought to be associated with improvements in pay, quality of work and job security – in other words, with a move towards more inclusionary forms of work. This chapter therefore uses this measure of progression to add a dynamic element to the picture.

Risks of exclusionary employment

For those in paid work in the PSE-UK survey, one in three is regarded as being in exclusionary employment: one in six is in in-work poverty (on the PSE-UK measure), one in ten is in insecure employment (poor work history) and one in six is in low quality employment. One way of looking at the overlaps between the different forms of exclusionary employment is to identify the proportion of individuals excluded on two or more dimensions. In other words, we are comparing people on the basis of a series of binary classifications (excluded or not) for each dimension. If we do this, the overlaps look relatively modest. While one in three has at least one form of exclusion, only one in twelve has two or more. Or, to put this another way, of those in exclusionary employment, fewer than one in four is excluded on two or more dimensions. See Figure 2 in Bailey (2016) for a visual representation of the overlaps.

This picture may be in part the result of the crude nature of our binary classifications: those just above the threshold for 'exclusion' on a given dimension are treated the same as those much further from the cut-off. A more subtle approach is to look at the risks for different groups of being excluded on each dimension (Table 6.1). We can also use logistic regression models to look at the influence of different factors, controlling for the others. Results are not shown for the latter since they change the picture very little but additional points which emerge from this are noted.

The groups most at risk of exclusionary employment are quite familiar, although it is striking how important age is, with adults under 35 having much greater risks of exclusion. Other factors include: being in the 'other' ethnic category (neither White nor Asian/Asian British); having children, especially if respondents are lone parents; having few qualifications; being in lower status occupations; or being in a household with low work intensity. In Table 6.1, working part-time is associated with higher risks of exclusion but this relationship disappears in the regression model. Similarly the greater risks of exclusion for those with a limiting long-term illness (LLTI) are much reduced when we control for other factors. Looking across the three elements which make up exclusionary employment, there is some consistency but also some variations in relationships. There is most similarity between poverty and insecurity (work history), reinforcing the importance of continuity of work for reducing poverty risks. For example, young adults and those in low status occupations face greater risks of exclusion on all three dimensions.

More than half of all lone parents (58 per cent) are in exclusionary employment, as are almost half of those with long-term health problems or disabilities (46 per cent). Moreover, both groups report low rates of progression in the labour market, implying that their exclusion is likely to be longlasting rather than transitory. The emphasis on driving up employment rates for these groups by reducing welfare entitlements appears particularly unsatisfactory.

If we look at occupational characteristics, risks of being in exclusionary employment are far higher for those in lower skilled occupations, particularly those in semi-routine or routine jobs where

61 per cent are excluded. People in these occupations have the highest levels of in-work poverty, the worst work histories and the poorest quality of employment. Those in lower supervisory occupations also face above average risks, largely due to their low quality of employment. Rates of progression are particularly low for those in semi-routine or routine occupations, with 40 per cent of the excluded reporting no progression over the last five years.

There is a group of service industries which all have high proportions of people in lower status occupations: wholesale and retail; transport; and accommodation and food. In these sectors, the risks of being in exclusionary employment are greater. To some extent, the risks reflect occupational mix but some differences remain even when we control for occupation (significance is just above the 1 per cent threshold). Risks are higher for this group on all three elements of exclusion and they also have the lowest rates of progression. Manufacturing and construction report particular problems of low quality (associated with poor physical working conditions especially) but they do not have the same problems with poverty or insecurity. Both the latter industries have far fewer people in routine or semi-routine occupations.

The self-employed are an interesting group, not least because numbers have been rising so rapidly in recent years, partly in response to falling levels of welfare entitlement. This group reports slightly lower risks of employment exclusion overall. While they have above average risks of being in the working poor group, they are less likely to be regard themselves as being in low quality work and they maintain a better work history. With relatively small numbers in the PSE-UK survey, it is difficult to disaggregate this group further although it would be useful to do so given there is likely to be extensive variation within it.

There are only limited variations between the countries of the UK or between labour market areas with higher or lower unemployment rates (results not shown). Scotland has slightly lower levels of exclusion than the rest of the UK, mainly due to lower risks of in-work poverty. Labour markets with higher unemployment rates have slightly higher levels of exclusion not because of higher working poverty but because of lower quality of work. There are slightly greater differences by urban–rural location, with people in rural areas least likely to be in exclusionary employment (31 per cent compared with 35 per cent in large urban areas) but it is the smaller urban location which have the highest risks (38 per cent). This pattern is apparent across all three aspects of exclusionary employment.

Table 6.1: Characteristics of those in exclusionary employment

		All employment excluded				Level of exclusionary employment		No progression (as % of excluded)
		All	Low pay	Insecure	Poor quality	One	Two or more	
All	All	35%	17%	10%	18%	27%	8%	15%
Sex	Male	37%	17%	9%	21%	28%	8%	17%
	Female	34%	18%	11%	15%	25%	8%	13%
Age	18-24	53%	19%	19%	32%	37%	15%	*
	25-34	41%	22%	12%	23%	29%	13%	18%
	35-44	33%	19%	8%	14%	27%	6%	14%
	45+	29%	13%	7%	15%	23%	6%	15%
Ethnicity	White	35%	17%	10%	18%	27%	8%	15%
	Asian/Asian British	34%	20%	10%	14%	26%	8%	13%
	Other	49%	33%	15%	24%	32%	17%	24%
Household composition	Single/couple	31%	10%	10%	18%	25%	6%	13%
	Adults (3+)	31%	*	*	21%	27%	*	*
	Couple & child(ren)	39%	25%	9%	18%	28%	11%	18%
	Lone parent & child(ren)	58%	41%	19%	24%	37%	20%	31%
	Adults(3+) & child(ren)	35%	18%	*	16%	26%	*	15%
Health/disability limits daily activity	No	34%	17%	9%	18%	26%	8%	14%
	Little or a lot	46%	25%	16%	23%	31%	15%	25%
Educational qualifications	Other/None	44%	23%	11%	24%	33%	12%	23%
	A Level or equivalent	31%	9%	8%	19%	28%	*	11%
	Degree or equivalent	21%	9%	8%	8%	18%	3%	6%

(continued)

		All employment excluded				Level of exclusionary employment		
		All	Low pay	Insecure	Poor quality	One	Two or more	No progression (as % of excluded)
Occupation (NS-SEC†)	Managerial/professional	20%	8%	6%	8%	17%	2%	5%
	Intermediate	32%	17%	8%	14%	26%	6%	10%
	Small employer/own account	33%	23%	8%	12%	25%	8%	16%
	Lower supervisory	43%	18%	*	27%	35%	*	19%
	Semi-routine/routine	61%	30%	19%	36%	41%	20%	40%
Industry (SIC2007)‡	Primary, manufacturing	35%	15%	6%	25%	26%	8%	18%
	Construction	39%	13%	9%	27%	33%	*	13%
	Wholesale, retail	53%	29%	15%	27%	39%	14%	34%
	Transport	49%	25%	*	31%	35%	14%	27%
	Accommodation, food	59%	34%	17%	35%	34%	25%	34%
	Other private services	22%	8%	7%	*	21%	*	*
	Admin., support services	41%	30%	*	13%	28%	13%	24%
	Public admin., education, etc.	27%	13%	9%	13%	21%	6%	7%
	Arts, entertainment, etc.	36%	19%	*	*	28%	*	*
Total hours worked	<16 hrs	46%	23%	20%	23%	31%	15%	20%
	16<30 hrs	49%	31%	19%	20%	32%	17%	30%
	30<40 hrs	30%	14%	8%	15%	24%	6%	12%
	40+ hrs	32%	14%	7%	19%	26%	6%	12%
Household work intensity§	<0.4	70%	52%	41%	25%	32%	38%	46%
	0.4 to 0.8	42%	26%	12%	19%	31%	11%	20%
	>0.8	30%	11%	6%	19%	24%	5%	10%
N (unweighted)		3075						1085

Notes:

*Fewer than 20 unweighted cases.

† NS-SEC – National Statistics Socio-Economic Classification.

‡ SIC2007 – Standard Industrial Classification 2007. 'Other private services' comprises: Information and Communications; Financial and Insurance; Real estate, Professional, etc.

§ 'Household work intensity' captures the extent to which working-age adults in the household (and not in full-time education) were in employment over the previous 12 months. '1' shows all adults worked full-time for all 12 months.

Relationships with other dimensions of exclusion

One of the main aims of the PSE-UK survey was to measure social exclusion in a truly multidimensional way for the first time in the UK. Each of the multiple domains identified in the B-SEM was operationalised in the survey (see the Introduction for a summary). We take advantage of this in constructing the measure of exclusionary employment, combining resource aspects (poverty) with participation and quality of life dimensions. This section takes the analysis further by focusing on three particular areas which might be expected to have relationships with exclusionary employment: health and well-being; social networks and participation; and housing and neighbourhood environment.

Health and well-being

The relationships between employment and health are of key concern to policy makers. On the one hand, poor health is a barrier to employment. In the UK, as in many other developed countries, the proportion of working-age people on long-term sickness benefits has been rising, leading to high fiscal costs as well as a reduced labour supply. Conversely, work is often seen as health-promoting, both indirectly as a result of higher income but also directly from the psychosocial benefits that follow from the sense of status, value or identity that can come from being in paid work (Waddell and Burton, 2006). Moving from unemployment back into work is usually good for both physical and mental health as well as for subjective well-being but it is also recognised that work can carry risks, particularly where the work is of poor quality. As a result, there has been a growing awareness that the quality of employment matters, and that government and employers can benefit from the promotion of higher job quality (Constable et al, 2009).

With the PSE-UK survey, it is not possible to explore whether exclusionary employment has a negative impact on health or well-being since we cannot rule out that the causal effect runs in the opposite direction: that those with poor health find it harder to secure well-paid, good quality jobs. In practice, there is likely to be a two-way relationship. We can however look at the simple associations (Table 6.2 and Figure 6.1). For health, we report the proportion of people who regard their general health as poor (responses 'fair', 'bad' or 'very bad'). For well-being, we use the subjective measure of satisfaction with day-to-day activities (answers from 0 to 10, with 4 or lower regarded

Table 6.2: Percentage reporting other aspects of exclusion by exclusionary employment status

Domain	Item	All in employment	Not excluded	Exclusionary employment				Level of exclusionary employment	
				All	Poor	Poor work history	Poor quality	One	Two or more
Health and well-being	Low satisfaction with daily life	10%	5%	19%	22%	18%	23%	17%	27%
	General health poor	14%	10%	21%	24%	24%	20%	19%	27%
	Workplace injury or illness in last year	10%	8%	15%	17%	12%	16%	14%	18%
Social networks and social participation	No/low contact with family	6%	5%	7%	7%	10%	7%	5%	11%
	No/low contact with friends	5%	4%	6%	7%	5%	7%	4%	10%
	Low sense of support	22%	18%	28%	31%	32%	29%	26%	37%
	Low social activities	13%	22%	52%	69%	54%	45%	46%	70%
Housing and neighbourhood environment	Private rent	13%	11%	17%	22%	19%	13%	16%	20%
	Dissatisfaction with housing	4%	2%	7%	12%	8%	5%	6%	13%
	Home in poor repair	5%	2%	9%	14%	11%	8%	8%	15%
	Home too cold last winter	35%	28%	47%	58%	51%	41%	42%	61%
	Dissatisfaction with local area	8%	5%	13%	15%	14%	13%	10%	19%
	Social problems in area	30%	26%	38%	44%	41%	37%	34%	51%

Figure 6.1: Health and well-being by level of exclusionary employment

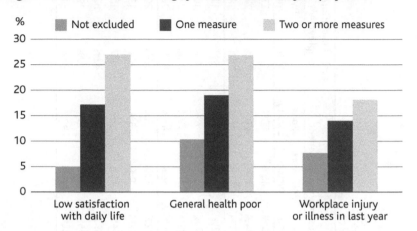

as low). We also look at the proportions reporting a workplace injury or illness in the last year to examine directly the risks of harm arising from employment.

People in exclusionary employment are much more likely to report low satisfaction with daily life and poor general health, and both of these problems rise as the level of exclusionary employment rises. Bailey (2016) shows that those in the lowest quintile on the job quality measure have lower well-being than those who are unemployed or inactive. The strongest relationship is with low satisfaction with daily life, where quality of work appears most important. Those in exclusionary employment who also report low progression in the labour market are even more likely to report low satisfaction with daily life (25 per cent, compared with 10 per cent overall). The relationship to exclusionary employment is weaker with general health, where we would expect ageing effects to be more important. It is the low paid and those with a poor work history who are more likely to report worse general health.

One area where we can gain some insight into the direction of the causal relationships between work and health is by looking at workplace injuries or illnesses. Figure 6.1 shows that those in exclusionary employment are much more likely to report having experienced a workplace injury or illness in the last year; this might be a physical problem such as back injury or a mental health problem such as stress. People in low paid work as well as those in low quality work were particularly like to report such problems. As Chapter 10 on harm shows more generally, the exposure to risks such as these are highly patterned, with low-income groups and others who are socially disadvantaged at much greater risk of a wide variety of harms.

Social networks and participation

Social networks and social participation do not form a single domain in the overall social exclusion framework but appear as two separate domains, part of the resources and participation groupings respectively (see Chapter 5 on social participation for a more detailed analysis). Social networks are regarded as a potential source of resources, as people with stronger networks of family and friends may be able to draw on these for financial or practical help, as well as for emotional support. Participation in social activities is regarded as one of the basic forms of participation in society, valued in its own right. As Townsend's (1979) definition of relative poverty notes, the ability to participate in customary activities or events declines as resources fall so that the inability to afford such participation forms part of the definition of relative poverty.

As employment tends to raise incomes, we expect it to have a positive impact on participation in social activities although, since it also reduces the time available for such activities, the effects may be curtailed – and even reversed – where people work long hours or spend a long time commuting. This might be particularly true for those in low paid employment, especially if they also have little control over working hours. We might also expect employment to widen social networks and increase opportunities for social interactions through friendships formed at work. Unemployment has long been regarded as leading to a narrowing of social circles and increased risks of social isolation (Bailey, 2006). On the other hand, for those in poverty, family connections in particular can play an essential role in helping people get by (Daly and Kelly, 2015).

In the PSE-UK survey, we look at levels of contact with family and with friends separately. In each case we ask about the number of people with whom the respondent is in contact and the frequency of contacts. From these, we construct two measures identifying those with low contact with family and with friends where contact is less than once a month (6 per cent and 5 per cent of those in employment respectively). The PSE-UK survey also captures quality of networks through a set of questions on the level of social support each person feels they have access to. Seven questions ask respondents about the level of support they believe they would get in relation to various practical tasks or emotional problems. Answers to all seven correlate highly, suggesting they provide a measure of a single underlying construct ('social support'); other attempts to measure social support find the same result (Thoits, 1995). The questions are therefore treated as a single scale, with scores averaged. People whose scores are in the lowest fifth are regarded as having low levels of support. For those in employment, 22 per cent fall into this category. The PSE-UK survey captures participation in 13 social activities such as 'going out socially once a fortnight' or 'having friends or family round once a month'. We regard people as having low social participation if they report six or fewer of these activities (13 per cent of those in employment).

Table 6.2 and Figure 6.2 show the relationships between levels of exclusionary employment and these measures of social networks and participation. At low levels of exclusionary employment, there is no difference in levels of contact with family or friends but at higher levels, people are twice as likely to report low contact in both cases. Respondents' sense of social support also falls as levels of exclusionary employment rise. With social participation, there is a particularly strong relationship with exclusionary employment. Here it is the resource aspects of employment which appear particularly important. Those in low paid work and those with a worse employment history report much lower levels of participation.

There is, however, a degree of circularity in the measures here, since the inability to participate in some of these social activities due to costs forms part of the measure of poverty included within the exclusionary employment definition. As Chapter 5 notes, five of the 13 are included as necessities items, where people do not participate in them as a result of being unable to afford them. There is some overlap in the PSE-UK poverty measure used to identify the employment excluded. There are other response categories (including not wanting to participate

Figure 6.2: Social networks and social participation by level of exclusionary employment

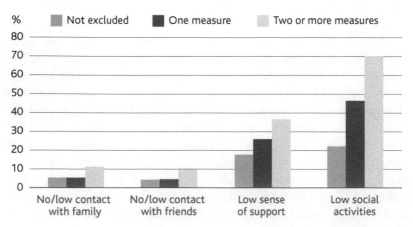

and being unable to for other reasons) so there is some independence between the measures. Using the eight items of the 13 which are not necessities does not change the picture (again, see Chapter 5 for a similar result).

Housing and neighbourhood environment

It would be surprising if there were no relationship between exclusionary employment and the domain of living environment since the economic resources derived from employment are crucial for securing access to better quality housing and more desirable neighbourhoods. It is possible that there also causal connections in the other direction, for example, as a result of 'neighbourhood effects' (van Ham et al, 2012). Table 6.2 shows a number of indicators of housing and neighbourhood quality. On housing, indicators come from separate questions on satisfaction with the dwelling, state of repair and whether it was too cold last winter. On the neighbourhood, there is a question about satisfaction with the area and whether there are any social problems in the area (such as noisy neighbours, people being drunk in the street, or people using or dealing drugs).

Table 6.2 also reports levels of private renting. This is not to suggest that private renting in itself is an indicator of social exclusion. The private rented sector has always been a very diverse tenure, home both to relatively affluent households who value it for its flexibility and choice, and lower income groups for whom it may be the only choice. In recent years, the sector has grown rapidly, encouraged in part by a range of government policies, so that private renting is now as large as the social rented sector, a major turnaround compared with the situation even 20 years ago (Kemp, 2015). However, private renting continues to be marked by short-term tenancies, high levels of insecurity and in some cases poor standards. The problematic aspects are likely to be greater for lower income households for whom the housing insecurity of private renting may compound other problems, not least those of insecure employment. As Figure 6.3 shows, people in the most exclusionary forms of employment are almost twice as likely to be in private rented accommodation (although the proportion is still only 20 per cent). It is those in low pay or with a poor work history who are most likely to be renting privately.

Figure 6.3 also shows that those in exclusionary employment experience much worse housing and neighbourhood conditions. They report markedly higher levels of dissatisfaction with housing, with problems of disrepair and heating both far greater. Beyond the dwelling

Figure 6.3: Housing and neighbourhood environment by level of exclusionary employment

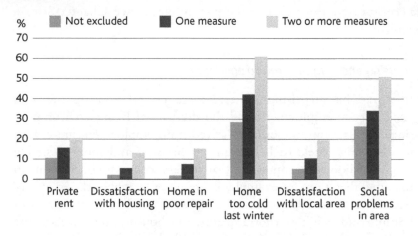

itself, the excluded employed report much greater dissatisfaction with their local area and a far higher incidence of social problems in the area in particular. In all cases, these problems increase rapidly with the level of exclusionary employment. It is the resource aspects of employment which are the most obvious explanation here.

Summary of relationships between dimensions

Figure 6.4 tries to show the inter-relationships between the different forms of exclusion in a single graphic. The three columns represent working-age adults in employment with different levels of exclusionary employment – not excluded (65 per cent), excluded on just one of the three aspects (27 per cent), or excluded on two or more (8 per cent). The width of the columns has been set to reflect the relative size of each group. Within each column, the bands show the proportions of people facing other forms of exclusion discussed in this chapter, recording whether they are excluded on one or more of these domains. The domains and the indicators for exclusion is each case are as follows, with the proportions of excluded on each in brackets at the end (for those in employment):

- Health and well-being: low satisfaction with daily life *or* poor general health (22 per cent);
- Social networks and participation: no or low contact with family *or* with friends, *or* low sense of support, *or* low social activities (36 per cent);

- Housing and neighbourhood environment: home in poor repair, *or* too cold last winter, *or* social problems in the area (53 per cent).

For each of these three dimensions, the individual is 'excluded' or not, and the number of such exclusions is then counted up. This is not meant to imply that, in some sense, each short list should be taken as a comprehensive definition of exclusion on a particular domain. This is simply a convenient way to try to summarise diverse aspects of exclusion across multiple dimensions.

Figure 6.4 shows clearly how exclusionary employment overlaps with and is potentially reinforced by other forms of exclusion. Looking at the people with none of the additional forms of exclusion (the top band), the overwhelming majority (84 per cent) are not in exclusionary employment either. They make up 32 per cent of that group (top left-hand column) but just 5 per cent of people with two or more aspects of exclusionary employment (top right hand column). Conversely, while those in exclusionary employment make up one in three of the working age population (35 per cent – the two right-hand columns), they account for half of the people with two or more of the other forms of exclusion (55 per cent). And for those with two or more aspects of exclusionary employment, the great majority (84 per cent) report two or more of the other aspects of exclusion.

Figure 6.4: Relationships between exclusionary employment and other forms of exclusion

Level of exclusionary employment

Conclusion

The first aim of this chapter was to provide a more detailed analysis of the characteristics of people who are in exclusionary employment. In general, it is clear that it is people with less human capital – less education, fewer skills, or younger and hence less experienced – as well as those who face barriers to securing employment due to health problems or disability, racial discrimination or caring responsibilities. In part, the problem occurs where people are unable to find full-time work or live in a household with low work intensity, although Bailey (2006) shows that a substantial proportion of those excluded through their employment work full-time and live with others working at or near full-time.

Two of the groups which have been most targeted by welfare reforms – lone parents and those with long-term health problems – have some of the highest rates of exclusionary employment. This is unsurprising given the barriers they face to securing well-paid, full-time employment, and it casts doubt on the logic of pursuing a strategy to push them back into work without further actions to ensure adequate conditions and quality of work. These groups face greater risks of ending up in insecure and poor quality work, reducing the chance that work will have transformative or restorative benefits (the role model effects for lone parents and the health benefits for those with health problems).

Perhaps of greatest concern is that exclusionary employment looks like a relatively durable situation for many groups. Around one in six of the excluded employed reported no progress over the past five years. Proportions were much higher for groups such as lone parents (almost one in three) or those in low status occupations (two in five). Again, the focus on policy needs to move beyond the efforts to drive people off welfare benefits and into employment regardless of conditions. Those in employment need access to a wider range of support to ensure that they can have greater change of progression over time.

The second aim was to explore the relationships between exclusionary employment and other aspects of exclusion. It shows clear associations between exclusionary employment and each of the other domains examined. As levels of exclusionary employment rise, so do the risks of exclusion on the other dimensions albeit at varying rates. We cannot make general inference about the directions of causality here but we can note some obvious variations. Low pay and insecure employment (or rather, poor work histories) have stronger relationships with some areas, notably quality of housing and neighbourhood as well as social participation. In other cases, notably subjective well-being, it is quality of employment which appears more important or at least as important. In broad terms, this validates the broader focus of social exclusion and underlines the multidimensionality of exclusion.

Note

[1] Satisfaction or sense of value is based on questions about whether the respondent feels: their work is interesting; their work is useful; they have supportive colleagues; and they are satisfied with their job. Control or flexibility is assessed by whether people feel they can: decide how they do each task; decide what time they start or finish; and take time off for personal matters. Physical environment depends on whether the respondent reports that: their work (not) physically demanding or tiring; their workplace is always a comfortable temperature; and there is (not) a lot of smoke, dust, fumes or noise in their workplace.

References

Bailey, N. (2006) 'Does work pay? Employment, poverty and social exclusion', in C. Pantazis, D. Gordon, and R. Levitas (eds) *Poverty and social exclusion in Britain: The Millennium Survey*, Bristol: Policy Press, pp 163-90.

Bailey, N. (2016) 'Exclusionary employment in Britain's broken labour market', *Critical Social Policy*, 36(1): 82-103.

Belfield, C., Cribb, J., Hood, A., and Joyce, R. (2016) *Living standards, poverty and inequality in the UK 2016*, London: Institute for Fiscal Studies.

Constable, S., Coats, D., Bevan, S., and Mahdon, M. (2009) *Good jobs. Research report 713*, London: HSE.

Daly, M. and Kelly, G. (2015) *Families and poverty: Everyday life on a low income*, Bristol: Policy Press.

DWP (Department for Work and Pensions) (2017) *Households Below Average Incomes: An analysis of the UK income distribution 1994/95-2015/16*, London: DWP.

Dickens, R., Gregg, P., and Wadsworth, J. (2003) *The labour market under New Labour: The state of working Britain*, Basingstoke: Palgrave Macmillan.

Gilbert, N. and Besharov, D. (2011) 'Welfare states amid economic turmoil: adjusting work-oriented policy', *Policy & Politics*, 39(3): 295-308.

ILO (International Labour Organisation) (1999) *Decent work. Report of the Director General, International Labour Conference, 87th Session*, Geneva: ILO.

Kemp, P. A. (2015) 'Private renting after the global financial crisis', *Housing Studies*, 30(4): 601–20.

Levitas, R. (1998) *The inclusive society? Social exclusion and New Labour*, Basingstoke: Macmillan.

Levitas, R., Pantazis, C., Fahmy, E., Gordon, D., Lloyd, E. and Patsios, D. (2007) *The multi-dimensional analysis of social exclusion*, Bristol: University of Bristol.

Machin, S. (2011) 'Changes in the UK wage inequality over the last forty years', in P. Gregg and J. Wadsworth (eds) *The labour market in winter: The state of working Britain*, Oxford: OUP.

OECD (Organisation for Economic Cooperation and Development) (2011) *Divided we stand: Why inequality keeps rising*, Washington: OECD.

Patrick, R. (2012) 'Work as the primary "duty" of the responsible citizen: a critique of this work-centric approach', *People, Place and Policy Online*, 6(1): 5–16.

Standing, G. (2011) *The precariat: The new dangerous class*, London: Bloomsbury Academic.

Thoits, P. A. (1995) 'Stress, coping, and social support processes: where are we? What next?', *Journal of Health & Social Behavior*, 36 (Extra issue): 53–79.

Townsend, P. (1979) *Poverty in the UK: A survey of household resources and living standards*, Harmondsworth: Allen Lane.

Trades Union Congress (TUC) (2010) *Fair work: Fighting poverty through decent jobs*, London: TUC.

van Ham, M., Manley, D., Bailey, N., Simpson, L. and Maclennan, D. (2012) *Neighbourhood effects research: New perspectives*, Dordrecht: Springer.

Venn, D. (2009) 'Legislation, collective bargaining and enforcement: updating the OECD Employment Protection Indicators', *OECD Social, Employment and Migration Working Papers No. 89*, Paris: OECD.

Venn, D. (2012) 'Eligibility criteria for unemployment benefits', *OECD Social, Employment and Migration Working Papers No. 131*, Paris: OECD Publishing.

Waddell, G. and Burton, A. K. (2006) *Is work good for your health and well-being?* London: The Stationery Office.

Watts, B., Fitzpatrick, S., Bramley, G. and Watkins, D. (2014) *Welfare sanctions and conditionality in the UK*, York: Joseph Rowntree Foundation.

SEVEN

Poverty, social exclusion and civic engagement

Eldin Fahmy

Introduction

Although political equality and political participation are basic assumptions of democratic theory, they are rarely combined in liberal democratic practice (Lijphart, 1997). Numerous random-sample surveys across these Western democracies have consistently demonstrated that participation in politics remains highly unequal, with socio-economic characteristics such as occupational class and educational attainment being key predictors of voting behaviour and more active participation (for example, Dalton, 2014; Marsh, 1990; Verba et al, 1995). These studies are also consistent with UK evidence showing political participation to be positively and strongly associated with socio-economic characteristics including higher socio-economic status and educational attainment (for example, Parry et al, 1992; Pattie et al, 2004; Fieldhouse et al, 2010; EHRC, 2010). The enduring strength of this connection has led some to refer to socio-economic status as the 'standard' or 'baseline' model of participation in the Western democracies (for example, Milbrath and Goel, 1977; Verba and Nie, 1972).

Since the responsiveness of political institutions and actors to public demands partly depends on citizen participation (Verba et al, 1995), systematic socio-economic inequalities in political participation mean that socially marginalised populations are in effect excluded from norms of effective democratic participation and representation. Inequalities in participation are most stark at the elite level, as reflected in the social characteristics of elected representatives to national assemblies, Parliaments and local authorities in the UK. Of MPs elected to Westminster in 2015, just 3 per cent had a manual occupational background, and over one third attended private (fee-paying) schools (Audickas, 2015). It is perhaps unsurprising therefore that, compared with manual workers, managerial and professional groups are considerably more likely to 'feel that they can influence decisions affecting their local area' (Taylor and Low, 2010).

However, to date poverty rarely features directly in debates about inequalities and political representation, and rigorous evidence in this area is limited. Recent years have seen increasing recognition of the importance of involving people experiencing poverty in the development of anti-poverty policies and practice (Lister, 2007a,b). This reflects growing acknowledgement of the importance of issues of recognition and voice in the experience of poverty and social exclusion (for example, Honneth, 1996; Fraser, 1995; Fraser and Honneth, 2003). Compelling evidence exists that people experiencing poverty are treated differently by public officials and service providers as a result of low income (for example, Beresford et al, 1999; UKCAP, 2002; Chase and Walker, 2013; Pemberton et al, 2016). Involving people experiencing poverty in the design and delivery of public services should therefore be a key priority.

Nevertheless, low income is not currently a 'protected characteristic' within the meaning of the 2010 Equality Act, and a legal requirement for public bodies to take steps to reduce socio-economic inequalities was scrapped in 2011.[1] It is therefore not subject to statutory monitoring or oversight with regard to political voice and representation. Whilst equalities analyses show political participation to be strongly associated with markers of social advantage (for example, education, occupation, ethnicity) (EHRC, 2010), with few exceptions the under-representation of people experiencing poverty in public life has received little comment. Few, if any, largescale random sample studies of citizen participation in politics make provision for reliable measurement of poverty status. Whilst respondents' self-reported personal income is a widely adopted measure in political science studies, it provides a poor guide to individual's command of resources over time and no direct insight into actual living standards. Drawing on the 2012 PSE-UK study, this chapter seeks to address this knowledge gap by investigating the relationship between poverty and political and civic participation. In doing so, it considers the extent to which poverty (as distinct from other dimensions of social disadvantage) is informative in understanding the determinants of political engagement. It begins by reviewing existing work in this area, before discussing the measurement of political and civic participation adopted here.

Poverty, social exclusion and political citizenship

It is more than fifty years since the US sociologist Michael Harrington commented on the political exclusion of the 'Other America' arising from poverty:

> The poor are politically invisible ... The people of the Other America do not, by far and large, belong to unions, to fraternal organisations, or to political parties. They are without lobbies of their own; they put forward no legislative program. As a group, they are atomized. They have no face; they have no voice. (Harrington, 1962: 6)

More than half a century later, the de facto exclusion of people experiencing poverty from full and effective exercise of political citizenship remains a live issue in the UK, not least in the context of the increased politicisation of poverty arising from the 2008 recession and subsequent austerity programme. The 1998 Human Rights Act enshrines in UK law commitments under the European Convention on Human Rights for protection from all forms of discrimination, including on the basis of property and social origin. Nevertheless, the pervasive climate of discrimination against people on the grounds of their poverty, or 'povertyism' (Killeen, 2008), within UK public debates in recent years has had the effect of marginalising the voices of people experiencing poverty. Lister (2007a,b) refers to this discursive marginalisation of the poor themselves arising from 'othering' processes of stigmatisation and shaming that are communicated both in people's everyday interactions, and in wider public discourse.

Despite growing acknowledgement of the importance of challenging the invisibility of the poor themselves in poverty debates, the wider exclusion of the poor from the equal exercise of political citizenship is rarely challenged. From a social policy perspective, understanding the interconnections between economic, social and political citizenship rights – and the conditions for their effective realisation – is central to addressing political exclusion. Lister (1990) highlights the disastrous consequences of material impoverishment in the 1980s for the effective exercise of social and political citizenship for low-income families. Poverty and social disadvantage constrain the personal and social resources needed to effectively engage in political action (for example, money, time, social networks, opportunities to engage), and force different, more pressing priorities on individuals and households in coping with financial hardship. Ward (1986: 33) similarly emphasises how limited resources militate against active citizen participation in politics:

> The methods by which policy is made and fought for, individuals selected for office, and essential political work carried out, all presuppose a fair amount of money at one's independent command, over and above the amount needed simply for survival. Those without this money are marginalised. (Ward, 1986: 33)

Whilst poverty has not featured prominently in academic political science accounts of citizen participation in politics, the 'civic voluntarism' model proposed by Sidney Verba and colleagues (for example, Verba et al, 1995; Schlozman and Verba, 1979; Verba and Nie, 1972) does emphasise the social determinants of participation. In addition to the direct material constraints associated with poverty in terms of time, money and the stress associated with making ends meet, people experiencing poverty are unlikely to benefit from the types of social and professional networks, or to participate in the kinds of organised civil associations which facilitate engagement and develop civic skills. Socially marginalised populations tend to lack the kinds of 'cultural capital' (for example, education, tastes and social sensibilities) needed to be influential within policy elites, and are often remote from the types of networks which might facilitate their engagement with formal political institutions. With good reason, people experiencing low income and socio-economic disadvantage tend to be less sanguine about the responsiveness of the political system to citizen demands, and exhibit lower levels of political trust, political interest, and satisfaction with the functioning of political institutions (Fieldhouse et al, 2010).

Understanding political and civic participation

However, how survey respondents respond to complex terms such as political trust, interest or participation remains poorly understood and reflects more basic questions about the definition of 'the political' itself. Feminist scholars have argued that the distinction between public and private realms obscures gendered norms of participation (Pateman, 1970), and that 'political' action typically excludes the kinds of informal, community-based modes of participation often favoured by socially marginalised groups (Lister, 1997). The growth of social movement politics since the 1970s has certainly widened the political repertoire of Western publics as previously 'unconventional' forms of protest activity have become mainstream. More contemporary innovations in local democratic practice associated with citizen deliberation also broaden the potential scope of political action. Recent studies of political participation have therefore usually adopted a relatively broad definition and this chapter focuses upon (legal) actions undertaken by citizens within the public realm with the aim of influencing the state and its representatives. Parry et al (1992) define political participation as 'action by citizens which is aimed at influencing decisions which are, in most cases, ultimately taken by public representatives and officials', and broadly similar definitions are adopted in other largescale studies (for example, Barnes and Kaase, 1979; Marsh, 1990; Klingemann and Fuchs, 1995; Pattie et al, 2004).

Nevertheless, pinning down the specifically 'political' dimension of political participation remains controversial. Critical to most definitions is a focus on action undertaken with the intention of influencing the state – directly or otherwise. Whilst this might exclude many kinds of informal community and civic engagement (for example, volunteering, community and interests group participation), such actions can have political consequences in reshaping social relations. Indeed, concerns about the apparent decline in social capital in America (Putnam, 1995) and Britain (Hall, 1999; Whiteley, 2014) have largely focused upon the extent and density of community ties as reflected in citizens' associational activity – their propensity to be 'joiners' of community groups, societies and associations – and its positive effects across a range of societal outcomes including voter turnout and citizen political action. In the analyses that follow I therefore seek to estimate the impact of respondents' associational activity on subsequent political action.

For this reason, I examine here both public participation in politics (encompassing conventional and protest action), and their wider civic engagement, that is, their membership of the kinds of voluntary associations of citizens (for example, social, cultural, sporting, environmental) which since de Tocqueville's classic study (1838) have been viewed by social capital theorists as highly supportive of democratic politics (see for example, Putnam, 1995). Our main indicator of political action is a binary variable measuring whether respondents had undertaken any political actions in the last 12 months aside from voting, based upon responses to nine question items on this topic (see Table 7.1). Our preferred measure of civic engagement is a binary variable measuring membership of any civil society group or organisation based upon responses to thirteen question items on this topic (see also Table 7.1).

Table 7.1: Indicators of political participation, civic engagement and political efficacy in the 2012 PSE-UK survey

		%
POLITICAL ACTION*	Voted in the last general election	58.0
	Signed a petition (in person or online)	30.9
	Contacted a local councillor or MP	13.0
	Attended a public meeting	12.3
	Taken part in an online campaign	11.4
	Boycotted certain products for political or ethical reasons	9.7
	Taken part in a strike or picket	4.2
	Taken part in a demonstration or protest	3.8
	Been an officer of a campaigning organisation or pressure group	1.3
	SPONTANEOUS ONLY: None of the above	30.9
	None of above actions except voting in general election	**57.6**
CIVIC ENGAGEMENT*	Sports, leisure or social club (e.g. gym, choir, trades club)	29.4
	Trade union or staff association (e.g. UNISON)	12.0
	Conservation or animal welfare group (e.g. The National Trust, RSPB)	11.7
	Religious organisation	9.2
	Neighbourhood or civic group (e.g. Residents Association, Rotary Club)	5.3
	Health, disability or welfare group (e.g. AgeUK, Royal British Legion)	3.7
	Women's group (e.g. Women's Institute)	2.5
	Humanitarian or peace group (e.g. Amnesty, CND)	2.3
	Environmental pressure group (e.g. Greenpeace)	2.2
	Youth group (e.g. Scouts, youth club)	2.1
	Political party	2.1
	Minority ethnic organisation (e.g. British Pakistani Association)	0.8
	Other group not listed above	8.5
	Not member of any of the above organisations	**43.4**
CIVIC EFFICACY	*'People like me have no say in what the government does'*	
	(Strongly) disagree	23.8
	Neither agree nor disagree	17.9
	(Strongly) agree	58.4
	'I think I could take an active part in political issues'	
	(Strongly) agree	28.4
	Neither agree nor disagree	20.1
	(Strongly) disagree	51.5
	'I can influence decisions affecting my local area'	
	(Strongly) agree	34.9
	Neither agree nor disagree	23.7
	(Strongly) disagree	41.5

Note: * All items refer to the 12 months preceding interview (excl. voted in most recent general election).

In addition to the personal resources (time, money, skills) and professional and social networks which facilitate participation, Verba and colleagues' civic voluntarism model (Verba et al, 1995) also identifies supportive civic attitudes as key drivers of citizen participation in politics. This encompasses a range of attitudinal measures, including sense of civic duty, perceptions of the efficacy of citizen action and of the responsiveness of institutions, trust in public and political institutions and actors, and so on. Although our data are limited here, the analyses that follow examine public perceptions of the efficacy of political action and the responsiveness of political institutions to citizen demands. (In particular, this chapter investigates responses to three 5-point Likert-type items relating to perceptions of citizen influence on local and national decision making (political efficacy), as shown in Table 7.1.)

Beyond voting in general elections, these data confirm that active participation in politics remains a minority experience for the UK public. Whilst nearly one third (31 per cent) of respondents had signed a petition in the 12 months prior to interview, not much more than one in eight respondents reported engaging in any of the more active forms of engagement listed here. Aside from voting, 57 per cent of UK adults took no other action about local problems or national issues in the last 12 months.

A broadly similar picture presents itself when looking at wider civic engagement as reflected in associational memberships. Sporting, leisure and social clubs continue to attract the membership of well over one quarter (29 per cent) of adult respondents but, aside from this, few respondents report membership of organisations with more overtly 'political' issue agendas. These data confirm that trades unions (just) remain the most popular membership organisations, with around one in eight PSE-UK adult respondents (12 per cent) reporting membership, followed closely by conservation and animal welfare groups and religious organisations. Beyond these, membership falls away dramatically and around 43 per cent of UK adults had not been a member of any group or organisation in the last 12 months.

These data also reveal disaffection with the UK system of government to be endemic. More than half of all UK adults feel that 'people like me have no say in what the government does' (58 per cent), and a similar proportion (52%) feel unable to 'take an active part in political issues'. These estimates are comparable with similar surveys revealing the extent of citizen disconnection with formal political institutions in the UK (Clarke et al, 2004; Fieldhouse et al, 2010; Hansard Society, 2013; Lee and Young, 2013). They are also consistent with compelling evidence documenting a long-term decline in levels of political trust and satisfaction with political institutions across Western democracies (for example, Norris, 1999). Moreover, most of these countries (including the UK) have also witnessed a long-term decline in turnout in national elections, prompting recurrent concerns of an apparent 'crisis' of democratic participation (for example, Whiteley, 2014). It may well be that these trends reflect changes in the participatory styles, social values and outlooks of Western publics associated with the growing appeal of political protest, direct action and more latterly online activism. Certainly, these previously 'unconventional' forms of political action have assumed a far greater role in the political repertoire of citizens in the UK and elsewhere (Parry et al, 1992; Dalton, 2014).

However, whilst these trends have been linked to wider processes of cultural post-modernisation and the growth of 'post-materialist' values and politics (for example, Inglehart, 1990; Dalton, 2014), little is known specifically about the changing socio-economic profile of citizen engagement in politics in the UK. Drawing on largescale survey sources, Li et al (2003) demonstrate that social class differences in the extent of associational memberships and civic participation have increased substantially in England and Wales since the 1970s. Hall's (1999) analyses similarly suggest that a dramatic decline in associational activity and civic action amongst working-class Britons has been the main driver of widening class disparities in participation. Alongside wider changes in class structure associated with the decline of manual employment in the UK, this also reflects the decline of trades union and labour movement activity amongst manual occupational groups over this period.

Despite this, rigorous evidence on the impacts of poverty and deprivation for citizen political participation remains scarce. By drawing on 2012 PSE-UK data, this chapter begins to redress this balance by addressing the following questions:

- What is the impact of poverty on overall levels of civic engagement and political action in the UK?

- Do inequalities in participation reflect different perceptions of the political system itself? Do they reflect unequal access to the material and human resources which promote effective democratic participation? Does material constraint directly restrict participation?

- Do these effects vary for different kinds of participation (for example, comparing conventional and protest action)?

In addressing the above agenda, the chapter is informed by the civic voluntarism model proposed by Verba and colleagues (Verba et al, 1995) by drawing upon detailed data on UK residents' socio-economic circumstances, social participation and networks, and their connections with political attitudes and behaviours.

As discussed above, one key issue in existing work in this area has been data limitations in operationalising poverty. There are many ways to operationalise an understanding of poverty as relative to prevailing normative standards, and it may be that no single measure of poverty is 'best' (Bradshaw and Finch, 2003). We therefore compare the following operational measures of poverty here: PSE poor (combined income/deprivation); deprivation (cannot afford 3+ necessities); subjective poverty (income insufficient to avoid poverty); and low income (less than 60 per cent PSE equivalised household median, after housing costs).

Findings

Poverty, political action and civic engagement

Table 7.2 shows the percentage PSE poor and non-poor adults reporting different forms of political action in the last 12 months, together with their reported organisational memberships over this period. It is clear that substantial disparities exist between poor and non-poor in their propensity to engage in political action, with PSE poor respondents being far less likely to report political activity than adults living in non-poor households. For example, more than two-thirds (68 per cent) of poor respondents had undertaken *none* of the actions listed here apart from voting, compared with a little over half (55 per cent) of non-poor respondents. There are no indicators where poor respondents report significantly higher levels of political participation. A very similar picture emerges in relation to associational activity, where the prevalence of memberships is typically much lower for poor respondents. For example, nearly two-thirds (64 per cent) of PSE poor respondents reported not being members of *any* local or national organisation in the previous 12 months, compared with just 37 per cent of non-poor respondents.

These data highlight important socio-economic gaps in the prevalence of civic participation between poor and non-poor respondents which is especially pronounced (in terms of absolute numbers) for sports, leisure and social clubs, conservation and animal welfare groups, and (interestingly) for trades unions and staff

Table 7.2: PSE poverty and political engagement in the UK (%)

		PSE poor (col %)		
		Poor	Not poor	Diff (a-b)
POLITICAL ACTION	Voted in the last general election	40.7	63.2	−22.5
	Signed a petition (in person or online)	23.9	32.9	−9.0
	Taken part in an online campaign	8.2	12.4	−4.2
	Contacted a local councillor or MP	10.1	13.8	−3.7
	Boycotted products for political or ethical reasons	6.8	10.5	−3.7
	Attended a public meeting	9.5	13.1	−3.6
	Taken part in a strike or picket	1.7	4.9	−3.2
	Been officer of campaigning or pressure group	1.7	1.2	0.5
	Taken part in a demonstration or protest	4.3	3.7	0.6
	None of above actions except voting in general election	**68.1**	**54.5**	**13.6**
CIVIC ACTION	Sports, leisure or social club	16.0	33.4	−17.4
	Conservation or animal welfare group	3.6	14.0	−10.4
	Trade union or staff association	5.5	13.9	−8.4
	Neighbourhood or civic group	1.8	6.3	−4.5
	Religious organisation	6.2	10.0	−3.8
	Health, disability or welfare group	2.0	4.2	−2.2
	Women's group	0.9	3.0	−2.1
	Youth group	1.1	2.3	−1.2
	Environmental pressure group	1.4	2.4	−1.0
	Other group not listed above	7.8	8.7	−0.9
	Humanitarian or peace group	2.4	2.3	0.1
	Political party	2.2	2.0	0.2
	Minority ethnic organisation	1.0	0.7	0.3
	Not member of any of the above organisations	**63.9**	**37.4**	**26.5**
CIVIC EFFICACY	*'People like me have no say in what the government does'* Agree/strongly agree	65.1	64.4	0.7
	'I think I could take an active part in political issues' Disagree/strongly disagree	53.5	51.0	2.5
	'I can influence decisions affecting my local area' Disagree/strongly disagree	49.6	39.0	10.6

associations. Aside from socio-economic inequalities in the more overtly 'political' activities reviewed above, these data again point to the effective exclusion of the poor from equal representation in civil society institutions in the UK. However, the absolute magnitude of the differences reported in Table 7.2 is obviously a function of their overall prevalence. It is therefore useful also to look at the relative risk of participation. Table 7.3 therefore shows relative risk estimates for political action and civic engagement items for the non-poor group relative to 'poor' respondents defined in terms of PSE, subjective, deprivation, and income measures.

Table 7.3: The probability of political disengagement by poverty status: PSE, subjective, deprivation and income poverty (relative risk ratios: ref=poor)

		PSE	Subjective	Deprivation	Income
POLITICAL ACTION	Taken part in a strike or picket	2.49	1.56	1.57	2.6
	Voted in the last general election	2.02	1.75	1.8	1.8
	Taken part in an online campaign	1.45	1.51	1.25	1.68
	Boycotted products for political or ethical reasons	1.45	1.82	1.32	1.58
	Signed a petition (in person or online)	1.42	1.36	1.26	1.32
	Attended a public meeting	1.33	1.47	1.15	1.5
	Contacted a local councillor or MP	1.32	1.44	1.33	1.38
	Taken part in a demonstration or protest	[0.88]	[1.13]	[0.93]	1.29
	Been officer of campaigning or pressure group	[0.79]	1.68	[0.99]	[1.19]
	SPONTANEOUS ONLY: None of the above	0.53	0.60	0.59	0.6
	None of above actions except voting in general election	**0.64**	**0.66**	**0.73**	**0.66**
CIVIC ACTION	Conservation or animal welfare group	3.57	3.14	2.54	2.26
	Neighbourhood or civic group	3.05	1.95	2.63	1.55
	Women's group	2.68	1.67	2.67	1.52
	Trade union or staff association	2.35	1.53	1.49	2.85
	Sports, leisure or social club	2.19	1.89	1.83	2.02
	Health, disability or welfare group	1.99	1.66	1.61	1.56
	Youth group	1.84	1.47	[1.18]	[0.94]
	Environmental pressure group	1.55	3.29	1.27	1.69
	Religious organisation	1.52	1.28	1.4	1.35
	Other group not listed above	[1.10]	1.28	1.16	1.23
	Humanitarian or peace group	[0.99]	1.57	[1.01]	2.57
	Political party	[0.93]	2.29	[1.19]	2.61
	Minority ethnic organisation	[0.75]	[0.82]	[0.78]	[1.65]
	Not member of any of the above organisations	**0.43**	**0.53**	**0.53**	**0.48**

Notes:

[] = p>0.05 (Pearson Chi Sq.)

Parameters are relative risk ratios for non-poor respondents relative to poor respondents. For example, compared to PSE poor respondents, non-poor respondents are twice as likely (RR=2.02) to have voted in the last general election (in 2010).

Overall, Table 7.3 shows a consistent pattern. Whether operationalised using subjective indicators or objective measures of income or deprivation (or a combination of these two), people experiencing poverty are less likely to engage in most forms of political action, and are similarly less likely to be a member of a variety of civil society bodies. In a few cases, it is not possible to draw wider inferences on the basis of these data due to the very low reported frequency of participation across the sample. However, the magnitude of relative differences in participation between poor and non-poor groups varies somewhat. With regard to political action, this socio-economic gap appears greatest for strike action, voting, online campaigning, and ethical consumption, but this difference almost disappears in relation to political protest and demonstrations. These data also point to similarly marked socio-economic disparities in civil society memberships, but especially for conservation and animal rights groups, neighbourhood and civic groups, women's groups, and trades unions and staff associations, where poor respondents are substantially less likely to report membership than non-poor respondents. Trends in trade union membership reflect the decline of union organisation amongst manual and private sector workers, and their concentration in public sector and white collar occupations (for example, Bryson and Gomez, 2002, 2005).

Poverty and political efficacy

Does political non-participation reflect disaffection with existing political institutions and/or opportunities for citizens to participate in political decisions? Certainly, the civic voluntarism model proposed by Verba and colleagues (1995) suggests that supportive attitudes (for example, political trust, personal political efficacy, satisfaction with democracy) are key drivers of citizen participation in politics. Conversely, it is sometimes suggested that non-participation may indicate satisfaction with existing political arrangements, certainly with regard to specific forms of participation such as contacting political representatives about individual concerns (for example, Barnes and Kaase, 1979). Whilst our data are somewhat limited in tapping respondents' wider political attitudes and orientations, the responsiveness of political institutions to citizen demands is clearly important for effective democratic practice. Table 7.4 therefore examines the bivariate relationships between poverty, political participation, and perceptions of political efficacy. These data show the relative risk of (dis)agreeing with three statements relating to political efficacy for poor compared with non-poor respondents by poverty status (for PSE, subjective, deprivation and income poverty measures) and participation status (political action beyond voting, and membership of any local or national group).

In virtually all cases, these comparisons are highly statistically significant (p<0.001) indicating social differences in perceptions of political efficacy by poverty and participation status not only for this sample but for the wider UK adult population. Whether measured by subjective perceptions of income adequacy, or more objective measures of deprivation and/or low income, people experiencing poverty are more likely to agree that 'people like me have no say in what the government does' than non-poor respondents. For example, seven out of ten (70 per cent) of respondents viewing their income as insufficient to avoid poverty share this view, compared with a little over half (55 per cent) of respondents classified as non-poor according to this measure. As with political action and civic engagement, this pattern is consistent across poverty measures. Less than two-fifths (37–39 per cent) of poor respondents report feeling unable to influence local decisions across these measures compared with around half (49–51 per cent) of non-poor respondents. These data appear to offer some support for the notion that supportive attitudes facilitate effective participation: more specifically, Table 7.4 suggests that people are more likely to engage in political action where they believe their actions to be capable of influencing decisions. For many UK citizens – and

Table 7.4: Poverty, political action and perceptions of civic efficacy in the UK: PSE, subjective, deprivation and income poverty measures (relative risk ratios: ref=poor)

	PSE	Subj	Dep	Inc	PolAct	SocAct
People like me have no say in what the government does (Strongly) agree	1.09	1.17	1.15	1.08	1.17	1.13
I think I could take an active part in political issues (Strongly) disagree	[1.03]	1.08	1.06	1.06	1.60	1.31
I can influence decisions affecting my local area (Strongly) disagree	1.11	1.15	1.18	1.10	1.57	1.30

Notes:

[] p>0.05 (Pearson Chi Sq.).

PSE=PSE Poor; Subj = income 'not enough to avoid poverty'; Dep = cannot afford 3+ necessities; Inc = income less than 60% equiv. household median; PolAct = no political action in last 12 months (excl voting); SocAct = member of local or national group, society or organisation.

especially for people experiencing poverty – this is demonstrably not the case. Moreover, Table 7.4 also shows that engaging in political action and associational memberships are both powerful predictors of positive civic attitudes – indeed these effects are mostly stronger than for poverty.

Understanding the determinants of participation

The above analyses reveal participation in politics and public life to be strongly socially patterned. Whether using subjective or objective measures – or direct (deprivation) or indirect (income) instruments – people experiencing poverty are substantially less likely to take political action, conventional or otherwise, and are similarly less likely to be members of voluntary citizen associations. Despite growing public acceptance of the legitimacy of protest action in the UK and elsewhere in recent decades, Table 7.1 above shows that, aside from voting, participation in politics remains far from being a social norm in UK society today. Nevertheless, poverty appears to erect additional obstacles to participation with regard to the material, social and personal resources which facilitate effective political action. Better understanding of their relative influence in shaping citizen's propensity to act politically is clearly important.

The remainder of this chapter therefore examines the determinants of citizen participation in politics and public life using multivariate methods. In doing so, it seeks to test the civic voluntarism model proposed by Verba et al (1995). They argue that people participate in politics: (a) when they have the personal resources to do so; (b) when they believe their actions to be capable of influencing decisions, and; (c) when they are provided with suitable opportunities to do so. In testing this, we model the probability of civic and political action (as previously operationalised) as a function of individual's personal resources (poverty status, education), their socio-political attitudes (political efficacy, social trust), and their 'opportunity structure' (social networks, class position, and associational activity). Since political participation is strongly associated with gender and especially age effects, we also control for these factors.

Table 7.5 presents the results of binary logistic regression analyses which model the probability (odds) of civic and political action for a variety of personal, attitudinal and social characteristics. Variables are entered sequentially in blocks based upon the civic voluntarism model proposed by Verba et al (1995). We begin by examining the human assets and material resources associated with civic action (Model 1) and political participation (Model 4). We then examine the additional effects of differences in political attitudes on civic action (Model 2) and political participation (Model 5), and how variations in respondents' social networks occupational status and (where applicable) associational activity impact upon citizen civic and political action (Models 3 and 6 respectively). Whilst associational action is important to the local opportunity structure in Verba et al's 1995 model, it is also central to social capital accounts of political participation (for example, Putnam, 1995; Whiteley, 2014). However, whilst these authors provide compelling evidence on the positive effects of associational activity for citizen political participation, the extent to which associational disengagement accounts for the under-participation of poorer citizens remains unclear. The final model (Model 6) therefore estimates the impact of poverty on political participation controlling for differences in associational activity.

In all models these multivariate odds estimate the likelihood of political action controlling for the independent influence of other model parameters and control variables (age, sex). Whilst these models are quite limited in their ability to explain variations in propensity to political action (as illustrated by quasi R squared values), they nevertheless do produce a statistically significant improvement at each step (as illustrated by model Chi Square values).

The odds ratios shown in Table 7.5 confirm the relationship between poverty and both civic disengagement and political non-participation. The connection between educational attainment and citizen participation in politics and public life is amongst the most well-established empirical findings in political science, reflecting differences in the politically-relevant skills and cultural capital necessary to political engagement. However, after controlling for differences in educational attainment (and in age and sex), non-poor respondents are nevertheless around 2.6 times more likely to be active in the associational life of their communities than PSE poor respondents (Model 1). They are also 60 per cent more likely to have engaged in political action in the past 12 months compared with PSE poor respondents (Model 3). These effects are somewhat attenuated when we take into account variations in perceptions of political efficacy, and social status and networks.

With regard to associational activity, despite important differences in education and class background and in the social networks that predict involvement, non-poor respondents are more than twice as likely (1: 2.3) to be active in civil society organisations than PSE poor respondents (Model 3).

Table 7.5: The determinants of civic and political action in the UK (logistic regression odds ratios)

Model:	Civic action			Political action		
	1	2	3	4	5	6
Age completed full-time education [ref: <16 yrs]						
16	1.30	1.28	[1.24]	[1.06]	[1.03]	[0.96]
17-18	1.94	1.83	1.56	1.43	1.31	[1.06]
19+	2.69	2.36	1.70	2.76	2.32	1.73
Not PSE poor [ref: poor]	2.66	2.58	2.15	1.57	1.49	1.33
'People like me have no say in what govt. does' [ref: (strongly) agree]		[1.08]	[1.02]		[0.93]	[0.90]
'I could take an active part in political issues' [ref: (strongly) disagree]		1.53	1.42		1.66	1.52
'I can influence decisions affecting local area' [ref: (strongly) disagree]		1.23	1.23		1.75	1.72
At least monthly contact with relatives			1.50			1.49
At least monthly contact with friends			[1.00]			[0.82]
NS-Sec occupational class [ref: semi(routine)]						
Professional			2.71			1.63
Intermediate			1.29			1.40
Member of voluntary group/assoc. [ref: no]						3.97
Interaction: Not PSE poor × Member of voluntary group/association						1.48
–2LL	5540	5476	5330	5845	5674	5374
Model Chi Sq (block)	286	63	146	245	170	300
Nagelkerke quasi R^2	0.086	0.104	0.145	0.072	0.120	0.201

It is only when we consider the interaction between respondents' associational memberships and poverty status (Model 6) that we begin to finally disentangle the complex relationship between poverty civic engagement action. Indeed, unsurprisingly, engagement in civil society organisations is the strongest predictor of political action, with the associationally active being four times as likely to report political action compared with other respondents (Model 6): 'joiners' tend to also be 'doers'. It appears that the wider exclusion of people experiencing poverty from the diverse social, cultural, political and civic institutions of civil society is a key driver of political exclusion. Nevertheless, poverty itself remains a significant direct predictor of political withdrawal: compared with the PSE poor, better-off respondents are around 30 per cent more likely to be politically active. Socio-economic differences associated with occupational class and educational attainment also remain influential.

Conclusion

Since 1966, the right of all citizens to opportunities to participate in public life has been enshrined in international law:

> Every citizen shall have the right and the opportunity [...]: To take part in the conduct of public affairs, directly or through freely chosen representatives; to vote and to be elected at genuine periodic elections which shall be by universal and equal suffrage and shall be held by secret ballot, guaranteeing the free expression of the will of the electors, [and]; to have access, on general terms of equality, to public service in his [sic] country. (Article 25, 1966 UN International Covenant on Civil and Political Rights)

However, whilst equal rights to electoral representation for all UK adults are now well-established, ensuring that all citizens have *real* opportunities to participate in public life remains a challenging agenda in the context of entrenched social and economic inequalities. Statutory monitoring of inequalities in public life has existed in the UK only since the 2006 Equality Act and does not currently encompass income inequalities. However, as this chapter shows, poverty is an important predictor both of civic engagement and political action, and this effect is not entirely explained by class and educational effects. Without a genuine political 'voice' it is unsurprising that many poor PSE-UK respondents report feeling unable to influence political processes, though again these attitudinal differences do not on their own explain this 'poverty gap' in participation.

Participation in UK politics therefore remains very much a classed, as well as a gendered and racialised phenomenon. Addressing this 'democratic deficit' in participation for socially marginalised populations requires concerted and urgent action to reduce social and economic inequalities. Beyond voting in general elections, citizen participation in politics in the UK remains a minority pursuit dominated by those with the material, human and social resources to secure effective influence. Since participation is pivotal in the allocation of public goods and resources, tackling the effective exclusion of the poor from the policy-making process should be an urgent priority. Reducing socio-economic inequalities through action to tackle poverty is clearly an important part of the solution here.

Nevertheless, institutional reform is also needed to ensure that democratic institutions better facilitate the styles of participation favoured by the public. The exercise of political citizenship should involve not simply a periodic right to representation via the ballot box, but also opportunities for active participation in political decisions. The growth of protest action and community activism in recent decades, in which politically marginalised groups have often played a prominent part, is indicative of a desire on the part of many citizens to exercise an influence upon decision-making processes which extends well beyond formal representation. Yet the UK remains wedded to a system of political representation and governance which has remained largely unchanged since 1918 in terms of the relationship between electors and representatives that it specifies. Encouraging more democratic participation therefore requires the development of new avenues of participation that facilitate people to exercise political influence in ways consistent with their own outlooks, values and priorities. This involves finding new ways of linking traditional representation via the ballot box with the type of informal, associational politics often favoured by politically marginalised populations.

Note

[1] The SNP government in Scotland is currently committed to (re)introducing the socio-economic duty in Scotland. See: https://www.holyrood.com/articles/news/nicola-sturgeon-plans-revive-legal-duty-public-bodies-reduce-inequalities.

References

Almond, G. and Verba, S. (1963) *The civic culture: Political attitudes and democracy in five nations*, Princeton: Princeton University Press.

Audickas, L. (2015) *Social background of MPs*, House of Commons Library Briefing Paper CBP 7483.

Barnes, S. and Kaase, M. (1979) *Political activity: Mass participation in five western democracies*, London: Sage.

Beresford, P., Green, D., Lister, R. and Woodard, K. (1999) *Poverty first hand: Poor people speak for themselves*, London: Child Poverty Action Group.

Bradshaw, J. and Finch, N. (2003) 'Overlaps in the dimensions of poverty', *Journal of Social Policy*, 32(4): 513-25.

Brady, H. E., Verba, S. and Schlozman, K. L. (1995) 'Beyond SES: a resource model of political participation', *American Political Science Review*, 89: 271-94.

Bryson, A. and Gomez, R. (2002) 'Marching on together? Recent trends in union membership', in A. Park, J. Curtice, K. Thompson, L. Jarvis and C. Bromley (eds) *British Social Attitudes: The 19th report*, London: NatCen.

Bryson, A. and Gomez, R. (2005) 'Why have workers stopped joining unions? Accounting for the rise in never-membership in Britain', *British Journal of Industrial Relations*, 43(1): 67-92.

Chase, E. and Walker, R. (2013) 'The co-construction of shame in the context of poverty', *Sociology*, 47(4): 739-54.

Clarke, H., Sanders, D., Stewart, M. and Whitely, P. (2004) *Political choice in Britain*, Oxford: Oxford University Press.

Dalton, R. (2014) *Public opinion and political parties in advanced industrial democracies*, (6th edn) University of California, Irvine.

EHRC (2010) *How fair is Britain? Equality, human rights and good relations in 2010, First Triennial Review*, London: EHRC.

Electoral Commission (2005) *Social exclusion and political engagement*, London: Electoral Commission.

Fahmy, E. (2003) 'Social capital, social exclusion and political participation in Britain: findings from the 1999 PSE-GB survey', *ESRC/ODPM Postgraduate Research Programme Working Paper 4*, London: Office of the Deputy Prime Minister.

Fieldhouse, E., Widdop, P., Ling, R., Li, Y., Cutts, D. and Morales, L. (2010) *Civic life: Evidence base for the EHRC Triennial Review*, Manchester: University of Manchester.

Fraser, N. (1995) 'From redistribution to recognition? Dilemmas of justice in a 'post-socialist' age', *New Left Review*, 212(1): 68-93.

Fraser, N. and Honneth, A. (2003) *Redistribution or recognition? A political-philosophical exchange*, London/New York: Verso.

Hall, P. (1999) 'Social capital in Britain', *British Journal of Political Science*, 29: 417-61.

Hansard Society (2013) *Audit of political engagement: The 2013 report*, London: Hansard Society.

Harrington, M. (1962 [1981]) *The other America: Poverty in the United States*, London: Penguin.

Home Office (2004) *Facilitating community involvement: practical guidance for practitioners and policy makers,* Development and Practice Report 27, London: Home Office.

Honneth, A. (1996) *The struggle for recognition: The moral grammar of social conflicts*, Cambridge, MA: MIT Press.

Inglehart, R. (1990) *Culture shift in advanced industrial society*, Princeton, NJ: Princeton University Press.

Killeen, D. (2008) *Poverty and human rights in the UK*, York: Joseph Rowntree Foundation.

Kilngemann, H.-D. and Fuchs, D. (eds) (1995) *Citizens and the state*, Oxford: Oxford University Press.

Lee, L. and Young P. (2013) 'A disengaged Britain? Political interest and participation over 30 years', in A. Park et al (eds) *British Social Attitudes: The 30th Report*, London: NatCen Social Research.

Li Y., Savage, M. and Pickles, A. (2003) 'Social capital and social exclusion in England and Wales (1972-1999)', *British Journal of Sociology*, 54(4): 497-526.

Lijphart, A. (1997) 'Unequal participation: democracy's unresolved dilemma', *The American Political Science Review*, 91(1): 1-14.

Lister, R. (1990) *The exclusive society: Citizenship and the poor*, London: CPAG.

Lister, R. (1997) *Citizenship: Feminist perspectives*, London: Palgrave.

Lister, R. (2007a) 'A politics of recognition and respect: involving people with experience of poverty in decision making that affects their lives', *Social Policy & Society*, 1(1): 37-46.

Lister, R. (2007b) 'From object to subject: including marginalised citizens in policy making', *Policy and Politics*, 35(3): 437–55.

Marsh, A. (1990) *Political action in Europe and the USA*, Basingstoke: Macmillan.

Milbrath, L. and Goel, M. (1977) *Political participation* (2nd edn), Chicago: Rand McNally.

Newell, P. and Wheeler, J. (2006) 'Rights, resources and the politics of accountability: an introduction' in P. Newell and J. Wheeler (eds) *Rights, resources and the politics of accountability*, London/New York: Zed Books.

Norris, P. (ed) (1999) *Critical citizens: Global support for democratic government*, Oxford: Oxford University Press.

Parry, G., Moyser, M. and Day, N. (1992) *Political participation and democracy in Britain*, Cambridge: Cambridge University Press.

Pateman, C. (1970) *Participation and democratic theory*, Cambridge: Cambridge University Press.

Pattie, C., Seyd, P. and Whiteley, P. (2004) *Citizenship in Britain: Values, participation and democracy*, Cambridge: Cambridge University Press.

Pemberton, S., Fahmy, E., Sutton, E., Bell, K. (2016) 'Navigating the stigmatised identities of poverty in austere times', *Critical Social Policy*, 36(1): 21-37.

Putnam, R. (1995) 'Tuning in, turning out: the strange disappearance of social capital in America', *PS: Political Science and Politics*, 28: 664-83.

Schlozman, K. and Verba, S. (1979) *Injury to insult: Unemployment, class and political response*, Cambridge, Mass.: Harvard University Press.

Taylor, E. and Low, N. (2010) *Citizenship survey 2008-2009: Empowered communities topic report*, London: CLG.

Tocqueville, A. de (1838) *Democracy in America* (3rd edn, translated by A. Reeve) London: Saunders and Otley.

UKCAP (UK Coalition Against Poverty) (2002) *Listen hear! The right to be heard. Report of the Commission on Poverty, Participation and Power*, Bristol: Policy Press.

UNESCO (2002) *Social capital and poverty reduction: Which role for the civil society organizations and the state?* Paris: UNESCO.

Verba, S. and Nie, N. (1972) *Participation in America: Political democracy and social equality*, Chicago: University of Chicago.

Verba, S., Schlozman, K. and Brady, H. (1995) *Voice and equality: Civic voluntarism in American politics*, Cambridge: Harvard University Press.

Ward, S. (1986) 'Power, politics and poverty', in P. Golding (ed) *Excluding the poor*, London: CPAG.

Whiteley, P. (2014) *Political participation in Britain: The decline and revival of civic culture*, Basingstoke: Palgrave Macmillan.

Part 3:
Quality of life

EIGHT

Poverty and health: thirty years of progress?

Lucy Prior and David Manley

Introduction

Health is a marker of the development of societies (Marmot, 2007). The wealth and prosperity of nations are embodied in the welfare of its citizens (Hoff, 2008). Overall, health has improved over the course of the twentieth century for many countries, particularly those forming part of the Organisation for Economic Cooperation and Development (OECD) (Marmot, 2007). However, disparities in the distribution of poor health persist between and within countries. Systematic differences in the risk of suffering a multitude of physical and mental illnesses by socio-economic groups reflects the organisation of societies, and specifically the distribution of wealth, resources and opportunities. Interest in the relationship of poverty and health, therefore, has come to focus on a moral concern with inequalities and the unfair, avoidable social structuring of poor health (Braveman and Gruskin, 2003).

On an international scale, systematic patterning in health is demonstrated by the variations in life expectancies that are observed between countries; in 2013 the range in life expectancy at birth between countries was 37 years for men, and 41 years for women (WHO, 2015). Marked inequalities have also been observed within countries and even in cities. For instance, life expectancies in the most affluent areas of Glasgow were reported at 82 years, compared to 54 years in one of the most deprived areas (Hanlon et al, 2006). The life expectancy for individuals in some deprived areas of Scotland was thus worse than the average in India (Marmot, 2007).

Inequalities in a variety of health outcomes have been demonstrated with a range of socio-economic and status measures. The *Black Report* produced by the Working Group on Inequalities in Health helped invigorate research and policy interest in health inequalities by demonstrating disparities in mortality rates based on social class

(Townsend et al, 1992). It identified material or socio-economic factors such as income, education and housing as the most important drivers of these inequalities. The WHO Commission on Social Determinants of Health compiled a wealth of evidence on the structuring of health by social conditions, demonstrating the 'poor health of the poor, the social gradient in health within countries, and the marked health inequities between countries are caused by the unequal distribution of power, income, goods, and services' (WHO 2008, p 1). UK inequalities in health have persisted and widened over time despite improvements in overall health, with enhancements in health for the poor failing to keep up with those enjoyed by the more advantaged (Graham, 2009; Smith et al, 2016).

Poverty represents a fundamental outcome of inequality, where people fall below the minimum standards deemed acceptable in a society (Mack and Lansley, 1985). The lack of financial and material resources that define poverty make it damaging to health. Individuals in poverty cannot afford the vital conditions for a healthy existence, such as decent housing, heating and diet (Mack and Lansley, 1985; Gordon, 2006). The plight of those in poverty is additionally compounded by perceptions of poorer social positioning, intensifying the negative psychosocial and health impacts these comparisons can induce (Runciman, 1966; Kuo and Chiang, 2013). Therefore, examining the health of those in poverty is a powerful tool for understanding the influence of social stratification on health.

Though poor health is most often considered a consequence of poverty, there is a school of thought which considers health as a *cause* of poverty. The 'health selection' hypothesis posits that those with poor health tend to drift down the social scale, leading to larger proportions of ill persons in lower social positions and poverty groupings. However, this explanation has largely been discounted as a having a substantial effect (Blane et al, 1993; Manor et al, 2003; Warren, 2009).

In the face of austerity measures, with past cuts to benefits evidenced as affecting those most in need the most severely (Stuckler and Basu, 2013), it is vitally important to understand the nature of the link between poverty and health. A report by the Institute for Fiscal Studies (Browne and Hood, 2016), projected household incomes at the bottom of the distribution will fail to keep up with forecasted overall growth in median income to 2020/21, increasing relative poverty. This forecast is attributed to planned cuts to benefits, which are also expected to increase child poverty (Browne and Hood, 2016). Further understanding will help to formulate and target social policies that aim to tackle inequalities in health and quality of life (Stewart et al, 2008).

In thematic sections centred on general health and mental health, this chapter will explore the relationship of current poverty measures, past poverty and changing circumstances, as well as key dimensions of social exclusion with health. Since questions on health in the PSE-UK 2012 survey are only asked of the adult population, all analyses reported below refer to people aged 18 or above.

General health

Health is conceptualised as more than the mere absence of disease or illness: it is an all-encompassing state of physical, mental and social well-being. To align analyses with such multidimensional understandings, a subjective measure of health is beneficial. Self-reported health measures can simultaneously tap into socially contextualised personal appraisals of multiple health components (Bowling, 2005).

Single item self-rated health measures are used extensively to assess general health status and have been widely validated as predictors of mortality and various morbidities (Bowling, 2005; DeSalvo et al, 2006). The general health measure is taken from the self-reported responses to the question: 'How is your health in general. Is it...?' Answers were scored on a 5-point scale from 'very good' to 'very bad', with a mid-point of 'fair'. For the following analyses, general health is dichotomised to contrast having (relatively) bad health (a state of 'fair' or worse – 27 per cent) with good or very good health.

Additionally, overall health status is accessed through a binary measure of long-term limiting illness or disability (LLTI), created through combining responses to the questions 'Do you have any physical or mental conditions or illnesses lasting or expected to last for 12 months of more?' and 'Does [your condition or illness/do any of your conditions or illnesses] reduce your ability to carry-out day-to-day activities?'; 22 per cent had a LLTI. LLTI provides an indication of poor health that impacts on everyday life, which is particularly important in regards to considering the interrelationship of social exclusion and health.

Poverty and general health

Descriptive results from the PSE-UK survey reinforce the picture of health inequalities demonstrated by other studies (Santana et al, 2002; Gunasekara et al, 2013; Saito et al, 2014) including previous *Breadline Britain* surveys (Gordon and Pantazis, 1997). However disadvantage is defined, the poor are disproportionately worse off in terms of their general health.

Figure 8.1 illustrates the extent of the inequality by three important measures of poverty: the UK government's standard low-income poverty measure, based on a threshold of 60 per cent of median income after housing costs; the consensual poverty measure developed by the PSE research project; and a subjectively determined measure based on whether respondents rated their standard of living as below average or not. (See the Introduction for detailed definitions.)

It is clear that those who are more disadvantaged experience worse health. For those classified as poor by the PSE poverty and low-income measures, 41 per cent report bad health, compared to 23 per cent for those who are not poor. The inequality in general health appears most marked for the subjective standard of living; the difference between those with a below average standard of living and those with average or better is 27 per cent. LLTI, which should capture problems with a greater ageing component, evidences the same trend of worse health for the more disadvantaged, though to a smaller extent in every case.

In order to develop a clearer picture of the nature of the disparities in health, it is necessary to control for the influence of key demographic and social factors. Health deteriorates with age, and at different rates for men and women, for example. Separate logistic regression models were run with general health and LLTI as the responses, controlling for age, sex, ethnicity, marital status, and household type. The first set of models tested the impact of the PSE poverty measure on general health and LLTI. In the second set, the relationships of income and

Figure 8.1: Percentage of adults with bad general health and LLTI by poverty definition

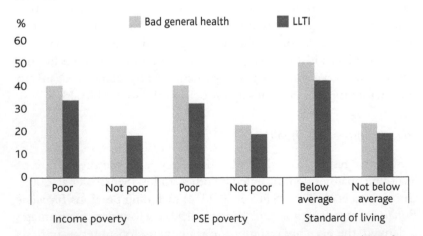

Note: Weighted cases between 8353 and 8365 for general health, and 8347 and 8361 for LLTI, depending on poverty measure.

deprivation with general health were tested in a single logistic model with controls for the same set of socio-demographic factors (but without PSE poverty included).[1]

Even after parcelling out the influence of age and other socio-demographic characteristics, the poor have a higher likelihood of worse health than those not poor. Across all adults, the mean predicted probability of bad health is 23 per cent for the not poor and 44 per cent for those in poverty, while for LLTI the probabilities for not poor and poor are 19 per cent and 35 per cent respectively. The modelled relationships of income and deprivation to general health are depicted in Figure 8.2. They both show the expected associations: the probability of being in poor health falls as income increases but rises as deprivation increases. Deprivation seems to have a more pronounced relationship with general health than income. The change in the predicted probability is approximately 29 per cent across the income range, compared to 43 per cent for deprivation. This finding echoes results from New Zealand by Gunasekara et al (2013); they found moving into deprived circumstances was associated with a larger decline in self-rated health than a move into a low-income group.

Past poverty and current health

Within the cross-sectional design of the PSE-UK, respondents were asked a set of questions relating to their past experiences of poverty as well as changes to their lives since last interview in the Family Resources Survey (FRS) (see the Introduction for details on the survey methodology). This offers the opportunity to signal how previous experiences of disadvantage are associated with current health. This is important in light of research which showcases the continuing influence of previous poverty on health, as well as the cumulative impact of longer periods spent in poverty (Benzeval and Judge, 2001; Ben-Shlomo and Kuh, 2002).

PSE-UK participants were asked to reflect on their lifetime and state how often there had been periods when they had lived in poverty by the standards of that time. Figure 8.3 demonstrates how, as time spent in poverty increases, so does the percentage of respondents with bad general health and LLTI. For those who have never lived in poverty, the percentages of bad health and LLTI are 21 per cent and 17 per cent respectively. This shifts to 57 per cent and 46 per cent for those who have lived in poverty most of the time. Pantazis and Gordon (1997) reported a similar relationship of history of poverty in respect to longstanding illness; 25 per cent of those reporting never having lived in

Figure 8.2: Predicted probability of being in bad health (by log income and deprivation index)

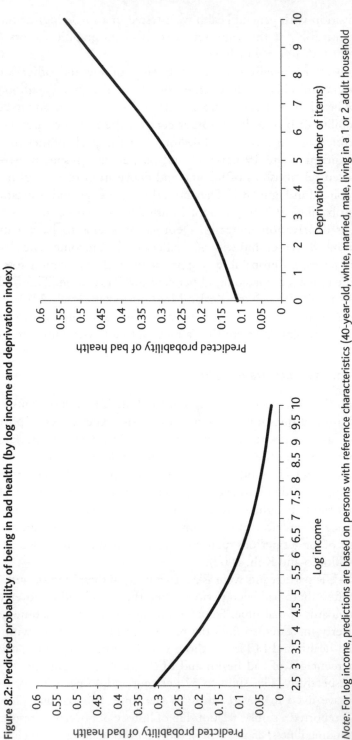

Note: For log income, predictions are based on persons with reference characteristics (40-year-old, white, married, male, living in a 1 or 2 adult household with no children or pensioners) and deprived of 0 items. For deprivation, predictions are based on adults with reference characteristics and mean income.

Figure 8.3: Percentage of adults with bad health and LLTI by history of poverty

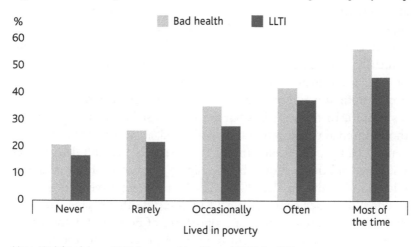

Note: Weighted cases 8363 for general health, and 8359 for LLTI.

poverty had a longstanding illness compared to 52 per cent for persons considering themselves to have lived in poverty for most of the time.

The influence of past circumstances on current health can be further explored by utilising participants' reports of whether their individual income had increased, decreased or stayed the same since the previous interview 12–18 months before. This measure provides an indication of the past financial situation of respondents, with those reporting an increase in income having been worse off previously; 40 per cent of adults reported an increase in income. The modelled relationship of a binary indicator of lower income in the past with bad health and LLTI appears to be significant, as tested in logistic models controlling for socio-demographic characteristics and PSE poverty. Across all modelled individuals, the mean predicted probability of bad general health for those who used to have a lower income was 32 per cent, compared to 28 per cent for those whose incomes were higher or the same. For LLTI, the respective mean predicted probabilities were 27 per cent and 22 per cent. These results support the lasting impact of historic circumstances on health.

Social exclusion and general health

Social exclusion offers a multidimensional appreciation for the domains through which different individuals may be excluded from full participation in society (Levitas et al, 2007). It is a broader concept than poverty, representing inequalities in the opportunities for and the distribution of social, cultural, and political resources and participation, alongside the material and economic factors more closely associated with poverty (Levitas et al, 2007; Bailey et al, 2016).

A vital dimension of social exclusion is economic participation, primarily through employment. Paid work is a major determinant of income and material circumstances, whilst poor health can restrict opportunities for labour market participation (see Chapter 6 for more discussion). In the PSE-UK survey, the worst health is displayed by those classed as permanently sick or disabled, at 92 per cent and 97 per cent for bad general health and LLTI respectively. Health deteriorates with age, and this is shown by the high proportions of retired adults with poor health in the PSE-UK: 45 per cent have bad general health and 39 per cent suffer a LLTI. Outside these categories, the unemployed show the highest proportions of poor health and LLTI, at 26 per cent and 21 per cent respectively, followed by the inactive (corresponding to students, those looking after home and family and other inactive) at 24 per cent for general health and 18 per cent for LLTI. Although those adults who are working, either full or part time, have the lowest proportions of bad self-rated health and LLTI (at 14 per cent and 9 per cent), the difference to the unemployed group is fairly small, at 12 per cent for both health measures.

The PSE-UK survey additionally asked respondents how long they had been unemployed for over the last five years. This offers insight into the role of poor health in transitions to unemployment. Logistic regression models were run with general health predicting a dichotomised length of unemployment variable, contrasting six months or more of unemployment (13 per cent of the adult population) with less than six months. Age, sex, marital status, ethnicity, and socio-economic status (SES) are also included in the model. Results reveal that poor health status significantly predicts longer unemployment. Across all modelled adults recording bad health, the probability of experiencing six or more months of unemployment is 16 per cent, compared to 11 per cent for those with good health. This result corroborates findings from other studies on health selective employment transitions (Ki et al, 2013; Webber et al, 2015).

Another important aspect of social exclusion is the living environment (see Chapter 9 for more discussion). In particular, the proximal household environment is an important influence on health (POST, 2011). Living in housing in a poor state is also a powerful marker of the inequality of disadvantage; having both a damp-free and a warm home have been consistently considered as necessities by the public (see Chapter 1). Participants of the PSE-UK survey were asked a range of questions relating to their living conditions. An examination of responses reveals a patterning of health by poor housing circumstances: 48 per cent of individuals who reported dissatisfaction with their housing circumstances were in bad health, compared to 26 per cent who were more satisfied; 39 per cent of respondents whose house was in a poor state of repair had poor health, compared to 26 per cent whose home was in a good or adequate state; and 33 per cent of participants whose home was too cold last winter reported bad health, in contrast to 24 per cent of individuals whose home was warm enough. Conditions such as damp, overcrowding, and poor maintenance can aggravate existing health conditions and precipitate experiences of ill health. In the PSE-UK survey, 34 per cent of the PSE poor and 31 per cent of the multiply deprived stated their housing situation had aggravated an existing health condition or brought on a new health issue, compared to 13 per cent and 8 per cent for the respective more advantaged groups. This represents a greater inequality than that reported in the 1990 *Breadline Britain* survey (Pantazis and Gordon, 1997).

Mental health

Mental health forms an essential element of a multidimensional, overarching appreciation of health and well-being. The WHO estimates of the Disability-Adjusted Life Years (DALYs) demonstrate the major contribution of mental health issues to the burden of disease globally (WHO, 2016). Mental health conditions are also linked to heavy incidence of physical health conditions and treatments, increasing the overall cost of mental illness. A report by the Centre for Mental Health (Naylor et al, 2012) estimated that between £8 billion to £13 billion of NHS expenditure on long-term physical health conditions was linked to co-morbid mental health issues. Previous studies have explored relationships between poverty and mental health at the area level and individually, demonstrating associations of poverty with a variety of mental health conditions and service use (Payne, 1997; Eibner et al, 2004; Fone and Dunstan, 2006; Butterworth et al, 2009).

Mental health within the PSE-UK survey was measured using the well-validated short form of the General Health Questionnaire (GHQ12). This instrument is used to indicate the presence of common mental disorder symptoms (Jackson, 2007). Respondents are asked a series of 12 questions, covering negative aspects such as 'Have you recently felt constantly under strain?' and positive elements, for instance 'Have you recently been able to enjoy your normal day-to-day activities?'. Each item has four possible answers, along the lines of 'not at all', 'no more than usual', 'rather more than usual' and 'much more than usual'. The following analysis implements the GHQ12 as a mental health continuum on a scale from 0 to 36,[2] with higher scores representing worse mental health. Additionally, where respondents had reported they suffered from a longstanding illness or condition, they could specify whether this took the form of a mental health condition (16 per cent of the adult population).

Poverty and mental health

It is important to consider the dynamics of age with mental health and poverty definitions. Unlike general health and LLTI, mental health has a younger age profile, as shown by the proportion of adults who reported a longstanding mental health condition by age band: 36 per cent of 18- to 24-year-olds had a serious mental health issue, compared to 25 per cent for those 45-54 years of age, and just 3 per cent for those 80 or more years old. Income measures of poverty are problematic in that they can overstate poverty in older age by failing to appropriately capture wealth in savings and assets accumulated over the life course. By comparison, measures driven primarily by deprivation, such as PSE poverty, highlight the younger poor; 30 per cent of 18- to 24-year-olds are classified as poor on this measure, compared to 10 per cent of people aged 80 or more.

The relationships of mental health and poverty to age help explain the pattern of inequalities found when examining the proportion of respondents with a mental health condition and a poorer mental health state (here taken as a score of 18 or more on the GHQ scale – 19 per cent). Figure 8.4 demonstrates that inequalities in mental health appear less prominent when assessed through an income dimension. The difference in poor mental states is 15 per cent between those above and below the 60 per cent threshold, whereas the difference between the PSE poor and not poor is 23 per cent. This is in contrast to general health and LLTI, where inequalities by income and PSE poverty were very similar. Overall, the case for the poor suffering worse mental health is substantiated in these descriptive analyses.

Given the indication of strong inequalities, it is important to explore models utilising the full scale of mental health. This is achieved using linear regression models predicting GHQ12 score by socio-demographics (age, sex, ethnicity, marital status, and household type) and a binary indicator of PSE poverty. From this model, it is clear that

Figure 8.4: Percentage of adults with poor mental states and reporting a chronic mental health condition by poverty definition

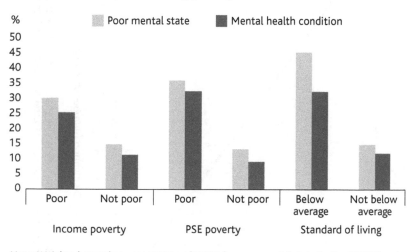

Note: Weighted cases between 7,909 and 7,948 for poor mental state by the GHQ12 and 2,801 and 2,803 for longstanding mental health condition, depending on poverty measure.

the poor are worse off. The estimated change in GHQ12 score for moving into the poverty grouping was 4.32 (99 per cent confidence intervals of 3.54 to 5.10). This signifies a significant effect of poverty. For all adult cases modelled, the effect of poverty corresponds to a mean predicted mental health score of 11 points for the not poor, compared to around 16 points for those in poverty.

The relationships of income and deprivation are examined in a linear regression model of GHQ12 score predicted by the same set of socio-demographic controls as previously, along with income (logged) and deprivation. Figure 8.5 shows that deprivation has a strong association with mental health; being more deprived relates to a markedly worse (higher) GHQ12 score. The predicted increase in mental health score for lacking a single extra item on the deprivation scale was 0.87 (99 per cent confidence intervals of 0.74 to 0.99). The models also revealed higher incomes were associated with better mental health scores but here the gradient was very shallow; the expected decrease in GHQ12 score for a 1 unit increase in log income was 0.21 points (99 per cent confidence intervals of -0.62 to 0.21). This suggests the association of mental health and income was not significant, as well as being relatively small in size. More proximal, material aspects such as deprivation are stronger factors in predicting mental health than income. This reinforces the need to consider poverty measures beyond the standard income threshold.

Figure 8.5: Predicted mental health score (by log income and deprivation index)

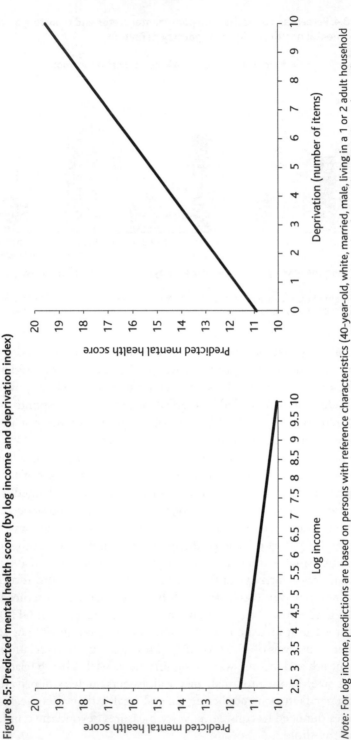

Note: For log income, predictions are based on persons with reference characteristics (40-year-old, white, married, male, living in a 1 or 2 adult household with no children or pensioners) and deprived of 0 items. For deprivation, predictions are based on adults with reference characteristics and mean income.

Past poverty and mental health

Mental health exhibits a similar relationship with history of poverty as general health, with a clear increase in the proportion of individuals rated as having a poor mental state as time spent in poverty increases. The percentage classed as having a poor mental state is only 12 per cent for those who have never lived in poverty, compared to 45 per cent for those who reported having lived in poverty most of the time. Similarly, the proportion of adults with a longstanding mental health condition is 10 per cent for those who do not consider themselves to have lived in poverty, and 39 per cent for those who have experienced the most spells of poverty. This substantiates the importance of poverty duration in predicting mental illness.

Exploring the relationship of previous income with mental health reveals a different pattern of association to that found for general health and LLTI. In models controlling for socio-demographics and PSE poverty status, having a lower income in the recent past was not associated with significantly worse mental health score (-0.46 point estimated change with 99 per cent confidence intervals of -1.04 to 0.12), whereas it was associated with worse general health. Conversely, a binary measure of previously higher income showed a relationship with worse mental health, relating to a 1.51 point increase in GHQ12 score (99 per cent confidence intervals of 0.68 to 2.34). These results suggest, in contrast to those for general health, that it is not necessarily previous *levels* of income which are important to mental health, but *changes* in income. A decline in income may itself be a source of stress and anxiety, or else may be associated with stressful circumstances, such as job loss, which negatively impact on mental well-being.

Social exclusion and mental health

Social exclusion and mental health are highly interlinked (Morgan et al, 2007), with those having mental health conditions identified as a major excluded group in society (SEU, 2004). Poor mental health can be both a cause and a consequence of social exclusion (Payne, 2006). Stigma and discrimination within the structure of society promote the exclusion of those with mental health problems (SEU, 2004). Mental health can also impact on opportunities and capacities to participate fully in the employment sector, with knock-on effects on income and material resources (Payne, 2006). Meanwhile, experiencing social exclusion can incite negative effects on mental health through feelings of low self-esteem, isolation and lack of support (Stewart et al, 2008).

The relationship between labour market exclusion and mental health is particularly complex, with mental health problems potentially acting as both cause and consequence of unemployment (see Chapter 6 for more discussion). We can gain insight into this complex relationship by examining the proportions of mental health issues by different categories of employment status. The lowest proportion of poor mental health was displayed by the retired group (11 per cent). This finding is likely explained by the younger age profile of mental health issues. The largest proportion of mental health issues resides in those categorised as permanently sick or disabled, although the percentage is around 57 per cent for poor mental state by the GHQ12, compared to over 90 per cent for general health and LLTI. Other economically inactive adults also showed relatively high rates of poor mental health, at 22 per cent. Not participating or the inability to participate in the labour market could restrict opportunities for positive self-esteem and social contact, while the stigma and low self-esteem associated with being inactive could negatively impact mental health and well-being. It should be noted that a proportion of the permanently sick or disabled will have chronic mental illness that perpetually excludes them from work. Mental health problems make up a growing proportion of long-term absences from work (CBI, 2008; Black and Frost, 2011).

A clear finding is the large proportion of adults (41 per cent) with a poor mental state within the unemployed category. This is markedly higher than the proportion seen in the working group (17 per cent), and is also higher than the percentages seen for general health and LLTI in the unemployed group. In an analysis of the PSE-GB 1999 survey, Payne (2006) similarly found the highest proportion of respondents with a mental disorder in the unemployed category. It appears mental health disparities by employment status have increased since 1999; the gap between the working and the unemployed was approximately 17 per cent in the PSE-GB 1999 survey, compared to 24 per cent for the PSE-UK 2012. It should be noted that Payne (2006) operationalised mental health through the binary GHQ12 scoring system, with a threshold score of 4 or more indicative of the presence of common mental disorder symptoms.

It is possible to further test the relationship of labour market exclusion to mental health by using history of unemployment (as a continuous scale of months of unemployment) to predict GHQ12 score, controlling for socio-demographics and current poverty status. The estimated coefficient for unemployment suggested a significant 0.03 point (99 per cent confidence intervals of 0.00 to 0.06) increase in GHQ12 score for each additional month of unemployment. This result substantiates the importance of unemployment for the mental health of individuals (Paul and Moser, 2009; Urbanos-Garrido and Lopez-Valcarcel, 2015).

As with general health, the local living environment can be a strong determining factor in generating variation in mental health. Thermal comfort, crowding, dampness and general state of repair are recognised as predictors of mental health (Evans et al, 2003). The proportion of individuals with poor mental health by standard of housing reveals an increasing gradient from good through adequate to poor, with percentages increasing from 15 to 26 to 37 per cent. Results from the 1990 *Breadline Britain* survey based on feelings of depression showed proportions of approximately 11, 20 and 41 per cent (Payne, 1997). Therefore, it appears the 2012 housing gradient in mental health is shallower than in 1990. Thanks to initiatives such as the Decent Homes Programme (POST, 2011), the condition of housing stock in the UK has improved over time. This means that what individuals class as 'poor' housing by today's standards could be better than what individuals in 1990 categorised as poor, hence the decreased mental health disparity.

Mental health is inherently a social phenomenon (Morgan et al, 2007) and social capital may act as a potential buffer to negative consequences from experiences of exclusion (Kawachi and Berkman, 2001). Therefore, exploring the social aspects of inclusion in terms of activity, participation and support is particularly relevant to mental health. Within the PSE-UK survey, participants were asked a series of questions relating to social support and social activity, as well as civic and political participation. Summary scales were created along each of these dimensions, affording the opportunity to analyse these different aspects of inclusion. Figure 8.6 shows the proportions of individuals classed as having a poor mental health state or not by binary indicators for low levels of social resources.

It is apparent that lower levels of social resources result in higher proportions of poorer mental health. However, civil participation (covering participation in organisations such as sports clubs and youth groups) and political participation (representing activities such as attending public meetings and demonstrations) appear to have weaker relations with mental health: the range for each group is small (5 per cent and 6 per cent respectively). These aspects of social inclusion could be considered as relating to structural dimensions of social capital (Harpham, 2008); this has previously been found to have weaker relationships to mental health (Fujiwara and Kawachi, 2008). The relationships of social activity and social support with mental health

Figure 8.6: Percentage of adults with poor mental states by social resources

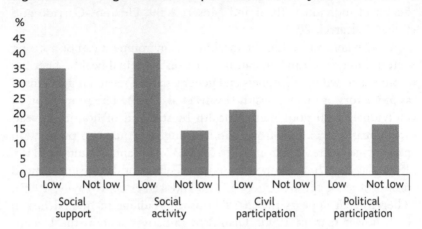

Note: Weighted cases between 7,909 and 7,955 depending on measure.

were substantiated in separate models of GHQ12 score controlling for PSE poverty status and the socio-demographic characteristics of individuals. Both appeared as significant predictors of mental health.

Conclusion

The persistent picture of health inequalities is reinforced by these findings; the poor are more likely to suffer worse general health, experience a LLTI, and have a poorer mental health state or longstanding mental health condition. The disproportionate disadvantage of the poor appears consistently across different definitions of poverty as well as after controlling for socio-demographic characteristics of individuals. Examinations of changing circumstances and past poverty further reinforce the issues of worse health for those in poor or worsening situations and provide stronger evidence for causal links from poverty to poor health.

The results also indicate the vital importance of considering broader aspects of poverty and social exclusion when relationships with health are of interest. Income measures still dominate much work on the effects of poverty. However, in this study, income was not found to be a significant predictor of mental health state once individual-level characteristics were controlled for, and income also demonstrated a weaker influence on general health than the consensual deprivation index. Furthermore, initial assessment of relationships of health to dimensions of social exclusion reveal interesting patterns by the health measure utilised. Though LLTI and general health showed consistently similar trends, assessments of mental health should take special consideration of the impacts of unemployment and social resources.

The conclusion remains the same as that offered by the previous *Breadline Britain* and PSE surveys: there are marked health inequalities associated with poverty and social exclusion in the UK. Despite 30 years of research and policy since the 1983 *Breadline Britain* survey, the poor are still suffering disproportionately worse general and mental health. Tackling issues of poverty and social exclusion remains the pathway to helping address such inequalities in health.

Notes

[1] The natural log of net weekly income after housing costs (PSE equivalised) is the income measure. Deprivation is a scale from 0 to 10 or more, indicating the number of items considered as necessities that adult participants lacked. Linear relationships of log income and deprivation with the log odds of bad health are assumed.

[2] There has been some concern raised over the slightly higher-than-expected reporting of mental health conditions in the PSE-UK, when using the binary scoring system for the GHQ12 and a cut-off threshold of 4. See Nandy et al for a discussion.

References

Bailey, N., Bramley, G. and Gannon, M. (2016) 'Poverty and social exclusion in urban and rural areas of Scotland', *Poverty and Social Exclusion UK Survey 2012 Working Paper*, Bristol: Poverty and Social Exclusion (PSE).

Ben-Shlomo, Y. and Kuh, D. (2002) 'A life course approach to chronic disease epidemiology: conceptual models, empirical challenges and interdisciplinary perspectives', *International Journal of Epidemiology*, 31, pp 285-93.

Benzeval, M. and Judge, K. (2001) 'Income and health: the time dimension', *Social Science and Medicine*, 52, pp 1371-90.

Black, C. and Frost, D. (2011) *Health at work – and independent review of sickness absence*, Report presented to Parliament by the Secretary of State for Work and Pensions, London: The Stationery Office Limited.

Blane, D., Davey-Smith G. and Bartley, M. (1993) 'Social selection: what does it contribute to social class differences in health?' *Sociology of Health and Illness*, 15(1), pp 1-15.

Bowling, A. (2005) 'Just one question: if one question works, why ask several?', *Journal of Epidemiology and Community Health*, 59, pp 342-5.

Braveman, P. and Gruskin, S. (2003) 'Poverty, equity, human rights and health', *Bulletin of the World Health Organisation*, 81, pp 539-45.

Browne, J. and Hood, A. (2016) *Living standards, poverty and inequality in the UK: 2015-16 to 2020/21. Report R114,* London: Institute for Fiscal Studies.

Butterworth, P., Rodgers, B. and Windsor, T. D. (2009) 'Financial hardship, socio-economic position and depression: results from the PATH Through Life Survey', *Social Science and Medicine*, 69, pp 229-37.

CBI (Confederation of British Industry) (2008) *At work and working well? CBI/AXA absence and labour turnover 2008*, London: Confederation of British Industry.

DeSalvo, K. B., Bloser, N., Reynolds, K., He, J. and Muntner, P. (2006), 'Mortality prediction with a single general self-rated health question: a meta-analysis', *Journal of General Internal Medicine*, 21(3), pp 267-75.

Eibner, C., Sturm, R. and Gresenz, C. R. (2004), 'Does relative deprivation predict the need for mental health services?', *The Journal of Mental Health Policy and Economics*, 7, pp 167-75.

Evans, G. W., Wells, N. M. and Moch, A. (2003) 'Housing and mental health: a review of the evidence and a methodological and conceptual critique', *Journal of Social Issues*, 59(3), pp 475-500.

Fone, D. L. and Dunstan, F. (2006) 'Mental health, places and people: a multilevel analysis of economic inactivity and social deprivation', *Health & Place*, 12, pp 332-44.

Fujiwara, T. and Kawachi, I. (2008) 'A prospective study of individual-level social capital and major depression in the United States', *Journal of Epidemiology and Community Health*, 62, pp 627-33.

Gordon, D. (2006) 'The concept and measurement of poverty', in C. Pantazis, D. Gordon and R. Levitas (eds) *Poverty and social exclusion in Britain*, Bristol: The Policy Press, pp 29-69.

Gordon, D. and Pantazis, C. (eds) (1997) *Breadline Britain in the 1990s*, Bristol: Summerleaze House Books.

Graham, H. (2009) 'The challenge of health inequalities', in H. Graham (ed) *Understanding health inequalities*, Maidenhead: Open University Press, pp 1-21.

Gunasekara, F. I., Carter, K. N., Crampton, P. and Blakely, T. (2013) 'Income and individual deprivation as predictors of health over time', *International Journal of Public Health*, 58, pp 501-11.

Hanlon, P., Walsh, D. and Whyte, B. (2006) *Let Glasgow flourish: A comprehensive report on health and its determinants in Glasgow and West Central Scotland*, Glasgow: Glasgow Centre for Population Health.

Harpham, T. (2008) 'The measurement of community social capital through surveys', in I. Kawachi, S. V. Subramanian, and D. Kim (eds), *Social capital and health*, Springer: New York, pp 51-62.

Hoff, A. (2008) 'Tackling poverty and social exclusion of older people – lessons from Europe', *Working Paper 308*, Oxford: Oxford Institute of Ageing.

Jackson, C. (2007) 'The general health questionnaire', *Occupational Medicine*, 57, p 79.

Kawachi, I. and Berkman, L. F. (2001) 'Social ties and mental health', *Journal of Urban Health: Bulletin of the New York Academy of Medicine*, 78(3), pp 458-67.

Ki, M., Kelly, Y., Sacker, A. and Nazroo, J. (2013) 'Poor health, employment transitions and gender: evidence from the British Household Panel Survey', *International Journal of Public Health*, 58, pp 537-46.

Kuo, C.-T. and Chiang, T.-L. (2013) 'The association between relative deprivation and self-rated health, depressive symptoms, and smoking behaviour in Taiwan', *Social Science and Medicine*, 89, pp 39-44.

Levitas, R., Pantazis, C., Fahmy, E., Gordon, D., Lloyd, E. and Patsios, D. (2007) *The multi-dimensional analysis of social exclusion: Report prepared for the Social Exclusion Unit*, Bristol: University of Bristol.

Mack, J. and Lansley, S. (1985) 'How poor is too poor?', in J. Mack and S. Lansley (eds) *Poor Britain*, London: George Allen & Unwin, pp 15-48.

Manor, O., Matthews, S. and Power, C. (2003) 'Health selection: the role of inter- and intra-generational mobility on social inequalities in health', *Social Science and Medicine*, 57, pp 2217-27.

Marmot, M. (2007) 'Achieving health equity: from root causes to fair outcomes', *Lancet*, 370, pp 1153-63.

Morgan, C., Burns, T., Fitzpatrick, R., Pinfold, V. and Priebe, S. (2007) 'Social exclusion and mental health', *British Journal of Psychiatry*, 191, pp 477-83.

Nandy, S., Payne, S., Gordon, D. and Patsios, D., 'A methodological note on the GHQ12 measure used in the 2012 Poverty and Social Exclusion Study', *Statistical Briefing Note No. 5*, Bristol: University of Bristol.

Naylor, C., Parsonage, M., McDaid, D., Knapp, M., Fossey, M. and Galea, A. (2012) *Long-term conditions and mental health: The cost of co-morbidities*, London: The King's Fund and the Centre for Mental Health.

Pantazis, C. and Gordon, D. (1997) 'Poverty and health', in D. Gordon and C. Pantazis (eds) *Breadline Britain in the 1990s*, Bristol: Summerleaze House Books, pp 135-57.

Paul, K. I. and Moser, K. (2009) 'Unemployment impairs mental health: meta-analyses', *Journal of Vocational Behaviour*, 72, pp 264-82.

Payne, S. (1997) 'Poverty and mental health', in D. Gordon and C. Pantazis (eds) *Breadline Britain in the 1990s*, Bristol: Summerleaze House Books, pp 159-77.

Payne, S. (2006) 'Mental health, poverty and social exclusion', in C. Pantazis, D. Gordon and R. Levitas (eds) *Poverty and social exclusion in Britain*, Bristol: The Policy Press, pp 285-311.

POST (Parliamentary Office of Science and Technology) (2011) 'Housing and health', *POSTNOTE No. 371*, Houses of Parliament: London, pp 1-4.

Runciman, W. G. (1966), *Relative deprivation and social justice*, London: Routledge.

Saito, M., Kondo, K., Kondo, N., Abe, A., Ojima, T., Suzuki, K. and the JAGES group (2014) 'Relative deprivation, poverty, and subjective health: JAGES cross-sectional study', *PLoS ONE*, 9(10), e111169.

Santana, P. (2002) 'Poverty, social exclusion and health in Portugal', *Social Science and Medicine*, 55, pp 33-45.

SEU (Social Exclusion Unit) (2004) *Mental health and social exclusion. Social Exclusion Unit Report Summary*, London: Office of the Deputy Prime Minister.

Smith, K. E., Hill, S. and Bambra, C. (eds) (2016) *Health inequalities: Critical perspectives*, Oxford: Oxford University Press.

Stewart, M., Reutter, L., Makwarimba, E., Veenstra, G., Love, R. and Raphael, D. (2008) 'Left out: perspectives on social exclusion and inclusion across income groups', *Health Sociology Reviews*, 17:1, pp 78-94.

Stuckler, D. and Basu, S. (2013) *The body economic: Why austerity kills*, Allen Lane: London.

Townsend, P., Davidson, N. and Whitehead, M. (1992) *Inequalities in health: The Black Report and the health divide* (2nd edn), London: Penguin Books.

Urbanos-Garrido, R. M. and Lopez-Valcarcel, B. G. (2015) 'The influence of the economic crisis on the association between unemployment and health: an empirical analysis for Spain', *European Journal of Health Economics*, 16, 175-84.

Warren, J. R. (2009) 'Socioeconomic status and health across the life course: a test of the social causation and health selection hypotheses', *Social Forces*, 87(4), pp 2125-54.

Webber, D. J., Page, D., Veliziotis, M. and Johnson, S. (2015) *Does poor health affect employment transitions? Joseph Rowntree Foundation report*, Bristol: University of the West of England.

WHO (World Health Organisation) (2008) *Closing the gap in a generation: Health equity through action on the social determinants of health. Final Report of the Commission on Social Determinants of Health*, World Health Organisation: Geneva.

WHO (World Health Organisation) (2015) *World health statistics 2015*, World Health Organisation: Geneva.

WHO (World Health Organisation) (2016), *Global Health Observatory (GHO): Disability-Adjusted Life Years (DALYs)*, www.who.int/gho/mortality_burden_disease/daly_rates/text/en/.

NINE

Housing and the living environment

Glen Bramley

Introduction

In the post-war British welfare state, housing was seen as one of the key sources of welfare, primarily through the vehicle of public housing but also through regulation of rents and standards and, increasingly, through the provision of Housing Benefits and Allowances. However, more recently, housing has been characterised as 'the wobbly pillar' of the welfare state, not least because of the increasingly market-dominated system of housing provision in UK and many other countries (Torgesen, 1987). Yet, for a number of reasons, housing can still be argued to be critical: some core housing conditions remain among the most universally supported of the 'essentials of life'; housing and related utility costs are a key driver of adverse patterns and changes in living standards; housing tenure is key to people's sense of security and control; and the state of the local neighbourhood is a major influence on people's quality of life. This chapter will discuss measures of housing (in)adequacy or housing need, and report on how these deprivations are associated with core and wider measures of poverty. It will look at changes over time, particularly since the 1999 PSE survey but also referring to analyses of UK longitudinal surveys (Bramley, 2016). Some of the key changes in the housing market, particularly in the balance of tenures, rent and price levels, will be discussed in terms of their impacts on housing-related aspects of poverty.

One particular housing-related issue is the cost of energy required to keep the home adequately warm and free from damp or related health-threatening problems. Given the combination of a relatively energy-inefficient housing stock and a dramatic rise in energy costs since the mid-2000s, 'fuel poverty' has become a massively bigger issue, contributing significantly to the deterioration in several housing-related material deprivations since 1999. However, changes in the measurement of fuel poverty have arguably obscured this significant policy failure. A later section of this chapter discusses fuel poverty.[1]

The neighbourhood dimension of the living environment has an important impact on people's quality of life, and hence indirectly on their health and well-being, as well as influencing their ability to access services, build social networks, and feel safe from crime or anti-social behaviour. The last part of the chapter will review the extent to which people report neighbourhood environmental and social problems, comparing socio-demographic groups and geographic area types. In particular, it will examine whether 'the poor' experience these problems more, and whether it is worse to be poor in a poor area.

Affordability and housing-related poverty changes

We may first consider what had been happening to housing affordability over the decade or so leading up to 2012, and how this relates to poverty. In addition to the two standard relative low-income poverty measures ('at risk of poverty', or AROP, before and after housing cost), we refer to two affordability indicators: (a) the proportion of households who are relatively poor (below 60 per cent of the median) *after* housing costs (AHC) but *not before* housing costs (BHC);[2] and (b) the ratio of housing costs to net income (Bramley, 2012 discusses affordability measures). Lastly we also consider change in the PSE poverty measure based on material deprivation. Figure 9.1 provides a summary of changes over this period in these measures for three main demographic groups.

The story is generally one of worsening housing affordability, particularly for working-age households. For all households and tenures, the proportion who are poor AHC but not BHC rose from 7.2 per cent in 1999 to 8.9 per cent in 2012, while the housing-cost-to-net-income ratio rose from 17.5 per cent to 24.3 per cent. In the early 2000s, these indicators fell, before rising back up to exceed their 1999 levels. Over the 13 years these increases affected families in particular, although the second measure increased for other working age as well, while pensioners saw a fall in the first measure and stability in the second. Affordability appeared to have improved *within* private renting on both measures, but the absolute rates in this tenure were higher throughout, so the large increase in the proportion of households in this tenure contributed to the overall worsening.

In this period, BHC poverty fell for families and especially for pensioners, but rose for other working-age households. AHC poverty fell by more for pensioners, while remaining static for families and rising for other working-age households. Our preferred PSE poverty

Figure 9.1: Changes in poverty risk and affordability problems, and PSE poverty by household type, 1999-2012

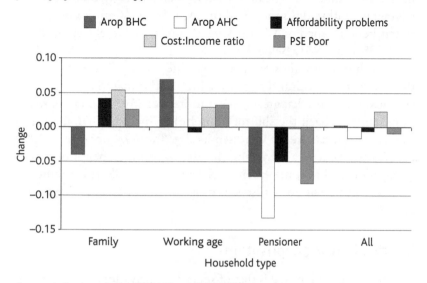

Source: Author's analysis of PSE-UK and FRS/HBAI data

measure, based on material deprivation as well as income, shows a strong pattern of rises in deprivation for families and working-age households, but falls for pensioners overall and in all tenures except private renting. The largest rise was for families in private renting, and looking at the tenures overall the largest rise was for private renting. This more adverse picture for poverty based on material deprivation reflects economic trends affecting living standards in this period, with living standards almost stationary in the mid-1990s and falling sharply between 2008 and 2011. The standard relative poverty measures do not pick up such adverse movements in absolute living standards, particularly when (as in this period) benefits were still indexed to inflation.

The analysis does show that housing costs play some part in explaining the adverse changes in living standards and poverty in Britain in this period, but these may not be the whole story. Other living cost factors, including fuel costs, are probably important. There is also a strong and uncomfortable story of a worsening position for working-age, non-family households (Aldridge et al, 2012). Policy has appeared to favour families, in trying to tackle child poverty, but these efforts have not succeeded in preventing a rise in material deprivation. The group which has really been favoured are pensioners, who benefit from the introduction of Pension Credits to top up state pensions, the availability of generous occupational pensions for the cohort who have now retired, the spread of owner occupation (free of mortgage payments) within this group, and the availability of other non-means tested benefits such as Winter Fuel Payments (Belfield et al, 2015: pp 34-35 and 46-51; Belfield et al, 2016: pp 58-60).

The other significant story here is private renting. It is not so much the rise in rents within the sector which is the main factor, as these rises have not been that great (except more recently in London). More important has been the shift of households (including families) into the sector as it has greatly increased its size (from 9.4 per cent in 1999 to 17.3 per cent of all dwellings in 2011), at the expense of owner occupation and to some extent social renting. While affordability in private renting has not worsened, more of the poor now live in this tenure.

Specific housing deprivations

The next topic addressed is that of specific deprivations and problems with housing itself, which might be termed 'housing needs', or rather shortfalls in housing conditions relative to general standards. The first group of indicators are housing deprivations, which are counted within the PSE's general material deprivation index. This small group of indicators have been included within the PSE and predecessor *Breadline Britain* surveys because they are among the items which very large majorities of people in Britain agree should be regarded as necessities. Table 9.1 shows values for the incidence of these over successive poverty surveys.

It is clear from this analysis that most of these problems have become more prevalent in the period 1999-2012, and in some cases they are worse in 2012 than they were even 30 years ago. The sharpest increase has been in the inability to afford to heat the home adequately to keep

Table 9.1: Proportion of households experiencing housing deprivations which are counted within general material deprivation index

Housing standards	1983	1990	1999	2012
Heating to keep home adequately warm (%)	5	3	3	9
Damp-free home (%)	6	2	7	10
Enough bedrooms for children (families) (%)	10		7	9
Keep home decently decorated (%)			15	20

Note: Housing deprivations which are agreed to be necessities by majority; proportion who lack item because they cannot afford it.

warm. The underlying factor here, rising fuel costs, is documented in a later section.

A second group of problems are covered by other housing-related questions asked in both 1999 and 2012 surveys, as shown in Table 9.2. Here the general picture is that there has been a deterioration in most indicators, although some have moved in a more favourable direction (for example, rot in doors and window frames) and some, such as disrepair, have been static. Leaks, damp and mould/condensation have all worsened considerably, and these are likely to impact adversely on health conditions (the latter two relating, again, to fuel poverty). Problems with payments for rent/mortgage and fuel costs, reflected in debt and arrears, have got considerably worse, reflecting the affordability changes discussed in the 'Introduction' section and part of a wider picture of financial stress discussed in Chapter 11. Crowding as reported in Table 9.1 solely refers to families with children. Crowding across all households has become more prevalent recently, as shown in Table 9.2 and confirmed in official statistics from the English Housing Survey and from the 2011 Census (Fitzpatrick et al, 2016, section 4.5).

Table 9.2: Proportion of households experiencing other housing-related problems in 1999 and 2012

Housing problem	1999 (%)	2012 (%)
Very dissatisfied with home	1.7	2.3
Poor state of repair	5.7	5.9
Any problem with accommodation, of which:	43.1	49.0
– too dark, not enough light	5.2	4.6
– inadequate heating*	6.6	7.7
– leaky roof	3.7	5.6
– damp	8.3	14.6
– rot	11.1	6.7
– mould/condensation*	5.9	11.1
– no place to sit outside	6.7	5.6
Five or more of accommodation problems above	1.4	3.9
In debt for rent, mortgage	3.8	6.8
In debt for utility bills	4.2	7.4
Cutting down on gas, elect*	10.3	21[†]

Notes:

* items subject to some change in wording or definition.

[†] 21% is most comparable measure ('Turned heating down or off, even though it was too cold in the house/flat'); any of 7 more specific ways of saving fuel were mentioned by 45%.

Housing needs: incidence over time

We can get confirmatory evidence of recent trends in housing needs by referring to Bramley (2016) based on analysis of the UK Household Longitudinal Surveys (now Understanding Society). Figure 9.2 summarises changes over five time periods in measures which were comparable. Three indicators showed general declines until the mid-2000s, followed by rises in 2009/11; one (affordability) started to rise from 2006, while the concealed families indicator rose at an increasing rate over the whole period. While all of the most recent rates are higher by statistically significant margins, it should be noted that the Understanding Society survey has some technical differences from its predecessor. Nevertheless, other sources such as the Census and several national surveys confirm these upward trends (ONS, 2014b; Fitzpatrick et al, 2016, section 4.5).

Bramley (2016) also showed that house condition problems, the largest category, had shown a marked longer term reduction up to 2006-08, as had some types of unsuitability, but that sharing and lack of amenities had increased, probably due to the rise in private renting.

We can go on to build from the PSE survey data for 2012 a picture of the incidence of housing need shortfalls in terms of a set of general

Figure 9.2: Selected housing needs incidence by time period, GB 1991-2011

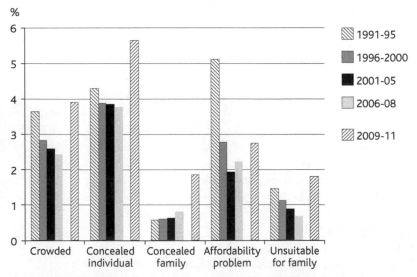

Source: Author's analysis of UK Household Longitudinal Surveys (BHPS & UKHLS), reproduced from Bramley 2016

categories, by combining information across a range of questions. Four core categories of housing need are defined as set out below.

- **affordability or insecurity problems**: likely to move in 1-2 years because cannot afford or due to eviction, repossession or end of tenancy; or in debt/arrears on mortgage, rent or fuel bills;
- **health- or disability-related housing problems**: likely to move in 1-2 years for health, disability, mobility reasons; or accommodation problems made existing health problem worse or brought on new health problem;
- **house condition problems**: poor state of repair of home, or cannot afford heating to keep home adequately warm, or cannot afford a damp-free home;
- **crowding affecting children**: not having enough bedrooms for children over 10 of different sex to have separate bedrooms.

This analysis of housing need follows a similar structure to that used in the official study for England (Bramley et al, 2010) and based mainly on English Housing Survey data for the period 1997-2007. Figure 9.3 shows the incidence of these core housing need in PSE-UK 2012 across broad household types and tenure.

Affordability/security problems affect nearly 12 per cent of all households (see note to Figure 9.3), with much higher incidence in both rental tenures and for families and other working-age households compared with older households. Housing-related health problems affect nearly 7 per cent of all households; again incidence is higher in the rental tenures, but this time incidence is somewhat higher for older households, as expected. House condition problems affect nearly 18 per cent of all households; again, the rental tenures are much worse, with this time private renting rather worse for working-age and older households and overall, although social renting families also have a high incidence. Of all owners 10 per cent, but as many as 16 per cent of family owners, are affected. Although disrepair in owner occupation is commonly seen as a particular problem for older households, that is not really reflected in these figures.

Overcrowding as measured here mainly affects families, and is notably high in social renting at 16 per cent of families, compared with only 8.1 per cent for all families or 2.4 per cent for all households. The broader category of 'other housing problems' (not included in these Figures) affects 21 per cent of all households, while rising to 51 per cent of all social renting families. Concealed potential households may be present in 3 per cent of all households, rising to

Figure 9.3: Core housing needs by broad household type and tenure, UK 2012

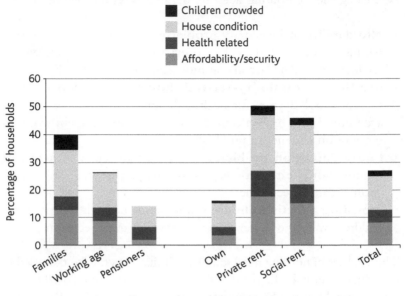

Note: Incidence of individual need types scaled down to discount overlap between needs, so that total bar height represents proportion experiencing any of these needs.

Source: Author's analysis of PSE-UK data

5.6 per cent of working-age owner occupiers, and it is noteworthy that this type of housing need is as prevalent in owner occupation as in renting tenures.

More than a quarter of all households have a core housing need of some sort, on this basis, but this rises to 40 per cent of all families, whereas only 14 per cent of elderly households are affected. The highest value is the 68 per cent for families in social renting. On the broader measure, 33 per cent of all households are affected. These figures are of the same order of magnitude as the proportion of households affected by multiple material deprivations – but they are not necessarily the same households.

The regional figures (not shown) confirm the concentration in London, particularly of affordability problems and crowding. That is no surprise given the spatial structure of the UK housing market. The North of England shows rather higher incidence than the South, Midlands or rest of UK. Of the other UK countries, Scotland shows the lowest overall housing needs, with better than average scores for each component except crowding, while Northern Ireland shows a slightly less favourable picture than the overall UK average.

Housing and welfare regimes

A broad view of the British welfare and housing systems would, in recent years, have been that the combination of a larger social rented sector and a comprehensive benefit system, including housing costs (for renters), has tended to weaken the link between poverty and housing needs (Bradshaw et al, 2008; Stephens et al, 2010). However, the PSE results (for example, Figures 9.1 and 9.3) suggest that this characterisation may no longer be so apposite. One striking finding from this evidence is that, in many cases, the worst-off group for housing need shortfalls is in fact social renters, particularly families in that sector. This is a cause for concern, because traditionally we would expect to see social renting as part of 'the solution' rather than as 'the problem'. The underlying explanation must be, in substantial measure, that the process of 'residualisation' of the social rented sector has led to it housing a high concentration of the poorest households. Such households are likely to be struggling financially and are therefore vulnerable to problems of debt and inability to afford fuel costs as well as housing costs themselves. The pressure on the sector, from demographic change and limited supply, is likely to have exacerbated these problems. The regional pattern tends to confirm this contention, by showing the higher incidence of needs in the most pressured region.

We can examine these propositions further using both PSE and longitudinal survey data. Firstly, we can look in PSE at the numbers of households experiencing various combinations of poverty and core housing need. Only 54 per cent of households experience none of these problems. A relatively small group demonstrate the independence of housing need from poverty, the 6.4 per cent who have a housing need but are not poor in either sense (income or material deprivation). Around 20 per cent, however, exemplify situations of households who are poor but who do not have core housing needs (that is, they could be said to have adequate housing). This is the same as the proportion who do exemplify the overlap or coincidence of poverty and housing need. This evidence seems to support the view that the UK housing system still protects the poor, to a considerable degree, from housing problems, which are clearly far from inevitable.

Bramley (2016) presents an analysis of the incidence of a rather similar housing need definition across England over a period of 12 years (1996–2008), distinguishing households who could afford to buy a home in their local market (and thus by implication move to solve their problem), by poverty status. This showed that the declines in need overall were mainly in the category of those who could buy, whereas the core group who were involuntarily in need tended to increase; and also that poverty greatly increased the risk of housing need, notably in the case of combined low income and material deprivation. This evidence suggested some tendency, within this period, for the association between poverty and housing need to increase.

Lack of space prevents full reporting of more detailed statistical modelling of housing need,[3] although it is worth mentioning some particular highlights. These models utilise binary logistic regression to predict the odds of individual households having any of the core housing needs discussed here. In general, the findings confirm the strong influence of poverty, especially material deprivation; when this is included as an explanatory variable, it has a very powerful effect, raising the odds of housing need by 6.5 times – this displaces much of the explanation associated with the income variables, and underlines that 'PSE poverty' is probably a better measure of real poverty than relative low income. In addition, this strong association underlines findings from the broader analyses of the patterns of social exclusion reported in Chapter 13, where it is shown that 'housing' deprivation is closely associated with economic deprivation.

The adverse effects of both rental tenures remain in these models, even when controlling for a wide range of other effects. The models also show that deprivation and housing needs are not simply generated by low income, but also that they are compounded by employment status (unemployment, workless households, larger households with fewer in work), lower occupational/qualification status, disability and poor physical and/or mental health conditions. The models confirm that certain demographic groups (larger households, female-headed, young) are more vulnerable while others (married, older households) seem to be more protected, although it should be noted that ethnic variables were not significant. Finally, the differences between the models suggest that some elements of housing need are driven by somewhat different factors, such as the level of house prices in the relevant market area.

The models as summarised here are essentially cross-sectional, although it is sometimes possible to include past experiences or conditions. Further analysis of longitudinal data such as UKHLS or birth cohort studies may help to strengthen conclusions about which factors are more clearly causal and which may be more coincidental or reflective of 'selection effects'.

Fuel poverty

Fuel poverty is a major issue in its own right, as well as being connected to some housing deprivations and financial problems. Although the UK government has had a target of eradicating fuel poverty by 2016, it is clear that this target has been missed by a large margin, and also that there are major differences in how this should be measured.[4] The traditional measure of fuel poverty was those households whose required fuel costs (applying a standard heating regime to their existing house) exceeded 10 per cent of their income. Although this measure was crude in some respects, it gave a reasonable and robust picture of the problem, and all the UK countries other than England still use it. For Scotland, this showed a rise in fuel poverty from 16 per cent in 2003 to 34 per cent in 2009, followed by some fluctuations (and definitional refinements) around a level of around 35 per cent. The key driver here has been the disproportionate rise in real domestic energy prices since the mid-2000s, with an 85 per cent real terms increase in 2003-14 (DECC ,2016, p 21). A new and apparently more sophisticated measure, the 'Low Income High Cost' index, was introduced in England, following the report by Hills (2012). However, this measure can be criticised for (a) producing some perverse results (for example, insulating all houses would not solve fuel poverty) while (b) seemingly discounting the effects of rising real fuel costs since the mid-2000s (Gordon, 2014). This results from the use of purely relative standards (if everybody's fuel costs double, the proportion below the median remains the same).

The inherited UK housing stock has generally had a low level of energy efficiency, and although considerable investment has been made in improving energy efficiency through better heating systems and more insulation (by 28 per cent between 2003 and 2014 [DECC, 2016, p 19]), this has not been sufficient to prevent the overall deterioration. Poorer households are not automatically protected from the effects by the benefit system, because fuel costs are not directly reflected in Housing Benefit, although they may be reflected in the price indices used for benefit uprating. Inadequate heating and the associated housing condition problems cause significant health problems, particularly for older and other vulnerable people, and the UK's poor performance in this respect is argued to be reflected in its high level of 'excess winter deaths' (at 43,900 in 2015-16, the highest this century [End Fuel Poverty Coalition, 2015]).

We can make limited comparisons with the PSE 1999 Survey, as Table 9.2 showed. Households in debt or arrears with their fuel bills have risen from 4.2 per cent in 1999 to 7.2 per cent in 2012. Households using less fuel because they cannot afford it have risen from just over 10 per cent to at least 21 per cent, and possibly as much as 45 per cent, depending on the measures taken to cut back on fuel. Households with inadequate heating systems have risen slightly, from 6.6 per cent to 7.7 per cent. However, as noted above, housing problems related to insufficient heating have risen dramatically, with damp rising from 8.3 per cent to 14.6 per cent and mould/condensation rising from 5.9 per cent to 11.1 per cent.

The PSE-UK survey does not enable us to generate conventional fuel poverty measures and hence we cannot directly resolve or contribute to the debate about target measures and how they may have changed over time. However, PSE does include some specific subjective and behavioural measures of people's experience of and response to the problem of heating their homes. These include a question on the level of warmth in the home last winter ('a lot colder/a bit colder than would have liked'), a question on whether and how they cut back on fuel last winter because they could not afford the costs, and a question on whether coldness affected household members' health, well-being, social activities or time spent at home or in bed. The responses provide a picture of some of the ways people were affected by fuel poverty, although the effects may also be displaced into other areas such as debt/arrears or skimping on other things like food or clothes. We can also combine them into indicators of subjective/behavioural 'fuel poverty'.

Of all households, 10 per cent were 'much colder' than they would have liked in the previous winter, but this rate was 29 per cent for PSE poor households, a risk ratio of nearly 3. Twenty-five per cent were 'a bit colder', rising to 33 per cent of the PSE poor. The 'much colder' rate was 26 per cent for the relative low-income poor (AHC), but no less than 52 per cent for the 'severely poor' (as defined in Chapter 3). The most common economising measures relating to fuel were to cut the number of 'heating-on' hours (28 per cent of all households, 45 per cent of the PSE poor), turn heating down/off although 'too cold' (45 per cent of poor), turn out more lights (38 per cent), and only heat/use part of the house (26 per cent).

It is clear that cold due to inadequate/unaffordable heating has adverse impacts on health and wellbeing. Ten per cent of all households, and 27 per cent of the PSE poor, reported that this made them feel anxious or depressed, while 15 per cent of the poor said it made an existing health problem worse, and 8 per cent said it brought on a new health problem for a household member. It is also clear that this problem curtailed daily living and social activities, with 20 per cent of the poor staying in bed longer, 13 per cent unable to invite friends round, and 8 per cent spending more time away from the home.

We have constructed composite indicators of problems from these data, a narrower core measure and a wider measure.

- **core fuel poverty impact**: households who were 'much colder' last winter, who cut back in more significant ways (turned heating down/off although too cold, less hot water or hot meals/drinks), and who were adversely affected in terms of either health or social activity;
- **wider fuel poverty impact**: includes the above plus households who were a bit colder and who cut back on fuel in any way, and who experienced adverse health/social effects or any debts/arrears on bills or who cut back/skimped on food or clothing.

The former core impact group comprises 5 per cent of all households, but 17 per cent of the PSE poor, whereas the wider impact affects 15 per cent of all households and 41 per cent of the PSE poor. Figure 9.4 shows the steep progression of both of these impact measures of fuel poverty as you move through households with financial pressures (as defined in Chapter 11), households who are PSE poor, and those who are severely poor (as defined in Chapter 3). The core measure

Figure 9.4: Core and wider fuel poverty impact by severity of poverty or financial pressure

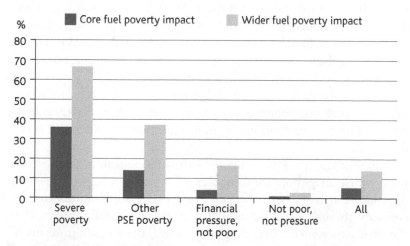

Source: Author's analysis of PSE-UK data

of fuel poverty impact is ten times higher for PSE poor households than for the non-poor, while the wider measure is six times higher.

This evidence underlines both the seriousness of the impacts of fuel poverty and their strong relationships with poverty.

Neighbourhood environment

While fuel poverty focuses on the environment within the home, the surrounding neighbourhood environment is also an important aspect of the housing experience and the quality of life which people enjoy and which contributes to their health and well-being. The PSE-UK survey asks standard questions on satisfaction with the neighbourhood as a place to live and also asks householders whether each of 16 common neighbourhood issues is a problem in this area. Rather than focus on individual problems, it is perhaps most helpful to group these together into three broad categories:

- **environmental problems**, such as poor lighting, potholes, lack of open spaces, illegal parking, graffiti, rubbish/litter, dogs/mess, poorly maintained homes and gardens, or vandalism;
- **pollution**, in the forms of noise, air quality or traffic hazards;
- **social problems**, such as joy riding, drunkenness, drug dealing/ use, harassment, or general dissatisfaction.

These are scored by counting the number mentioned as a proportion of the maximum possible, with overall scores around 0.065 for social, 0.095 for pollution and 0.15 for environmental. There are some differences between countries, with Scotland scoring worse than England on social and environment but better on pollution, while Wales and Northern Ireland score better on all domains. Figure 9.5 looks at these scores across the urban–rural and poor–non-poor dimensions, both individual and area-based.

It is perhaps only to be expected that rural areas will score better than urban on these neighbourhood problems, although it is interesting to note that on the (perceptions of) pollution issue the difference is not that great.

With regard to poverty, while the primary question is 'do the poor suffer worse neighbourhood problems?', there is a further question of whether it is worse to be poor in a poor neighbourhood. It is certainly the case, in 2012 as it was in previous PSE surveys, that the poor experience worse neighbourhoods, particularly in terms of social problems (three times worse) but also pollution (1.7 times) and

Figure 9.5: Neighbourhood problem scores by urban, rural, individual and area poverty levels

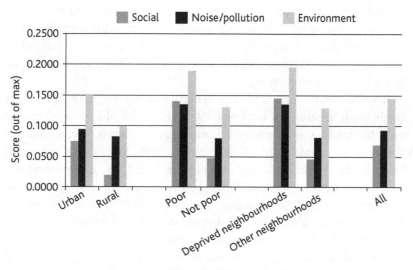

Source: Author's analysis of PSE-UK data

environment (1.5 times). This is equally true whether measuring for poor households or poor neighbourhoods. With regard to the second question, it is clearly worse to be poor in the poor neighbourhoods, so far as the experience of neighbourhood problems is concerned – double the incidence of social problems and one-third more of the pollution and environmental problems. So concentrated poverty may contribute to neighbourhood problems, and this may make such neighbourhoods unattractive to the non-poor, but poor people themselves suffer disproportionately from the adverse impacts.

Conclusion

This chapter has demonstrated that housing conditions and costs are important factors in overall living standards as well as material poverty. They also impact more widely on health and quality of life.

Housing affordability and poverty both partly reflect changes in real household income levels, which grew only sluggishly up to 2007 before falling in the post-2008 crisis period. Indicators of housing unaffordability increased between 1999 and 2012, although this deterioration was concentrated in the later part of this period. Falls in BHC poverty were partially offset by higher housing costs, making for adverse changes in AHC poverty for families and working-age households. Although these ratios did not increase within the private rented sector, because the level is higher within this tenure and the scale of private renting increased dramatically, this also contributed to the overall deterioration. Pensioner households saw an overall fall in AHC poverty and affordability issues, while working-age, non-family households saw an increase.

A similar but stronger picture emerges when we look at changes in material deprivation between 1999 and 2012. There were strong rises for families and other working-age households, but reductions for pensioner households. Core housing costs are part of this story, but rises in real living costs, particularly fuel costs, exacerbated the deterioration in living standards. However, pensioners were more protected from these changes, thanks to more favourable benefit rates, occupational pensions, and more widespread owner occupation generally free of mortgage commitments.

Some of the increase in material deprivation is directly attributable to housing items in the list of essentials (adequate heating, damp-free homes, bedrooms for children), which all deteriorated markedly in this period. It was not just housing items which increased, although for some items like clothing there was more stability. A wider set of housing problems also displayed a general picture of worsening over this period, as did measures of social exclusion and financial insecurity.

The PSE-UK survey data can be used to present measures of housing need shortfalls in 2012. These are clearly much more prevalent in the rental tenures, and in most cases less prevalent for older households. A quarter of all households have some housing needs, rising to a third on a somewhat wider definition of problems. Needs are highest in London, where market pressures are greatest, but also quite high in 'poor' regions like the North East, and much higher in poor neighbourhoods, while being generally lower in Scotland.

The view that the British housing and welfare system partially protects the poor from having poor housing as well as other forms of deprivation is somewhat challenged by the evidence that needs incidence is greatest in social renting and in poor neighbourhoods. However, it is still true that a proportion of needs is suffered by households who are not poor or materially deprived, while half of poor/deprived households do not experience housing need shortfalls. However, models to predict housing needs show that poverty (especially if confirmed by material deprivation) is strongly associated with needs.

Fuel poverty is partly related to housing quality and condition, but the biggest influence recently has been the large rise in energy costs. This has led to a significant worsening, notwithstanding some official measures which appear to suggest otherwise, making a nonsense of the target of eradicating fuel poverty by 2016. Composite measures of the adverse impact of fuel poverty (on health, social activities, well-being, financial stress and hardship) show that the poor are between six and ten times more likely to experience these.

It remains true that the poor experience worse neighbourhoods, particularly in terms of social problems but also pollution and environment, and it is clearly worse, in this as well as other respects, to be poor in a poor neighbourhood.

Notes

[1] The impact of fuel poverty on one particular vulnerable group is discussed by Patsios (2017).

[2] This measure is effectively the difference between the two relative low income 'AROP' measures.

[3] PSE-based models for housing need and poverty were reported in Bramley and Besemer 2013, while models based on the British Household Panel Survey are reported in Bramley, 2016.

[4] These issues were underlined in a very telling *Panorama* documentary 'Too poor to stay warm' first broadcast on BBC1 in March 2016 (http://www.bbc.co.uk/news/magazine-35834733).

References

Aldridge, H., Kenway, P., MacInnes, T. and Parekh, A. (2012) *Monitoring poverty and social exclusion 2012*, York: Joseph Rowntree Foundation and New Policy Institute.

Belfield, C., Cribb, J., Hood, A. and Joyce, R. (2015) *Living standards, poverty and inequality in the UK: 2015*, London: Institute for Fiscal Studies.

Belfield, C., Cribb, J., Hood, A. and Joyce, R. (2016) *Living standards, poverty and inequality in the UK: 2016*, London: Institute for Fiscal Studies.

Bradshaw, J., Chzehn, Y. and Stephens, M. (2008) 'Housing: the saving grace in the British welfare state?', in S. Fitzpatrick and M. Stephens (eds) *The future of social housing*, London: Shelter.

Bramley, G. (2012) 'Affordability, poverty and housing need: triangulating measures and standards', *Journal of Housing and the Built Environment*, 27(2): 133-51.

Bramley, G. (2016) 'Housing need outcomes in England through changing times: demographic, market and policy drivers of change', *Housing Studies*, 31:3, 243-68.

Bramley, G. and Besemer, K. (2013) 'The role of housing in the impoverishment of Britain', *Conference Paper, Workshop 03*, June 2013, European Network for Housing Research Conference, Tarragona, Spain.

Bramley, G., Pawson, H., Pleace, N., Watkins, D. and White, M. (2010) *Estimating housing need*, London: Communities and Local Government.

DECC (Department of Energy and Climate Change) (2016) *Annual Fuel Poverty Statistics Report*, www.gov.uk/decc.

End Fuel Poverty Coalition (2015) 'Winter deaths surge', News release, 26 November 2016, http://www.endfuelpoverty.org.uk/winter-deaths-surge/.

Fitzpatrick, S., Pawson, H., Bramley, G., Wilcox, S. and Watts, B. (2016) *The homelessness monitor: England 2016*, London: CRISIS.

Gordon, D. (2014) 'Fuel poverty in Scotland'. Presentation to Poverty and Social Exclusion in Scotland and the UK, http://www.poverty.ac.uk/take-part/events/Scotland-conference.

Gordon, D. et al (2013) *The impoverishment of the UK: PSE UK first results: Living standards*, http://www.poverty.ac.uk/pse-research/pse-uk-reports.

Hills, J. (2012) *Getting the measure of fuel poverty. Final report of the Fuel Poverty Review*. CASE Report 72, London: Centre for Analysis of Social Exclusion, London School of Economics.

Levitas, R., Pantazis, C., Gordon, D., Lloyd, E. and Patsios, D. (2010) *The multi-dimensional analysis of social exclusion*, Report by Bristol University to Department of Communities and Local Government, Bristol: University of Bristol.

ONS (2014a) *Large increase in 20 to 34 year olds living with parents since 1996*, http://www.ons.gov.uk/ons/rel/family-demography/young-adults-living-with-parents/2013/sty-young-adults.html.

ONS (2014b) *What does the 2011 Census tell us about concealed families living in multi-family households in England and Wales*, www.ons.gov.uk

Pantazis, C., Gordon, D. and Levitas, R. (2006) *Poverty and social exclusion in Britain: The Millennium Survey*, Bristol: Policy Press.

Patsios, D. (2017) 'Poverty and social exclusion among older people', in E. Dermott and G. Main (eds) *Poverty and social exclusion in the UK: Vol. 1 – The extent and nature of the problem*, Bristol: Policy Press.

Stephens, M., Fitzpatrick, S., Elsinga, M., Steen, G. V. and Chzhen, Y. (2010) *Study on housing exclusion: Welfare policies, labour market and housing provision*, Brussels: European Commission.

Torgesen, U. (1987) 'Housing: the wobbly pillar under the welfare state', in J. Kemeny, B. Turner and L. Lindqvist (eds) *Between state and market: Housing in the post-industrial era*, Stockholm: Angqvist and Wiksell, pp 116-28.

TEN

Poverty and social harm: challenging discourses of risk, resilience and choice

Simon Pemberton, Christina Pantazis and Paddy Hillyard

Introduction

In recent years interest has grown in the concept of social harm as a form of social enquiry that can provide accurate and systematic analyses of injury in late capitalist societies (see Hillyard et al, 2004; Pemberton, 2015). A key concern of this approach has been to contextualise harm and to consider the forms of injury that have the greatest social impact. In doing so, it has sought to build a more sophisticated picture of the lived reality of injury focusing, for example, on the interrelated nature of harm, its social patterning, and how harms accumulate across the life course from the 'cradle to the grave'. One of the principal motivations driving this work is to foreground structural harms within social science analysis, to understand the varied ways that the organisation of societies serves to injuriously compromise human flourishing.

Poverty constitutes one of the most significant forms of harm in contemporary Britain in terms of its scale and severity. According to the PSE method, one quarter of citizens in the United Kingdom are poor (see the Introduction) and are therefore likely to experience increased vulnerability to a range of injuries: reduced life expectancy (see also Thomas et al, 2010); life-limiting illnesses (Chapter 8); lower levels of educational achievement (Bradshaw, 2002) and so on. The point is, poverty as a condition deleteriously impacts physical well-being, desired forms of human flourishing, social participation and the formation of meaningful relationships, as well as providing a context in which related harms are experienced. Yet it is seldom that social science analyses consider the injuries of poverty in the round. Rather, focus tends to fall on the discrete aspects of harm. However, without a fully articulated concept of harm, the lived realities of poverty, the limits that poverty imposes on individuals, and how it shapes individuals' responses to the circumstances in which they find themselves, can only be partially understood.

This chapter investigates poverty as both a structural outcome and a process; as a harmful state and a generative context in which related harms are experienced. Moreover, poverty is viewed as a 'structural symptom' of capitalist societies where the underlying organisation of these societies serves to maldistribute resources and respect in equal measure. It is argued that recent trends in both academic and policy discourses have seen the structural features of poverty either airbrushed out of discussions or remain implicit, rather than being explicitly articulated. The value of a social harm lens is that it allows for a better understanding of the ways in which individuals' lives are injuriously compromised through the structural constraints that limited resources place on the opportunities to flourish, rather than to simply exist. The chapter offers a contribution to understanding poverty as a phenomenon. In doing so, it highlights the limitations of three dominant discourses to the study of poverty which, respectively, emphasise risk, resilience and choice.

The **risk discourse** on poverty, which stems from the work of Beck (1992), assumes that injuries do not conform to a hierarchical logic. According to Beck the experience of harms is not patterned according to socio-economic position, and therefore individual biographies of risk navigation become the key element. Whilst the influence of the 'risk society' thesis on policy is particularly associated with the New Labour years, its legacy continues to shape academic and policy debates – particularly in relation to the placing responsibility on benefit claimants through 'active labour market' policies (see Olofsson et al, 2014).

The emergence of the **resilience discourse** within the social sciences owes much to the risk society thesis and focuses on how people adapt to pressures. Resilience, then, refers to a 'dynamic process encompassing positive adaption within the context of significant adversity' (Luthar et al, 2000: p 543). It has witnessed a considerable renaissance in the wake of the 2007-8 recession, with a particular policy focus on building adaptive capacity amongst the 'poor' and, alongside the 'Big Society', establishing resilience within communities (see Levitas, 2012; Andres and Round, 2015). In this conceptualisation, individuals are re-imagined as active agents who adapt to harm and use it as a positive catalyst, rather than being viewed as passive victims of poverty simply experiencing the associated injuries (see, for example, Batty and Cole, 2010; Davidson, 2008).

The third discourse conceives of poverty as a **lifestyle 'choice'** (see Pantazis, 2016). Following the credit crunch and the era of austerity, policy discourse has been dominated by behavioural accounts of poverty in which the idea of choice dominates. The Coalition government and the current (2015-17) Conservative administration have focused on nudging those people deemed to have made 'wrong choices', so consigning themselves and their families to a life on benefits (Wiggan, 2012; Pantazis, 2016), into making the 'right choices'. Universal Credit has been developed in order to provide an 'architecture of choice' (Standing, 2011), while technologies offered by the Cabinet Office's Behavioural Insights Team such as 'commitment devices' seek to re-programme benefits claimants into work (Standing, 2011). Thus, government policy has become focused on seeing poverty (alongside a host of other harms such as truancy, obesity) as a form of self- inflicted injury.

Whilst there are considerable differences between these discourses, it remains the case, we argue, that these approaches overstate the agency of those living in poverty. The question of structure and agency within poverty research is not new. There exists important work from the 1990s and early 2000s that thoughtfully sought to address overly deterministic accounts and tried to foreground the agency of those in poverty within the structural constraints imposed by low income (Beresford and Croft, 1995; Lister, 2003). Yet, as we have argued, the lessons of this work have been lost on current debates. The social harm approach offers an opportunity and potentially novel way to re-articulate the structural understandings of poverty.

In addressing these concerns, the chapter is divided into three principal parts. The first section outlines the social harm lens adopted for the purposes of this analysis and details the subsequent research design that drew on data from the Poverty and Social Exclusion-UK Living Standards 2012 survey (the 'PSE-UK survey') and the qualitative Life on a Low Income in Austere Times project, both part of the Poverty and Social Exclusion Study (see the Introduction). Drawing upon analysis of these data sources, the second section presents detailed empirical evidence on the extent and interrelated nature of the harms of poverty. The final section concludes by considering the implications of the data and analyses for understanding poverty and how these might challenge the portrayal of injury in the discourses of risk, resilience and choice.

Measuring the harms of poverty and understanding injurious consequences

Accurately documenting the harms of poverty requires a sufficiently broad notion of injury to encompass the varied and many ways that poverty compromises human flourishing and self-actualisation. Key to such a notion of human development is the satisfaction of a web of interrelated and identifiable human needs without which identifiable forms of injury arise (Doyal and Gough, 1991). Our analyses are guided by Pemberton's (2015) definition of social harm that identifies three categories of injury arising from the non-fulfilment of need: physical and mental health; autonomy; and relational.

Physical and mental well-being are necessary to be able to successfully pursue one's life goals, as well as being desirable end states in their own right (Doyal and Gough, 1991). This chapter will explore the ways in which material deprivation impacts on physical well-being (Pemberton 2015). In addition, it will examine the injuries that poverty inflicts in relation to mental well-being, principally through the financial strains and emotional pressures that are brought to bear on individuals as they attempt to make ends meet and negotiate the stigma of low income.

Autonomy harms result from the inability of individuals to lead lives of their own choosing and ultimately to realise self-actualisation in the forms they may desire (Pemberton, 2015). This is explored through the ways in which poverty curtails autonomy by restricting individuals' ability to exert control over key aspects of their lives. Being unable to influence decisions or exercise sufficient control over economic and social resources that facilitate life choices can feed injurious states of insecurity and powerlessness (Pemberton, 2015).

Relational harms result from the inability to facilitate and maintain positive relationships with others. The chapter considers two forms of injury in the context of poverty that result when 'being with others' is restricted. First, we will examine the ways that poverty serves to compromise the ability to maintain and nurture personal relationships, and how in doing so it leads to deleterious emotional states. Second, 'being with others' can be frustrated when individuals are unable to present their own identity in the way that they might choose. If 'public identities' are imposed on individuals by others within society, and presented as 'spoiled' or 'blemished', so that they are viewed as 'other' and therefore distinct from mainstream society, this can serve to harmfully marginalise (Goffman, 1963).

A social harm method

A mixed methods approach was developed in order to operationalise the harm categories detailed above. This chapter presents quantitative data from the PSE-UK survey to identify the prevalence and patterning of the harms of poverty alongside qualitative data gathered as part of the wider PSE study. Together, the data enable us to provide a detailed assessment of poverty as a 'social' injury and help us to better understand the implications of poverty not only as a harmful outcome in its own right but also as a process which produces a set of secondary harms. Full details of sampling and methods in relation to these studies are documented elsewhere (see the Introduction in relation to the survey and Pemberton et al (2014) in relation to the qualitative work).

The quantitative analysis is based on responses from 9,071 respondents who answered questions from the Harm, Crime and Criminalisation section of the survey, which was designed to capture the experience of physical and financial harms, as well as harms of misrecognition.[1] Other harm indicators from additional sections of the survey were utilised in order to capture as wide a range of social injuries as possible. The main measure of poverty ('PSE poverty') used in the analysis is based on the combination of deprivation and low income (see the Introduction for details). A series of crosstabulations with tests for statistical significance were conducted to map associations between the PSE-poor measure and specific harms – with an alternative low-income poverty measure used in relation to social participation to avoid spurious correlation (see the Introduction for details on measures). Analyses to test the influence of demographic factors were not possible due to the small numbers of survey participants experiencing many of the harms (survey questions limited the experience of harm to the last 12 months); similarly this precluded the use of regression models.

The chapter presents the quantitative results alongside the qualitative component of the PSE. Qualitative data were collected in the form of semi-structured testimonies from a purposive heterogeneous sample of 62 participants (female=38/male=24) living on low income in Birmingham (n=18), Glasgow (n=23), and Gloucestershire (n=21) during 2012-13. The sample had representation across the minority British ethnic categories (n=15) and the majority of participants (n=53) were unemployed. Recruitment for the study was facilitated through community and voluntary organisations working with people living on a low income. Data were coded according to injuries that reflect the threefold definition and subsequently analysed through a thematic framework approach (Ritchie and Lewis, 2003) using the

Atlas TI CADAQS package. From this initial coding frame, individual codes were reorganised through an explanatory phase of analysis, with codes ordered into overarching thematic containers that reflect the testimonies of participants and with the links and interrelationships between these codes subsequently built to reveal the cumulative and overlapping nature of these injuries. The empirical findings that follow reflect the outcome of an operationalisation of the social harm concept in this context. It was a conscious decision to allow the findings of the qualitative work to shape the thematic structure of the chapter from this point.

Documenting poverty harms

The physical injuries associated with poverty

Apart from curtailing life expectancy, poverty causes a number of physical and mental health injuries. It compromises physical health to such an extent that it often becomes impossible for people to lead lives of their own choosing (see Chapter 8). Alongside these direct injuries, poverty exposes individuals and households to a series of risks that result in a host of secondary harms. For example, poverty presents stark 'choices'. Many participants in the qualitative phase revealed they were regularly required to choose whether to 'heat or eat'. At the point this research was conducted, these choices were even starker. As Cribb et al (2015: 2) note, low-income households have been subject to 'higher-than average inflation since 2007–08', largely due to rising food and energy prices. However, as prices rose, incomes failed to recover from the recession. As Belfield et al (2014: 2) report, 'real median income in 2012/2013 was 5.8% below its 2009-2010 peak'. For participants the deleterious health consequences of these 'choices' or adaptive responses were clearly articulated, with many unable to sustain healthy diets or dietary plans necessary to manage long-term health conditions, or maintain damp-free and warm homes:

> 'I can't buy the nice branded stuff ... basic budget brands ... I tend to go to 'Iceland' [a budget supermarket] a lot because they do a lot of things for a pound ... it tends to end up being a lot of rubbish food, processed stuff, things I don't want to be eating and things I don't want my kids eating, but we have no choice really because it is cheaper.'
> (Lone parent, female, Gloucestershire)

'The cost of living in general has gone up. Obviously fuel ... that has had a big impact because I can't afford to heat my home sometimes. We have had times where we have had to sit with no heat, because that's how bad things are. In general it is pretty tough because of what is happening out there and you just can't seem to get by.'

(Lone parent, female, Birmingham)

This picture of poverty having negative repercussions on health is also supported by the survey data, which found that among respondents with a limiting long-term illness (LLTI) and living in poverty, nearly two-thirds (61 per cent) reported that their health over the previous 12 months was affected by a lack of money ($p<0.01$ level). The epidemiological literature appears to further support these observations. Take, for example, the impact of damp and cold housing. Whilst it has long been understood that 'excess winter deaths' are largely a result of thermally inefficient housing stock and fuel poverty – with currently an estimated 40,000 lives ending prematurely in the UK annually – recent studies have documented 'the enduring and potentially cumulative health effects ... associated with living in cold conditions ... which include increased risk of influenza, pneumonia, asthma, arthritis and accidents at home' (Liddell and Morris, 2010: 2988). Indeed, it is the cumulative physical impact of the 'heat or eat trade' that emerges strikingly from this literature. As Beatty et al (2014: 292) conclude, this *'trade ... may run down the stock of health capital and have medium to long term effects'*.

Poverty serves as a generative context for a range of secondary physical injuries. It increases the risk of physical injury in workplaces and home environments because physical harms are rarely random events but are more often socially patterned (see Table 10.1). Although relatively few respondents to the PSE-UK survey had experienced a physical harm in the last 12 months, the data shows that adults living in poverty were significantly more likely to experience physical harms such as a workplace injury (1.9 times as likely), or to have a health problem made worse by a medical intervention (2.4 times as likely). According to the existing literature, poverty increases vulnerability to unintentional physical harm. As Laflamme et al's (2010: 19) systematic review of unintentional injuries reveals, deprivation plays a key role in the experience and gravity of these injuries; insofar as the resources and items necessary 'to protect one's health and safety are socially distributed ... people of higher SES (Socio-Economic Status) hold an advantage in warding off threats to their — and their offspring's —

Table 10.1: Percent of adults experiencing physical harms in the previous 12 months

Physical harm	PSE poor	Not poor	All
***A workplace injury or illness, e.g. back injury/stress [†]	16.5	8.4	9.9
**An accident or injury around the home	6.8	4.3	4.9
A road traffic accident	3.3	4.1	3.9
***A health problem made worse as a result of medical advice or treatment, e.g. hospital infection, wrong treatment	5.9	2.5	3.3
***A physical attack by a stranger or acquaintance	5.6	1.2	2.1
***A physical attack (e.g., involving hitting, slapping, kicking) by a partner or ex-partner [‡]	5.6	1.2	1.9
A serious incident of food poisoning	2.0	1.2	1.4

Notes:

Statistically significant at ***p<0.001, **p<0.01, *p<0.05 crosstabulations with test for statistical significance (Pearson Chi Square).

[†] Among respondents who had worked in the previous 12 months.

[‡] Answer provided by respondents in self-completion part of the questionnaire.

wellbeing'. Whilst these injuries may appear to be random or chance happenings, these 'accidents' conform to and are determined by a social logic of which poverty plays a key determining role.

Some of the largest discrepancies that exist between 'poor' and 'non-poor' in relation to physical harm relate to the experience of violence. People living in poverty were nearly five times as likely as others to report being attacked by a stranger or hit by a partner or ex-partner in the previous year. The relationship between poverty and violence is also reflected more generally in the findings of homicide studies (see Pridemore, 2010), as well as more specifically within reviews examining links between deprivation and domestic violence (Fahmy et al, 2016). It appears to lend credence to theories linking interpersonal conflict to poverty and inequality, although caution should be taken when seeking to interpret this association as causality might work both ways. For Wilkinson and Pickett (2010), such a relationship might be best explained by the feelings of shame and humiliation that result from socio-economic inequalities. Thus, whilst status in hierarchical market societies is predominantly determined by material possessions and an ability to consume, the 'poor' are more likely to exist in public spaces and be in relationships whereby markers of status and success are less readily available, with violence providing a channel to assert status.

Compromised autonomy: losing control, insecurity and anxiety

Testimonies in the qualitative interviews demonstrate the ways that low income serves to deleteriously impact the autonomy people exercise over all aspects of their lives: the friendships and relationships they are able to sustain and nurture; the leisure activities and hobbies they pursue; and the influence they exert over the decisions that impact their lives. Participants articulated the relationship between financial resources and personal autonomy whilst they reflected that without sufficient income, freedom was an illusory and intangible notion:

> 'Money to me buys you a certain amount of freedom and relying on money you are not financially free ... you just wish you were in a free situation ... and be independent, which is how you are meant to be.'
>
> (Young unemployed, Birmingham)

Low income does not only restrict choices on a day-to-day basis, it also diminishes the possibility of formulating and achieving broader life goals, undermining capacity for meaningful self-actualisation. Without sufficient autonomy, our participants find themselves in an enforced state of dependence on others through informal familial or friendship networks, community organisations, and the state.

> 'No I haven't really got control over my budgeting – the government has. Yes, every fortnight I get paid, but there is always that fear that I am going to go there and my money is not going to be in. So they are always going to have control over my life ... there are a couple of times when the social has not paid my money and I have been like 'what's going on?' and they say "oh the computers have gone down, come back the next day" and that is panic. They are always going to have control over me until I get myself a job.'
>
> (Long-term illness, male, Gloucester)

This sense of a lack of control is underlined by the experience of financial loss that disproportionately impacts the poor, affecting the constancy of resource necessary for secure lives (see Table 10.2). The precariousness of poor people's lives, in terms of casualised and poorly paid employment with the attendant risks of redundancy, exposes them to the higher risks and perils of financial harm. One in three people living in poverty said that they had experienced a significant

Table 10.2: Percent of adults experiencing financial harms in the previous 12 months

Financial harm	PSE poor	Not poor	All
***A significant loss of income, e.g. losing your job, benefit changes, or through divorce	29.6	9.2	13.9
**A large fall in the value of your pension or other financial assets, e.g. property, savings, etc	8.1	12.4	11.4
***Have fallen behind with bills	19.8	2.7	6.3
The loss of a public service, e.g. library, crèche/nursery facilities	4.7	3.0	3.4
*Had your home broken into and something stolen	4.4	2.6	3.1

Note: Statistically significant at ***p<0.001, **p<0.01, *p<0.05 crosstabulations with test for statistical significance (Pearson Chi Square).

loss of income in the previous year. However, the higher risks also reflect the dynamics of poverty: the 'poor' are not a static category – those currently classified as 'poor' will almost certainly include people who were previously not poor but for whom the loss of a job has pushed them into this category. Falling into debt is all too common an experience for people living in impoverished situations; poor people were seven times as likely to have fallen into arrears with their financial commitments compared to others (see Chapters 3 and 11). The vast majority of people living in poverty reported either 'falling behind' with bills or 'keeping up but constantly struggling'. It is in these circumstances individuals are often driven into borrowing from friends and family, and in the most desperate situations, end up resorting to credit sources attracting high interest payments; 16 per cent of poor people had used pawnbrokers, money lenders or loan sharks in the previous 12 months.

Powerlessness also gives rise to a pervasive sense of insecurity. Life on a low income inevitably is precarious; without sufficient income it is difficult for individuals to assert control over their lives. Feeling powerless gives rise to anxiety and speculation over anticipated events that lie beyond the control of those living on low income (Giddens, 1991). Testimonies made reference to insecurity in numerous forms, but primarily to financial insecurity, as an inability to control the constancy and adequacy of incomes. The survey data corroborates participant testimony: three in every four people living in poverty reported that they were worried about the loss of income as a result of losing their job, benefit changes or divorce, whilst more than two-thirds were worried about the loss of a public service (see Table 10.3; see also Pantazis, 2000; 2006).

Powerlessness is anxiety-provoking: without the resources to respond to events, participants can only worry about the future possibility of additional expenses or threats to their income that lie beyond their control. Testimonies in qualitative interviews made persistent references to feeling worried, anxious, stressed, or being unable to sleep, or what Edin and Schaeffer (2015: 88) might term to be the 'toxic stress' of poverty:

> 'I hate being in debt, it feels like a big pressure on me it is always on my mind how much I owe. It does affect you. Worrying about money is the biggest stress ever I think, it is just awful.'
>
> (Unemployed, female, Gloucester)

Inevitably the persistent nature of these pressures and struggles may lead to serious consequences for mental health. As the PSE-UK survey data demonstrate, one in three people living in poverty reported suffering from a mental health illness or condition in the previous 12 months, in contrast to just 9 per cent of those not defined as 'poor' (33 per cent versus 9 per cent, $p<0.00$).

Numerous injurious states coalesce: the continual strain of making ends meet, the sense of personal failure (detailed in the following section), the lack of control and influence and the sense of isolation. Participants made reference to being prescribed anti-depressants by their General Practitioner as a response to these pressures. Depression is hardly surprising given the messages that people living on low

Table 10.3: Percent of adults expressing that they are fairly or very worried about possibility of experiencing financial harms

Financial harm	PSE poor	Not poor	All
***A significant loss of income, e.g. losing your job, benefit changes or through divorce	75.7	43.9	51.3
***Worried about the loss of a public service, e.g. library, crèche/nursery facilities	63.7	47.2	51.1
**A large fall in the value of your pension or other financial assets e.g. property, savings, etc	53.7	45.5	47.2
***Had your home broken into and something stolen	51.9	34.4	38.5

Note: Statistically significant at ***$p<0.001$, **$p<0.01$, *$p<0.05$, crosstabulations with test for statistical significance (Pearson Chi Square).

income receive – and that many internalize – resulting in a sense of personal failure or inadequacy for 'poor life choices' or 'financial mismanagement':

> 'I have had nervous breakdowns and been left with very bad depressions, because of the money ... I was signing onto the dole and you have got them rabbiting in your earhole threatening to stop your money ... they treat you as a number and not a person, they have got the job and you should be out there looking for work, you shouldn't be ill, you should be looking for this, that and the other. That is how they speak to you. You need to look for four jobs and if you don't bring those in we will stop your money ... The last time that was said to me, I broke down there and cried my eyes out, went to my doctor, and he said, "Oh, Mrs Jones, you have just had a nervous breakdown."'
>
> (Retired, female, Gloucester)

To summarise, poverty engenders a state of powerlessness whereby autonomy is injuriously curtailed. The structural constraints of poverty are tangible and serve to reduce the choices of the 'poor' to a series of budgeting decisions. These analyses suggest that trying to make ends meet and the anxieties life on a low income prompts have a profound impact on mental health, giving rise to a host of associated injuries.

Symbolic injuries: misrecognition and loss of self-esteem

'Othering', as Lister (2003: 100-01) suggests, encompasses 'the many ways in which the "poor" are treated as different from the rest of society'. It is a process 'animated by the non-poor' that serves to differentiate and demarcate a 'line between 'us' and 'them'; ultimately, a line that is 'imbued with negative value judgements' (Lister, 2003: 101). 'Othering' represents one aspect of the intersubjective process of 'misrecognition'. As Taylor (1994: 25) highlights, misrecognition relies on 'dialogical relations with others' that not only serve to shape others' opinions of us, but that also structure our own understandings of who we are and our 'fundamental characteristics as a human being'. Taylor's (1994: 25) discussion of the injury that results from misrecognition is instructive, as he argues 'misrecognition, can inflict harm ... imprisoning someone in a false, distorted and reduced mode of being ... It can inflict a grievous wound, saddling its victims with a crippling self hatred'.

Numerous social cues and physical signs associated with the experience of poverty serve to 'discredit' the 'poor' in the eyes of others. Participants' testimonies revealed the injurious impacts of being publicly 'outed' as poor and detailed the mundane aspects of everyday life that served to distinguish them as 'other' in mainstream society:

> 'My boy since he has started high school, he was like can I have this before I go back to school, they want all the designer stuff, I can't do it, the trousers I can get from Asda or whatever, but when it comes to the jacket or the shoes, they want the expensive stuff ... I think he feels out of place, he has to conform to what everyone else is wearing, which I don't agree with at all, but obviously he is at that age ...'
> (Low wage worker, female, Glasgow)

Disrespect is a relational injury that results when the 'poor' are treated as a distinct group and consequently as citizens of 'unequal worth' (Lister, 2003:121). Thus, being identified and 'outed' as being 'poor' gives license to the 'non-poor' to treat our participants without the same measure of respect they would afford to others. The testimonies revealed numerous examples of disrespect that resulted from painful everyday interactions with strangers in public spaces:

> 'I have had it when out and about or going to different places, maybe meeting someone who considers themselves to be one or two rungs up the ladder of the class system ... you can get people who work in shops or restaurants and they look at you like, "what the hell are you doing in here?" It's horrible.'
> (Low wage worker, male, Glasgow)

> 'The church gave me a voucher so that I could do some food shopping. The women on the till looked at me as though I was disgusting.'
> (Lone parent, female, Birmingham)

Some of the study participants noted that media coverage and political debates appeared to give 'license' or 'permission' for those within mainstream society to 'hate' (Poynting and Mason, 2006) or 'denigrate' the 'lifestyles' of those living on low income. PSE-UK survey respondents were categorised as having experienced misrecognition if they reported that they had been 'harassed, abused or made to feel uncomfortable' or 'treated less favourably by people in a position of authority' because of reasons relating to their identity or personal characteristics. People living in poverty were significantly more likely to experience misrecognition with respect to seven of the nine indicators (see Table 10.4). Differences in the experience of misrecognition emerged between people living in poverty and those not poor; 30 per cent of poor people reported some form of misrecognition (versus 14 per cent of non-poor). However, these differences are not as great as might be expected given the weight of qualitative testimony; consideration to the way these issues are framed in survey questions should guide future research.

The largest differences emerged in relation to social class and disability, where PSE-poor respondents were nearly eight and six times respectively more likely to report having experienced some form of misrecognition. These differences should not be surprising given that the research was conducted at the point at which the Coalition government's austerity policies were being promoted, policies that focused intensely on working-age benefit recipients and specifically on those receiving forms of disability benefit. Hostile political rhetoric through the oft-cited 'shirkers versus workers' metaphor has served to focus public vitriol on social security claimants (see Walker and Chase, 2013; Baumberg et al, 2012).

Stigma and disrespect are externally inflicted injuries. Yet when these pejorative social judgements are internalised, secondary injuries of shame and low self-esteem result. This interrelationship is clearly articulated in Chase and Walker's (2013: 740) concept of shame, as 'co-constructed' through 'the internal judgement of one's own frailties'

Table 10.4: Percent of adults reporting misrecognition in the previous 12 months

Harms of misrecognition	PSE poor	Not poor	All
**Ethnicity or religion	6.5	3.5	4.2
**Age	6.1	3.5	4.1
***Social class	7.7	1.0	2.6
Gender	3.9	2.2	2.6
***Disability	5.6	1.0	2.1
Sexuality	1.2	1.1	1.1
***Other	6.7	3.4	4.2
Total			

Note: Statistically significant at ***p<0.001, **p<0.01, *p<0.05, crosstabulations with test for statistical significance (Pearson Chi Square).

and the 'anticipated assessment of how one will be judged by others ... considered socially and morally superior'. This 'co-construction' was clearly reflected within participants' testimonies:

> 'If someone repeats something to you over and over, you are going to start believing it yourself, bringing yourself down, you look at yourself in a particular way, which can cause more harm than good ... it does make you look at yourself and think "are they really right? Is it because you are lazy that you are not in a job?" ...

> *Interviewer.* Do you ever feel embarrassed?

> 'Definitely! To be seen with a sign-on book for example. You would not want to let anyone see that you sign on, because of what you think they will think. That is because of the picture that has been put in your head by when you walk into that Job Centre, you just think "oh, everybody thinks you are lazy and on Job Seeker's". That has gone through my head on more than one occasion, I wouldn't want anyone to see me with that booklet.'
>
> (Unemployed, female, Birmingham)

To feel embarrassment was a feature of life on low income for those reporting to the PSE-UK survey. Half of all PSE poor respondents said they had felt 'embarrassed' *because* they had a low income. Whilst 'embarrassment' may pass, as participants' testimonies suggest, 'feeling ashamed' has a lingering and more corrosive impact (see Lynd, 1958) and was often framed in terms of a loss of status:

> 'I felt like I had failed. I felt like I had let myself down. I have been on benefits for four years so I feel like I have got used to it. Although, I still don't feel I should living like this ...I t felt wrong, I used to be one of those people who thought "oh single parent on benefits" and all that ... I am not working for the money I am getting and it feels wrong, but I need it.'
>
> (Lone parent, female, Gloucester)

Here lies the double bind of poverty: an enforced state of compromised autonomy that conflicts with the societal norms of self-sufficiency, resulting in what Sennett (2003: 101) terms the 'shame of dependence'.

Feeling ashamed is a deeply damaging emotional state that serves to erode self-esteem and provides the context in which so-called 'choices' are made, encompassing seemingly self-destructive injuries.

Fragmented and fractured lives: harmful isolation and deteriorating relations

Life in poverty places untold pressures on relationships. These pressures take their toll on the ability to sustain familial relationships as well as form and maintain wider friendships. The scarcity of household income, overlaid with pressures of debt and the requirement to forego 'necessities' and spending more time in the home, can place intolerable strains on intimate relationships (Kempson, 1996). As our participants' testimonies demonstrate, trying to sustain relationships amidst pressures of making ends meet leaves little space for personal relationships to flourish. The pressures exacted on relationships are underlined by the reported levels of domestic violence in lower income households documented earlier in the chapter.

It is not only relationships within the home that are damaged by low income, but wider familial relationships and friendships. 'Going without' often means being unable to afford to go out, to attend birthday parties or special occasions; in other words, to take part in activities in which people may be expected to take part, in order to sustain friendships and familial relations. The PSE-UK analysis demonstrates the extent to which poverty acts as an impediment to engaging in socially approved activities (See Table 10.5).

A lack of resources is only part of this picture. The necessity to avoid shame plays a significant role in the deterioration of existing relationships and social networks. To avoid being identified as being 'poor' means participants in the qualitative study either avoided specific social occasions or in extreme circumstances withdrew altogether from particular friendships – a process that Wacquant (2010: 217) terms 'symbolic self defence'. It is unsurprising, given the painfully injurious experience of stigma, disrespect and shame already documented, that participants sought to minimise relational and emotional injuries where possible. Testimonies identified strategies that are developed to minimise potentially painful interactions that reveal the 'actual identities' of our participants (Goffman, 1963). Whilst these strategies undoubtedly mediate the most corrosive and painful aspects of the injuries of othering, the adaptive responses beget further injury. In many instances, unexplained withdrawal from these relationships caused irreparable damage to friendships, as it is often perceived that

Table 10.5: Percent of adults reporting going without social participation because they cannot afford activity

Social activity	Low-income poor[+]	Not poor	All
***Friends or family round for a meal or drink at least once a month	18.1	6.6	9.3
***Going out socially once a fortnight	32.6	12.0	16.9
***Celebrations on special occasions such as Christmas	7.1	1.8	3.0
***A meal out once a month	38.0	13.9	19.6
***Visits to family or friends in other parts of the country 4 times a year	37.6	15.6	20.8
***Going out for a drink fortnightly	28.2	10.1	14.4
***Attending weddings, funerals and other such occasions	6.1	1.5	2.6

Notes:

Statistically significant at ***$p<0.001$, **$p<0.01$, *$p<0.05$, crosstabulations with test for statistical significance (Pearson Chi Square).

[+] 'Low-income poor' = below 60 per cent median equivalised income after housing costs (AHC)

participants had actively and deliberately chosen not to engage in particular social activities. Consequently some study participants experienced what Abramsky (2013: 5) terms the 'sheer loneliness of poverty':

> 'I don't go out ... the last time was probably eight years ago, that I went out socially.'
>
> (Lone parent, female, Birmingham)

> 'I am just a loner, I have got my boys and they are my world. I have got friends, but I don't really go out, I haven't got the money anyway. It is tough.'
>
> (Unemployed, female, Glasgow)

Friendships and family remained important aspects of participants' lives and, where possible, participants went to great lengths to maintain contacts with significant others in their lives. Yet the quality of these relationships was impacted by the inability to participate socially to the same degree that others within society would take for granted. Over a third of those living in poverty (according to an income measure) reported being unable to afford 'going out socially': 'a meal out socially once a month' or 'to visit family or friends in other parts of the country 4 times a year'. Each rate was two times greater than the non-poor (see Table 10.5). Nevertheless, these fragile social networks provided important support at points of crisis and were often critical to mediating the harms of poverty, particularly familial networks. This analysis appears to be corroborated by the PSE-UK survey data that show that people living in poverty are less likely to have frequent contact with friends but seek to maintain family relationships (see Chapter 5 on social participation).

Conclusion

Poverty can be an all-consuming experience that injuriously impacts many aspects of being, damage that is not simply restricted to the ability to afford commonly held items or activities. At worst, poverty leads to a shorter life and at best it is an assault on self: it undermines the ways that individuals are able to develop, compromises the ability to be with others, damages public identity, as well as deleteriously impacting self-image. It follows then from our analyses that the longer poverty is experienced, the heavier these injuries weigh and the more likely the deleterious impacts will accumulate. But what does social harm add to our understanding of poverty in relation to risk, resilience, choice?

First, in relation to the risk society thesis, the chapter confirms much of what is already known empirically speaking, in the sense that harm and injury do not conform to a more individualised logic. Indeed, leaving aside the fact that poverty is a harm in its own right, we have demonstrated that the survey respondents who were identified as poor are more likely to experience a host of secondary harms in terms of physical and mental health. The point is that this is not a matter of individual risk navigation, when those already on the margins with few resources are unable to avoid these injuries.

Second, in terms of resilience, without doubt those living on low income are not merely passive actors and the qualitative data reveals this, demonstrating how resourceful and inventive those on low income can be in the face of significant personal adversities (see Kempson, 1996; Dominy and Kempson, 2006). However, the analysis suggests that people's resourcefulness is a fragile and finite state, to the extent that it becomes difficult to habitually 'bounce back'. Here we wish to elaborate on the criticisms of the resilience agenda highlighted by Harrison (2013). Harrison (2013: 107) correctly, according to our analysis, speculates that it is 'too easy to emphasize the positive aspects of resilience – the strategizing, cutting back, ... but overlook the costs'. This analysis adds weight to this argument; what Harrison euphemistically terms to be the 'cost' can be accurately described as 'injury' according to our analysis. Indeed, what has been demonstrated is that 'going without' in order to make ends meet or withdrawing from social participation to avoid the stigma of poverty leads onto a series of related harms and harmful states. It also takes its toll emotionally. The continual struggle to make ends meet inflicts significant psychological injuries, and the pressure of low income is unremitting, resulting in a host of injuries in terms of stress, and anxiety through to long-term forms of depression. The point is that 'coping' with the injuries of poverty requires significant emotional resource; resource which is not infinite, but is likely to be eroded across time, the longer an individual is forced to endure the rigours of deprivation.

Third, the idea that a 'life on benefits' and by logical extension, life in poverty, is a lifestyle choice, is thrown into sharp relief by our analysis. It might be a glib point, but it remains an important one, even within the utilitarian logic of the nudge paradigm, the harms and injuries associated with poverty are so unpleasant and damaging that the idea that people are opting to endure them is indeed fanciful. However, our analyses reveal a further, more critical point. As Leggett (2014: 11) argues, 'nudge theory lacks an adequate conception of social environment', neglecting that 'agents' uneven access to economic, cultural and other forms of capital will filter and constrain (or enable) their choices and action'. It is our contention that a fundamental omission of recent nudge approaches to social security reform is the injurious context of poverty. Thus whilst nudge practitioners and theorists focus on, as Standing (2011:28) puts it, 'character deficiency … persistent misguidedness, ignorance or laziness' of the poor, our analyses demonstrates that a fundamental harm poverty inflicts is the injurious restrictions and constraints it places on personal autonomy. An irony of the various 'carrots and sticks' envisaged within this policy agenda, through which technocrats attempt to nudge benefits claimants into 'good behaviours', is that this inflicts further autonomy harms by 'infantilising' the objects of these behavioural technologies (Standing, 2011: 31).

Ultimately poverty results from the maldistribution of resource and respect in our societies; as a structural harm it injuriously constrains the lives that the 'poor' may lead. We require social science analyses that articulate this reality – a social harm analysis offers this possibility.

Note

[1] 'Misrecognition' is a general term for situations where inappropriate social labelling or categorisation of people may adversely affect their social standing, opportunities or well-being, through such mechanisms as stigma or prejudice. See also discussion in this chapter of 'Relational harms' and 'Symbolic injuries'.

References

Abramsky, S. (2013) *The American way of poverty: How the other half still lives*, New York: Nation Books.

Andres, L. and Round, J. (2015) 'The role of "persistent resilience" within everyday life and polity: households coping with marginality within the "Big Society"', *Environment & Planning A*, 47(3): 676-91.

Batty, E. and Cole, I. (2010) *Resilience and the recession in six deprived communities: Preparing for worse to come?* York: Joseph Rowntree Foundation.

Baumberg, B., Bell, K. and Gaffney, D. (2012) *Benefits stigma in Britain*, London: Elizabeth Finn Trust.

Beatty, T., Blow, L. and Crossley, T. (2014) 'Is there a "heat-or-eat" trade-off in the UK?', *Journal of the Royal Statistical Society*, 177(1): 281-94.

Beck, U. (1992) *Risk society: Towards a new modernity*, London: Sage.

Belfield, C., Cribb, J., Hood, A. and Joyce, R. (2014), *Living standards, poverty and inequality in the UK: 2014*, London: Institute for Fiscal Studies.

Beresford, P. and Croft, S. (1995) 'It's our problem too', *Critical Social Policy*, 15(2/3): 75-95

Bradshaw, J. (2002) 'Child poverty and child outcomes', *Children & Society*, 16(2): 131-40.

Chase, E. and Walker, R. (2013) 'The co-construction of shame in the context of poverty: beyond a threat to the social bond', *Sociology* 47(4): 739-54.

Cohen, R., Coxall, J., Craig, G. and Sadiq-Sangster, A. (1992), *Hardship Britain: Being poor in the 1990s*, London: Child Poverty Action Group.

Cribb, J., Hood, A. and Joyce, R. (2015) *Living standards: Recent trends and future challenges*, London: Institute for Fiscal Studies.

Davidson, R. (2008) 'More than "just coping": the antecedents and dynamics of resilience in a qualitative longitudinal study', *Social Policy & Society*, 8(1): 115-25.

Dominy, N. and Kempson, E. (2006) *Understanding older people's experiences of poverty and material deprivation*, Norwich: HMSO.

Doyal, L. and Gough, I. (1991) *A theory of human need*, Basingstoke: Palgrave Macmillan.

Edin, K. and Schaeffer, L. (2015*) $2.00 a day: Living on almost nothing in America*, New York: Houghton Mifflin Harcourt.

Fahmy, E., Williamson, E. and Pantazis, C. (2016) *Evidence and policy review: Domestic violence and poverty*, York: Joseph Rowntree Foundation.

Giddens, A. (1991) *Modernity and self-identity*, Cambridge: Polity Press.

Goffman, E. (1963) *Stigma: Notes on the management of spoiled identity*, Englewood Cliffs, NJ: Prentice-Hall.

Harrison, E. (2013) 'Bouncing back? Recession, resilience and everyday lives', *Critical Social Policy*, 33(1): 97–113.

Hillyard, P., Pantazis, C., Tombs, S. and Gordon, D. (eds) (2004) *Beyond criminology: Taking harm seriously*, London: Pluto Press.

Kempson, E. (1996) *Life on a low income*, York: Joseph Rowntree Foundation.

Laflamme, L., Hasselberg, M. and Burrows, S. (2010) '20 years of research on socioeconomic inequality and children's unintentional injuries: understanding the cause-specific evidence at hand', *International Journal of Pediatrics,* doi:10.1155/2010/819687.

Leggett, W. (2014) 'The politics of behaviour change: nudge, neoliberalism and the state', *Policy & Politics*, 42(1): 3-19.

Levitas, R. (2012) 'The just's umbrella: austerity and the Big Society in Coalition policy and beyond', *Critical Social Policy*, 32: 320-42.

Liddell, C. and Morris, C. (2010) 'Fuel poverty and human health: a review of recent evidence', *Energy Policy*, 38: 2987-97.

Lister, R. (2003) *Poverty*, Cambridge: Polity Press.

Luthar, S., Cicchetti, D. and Becker, B. (2000) 'The construct of resilience: a critical evaluation and guidelines for future work', *Child Development*, 71, 543–62.

Lynd, H. (1958) *On shame and the search for identity*, New York: Harcourt Brace.

Olofsson, A., Zinn, J. O., Griffin, G., Nygren, K. G., Cebulla, A., and Hannah-Moffat, K. (2014) 'The mutual constitution of risk and inequalities: intersectional risk theory', *Health, Risk & Society*, 16(5): 417-30.

Pantazis, C. (2000) ' "Fear of crime", vulnerability and poverty', *British Journal of Criminology*, 40(3): 414-36.

Pantazis, C. (2006) 'Crime, "disorder", insecurity and social exclusion', in C. Pantazis, D. Gordon, and R. Levitas, (eds) *Poverty and social exclusion in Britain: The Millennium Survey*, Bristol: The Policy Press.

Pantazis, C. (2016) 'Policies and discourses of poverty during a time of recession and austerity', *Critical Social Policy*, 36(1): 3-20.

Pemberton, S. (2015) *Harmful societies: Understanding social harm*, Bristol: Policy Press.

Pemberton, S., Sutton, E., Fahmy, E. (2014) 'Life on a low income in austere times', *PSE Working Paper – Analysis Series*, Bristol: University of Bristol.

Poynting, S. and Mason, V. (2006) '"Tolerance, freedom, justice and peace"?: Britain, Australia and anti-Muslim racism since 11 September 2001', *Journal of Intercultural Studies*, 27(4): 365-91.

Pridemore, W. (2010) 'Poverty matters: a reassessment of the inequality-homicide relationship in cross-national studies', *British Journal of Criminology*, 51: 739-72.

Ritchie, J. and Lewis, J. (eds) (2003) *Qualitative research practice: A guide for social science students and researchers*, London: Sage.

Sennett, R. (2003) *Respect*, London: Penguin.

Standing, G. (2011) 'Behavioural conditionality: why the nudges must be stopped – an opinion piece', *Journal of Poverty and Social Justice*, 19(1): 27-38.

Taylor, C. (1994) 'The politics of recognition' in A. Gutmann (ed) *Multiculturalism and the politics of recognition*, Princeton: Princeton University Press, pp 25-73.

Thomas, B., Dorling, D. and Davey Smith, G. (2010) 'Inequalities in premature mortality in Britain: observational study from 1921 to 2007', *British Medical Journal*, Vol. 341, pp 3633-9.

Wacquant, L. (2010) 'Urban desolation and symbolic denigration in the hyperghetto', *Social Pyschology Quarterly*, 73(3): 215-19.

Walker, R. and Chase, E. (2013) 'Separating the sheep from the goats: tackling poverty in Britain for over four centuries', in E. Gubrium, S. Pellissery and I. Lødemel (eds) *The shame of it: Global perspectives on anti-poverty policies*, Bristol: Policy Press.

Wiggan, J. (2012) 'Telling stories of 21st century welfare: the UK Coalition Government and the neo-liberal discourse of worklessness and dependency', *Critical Social Policy*, 32(3): 383-405.

Wilkinson, R. and Pickett, K. (2010) *The spirit level: Why equality is better for everyone*, Harmondsworth: Penguin.

ELEVEN

Financial inclusion, financial stress and debt

Glen Bramley and Kirsten Besemer

Introduction

This chapter discusses the concepts of debt and financial exclusion, and considers the significance of the findings of the PSE-UK survey in the light of policy and social developments in this area in the UK over the past decade. At the time, the Millennium (PSE) Survey in 1999 was one of the first to look the relationships between poverty, debt and financial exclusion (McKay and Collard, 2006). Since then, there has been increasing interest in the way debt problems and financial exclusion may contribute to a range of economic, social and health outcomes, as well as interest in the multidirectional causal linkages between financial exclusion and debt (Salignac, Muir and Wong, 2016; Simpson and Buckland, 2009; Sinclair, 2013).

Financial exclusion research originated in the context of the UK's early-1990s financial crisis, at a time when banks became increasingly restrictive in their service delivery, withdrawing from vulnerable social groups and disadvantaged localities in order to reduce risk (Fuller, 1998; Leyshon and Thrift, 1995). The term 'financial exclusion' emerged as a general concept to describe the process by which social groups and individuals were excluded from access to financial services, including loans and bank accounts (Leyshon and Thrift, 1995). Over the course of the 1990s, technological developments in electronic banking meant that the importance of banks' geographical locations diminished relative to a much broader range of barriers preventing certain social groups from accessing appropriate and affordable financial products and services (Mitton, 2008). Over this period, research has similarly broadened from a narrow focus on the consequences of exclusionary criteria and costs associated with specific financial products or services (Devlin, 2005), to include a much wider range of causal processes associated with non-use. These include problems relating to a lack of financial capability, defined as the knowledge, skills and ability to identify appropriate financial products and services and to effectively manage finances (Taylor, 2011). In many countries, such problems are found to be concentrated among poorer and more disadvantaged populations (Hogarth et al, 2005; Carbo et al, 2007). Financial exclusion also needs to be understood in terms of a wider societal shift towards 'financialisation' (Sinclair, 2013; Marron, 2013), whereby financial institutions, markets and services become more embedded in different aspects of social, institutional as well as economic life.

Processes of financial exclusion and indebtedness are, it is argued, inexorably linked through a variety of causal pathways. First, debt may be a consequence of financial exclusion. Individuals and households without access to mainstream banking services are more reliant on more expensive forms of credit when facing financial shortfalls. The need to use more expensive sources of credit may subsequently contribute to higher debts (Gritten, 2011; Hogarth et al, 2005; McKay and Collard, 2006). It has also been suggested that, where households only have access to more expensive forms of credit (such as loans on credit cards), getting into arrears on regular payments like utility bills may be a considerably lower cost means of borrowing (Bridges and Disney, 2004). Conversely, however, the build-up of high levels of expensive debt, as well as patterns of arrears on utility bills, may also cause households to be considered 'high risk', as measured through credit scoring and referencing systems. This results in difficulty in obtaining a bank account and further reducing the sources of credit available to them, while increasing their financial need. Consequently, household indebtedness can be seen as both a cause and a consequence of financial exclusion, and indeed as a key mechanism compounding the descent into more severe poverty (see Chapter 3 and Fitzpatrick et al, 2016).

In recognition of the variety of processes through which financial exclusion may operate, financial exclusion is increasingly seen as a multidimensional concept, captured through a range of indicators extending to financial vulnerability and financial capability as well as access to, and use of, more specific banking services (Taylor, 2011). Consequently, this chapter will focus on two key groups of indicators: indicators relating to **exclusions from banking services** (such as bank accounts, credit cards and bank loans), **as well as other financial services** (such as home contents insurance); and, indicators relating to **financial vulnerability**, including the ability to build up savings, and conversely, the extent and nature of borrowing, debt and arrears.

This chapter will first review policy responses to financial exclusion, particularly in the UK but with some reference to other countries, before reporting changes in these key indicators and their relationship with poverty since the PSE Survey in 1999. It will consider the extent to which cross-temporal changes can be explained by policy changes or other contextual events in the UK over the past decade or so. The chapter then proceeds to look at wider subjective indicators of financial stress and some evidence on how people cope with financial pressures at different levels on the poverty spectrum. It looks at how financial stress and debt relate to the wider range of social exclusions, paying particular attention to the question of whether and how far 'social capital' may play a role in alleviating financial stress and exclusion. Finally, it reflects on societal trends which may be exacerbating or changing the nature of these issues.

UK policy responses to financial exclusion

Financial exclusion first emerged as a UK policy concern in the late 1990s, both as part of the New Labour government's policy emphasis on social exclusion, and in response to increasing concerns about the number of people who were excluded from the most basic banking services, especially current accounts (Marron, 2013).

These concerns developed into a series of policies aimed at the expansion and consolidation of the credit union network and community-based loan schemes, the provision of low-cost insurance schemes for public housing tenants and the promotion of 'basic bank accounts' – accounts with reduced overdraft facilities, which are therefore accessible to people who face barriers to accessing regular bank accounts (Collard, 2007; Marshall, 2004; Mitton, 2008). While these initial measures helped to overcome a number of barriers associated with uneven financial services access, and were especially effective in reducing the number of 'unbanked adults', they did little to address a growing problem of over-indebtedness among poor consumers (Collard, 2007). Between 1995 and 2003, the average level of outstanding consumer credit per UK household had effectively tripled, a momentous rise that was largely attributed to an increase in irresponsible lending practices alongside growing flows of funds available at lower cost. In 2003, the Department of Trade and Industry responded to this debt crisis with a White Paper on the consumer credit market, which formed a foundation for a national overhaul of consumer credit laws (DTI, 2013). The main purpose of the reforms was to eliminate unfair lending practices, and promote greater transparency in the provision of credit, in order to ensure that consumers could make more informed borrowing choices and avoid particularly unfavourable terms (Marron, 2012; Collard and Kempson, 2005). To some extent, the reform of the credit market, which also included stricter licensing laws, reversed the effects of the deregulation of consumer credit legislation by consecutive Conservative governments in the 1980s and 1990s (Ryder and Thomas, 2011).

Other national-level financial inclusion measures gained a new impetus following the Labour government's 2004 spending review, in which the government announced the establishment of a Financial Inclusion Fund providing sustainable funding for both existing and further financial inclusion commitments, as well as the establishment of a Financial Inclusion Taskforce to monitor progress (House of Commons Treasury Committee, 2006).

Although policy and research interest for 'financial exclusion' is not exclusive to the UK, the concept only slowly gained attention in other countries. The first comparative overview of financial exclusion across Europe (Carbo et al, 2007) found that, as in Britain, screening practices such as credit scoring excluded some poor people from the use of banking services in some countries, particularly in Southern Europe (Italy, Portugal and Greece), Austria, and Ireland. The review directly related these problems to financial deregulation, which had allowed banks greater flexibility to direct and restrict services to wealthier consumers. Of the six countries where lack of access to financial services affected a sizeable proportion of the population, the UK was the only country with a national financial exclusion strategy. However, in many other European countries, cultural principles of solidarity and public responsibility nevertheless resulted in a variety of social banking solutions, despite the absence of explicit national financial exclusion policies (Carbo et al, 2007).

The early twenty-first century marked an increasing disconnect between policy in many European countries and that in the UK. While policy in many Western European countries continued to be largely focused on the social responsibility of financial institutions to provide accessible services, UK policy increasingly shifted towards financial inclusion policies aimed at the adjustment of consumer behaviour (Carbo, 2007; Fenge 2012). In the UK, face-to-face money advice services, civil legal aid services and debt advice thus became increasingly central to the overall social inclusion strategy. In addition, curricula for schools in England and in the devolved administrations were revised to cover personal finance (Mitton, 2008; Marron, 2013).

When the Conservative-led Coalition government took office in 2010, New Labour's Financial Inclusion Taskforce and Financial Inclusion Fund were still in operation, but these were discontinued in 2011. Since then, a declining interest in the social exclusion rhetoric, accompanied by a stronger policy focus on spending reduction, meant that many financial inclusion initiatives lost funding. Indeed, the term 'financial inclusion' was rarely used in any Coalition government publication and that government withdrew some or all funding from a variety of financial advisory services as well as government-subsidised savings schemes (including the Child Trust Fund (CTF), the Saving Gateway and the Social Fund, a grant and borrowing scheme for people in acute financial need (Appleyard, 2015)).

There have, however, been some recent indications of a possible revival of social inclusion policy interest. The Child Poverty Strategy 2014–17 included a variety of relevant strategies, including investment in credit union expansion, greater restrictions on payday lending and investments in money management support, and debt advice. Furthermore, prior to the 2015 elections, a Financial Inclusion Commission was formed with the explicit aim 'to put financial inclusion back on the political agenda' (Financial Inclusion Commission, 2015). Some recommendations from the Commission's report (notably designating responsibility to a senior minister) have not as yet been implemented. However, the inclusion of problematic debt as one of the 'root causes of poverty' in the new legislation in the Welfare Reform and Work Act 2015 may be seen as a potential signal of a renewed interest in financial inclusion as a policy goal (Hartfree and Collard, 2015). At the same time, there has been a pronounced increase in attention to financial inclusion on the wider international stage (Beck et al, 2007; Čihák et al, 2012; Demirgüç-Kunt, 2015).

Trends in financial exclusion

Table 11.1 suggests a number of different trends in key financial exclusion measures. For financial services exclusion, there has been a significant improvement in terms of reducing the proportion of households without a bank account, which dropped from 16 per cent in 1999 to only 5 per cent in the 2012 data. Indeed, the poor are now as likely to have bank accounts as other households. Aside from improvements in access to banking services over the preceding period, this shift may also reflect changes in payment methods for both wages and benefits, as part of the wider move towards a 'cashless society'.

The proportion of *individuals* without accounts is slightly higher than the proportion of households without accounts, particularly among the PSE poor. A much larger proportion of individuals report that they make limited use of banks because of dissatisfaction with the service offered. This dissatisfaction with banks, which is not strongly associated with poverty, may be related to the shrinkage of the branch network or service rationalisations following the 2007 banking crisis, as well as aspects of the behaviour of banks during and after the financial crisis.

Inability to afford home contents insurance remains quite strongly related to poverty and has *increased* its share of all households (particularly the non-poor) since 1999. We would see this as a significant marker of increased financial stress more widely in society. In 2008, according to the Living Costs and Food Survey, more than half of poor households did not have any home insurance, a level that was the same as measured in 1998/9 in the then Family Expenditure Survey (ONS 1999; Whyley et al, 1998). While it is quite likely that this figure may include households who voluntarily opt out, for example because they have few valuable possessions, lack of home insurance is a worrying indicator. Previous research has shown that households with no home contents insurance are more than three times as likely to be burgled as those with insurance (McKay and Collard, 2006; pp 200-01). As the cost of home insurance is dependent on the level of risk associated with the neighbourhood, policies can be significantly more expensive in poor areas with higher levels of crime, perversely pricing out those tenants and home-owners who are also most at risk (an aspect of the so-called 'poverty premium'). Lack of home insurance is also correlated with poor mental health (Payne, 2000).

Part (b) of Table 11.1 shows marked increases in all three key markers of problems in relation to credit, debt and savings. For all households, these issues are affecting between a third and a half more households than in 1999. As expected, the incidence of these problems is markedly higher for poorer households, and especially so for PSE poor. Comparing those on relative low income after housing costs in 2012 with the equivalent group in 1999, we can see that the use of informal borrowing has now increased for people on low incomes. Being behind on bills or credit has remained steady for the low-income group, and being unable to afford regular saving has fallen within this group (although still affecting a majority). While the apparent absence of a further increase of debt and repayment problems among the income-poor may seem to be a positive feature, their risk

Table 11.1: Key financial exclusion measures over time and by poverty status (percent within each year/poverty group)

(a) Financial services

| | | | Poor (AROP) | | Poor |
| | All | All | BHC | AHC | PSE |
Exclusion indicators	1999	2012	1999	2012	2012
No bank account (individual)		5		6	7
No bank account (household)	5	4	16	5	3
Limited/inadequate banks	13	16	19	15	13
Can't afford home contents insurance	8	13	30	31	44

(b) Credit/debt/savings

| | | | Poor (AROP) | | Poor |
| | All | All | BHC | AHC | PSE |
Measures	1999	2012	1999	2012	2012
Used informal borrowing	11	22	34	44	60
Behind on bills/credit (year)	14	20	42	41	55
Can't afford regular savings	24	32	75	57	79

Note: 'Poor' households in 1999 identified using the standard 'at risk of poverty' (AROP) measure of below 60% of median equivalised income before housing costs (BHC); for 2012 figures we use poverty after housing costs (AHC) and PSE poverty based on material deprivation.

of such problems remains two to-three times higher than the non-poor.[1] The trends also indicate that these problems have increased disproportionately among the non-poor. Over the next section, we return to this group of additional financially stressed households, to look at their profile and the factors associated with this phenomenon.

Borrowing, debt and arrears

The problem of debt among households in the UK has risen significantly since the late 1990s, although there has been some level of reduction in some types of debt (for example, mortgages) since the period of financial crisis around 2008-10. Levels of borrowing have become increasingly problematic, both in terms of the growing proportion of people using 'informal' sources of borrowing to meet everyday living requirements and in those who are struggling with repayment problems (Bridges and Disney, 2004). Informal systems are typically more expensive, and may have additional risks attached to them. While this is most concerning with sources such as pawnbrokers, money and payday lenders, even loans from friends or family may strain social relationships.

As shown in Table 11.2 (columns 1-2), there has been a notable increase in the proportion of households using such borrowing, particularly in the categories of 'pawnbroker/cash converter' and 'money lender/payday lender/doorstep lender', and a more than doubling in borrowing from families. Some of this increase will be explained by the rapid growth of payday lending companies in this period. Such companies offer loans with few or no credit checks, but at annualised interest rates as high as 4000 per cent (Skiba and Tobacman, 2007). The rapidly increasing visibility of such lenders on UK high streets in the years following the financial crisis has attracted considerable media attention. However, the increase in borrowing from other sources, including friends and family, suggests an increase in the need/demand for borrowing arising from financial pressures.

Informal borrowing is three to four times more likely for PSE-poor households in 2012, and it can be seen that the increase in borrowing is marked among the poor as much as in the overall population. It is interesting to note that PSE poverty shows a somewhat greater association with informal borrowing than relative low income (after housing costs, 'AHC'), again confirming that PSE poverty is a better poverty measure. However, people who subjectively feel poor 'all the time' are even more likely to report reliance on informal borrowing than the PSE poor group. This may suggest that this subjective poverty indicator is an even more sensitive indicator of current poverty

Table 11.2: Lenders used for borrowing to meet day-to-day needs, 1999 and 2012 and by poverty indicator (percent of households within each year/ poverty group)

Type of lender used for day-to-day needs	All 1999	All 2012	PSE poor 1999	PSE poor 2012	Low income AHC 2012	Feel poor all the time
Pawnbroker/A&B/cash converter	1	2	2	8	6	14
Money lender/payday/doorstep	2	5	6	15	9	18
Unlicensed lender		0		0	0	0
Social Fund		4		13	9	18
Credit union		1		3	3	4
Friends	4	7	14	22	16	30
Family	8	17	22	44	32	53
Any 1-3	2	6	8	18	12	25
Any	11	22	32	60	44	71

Note: A&B = Albermarle and Bond; AHC = after housing costs.

experience, and/or that being forced to rely on informal borrowing is a painful reminder of financial stress and poverty.

The reliance on borrowing from family, both in terms of its level and its increase, is noteworthy, and echoes findings on severe poverty and destitution reported in Chapter 3. It is particularly noteworthy that over half of people who are, by their own estimate, in poverty 'all the time' use their family as a source of credit. As the family providing such credit is also often likely to be poor, this may have wider repercussions on the lending as well as the receiving household. This certainly highlights the importance of social networks, and particularly family, for those who are struggling to get by (see also Bailey et al, 2015, and Chapter 5 in this volume).

While taking on informal loans is one side of problem debt, falling behind on regular bills/payments represents another very common form and further evidence of financial stress. The PSE surveys show that the prevalence of these types of debt or arrears has risen by half since 1999. Figure 11.1 shows the pattern across different types of bill, and highlights particularly sharp increases in housing and energy arrears as well as in consumer credit (credit cards, hire purchase) and TV licence arrears. In no case have arrears become less common. More than one in every 15 people now has arrears on their rent or mortgage, so risking possible loss of their home, while more than one in five people is in arrears on at least one kind of bill. For poor people, short-term shortfalls leading to arrears are more likely to necessitate borrowing from expensive, high-interest credit providers (Gritten, 2011) while also damaging credit scores and thereby limiting access to formal credit in future.

The descent of a household from going into arrears on some bills to finally suffering from severe indebtedness can be seen as a journey along a continuum. Household and personal savings, as well as help from friends and family, can reduce financial vulnerability, but at the same time arrears on bills and debts, especially with informal lenders, contribute to such vulnerability. Early warning signs include a lack of savings, difficulty getting to the end of the month and a build-up of arrears. Households which are already suffering from such financial vulnerability have much less resilience in the face of sudden expenses or a loss of income, for example resulting from illness, unemployment or the breakdown of an essential household item. The outcome in some cases can be severe poverty or destitution, as described in Chapter 3.

Belfield et al (2015) review trends since 2004 in arrears on household bills alongside other indicators such as material deprivation, for different broad household groups, based on Family Resource Survey

Figure 11.1: Households with arrears/'behind' by type of bill/payment, 1999 and 2012 (percent)

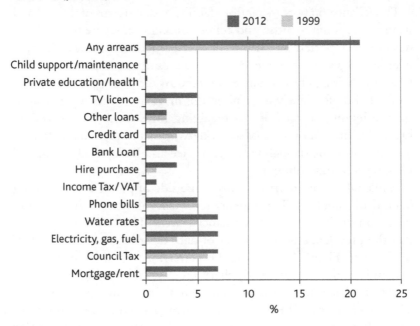

(FRS) data. Given differences in the exact time period and bills covered it is difficult to make precise comparisons, but their analysis shows only moderate increases up to 2010, some reduction after that but a resumed increase in 2013. It is possible that much of the increase shown in Figure 11.1 occurred between 1999 and 2004, when credit liberalisation was particularly noticeable. Belfield et al (2015) are not able to readily account for these recent fluctuations, except that the 2013 increase seems to be associated with the localisation of Council Tax support and other benefit reforms.

Figure 11.2 clearly shows the relationship between such arrears and the degree of poverty. Of those in 'severe poverty' (based on combination of objective and subjective criteria), a third or more are in arrears on each of the following: mortgage or rent, Council Tax, energy bills, water charges and TV licence. This underlines the significance of both housing and fuel costs for poverty, but also perhaps reflects the point that these can be, effectively and within limits, cheaper forms of borrowing to get by on. It is also noteworthy that these types of arrears are much more common for the poor groups than are the various forms of consumer credit, which are often linked in popular comment to financial difficulty. Whereas consumer credit may be incurred to meet discretionary or 'inessential' expenditures, rent/mortgage, fuel/

Figure 11.2: Households with arrears/'behind' by type of bill/payment and degree of poverty (percent)

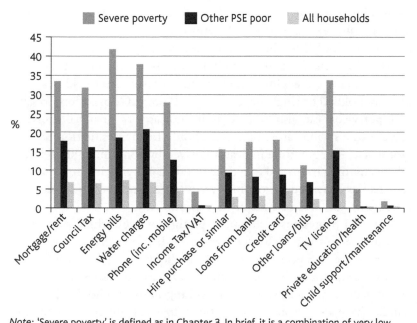

Note: 'Severe poverty' is defined as in Chapter 3. In brief, it is a combination of very low income, material deprivation and subjective poverty.

utilities and Council Tax are all 'essential' and (ultimately) relatively unavoidable. They are also, interestingly, more under national or local government control, as underlined in Chapter 3.

Subjective assessments of financial stress

A further set of measures describe people's own perception of the extent to which their household is managing to keep up with bills. Some research has suggested that differences in perceptions of indebtedness may be influenced by factors other than the actual level of debt. Respondents suffering from depression or other mental health problems are considerably more likely to consider their financial situation problematic, while other socio-demographic factors may also influence the level of financial difficulty considered problematic (Bridges and Disney, 2010). On the other hand, subjective measures of arrears also give a better understanding of the extent to which the financial problems are experienced as problematic. Research has also shown that stress arising from debt and arrears may be associated with, and may well cause, mental as well as physical health problems (Payne, 2000; McKay and Collard, 2006; Gathergood, 2012).

We constructed a composite indicator of households who considered themselves subject to 'financial pressure' reporting that: it is 'a constant struggle' to keep up with bills; they are not keeping up; could not meet a major expense of £500; cannot spend money on self; their income is a lot below the amount they consider they need to avoid poverty. We classify these households as under 'financial pressure'. This is actually quite a broad definition, capturing nearly 42 per cent of households. The single deprivation indicator of 'can't afford to save £20 per week' can also be used as an indicator of financial stress, as can a group of indicators of a household's financial situation having 'got worse' – a composite indicator derived by combining households where anything happened to reduce standard of living in last 2 years or who had experienced various life events (including divorce, separation, retirement, job loss, or a major health problem).

Figure 11.3 presents a summary picture of these three subjective indicators across key socio-demographics. It shows that all are much higher for the PSE poor than for all households, as well as for informal borrowers and for both types of renters. Older households clearly have less subjective financial stress than working-age households, although families have a lower incidence of their financial situation having got worse; this may reflect the impacts of retirement and ill health on the older group. Interestingly, these subjective financial problems are not so much higher for households with no bank account, and in one case ('got worse') they are less prevalent. This suggests that the bank

Figure 11.3: Indicators of financial pressure by poverty, financial exclusion, household type and tenure

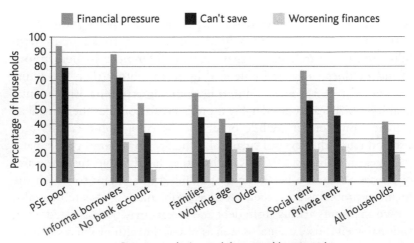

Poverty, exclusion and demographic categories

account issue is less critical for the more problematic contemporary aspects of financial exclusion.

Can we get more of a sense of how serious these 'financial pressures' are, relative to core poverty? One way of doing this is to look at the PSE-UK financial hardship indicators, which include a variety of economising behaviours suggestive of acute financial need. Individuals report on these behaviours in answer to the general question:

> In the last 12 months, to help you keep your living costs down, have you:
>
> - skimped on food yourself so that others in the household would have enough to eat?
> - bought secondhand clothes for yourself instead of new?
> - continued wearing clothes/shoes that had worn out instead of replacing them?
> - cut back on visits to hairdresser/barber?
> - postponed visits to the dentist?
> - spent less on hobbies than you would like?
> - gone without or cut back on social visits, going to the pub or eating out?
> - cut back on or cancelled pension contribution?
>
> (PSE-UK 2012
> Living Standards Survey Questionnaire)

In the survey, individuals were given a number of options to indicate the frequency at which such economising responses occurred. In Figure 11.4, we show the proportion of household representatives responding 'often' to each case as a marker of significant economising, and compare its incidence between households who are PSE poor and other households whom we have classified as experiencing subjective financial pressure (the first of the three measures described above), as well as households in neither of these categories.

The patterns of response are broadly as expected. PSE-poor households show more frequent and more severe economising behaviours: 25–30 per cent of such households skimp food, cut clothes, dentist, or pension contributions; while around 50-60 per cent cut hairdresser, hobbies, social life/pub/meals out. Financially stressed households who are not PSE poor still have to make similar adjustments, although the proportion making these is rather less than those who are PSE poor as well.

Financially pressured households account for 43 per cent of all households; within this, 23 per cent are PSE poor and 20 per cent

Figure 11.4: What households cut back on 'often' by poverty and financial pressure status (percent)

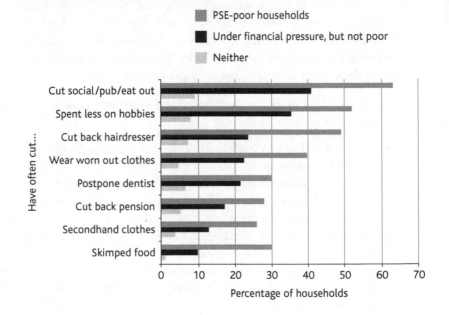

are not. This latter is a key group whose position appears to have deteriorated quite a lot, with the greater incidence of arrears, informal borrowing and other indicators of financial stress discussed above. This may be seen as one further manifestation of the growth of a 'precariat' in the UK (Standing, 2011).

Financial exclusion and social exclusion

This chapter so far has looked at objective and subjective ways of measuring financial exclusion, with a particular focus on changes over time and on the relationship with our core measures of poverty. But how does financial exclusion fit with the wider picture of social exclusion? Is it mainly just related to, or through, poverty, or are there relationships with other dimensions of exclusion?

We explore these questions by looking at a composite flag indicator for 'problem debt', which highlights households who have three or more of the debts listed in Figure 11.1, or who have borrowed from two or more of the lenders in Table 11.2, or from any one of the first four, or who are falling behind with bills. This affects 16 per cent of households, but the proportion of PSE-poor households affected is three times that, at 47 per cent. This relative risk ratio for problem debt of around 3 in the case of PSE poverty is the highest for any of the binary indicators of different domains of social exclusion (as defined in the Appendix to Chapter 3). In other words, problem debt is most closely related to poverty in terms of economic/material resources. The next highest is the employment domain, at 2.7, indicating a clear link with current or recent unemployment. Other moderately high risks are associated with exclusions in terms of social activities, housing conditions and health (between 2.1 and 2.5). The relationship with other domains of exclusion is weaker.

We can use a multivariate logistic regression model to predict the incidence of problem debt across the PSE-UK household sample, in order to highlight the relative influence of different socio-demographic factors alongside poverty and unemployment. Quite a reasonable model can be fitted with 13 significant explanatory variables, accounting for approaching half of the variation (Nagelkerke r-square 0.46) and correctly predicting 49 per cent of positive cases and 88 per cent of all cases. This confirms the strong effect of PSE poverty and the significant effects of current and recent unemployment, while also showing quite strong positive effects of younger age versus negative for retirement age. The model shows that problem debt is also related to female-headed households, number of children, rented (especially social) housing, bad health, and receipt of income-related benefits. Living in a poor neighbourhood, particularly the worst 10 per cent of areas, also significantly increases the odds of problem debt. The latter features pick up the theme from the 1990s literature, on the geographical dimension of financial exclusion, but may also reflect cultural and behavioural factors, including an element of (lack of) financial management capability.

What about causality running in the other direction? Are problem debts a key factor adversely affecting other key outcomes, whether as an original cause, key trigger or intervening factor? We have already referred to some literature which has drawn a link with mental health problems. There are indications that these problems may impact on individuals' wider sense of well-being and happiness, as discussed in the following chapter (Chapter 12). Problem debt is also clearly related to the experience of severe poverty and the risk of destitution, as discussed in Chapter 3.

Social capital and financial exclusion

There is a body of literature which underlines the importance of reciprocal social support networks in the mitigation of acute financial hardship for poor families. The extent of borrowing from family and friends shown in Table 11.2 is striking evidence of the importance of this link, and of the notion that the social capital embodied in such relationships can translate literally into financial capital, thereby providing a buffer enabling households to absorb financial shocks. However, not everybody enjoys the same level of potential support through family and other relationships, whether because of limitations in the extent or closeness of kinship or friendship networks or because of the economic situation of those key friends and relations. To some extent, these limitations seem to correlate with poverty at individual and area level (Bailey et al, 2015).

We looked slightly further into the PSE data to see to what extent we could observe these relationships working to buffer financial pressure and poverty. In particular, we looked at the relationship between measures of the strength of relationships with relatives and friends, in terms of numbers (implying broader 'bridging' ties) and frequency (implying stronger 'bonding' ties), and the frequency of risky informal borrowing versus borrowing from family or friends, at different levels in the pressure–poverty spectrum. Some relationships are as expected: people with low supportive networks under financial pressure or poverty are more likely to incur risky borrowing; people with high frequency contact with relatives, when under financial pressure or poverty, are very likely to borrow from family. The same is true to a lesser extent where there are high frequency contacts with friends. Those who have relatively low contact with families or friends and are under financial pressure (but not poor) are very unlikely to borrow from them. Some other relationships seem a little perverse: high frequency contact with relatives is associated, for people in poverty or under financial pressure, with somewhat higher levels of risky borrowing – this may be because the capacity of relatives to lend has been exhausted, or perhaps in some instances due to a desire to keep up with relatives (for example, in buying things for children).

Societal trends and financial exclusion

Over the past three decades, banking services have become increasingly interwoven into the everyday lives of individuals, a process referred to as 'financialisation' (Marron, 2013; Coppock, 2013; Sinclair, 2013). However, as modern society moves inexorably towards a near-universal take-up of banking, non-use of such services has grown into an indicator of exclusion from normal social life. The past decades have seen a shift in perception, and the use of a bank account has become a societal expectation rather than a personal choice. Indeed, deprivation from bank accounts arguably matters primarily *because of* that societal expectation (Coppock, 2013).

In the UK, these processes have led to a policy shift from the provision of basic financial services to an increasing emphasis on promoting financial capability. Concurrently, having a bank account has become a requirement to receive an increasingly large variety of benefits, including Tax Credits and Child Benefits, and in due course, to receipt of Universal Credit incorporating Housing Benefits. Meanwhile, as bank branches were withdrawn and electronic banking gained prominence, bank use changed from what was once a face-to-face service into a much more individual and impersonal experience (Devlin, 2005; Mitton, 2008; Marron, 2013). Concurrently, it has been argued that an ongoing trend of reduced access to affordable credit for poorer families and communities has led to a much greater reliance on more expensive 'sub-prime' lenders, including doorstep moneylenders, payday loans or high-interest deferred payments for goods, the number of which has soared in response (Fuller and Mellor, 2008). Evidence on the growth of some of those was presented earlier.

As a result of these cumulative changes, the complexity of financial management has increased considerably for financial service users, placing greater demands on their financial capability, computer skills and literacy than in the past. Difficulties associated with the non-use or under-use of banking and financial services are no longer primarily reflected in problems with geographical access or the conditions associated with specific products, but need to be understood as in the context of broader inequalities, including disparities in the social networks, education and the skills to cope with the requirements of increasing complexity of financial service use (Taylor, 2011).

The results of the 2012 PSE-UK survey have shown that poverty is still the main predictor of financial exclusion, particularly problem debt, in the UK, and that it is still associated with exclusion from some financial products, such as home contents insurance. However, few households now lack a bank account and this is less related to poverty than previously. They show that financial pressure is experienced more widely across the population, many of whom are living in varying degrees of financial precariousness, and responding to this in various ways including cutting back on a range of items. Financial inclusion policies discussed earlier in this chapter have addressed some of the problems which were known to act as barriers to banking service take-up of low-income households. Future policies should reflect a more heterogeneous population of socially or financially excluded or stressed households, with a greater variety of financial service needs. However, it is unclear how much practical commitment there is within the current UK government to these issues, nothwithstanding high-level statements of empathy with people's everyday struggles to get by.

Conclusion

From comparing PSE data from 2012 with 1999 we show clear evidence that the problem issue of non-use of financial services, particularly bank accounts, is contained or reducing, although there are growing concerns about the quality of service from the financial providers. By contrast, the main indicators of financial stress and problem debt have greatly escalated in recent years. In addition, it is these latter indicators that are strongly related to poverty, whereas the former are not.

The evidence on coping strategies and the read-across to severe poverty and destitution (Chapter 3) show the important role of financial stress in the dynamics of poverty for individual families. At the same time, financial stress indicators affect a wider section of the population than 'the poor' as normally defined, particularly a substantial group of working families (mainly in rented housing) for whom financial stress is a significant issue and who may be vulnerable to future experience of poverty and material deprivation. Financial stress may also impact on health and well-being. We also explore the role of social capital in enabling mutual support in times of financial stress, finding some evidence for the expected buffering role but also highlighting limitations. It is unclear whether the momentum of previous policies towards financial inclusion will be maintained, and we suggest that these need to re-orient somewhat towards financial capability including computer literacy. Meanwhile, the broader spread of financial stress and debt problems suggests a questioning of societal trends to greater financialisation and reliance upon debt.

Note

[1] The 1999 survey measure of low income is on a 'before housing costs' basis, so there may not be complete comparability.

References

Appleyard, L. (2015) 'Financial inclusion: review of Coalition Government policies 2010-2015', *Briefing Paper BP4/2015*, Centre on Household Assets and Savings Management, Birmingham: University of Birmingham, http://www.birmingham.ac.uk/Documents/college-social-sciences/social-policy/CHASM/briefing-papers/2017/BP4-2017-Magda-Nowakowska-James-Gregory.pdf.

Bailey, N., Besemer, K., Bramley, G. and Livingston, M. (2015) 'How neighbourhood social mix shapes household resources through social networks and services', *Housing Studies*, 30(2), 295-314.

Beck, T., Demirguc-Kunt, A. and Peria, M. (2007) 'Reaching out: access to and use of banking services across countries', *Journal of Financial Economics*, Elsevier, Vol. 85, pp 234-66.

Belfield, C., Cribb, J., Hood, A. and Joyce, R. (2015) *Living standards, poverty and inequality in the UK: 2015*, London: Institute for Fiscal Studies.

Besemer, K. and Bramley, G. (2011) *Housing and the living environment indicators in the PSE survey*, PSE Working Paper No. 6, Poverty and Social exclusion in the UK (PSE), http://www.poverty.ac.uk.

Bridges, S. and Disney, R. (2004) 'Use of credit and arrears on debt among low-income families in the United Kingdom', *Fiscal Studies* 25(1), 1-25.

Bridges, S., and Disney, R. (2010) 'Debt and depression', *Journal of health economics*, 29(3), 388-403.

Carbo, S., Gardener, E. P. M. and Molyneux, P. (2007) 'Financial exclusion in Europe', *Public Money & Management*, 27(1), 21-2.

Čihák, M., Demirgüç-Kunt, A., Feyen, E. and Levine, R. (2012) *Benchmarking financial systems around the world*, World Bank Policy Research Working Paper (6175), Washington, DC.

Collard, S. (2007) 'Toward financial inclusion in the UK: progress and challenges', *Public Money and Management*, 27(1), 13-20.

Collard, S., and Kempson, E. (2005) *Affordable credit: The way forward*, Bristol: Policy Press.

Coppock, S. (2013) 'The everyday geographies of financialisation: impacts, subjects and alternatives', *Cambridge Journal of Regions, Economy and Society*, 6(3), 479-500.

Demirgüç-Kunt, A., Klapper, L. F., Singer, D. and Van Oudheusden, P. (2015) *The global Findex database 2014: measuring financial inclusion around the world*, World Bank Policy Research Working Paper (7255), Washington, DC.

Department for Education (2014) *Child Poverty Strategy 2014 to 2017*, Policy document, London: DfEE.

Devlin, J. F. (2005) 'A detailed study of financial exclusion in the UK', *Journal of Consumer Policy*, 28(1), 75-108.

DTI (Department of Trade and Industry) (2013) *Fair, clear and competitive: The consumer credit market in the 21st century*, Cm 6040, London: The Stationery Office.

Fenge, L.-A., Hean, S., Worswick, L., Wilkinson, C., Fearnley, S. and Ersser, S. (2012) 'The impact of the economic recession on well-being and quality of life of older people', *Health & Social Care in the Community*, 20(6), 617-24.

Financial Inclusion Commission (2015) *Financial inclusion: Improving the financial health of the nation*, http://www.financialinclusioncommission. org.uk/pdfs/fic_report_2015.pdf

Fitzpatrick, S., Bramley, G., Sosenko, F., Blenkinsopp, J., Johnsen, S., Littlewood, M., Netto, G. and Watts, B. (2016) *Destitution in the UK: Final Report*, York: Joseph Rowntree Foundation.

Fuller, D. (1998) 'Credit union development: financial inclusion and exclusion', *Geoforum*, 29(2), 145-57.

Fuller, D. and Mellor, M. (2008) 'Banking for the poor: addressing the needs of financially excluded communities in Newcastle Upon Tyne', *Urban Studies*, 45(7), 1505-24.

Gathergood, J. (2012), 'Debt and depression: causal links and social norm effects', *The Economic Journal,* 122(563), 1094-114.

Gritten, A. (2011) 'New insights into consumer confidence in financial services', *International Journal of Bank Marketing,* 29(2), 90-106.

Hartfree, Y. and Collard, S. (2015) 'Locating credit and debt within an anti-poverty strategy for the UK', *Journal of Poverty and Social Justice* 23(3), 203-14.

Hogarth, J. M., Anguelov, C. E. and Lee, J. (2005) 'Who has a bank account? Exploring changes over time, 1989–2001', *Journal of Family and Economic Issues*, 26(1), 7-30.

House of Commons Treasury Committee (2006) *Financial inclusion: The roles of the Government and the FSA, and financial capability*, First Report of Session 2006–07, London: The Stationery Office.

Kempson, E., Atkinson, A., and Pilley, O. (2004) *Policy level response to financial exclusion in developed economies: lessons for developing countries*, Bristol: Personal Finance Research Centre, University of Bristol.

Kempson, E., and Whyley, C. (1999) *Kept out or opted out: Understanding and combating financial exclusion*, Bristol: The Policy Press.

Leyshon, A. and Thrift, N. (1995) 'Geographies of financial exclusion: financial abandonment in Britain and the United States', *Transactions of the Institute of British Geographers*, 20(3), 312-41.

Marron, D. (2012) 'Producing over-indebtedness', *Journal of Cultural Economy*, 5(4), 407-21.

Marron, D. (2013) 'Governing poverty in a neoliberal age: New Labour and the case of financial exclusion', *New Political Economy* 18(6), 785-810.

Marshall, J. N. (2004) 'Financial institutions in disadvantaged areas: a comparative analysis of policies encouraging financial inclusion in Britain and the United States', *Environment and Planning A*, 36(2), 241-62.

McKay, S. and Collard, S. (2006) 'Debt and financial exclusion' in C. Pantazis, D. Gordon and R. Levitas (eds) *Poverty and social exclusion in Britain*, Bristol: The Policy Press, pp 191-216.

Mitton, L. (2008) *Financial inclusion in the UK: Review of initiatives to tackle financial exclusion*, York: Joseph Rowntree Foundation/ University of Kent.

ONS (Office for National Statistics) (1999) *Family Spending 1998/9*, London: The Stationery Office.

Payne, S. (2000) 'Poverty, social exclusion and mental health: findings from the 1999 PSE Survey', *Working Paper (15)*, Townsend Centre for International Poverty Research, Bristol: University of Bristol.

Ryder, N. and Thomas, R. (2011) 'Convenient credit and consumer protection – a critical review of the responses of Labour and Coalition Governments', *Journal of Social Welfare and Family Law*, 33(1), 85-95.

Salignac, F., Muir, K. and Wong, J. (2016) 'Are you really financially excluded if you choose not to be included? Insights from social exclusion, resilience and ecological systems', *Journal of Social Policy*, 45(02), 269-86.

Simpson, W. and Buckland, J. (2009) 'Examining evidence of financial and credit exclusion in Canada from 1999 to 2005', *The Journal of Socio-Economics*, 38(6), 966-76.

Sinclair, S. (2013) 'Financial inclusion and social financialisation: Britain in a European context', *International Journal of Sociology and Social Policy*, 33(11/12), 658-76.

Skiba, P. and Tobacman, J. (2007) *The profitability of payday loans*, mimeo, University of Oxford.

Standing, G. (2011) *The precariat: The new dangerous class*, London: Bloomsbury.

Taylor, M. (2011) 'Measuring financial capability and its determinants using survey data', *Social Indicators Research*, 102(2), 297-314.

Whyley, C., McCormick, J. and Kempson, E. (1998) *Paying for Peace of Mind*, London: Policy Studies Institute.

TWELVE

The poverty of well-being

Mike Tomlinson and Lisa Wilson

Introduction

The main aim of this chapter is to explore the material basis of well-being using data from the Poverty and Social Exclusion UK (PSE-UK) 2012 survey. The chapter begins by reviewing contemporary discussions of well-being and the ubiquitous presence of the concept in public and private sector discourses. It explores the ideas behind the rise of the 'happiness industry' and shows how the measurement of well-being has been at the forefront of some recent developments in official statistics, principally through survey questions on life satisfaction, happiness and anxiety.

Using the PSE-UK data, we analyse the relationship between poverty and satisfaction/dissatisfaction with various circumstances such as employment, accommodation and neighbourhood, as well as between poverty and overall satisfaction with life and feeling part of the community. Several measures of income poverty and deprivation are used to explore the consistency of relationship between very low levels of satisfaction with life and poverty. We also use regression analysis to distinguish the impact on overall well-being of factors such as material deprivation, long-term illness, age and employment status.

The chapter concludes with a discussion of well-being and social policy. One of the consequences of the mainstreaming of well-being is that subjective happiness scores are now receiving much more attention than traditional measures of social justice (such as unemployment, poverty and mortality rates). The explicit assumption is that how people feel is more important to both the outcomes of policies and to the way governments seek to achieve social policy goals in the era of austerity – by 'nudging', and in many cases compelling, individuals towards healthier and more enriching behaviours. On the basis of the PSE-UK evidence, we argue that substantial gains in well-being are most likely to be achieved by reducing poverty and providing more support to those with long-term illnesses and disabilities.

The ubiquity of well-being

The promotion of well-being has lately become all things to all people. 'Well-being' and the associated concepts of 'happiness' and 'quality of life' are liberally used in public and private sector discourses as if there is now universal agreement on the common purpose of corporate effort and activity (Scott, 2012). As a policy goal, the improvement of well-being is suitably vague and all-encompassing. Such is the non-specific nature of the term that it typically needs to be qualified in order to clarify what is under discussion – workplace well-being, environmental well-being, financial well-being and so on. Well-being is no longer the exclusive purpose of health professionals, but is also a matter for companies, institutions and, indeed, countries such that 'national well-being' indexes quantifying the metaphorical health of the nation are proliferating.

This is a welcome development, according to Layard (2005) who, more than ten years ago, called for a revolution across academia and government to make happiness the overall purpose of public policy. All policies he argues, including for example taxation, or the regulation of work and pay, the environment, education and mental health, need to be evaluated and calibrated in terms of their happiness outcomes. This is clearly a radical departure from a policy framework based on social justice (Burchardt, 2006) and represents an approach that focuses on subjective and qualitative aspects of life, and 'valorises people's assessments of their situation, challenging the tendency for researchers and other experts to "know" without consulting people' (Daly, 2011, p 41). From Layard's Action for Happiness project, it is evident that individuals themselves, rather than governments or employers, are seen as the real drivers of well-being. While the 'science of well-being' can inform changes at the level of institutional policies, the priority is for individuals to realise that happiness is 'heavily influenced by our choices – our inner attitudes, how we approach our relationships, our personal values and our sense of purpose' (www.actionforhappiness. org). Happy and positive people are 'contagious' and can not only turn around their own lives but also increase the well-being of their families, friends, neighbours and work colleagues.

Populist presentations around the 'most and least happy places' to live in the UK are now a regular event (BBC, 2016). The latest revelation is that the Western Isles has the highest happiness, while 'Liverpool and Wolverhampton are the saddest' places in the UK (Mailonline, 2016). Just six months earlier, Fermanagh and Omagh were announced as the happiest places in the UK, while Bolsover in Derbyshire was the saddest (BBC, 2015). For all the emphasis on the happiest places to work, the happiest cities on earth and the happiest countries, the geographical league-table approach to well-being misses the point according to Dolan (2014). While we may imagine that a move to a Scottish island will improve our well-being, the structures of place, employment status or income matter less than the focus on how individuals can learn to improve their own well-being by means of deliberate choices around the experience of pleasure and purpose.

The 'happiness industry' is more contradictory and manipulative than the promoters of well-being suggest, argues Davies (2015). At its core, the well-being business reflects an emerging alliance between positive psychology (Seligman, 2002) and economics. Neo-classical economists construct models based on the supposedly rational market choices of consumers and other economic actors, but the starting point for 'behavioural economics' is that choices are influenced by emotions and the behaviours of those around us (Kahneman and Tversky, 1979; Kahneman, 2003). Hence the focus is on 'choice architectures' and 'nudging' people towards better lifestyle and consumer choices (Thaler and Sunstein, 2009).

Davies sees the measurement of subjective well-being as a key characteristic of the happiness industry. Data on well-being as 'a bio-psycho-social capacity' (Davies, 2011) are needed in order to explore the mismatch between economic development, material circumstances and how people feel about their lives, and as a starting point for addressing neo-liberalism's various crises. It is no accident, therefore, that the impulse towards subjective indicators is particularly associated with periods of conservative political ascendancy and restrictive economic policies (Scott, 2012, p 20). In such times, there is less interest in measuring social progress in terms of unemployment, poverty, and inadequate housing, for example, and more concern with individual behaviours and psychologies: the problem is the behaviour of the poor, not the distribution of income, culminating in social policies that coerce or 'nudge' people off benefits.

Without question, the demand for well-being indicators based on asking people how they feel about aspects of their lives has grown considerably in recent decades and is supported from diverse quarters. While the ascendancy of positive psychology and behavioural economics have been central in the recent promotion of the well-being agenda, we should also note the part played by climate change and the limits to growth – going 'beyond GDP' (Stiglitz et al, 2009) – as well as the political and academic investments in the indicators themselves, including the flourishing 'science of happiness' (Tomlinson and Kelly, 2013).

Measuring well-being

In the UK context, the Conservative Party has put most political weight behind subjective well-being indicators, led by the Quality of Life policy group established in 2005. This recommended that any future Conservative government should introduce a well-being index intended to link subjective well-being to crime and divorce rates, among other indicators (Tomlinson and Kelly, 2013, p 140). There had been some earlier developments under the Blair government, notably from the Department for Environment, Food and Rural Affairs (DEFRA) which, from 2007, introduced survey questions on life satisfaction generally and in relation to 11 specific aspects of life (personal relationships, health and so on) (DEFRA, 2005). In 2010, Prime Minister Cameron announced that from April 2011, the Office of National Statistics (ONS) would start collecting data on subjective well-being, which would be included in a National Well-being Index under the domain of 'individual well-being'. There were nine other proposed domains: our relationships (family and social life), health, what we do (work and leisure), where we live (neighbourhood, crime, fear, green spaces), personal finance, education and skills, governance (voting, trust in political institutions), the economy (GDP, household income, price inflation), and the natural environment (air pollution, emissions, renewables) (Beaumont, 2012).

To measure individual well-being, ONS introduced four new 'happiness questions'. On a scale of 0 to ten, where 0 is 'not at all' and 10 is 'completely', people are asked:

1. Overall, how satisfied are you with your life nowadays?
2. Overall, to what extent do you feel the things you do in your life are worthwhile?
3. Overall, how happy did you feel yesterday?
4. Overall, how anxious did you feel yesterday?

The results are typically presented in two ways: as an average score for a selected variable, such as region or occupational status, or as the proportion with low, medium or high banded scores. The latest available results (ONS, 2015a) reveal that personal well-being across the UK has improved each year since 2011/12. The average life satisfaction score, for example, was 7.6 (out of 10) for 2014/15 compared to 7.4

in 2011/12, representing a statistically significant year-on-year change from 2011/12. The average score for feeling that the things people do in life are worthwhile has risen to 7.8 for 2014/15, an increase of 0.16 since 2011/12. Looking at the proportion with low well-being (scoring 0-4) and high well-being (scoring 9-10), there are similar improvements. In 2014/15, 4.8 per cent had low well-being compared to 6.6 per cent in 2011/12. Just over a quarter (26.1 per cent) had high well-being in 2011/12 but this rose to 28.8 per cent by 2014/15. Clearly, in recent years, things are only getting better, on average.

There are, however, marked variations by health and employment status, and some by age. While the mean life satisfaction score for all adults in the UK was 7.61 for 2014/15, the score for those with a disability was 6.90 and for the unemployed, 6.80 (ONS, 2015b). Those with no disability scored 7.85 and those in employment, 7.71. The biggest variation in scores is in relation to self-reported health. Those whose health was 'very good' had a life satisfaction score of 8.10, compared to 4.97 for those with 'very bad' health. Those in 'bad' health had an average score of 5.96 and those in 'good' health, 7.69. Life satisfaction scores vary much less by age group. They are highest for younger and older groups (7.91 for 16- to 19-year-olds and 7.93 for 70- to 74-year-olds), with the lowest average score of 7.27 for 50- to 54-year-olds. Every five-year age band between 35 and 54 has a below average life satisfaction score.

There are some indications that inequalities in life satisfaction scores may be widening. For instance, the gap between the employed and the 'inactive' average life satisfaction scores was 0.10 in 2011/12 (derived from ONS, 2012) but 0.17 by 2014/15. Similarly, the gap in average scores between those with a disability and those without was 0.8 in 2011/12 but had grown to 0.95 by 2014/15. Overall, the higher well-being scores recorded for 2014/5 resulted less from a reduction in the proportion of people with low scores and owe more to a growth in the proportion with high scores which 'suggests growing inequality in reported personal well-being' (ONS, 2015a, p 17).

To date, the ONS has not published any papers exploring subjective well-being in relation to poverty or aspects of social exclusion, with the exception of scores for disability, unemployment and labour market inactivity. There are, however, two papers that explore the subjective well-being data in relation income and wealth. Using the Wealth and Assets survey of 2011/12, Chamberlain (2015) found that the higher an individual's wealth, the higher the life satisfaction, happiness and feeling life is worthwhile, and the lower the anxiety (controlling for nine factors including sex, age, health and employment status). With income, the relationships held good for life satisfaction and happiness but not for anxiety and feeling life is worthwhile (Chamberlain, 2015, p 14-15). Chamberlain also looked at the distribution of wealth and income, finding that the only significant differences for wealth in relation to life satisfaction were between decile one and decile five, and between decile one and decile ten. For income, individuals in households in the top three income deciles 'are more likely to report higher life satisfaction than those living in households in the fifth income decile and individuals living in households in the bottom 2 income deciles are more likely to report lower levels of happiness than those living in the fifth wealth decile'. But when the other variables are controlled for, 'there are far fewer significant differences in the levels of well-being reported across the varying household income deciles' (Chamberlain, 2015, p 19).

The other ONS paper (Lewis, 2014) looks at income and expenditure. The headline findings are that individuals living in higher income households have 'higher life satisfaction and happiness, and lower anxiety on average, but do not give significantly different ratings to their sense that the things they do in life are worthwhile, holding other factors equal' (Lewis, 2014, p 5). This paper also looked at income quintiles, finding that 'the biggest difference in all four measures of personal well-being between individuals in neighbouring fifths of the income distribution is between the bottom and second fifths' (Lewis, 2014, p 5). For individuals in the top household income quintile, life satisfaction is significantly greater than for those in any other quintile. This is not the case for anxiety, happiness or sense of worth.

The PSE-UK 2012 survey included a number of questions that contribute to the discussion of subjective well-being. Of the four new ONS happiness questions, however, only the overall life satisfaction question was included. The two 'affective' ONS questions (numbers 3 and 4 above) were ruled out largely on the grounds that the immediacy of mood sheds little light on the medium- and long-term relationship between poverty, forms of social exclusion and mental well-being. As questions, too much ambiguity surrounds phrases such as 'how anxious' or 'how happy' a person feels, and the immediacy of asking about 'yesterday' was thought to be of little value. These issues are picked up in guidelines published by the Organisation for Economic Cooperation and Development on measuring subjective well-being which point out, among other things, that the English word 'happy' does not translate well (OECD, 2013, p 70-1). Similar criticisms apply to the overarching question on feeling that 'the things you do in your life are worthwhile'. Rather than ask this, the PSE-UK survey is able to gauge comprehensively (and less bluntly and even intrusively) what people feel about specific aspects of their lives by asking them about, for example, social networks, employment and working conditions, poverty, personal relationships, social and political life, their health, and so on.

Well-being and poverty

In this section, we use the PSE-UK survey data to show how poverty is associated with significantly lower well-being scores. Well-being is captured through three main questions gauging how satisfied people are with (a) day-to-day activities, (b) feeling part of the community and (c) life overall (one of the ONS questions). As in the ONS surveys, an eleven-point scale (0 being completely dissatisfied and 10 being completely satisfied) is used for these three questions. The PSE-UK survey also asked people to rate their satisfaction with five other things: personal relationships, the management of personal finances, jobs, accommodation and area as a place to live. For these questions a five-point scale was used (very satisfied through to very dissatisfied).

Income poverty

As noted, the PSE-UK survey asked the ONS 'life satisfaction' question: 'How satisfied are you with your life nowadays?'. The average for all individuals (aged 18 and over) was 7.2, compared to the ONS result for 2011/12 which was 7.4.

The first part of Table 12.1 shows the average scores for the life satisfaction (out of 10) of adults for two income poverty measures: the below Minimum Income Standards (MIS) poverty line and PSE 'at-risk-of-poverty' (AROP – below 60 per cent of median household income) for income after housing costs (AHC) are deducted. Across both measures those identified as income-poor have life satisfaction scores well below the average and all of the differences between the 'not poor' and 'poor' are statistically significant. The highest life satisfaction score for any poor group is for those poor on the MIS measure, which is the broadest (42.9 per cent of adults are below this standard). Those in poverty by the PSE low-income poverty measure have the worst life satisfaction, with a score of 6.23. This is considerably below the average of 6.63 for people with a longstanding illness or disability.[1] Of all the income poverty measures calculated from the PSE-UK survey (only two are shown in Table 12.1), the PSE-UK measure gives the widest gap in life satisfaction scores between 'not poor' and 'poor'.

Table 12.1: Satisfaction with life by income poverty, deprivation and combined income and deprivation poverty

Mean scores of individuals (adults)	Not poor	Poor	% poor
Income poverty			
Below Minimum Income Standards poverty line 2012	7.62	6.65	42.9
PSE 'at-risk-of-poverty', AHC	7.54	6.23	23.5
Deprivation			
Child Poverty Act deprivation	7.52	5.67	17.4
PSE deprivation	7.82	6.08	34.0
Combined income and deprivation poverty			
PSE poverty	7.63	5.86	21.2
Child Poverty Act: combined low income and material deprivation	7.39	5.34	9.6

Note: Differences between 'poor' and 'not poor' all significant at p<0.001 level.

Deprivation

Deprivation appears to result in lower life satisfaction scores than income poverty. Table 12.1 shows two deprivation measures: one based on the PSE deprivation items and the other based on the reduced set of items used in the Child Poverty Act measure until its abolition (see Chapter 1). People deprived on the PSE measure have markedly lower life satisfaction on average than those poor on any of the low-income measures, although this is not a small group. The smaller group regarded as poor on the Child Poverty Act measure have lower satisfaction still.

If we look in more detail at the relationship between deprivation and life satisfaction, we find a continuous decline as deprivation increases (Figure 12.1). With no items lacking, individuals have a relatively high average life satisfaction score (8.02) compared to the average (7.22). At three items lacking, the life satisfaction score drops below the average and at five items lacking (6.43) there is a sharp drop of .60 points. For those lacking three *or more* items (one third of adults) the average life satisfaction score is 6.08 (not shown), again a score which is below those for income poverty. The score for those lacking five or more items (22 per cent of adults) is 5.53 (not shown).

Income poverty and deprivation

Going back to Table 12.1, we have two measures combining income poverty and deprivation. Those in poverty on both the PSE and the Child Poverty Act measures have much lower life satisfaction scores

Figure 12.1: Average satisfaction with life scores by number of deprivation items lacking (all individuals)

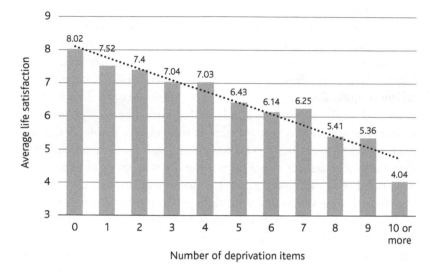

than the income poor. In the case of the PSE measure, this represents 10.5 million adults who lead lives that are considerably less satisfying than those of people with a longstanding illness or disability.

Poverty, low income and dissatisfaction

As we have seen, the ONS work on well-being defines 'low satisfaction' where people score between 0 and 4 on the eleven-point scale. In Table 12.2 we give the results for low satisfaction for the three questions asked in the PSE–UK survey using this scale. A fifth of people gave a low satisfaction score when asked about feeling part of the community, whereas about a tenth gave low satisfaction scores for life overall. Low satisfaction with day-to-day activities comes halfway between the two. Table 12.2 also gives the proportions with low satisfaction scores for the PSE poor and income poor. One third of those in PSE poverty have low satisfaction scores when it comes to feeling part of the community and for feeling that day-to-day activities

Table 12.2: PSE poverty and low satisfaction

% of adults with low satisfaction	Life overall	Day-to-day activities	Feeling part of the community
All adults	10.5	14.5	19.9
PSE income poor	23.0	26.9	30.7
PSE poverty	26.1	32.9	32.9

are worthwhile. Over one quarter have low satisfaction with their lives overall. The low satisfaction scores for PSE income poverty are slightly lower across the board.

As indicated earlier, the PSE-UK survey also asked about satisfaction with a number of specific aspects of life, using a five-point scale. Table 12.3 shows the proportions poor and not poor saying they were either 'slightly' or 'very' dissatisfied with their accommodation, personal relationships and so on, using the PSE poverty measure. The findings presented in Table 12.3 make clear that the effects of poverty on satisfaction stretch into many different areas of life. Those in poverty are just over twice as likely to be dissatisfied with personal relationships than those who are not poor. They are more than twice as likely to be dissatisfied with their job (if they have one) and the area they live in, over four times as dissatisfied with their accommodation and five times as dissatisfied with the way their household finances are managed.

The PSE-UK survey also measures poverty using a number of 'subjective' measures (see the Introduction for details). In Table 12.4, we show average satisfaction on the three broad measures across the four subjective poverty measures. Those who 'could genuinely say' they are poor now, 'all the time', record the lowest averages for satisfaction with life overall and in relation to day-to-day activities, and the joint lowest average for feeling part of the community. This suggests that the depth and duration of poverty has a powerful impact on social isolation and feeling that there is little satisfaction in life.

Figure 12.2 shows how overall life satisfaction rises as income rises. As with deprivation, this shows continuous change across the spectrum but it also reveals an additional important relationship. The gains in well-being from increasing incomes are much greater for poorer than for richer households. Moving from the lowest quintile to the second, average well-being rises by 0.98, but moving from the fourth quintile to the fifth, it rises by just 0.16. This suggests that, at least in relation to well-being, income redistribution is not a 'zero sum' game. Rather

Table 12.3: PSE poverty and dissatisfaction

% of adults 'slightly' or 'very' dissatisfied	Personal relationships	Way household finances are managed	Accommodation	Area as place to live	Job
Poor	12.8	12	11.6	15.3	12.1
Not poor	6.2	2.4	2.7	6.4	5.2
Ratio poor to not poor	*2.06*	*5.00*	*4.30*	*2.39*	*2.33*

Note: Differences between 'poor' and 'not poor' all significant at p<0.001 level.

Table 12.4: Subjective poverty and satisfaction

Mean scores of individuals		Life overall	Day-to-day activities	Feeling part of the community
How often have there been times in your life when you think you have lived in poverty by the standards of that time?	Never	7.7	7.13	6.47
	Most of the time	5.35	4.89	4.38
Do you think you could genuinely say you are poor now?	Never	7.81	7.25	6.54
	All the time	4.82	4.37	4.39
Have you ever felt embarrassed because you have a low income?	No	7.6	7.0	6.34
	Yes	5.89	5.31	5.22
Have you ever been made to feel small because you have a low income?	No	7.48	6.88	6.27
	Yes	5.85	5.28	5.17

Note: Differences between 'poor' and 'not poor' all significant at p<0.001 level.

Figure 12.2: Overall life satisfaction by income quintiles

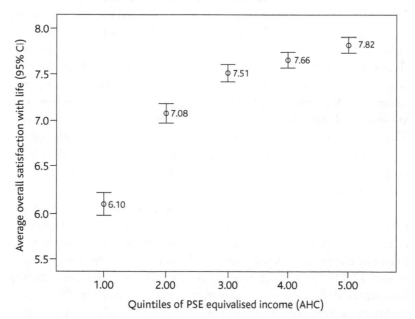

Note: CI = Confidence Interval.

it would produce a significant net increase in life satisfaction for the country.

Overall, these results show that poverty dramatically increases the risk of feeling that life is not satisfying. People who are living in poverty according to the PSE measure are more than four times as likely to be very dissatisfied with their lives, than people not in poverty. For those deprived of three or more of the PSE deprivation items, the risk of low satisfaction with life rises to more than five times. Nevertheless, we need to know the extent to which demographic and other factors are contributing to these differences. We now explore these factors and use regression analysis to establish the part played by poverty in explaining low well-being.

The social profile of low satisfaction

In Table 12.5, the proportions of those adults with low satisfaction with life are shown for a number of social variables. If the difference between those with low satisfaction and those not in this category is statistically significant (using ANOVA), this is shown in the last column. Within the category, the figure for the total adult population is the reference. Values are shaded where the cell sizes fall below 20 cases. As can be seen, the differences by gender are not significant. In terms of ethnic categories (which were merged to create sufficient cell sizes) only 'Black or Black British' was significantly more likely to have low satisfaction. Lone parents were significantly more dissatisfied than other family types. Indeed, some of the statistical significance is in the reverse direction: couples with children have significantly lower 'low life satisfaction' scores. Under marital status, people who are separated (but still married) have the highest low satisfaction score. The variations in scores by age band vary less than in some of the other categories but are still significant for a number of bands. Under employment status, unemployment stands out, as does 'permanently sick/disabled'.

As a basis for developing a regression model to explore the relationship between low satisfaction with life and poverty, Table 12.5 suggests that gender, ethnic group and possibly age are unlikely to be useful in the model. While Table 12.5 includes a long-term limiting illness (LLTI) factor, with more than a quarter (27 per cent) having low satisfaction, a more useful variable comes from the PSE survey question on whether 'health in past year limited ability to participate in society'. Four responses could be given to this question, ranging from 'not at all' to 'a lot'. Those whose health limited their ability 'a lot' were 4.5 times as likely to have a low satisfaction score compared to the 'not at all' respondents. The results for this question are not included in Table 12.5. Nor do we show the results for tenure, where those living in social housing are twice as likely as those who own a house with a mortgage to have a low satisfaction score.

Table 12.5: Low satisfaction rates for key social variables

% of adults		Low satisfaction	Share of category	Sig.*
All adults		10.5	100	
Gender	Female	10.9	55	
	Male	10.1	45	
Ethnic group	White	10.4	90.4	
	Asian or Asian British	9.7	4.8	
	Black or Black British	15.9	3.5	*
	Other	11.9	1.3	
Family type	Pensioner couple	6.2	8.1	*
	Pensioner single	10.9	10.4	
	Couple with children	8.6	22.3	*
	Couple without children	5.7	14.3	*
	Lone parent	25.6	13.2	*
	Single without children	16.8	31.8	*
Marital status	Single, never married	14.3	39.7	*
	Married and living with husband/wife	6.2	30.3	*
	Civil partnership	0.2	0.0	
	Separated from husband/wife	24.0	5.1	*
	Divorced	16.4	14.7	*
	Widowed	13.9	10.1	*
Age	18-34	10.0	26.1	
	35-54	12.0	40.3	*
	55-74	9.7	25.0	
	75 and over	8.7	8.6	
Employment status	Employed (full-time, part-time and self-employed)	6.6	37.6	*
	Unemployed (looking and available for work)	26.6	15.5	*
	Retired	7.6	14.1	*
	Student	5.5	1.9	*
	Looking after family/home	11.6	6.6	
	Permanently sick/disabled	50.1	22.1	*
	Other inactive	26.8	2.2	*

Note: ▬ = Cell count below 20; * Significance = p<0.05.

Of the categories in Table 12.5, marital status was excluded from Model 3 presented in Table 12.6. It had little effect in various models, with or without the inclusion of family type which was significant for single people and lone parents.

In Model 1, the PSE deprivation poverty measure (lacking three of 25 items) accounts for around 15 per cent of the variation in low

Table 12.6: Binary logistic regression results for factors associated with low satisfaction with life

	Model 1			Model 2			Model 3		
Nagelkerke R²	0.155			0.281			0.339		
Variables	B	Sig. level	Exp(B) – odds ratio	B	Sig. level	Exp(B) – odds ratio	B	Sig. level	Exp(B) – odds ratio
Constant	-3.164		0.042	-3.19		0.041	-4.249		0.014
Lacking three or more deprivation items (out of 25) (Reference category: Not deprived)	1.933	***	6.909	1.370	***	3.936	1.088	***	2.967
Health in past year limited ability to participate in society (reference category: Not at all)									
Slightly				0.887	***	2.429	0.681	***	1.977
Quite a lot				1.539	***	4.658	1.110	***	3.035
A lot				2.177	***	8.824	1.523	***	4.588
Employment status (reference category: Employed)									
Unemployed (not working but looking for work and available for work)							0.752	**	2.121
Retired							0.609	*	1.839
Student							-0.547		0.579
Looking after family/home							0.442		1.556
Permanently sick/disabled							1.148	***	3.153
Other inactive							1.023	*	2.781

(continued)

302

Nagelkerke R²	Model 1 0.155			Model 2 0.281			Model 3 0.339		
Variables	B	Sig. level	Exp(B) – odds ratio	B	Sig. level	Exp(B) – odds ratio	B	Sig. level	Exp(B) – odds ratio
Family type (reference category: Couple with no children)									
Pensioner couple							-0.155		0.856
Pensioner single							0.058		1.060
Couple with children							0.222		1.249
Lone parent							1.166	***	3.208
Single without children							0.458	*	1.580
Age (reference category: 18-34)									
35-54							0.604	**	1.830
55-74							0.559	*	1.748
75 and over							0.340		1.405
Tenure (reference category: Owned with mortgage)									
Owned outright							0.288		1.334
Social housing							0.651	**	1.917
Private rented							0.174		1.190

Note: *p<0.05; **p<0.01; ***p<0.001.

satisfaction but that figure rises to 28 per cent in Model 2, which includes the variable 'health in the past year limited ability to participate in society'. Controlling for this health factor along with employment status, family type, housing tenure and age (Model 3), deprivation increases the odds of low life satisfaction by three times. This is very similar to the effect of being a lone parent as opposed to being married, or the effect of permanent sickness and disability relative to being employed. The effect of being unemployed is to increase the odds of low life satisfaction by 2 times, slightly above the effect of being retired, which is 1.8 times. Deprivation accounts for almost a quarter of the effects in the model (23 per cent) while the limiting effects of ill-health account for 60 per cent of the total. Of the factors with the least effect, housing tenure and age band, living in social housing means that the odds of people expressing low satisfaction with life are 1.9 times compared to those who own outright. The strongest effect of age, relative to 18- to 34-year-olds, is in relation to the 35-54 age group. The results with the PSE poverty measure in the model are very similar though slightly weaker.

To test the effect of the other satisfaction variables on overall life satisfaction, another model was developed using 'feeling part of the community' and 'satisfaction with day-to-day activities and accommodation' as explanatory factors (results not shown). Job satisfaction was excluded as very few people expressed dissatisfaction with their job (6.3 per cent). Also, satisfaction with the area people live in appears to have no statistical relationship to whether they are dissatisfied with their lives overall or not. The model accounts for about 40 per cent of the variation in overall life satisfaction scores (Nagelkerke R^2=0.410). As might be expected, satisfaction with day-to-day activities is strongly associated with low satisfaction with life overall, suggesting that people conceptualise life satisfaction very much in terms of what they do on a daily basis. Controlling for satisfaction with community and satisfaction with accommodation, being dissatisfied with day-to-day activities increases the odds of being dissatisfied with life overall by 60 times. The odds of low life satisfaction for those not feeling part of the community were 2.6 times the odds for those highly satisfied with feeling part of the community.

In population terms, the PSE data show that around five million (4.8) adults have low life satisfaction and over a million of these are either completely dissatisfied with their lives (score of zero) or gave a score of one. Of the five million, some 1.6 million, including 600,000 lone parents, are caring for children. Around 700,000 (or 15 per cent of the total dissatisfied) have no job and are looking for work. Three-quarters (74.2 per cent) of the dissatisfied are PSE deprived and three-fifths (57 per cent) are PSE poor. Almost a quarter (24 per cent) are full-time employees.

Conclusion

The evidence presented above challenges the contemporary framing of well-being in a number of ways. The first concerns the emphasis in well-being debates on individual psychology, or subjective well-being, and positive psychology's agenda for individual transformation. The positive psychology movement (Seligman and Peterson, 2003) is quite explicit about promoting psychological well-being for all, as a break from the 'negativity' of traditional psychology's preoccupation with mental pathology and the social needs of a minority (Seligman, 2002). The alliance with some economists takes this a step further into positivity in the workplace, the connecting of positive emotions to consumption, and creating strategies to 'nudge' people towards behaviour change in the most resource intensive areas of social policy: social security and health. Yet the new culture of positivity exists alongside a mental health crisis arguably associated at least in part with the intensification of work, the precarious nature of work (Standing, 2011), the austerity-driven erosion of public services, rising levels of poverty and an unprecedented attack on the living standards of working-age long-term sick and disabled people. The PSE-UK evidence on (dis)satisfaction underlines the misery of many people deprived of adequate incomes and other resources. We have shown that there is a close association between poverty and low satisfaction with life, and a clear gradient between income or deprivation and levels of well-being. The more readily available evidence of low satisfaction with life, with feeling part of the community and with day-to-day activities should be bringing us back to the social determinants of misery, rather than fuelling the intensification of psychologically based interventions. In Davies' words, 'even a cursory examination of the evidence on unhappiness in neo-liberal societies draws the observer beyond the limits of psychology, and into questions of political economy' (Davies, 2011, p 70).

The second aspect of the framing of well-being is its apparent universal and consensual appeal. As a recent Carnegie Trust (2015, pp 1-2) initiative puts it 'well-being provides a way to understand what is required and how best we can all work together to improve our lives in a complex world'. Whatever the advantages and appeal of such an agenda, there is a danger that political and administrative style prevails over policy content and masks where the real challenges lie.

In privileging well-being there needs to be an understanding that the biggest improvements need to be made, and are more possible to make, in the lower half of the income or deprivation spectrum. As we have seen, average satisfaction with life falls increasingly fast as household incomes fall so there are particular gains to be had from focusing on the material needs of the most disadvantaged. Increases in income for the top 40 per cent lead to only very marginal improvements in well-being scores. Rather than a strategy of mass distress (Tomlinson, 2016), for example, the administered lives of the long-term sick and disabled would be measurably improved by raising their household income levels and servicing their health needs and by abolishing stressful forms of testing. Addressing poverty and deprivation, long-term ill health and the first two quintiles of low household incomes will reduce low satisfaction substantially and raise average well-being. Income redistribution would be a non-zero-sum game.

Our third concluding point is to challenge the idea that personal and collective well-being is (mainly) 'all in the mind' and somehow detached from material resources. Whether born of resignation in the wake of the reduced role of the austerity state (Taylor-Gooby and Stoker, 2011) or part of discussions of 'happy slaves' (see *Guardian*, 2016; also, Oishi and Diener, 2014) and the 'happy poor' (Ward and King, 2016), the notion that real change lies with private citizens taking control of their own well-being, supported by a burgeoning private market in happiness, is not supported by the evidence presented here. There is a systematic relationship between dissatisfaction with life and poor material circumstances that no amount of moralising about striving or positivity will shift. At best, the well-being agenda can help to support the eradication of poverty and social exclusion, and can strengthen the argument for a traditional social policy focus on delivering social justice; at worst, it represents an extreme form of the privatisation of public issues.

Note

[1] People answering 'yes' to the question: Do you have any physical or mental health conditions or illnesses lasting or expected to last for 12 months or more?

References

Alter, A. (2014) 'Do the poor have more meaningful lives?' *The New Yorker*, 24 January, http://www.newyorker.com/business/currency/do-the-poor-have-more-meaningful-lives.

BBC (2015) 'Well-being survey: Fermanagh and Omagh "happiest in UK"', 23 September, http://www.bbc.com/news/uk-34336951.

BBC (2016) 'Most and least happy places revealed in major ONS report', 3 February, http://www.bbc.com/news/uk-england-35470725.

Beaumont, J. (2012) *Measuring national well-being: Report on consultation responses on proposed domains and measures*, London: Office for National Statistics.

Burchardt, T. (2006) 'Happiness and social policy: barking up the right tree in the wrong neck of the woods', in L. Bauld, K. Clarke and T. Maltby (eds) *Social policy review 18*, Bristol: The Policy Press, pp 145-64.

Carnegie Trust (2015) *Towards a wellbeing framework: Findings from the roundtable on measuring wellbeing in Northern Ireland*, www.carnegieuktrust.org.uk.

Chamberlain, E. (2015) *Wealth in Great Britain Wave 3: Relationship between wealth, income and personal well-being, July 2011 to June 2012*, London: ONS.

Daly, M. (2011) *Welfare*, Cambridge: Polity Press.

Davies, W. (2011) 'The political economy of unhappiness', *New Left Review*, 71, 65-80.

Davies, W. (2012) 'The emerging neocommunitarianism', *Political Quarterly*, 83, 767-76.

Davies, W. (2015) *The happiness industry*, London: Verso.

DEFRA (2005) *The UK government sustainable development strategy*, Cm 6467, London: HMSO.

Dolan, P. (2014), *Happiness by design*, London: Allen Lane.

Guardian (2016) 'George Washington book slave controversy', 18 January, http://www.theguardian.com/us-news/2016/jan/17/scholastic-george-washington-book-slave-controversy.

Kahneman, D. (2003) 'A psychological perspective on economics', *American Economic Review*, 93(2), 162-8.

Kahneman, D. and Tversky, A. (1979) 'Prospect theory: an analysis of decision under risk', *Econometrica*, 47(2), 263-91.

Layard, R. (2005) *Happiness: Lessons from a new science*, London: Allen Lane.

Lewis, J. (2014) *Income, expenditure and personal wellbeing, 2011/12*, London: ONS, http://webarchive.nationalarchives.gov.uk/20160105160709/http://www.ons.gov.uk/ons/rel/wellbeing/measuring-national-well-being/income--expenditure-and-personal-well-being/art--income--expenditure-and-personal-well-being.html#tab-abstract.

Mailonline (2016) 'Revealed: The Western Isles is the happiest place to live in the UK – but Liverpool and Wolverhampton are the saddest', 2 February, http://www.dailymail.co.uk/news/article-3428730/ Western-Isles-happiest-place-live-UK-Liverpool-saddest.html.

OECD (2013) *Guidelines on measuring subjective well-being*, Paris: OECD Publishing, http://dx.doi.org/10.1787/9789264191655-en.

Oishi, S. and Diener, E. (2014) 'Residents of poor nations have a greater sense of meaning in life than residents of wealthy nations', *Psychological Science*, February, 25(2), 422-30.

ONS (2012), *Personal well-being dataset for 2011/12*, http://www. ons.gov.uk/peoplepopulationandcommunity/wellbeing/datasets/ personalwellbeingestimatespersonalcharacteristics.

ONS (2015a) *Personal well-being in the UK, 2014/15*, http://www. ons.gov.uk/peoplepopulationandcommunity/wellbeing/bulletins/ measuringnationalwellbeing/2015-09-23.

ONS (2015b) *Personal well-being dataset for 2014/15*, released 23 September 2015, http://www.ons.gov.uk/peoplepopulationandcommunity/ wellbeing/datasets/personalwellbeingestimatespersonalcharacteristics.

Scott, K. (2012) *Measuring wellbeing: Towards sustainability?*, London: Routledge.

Seligman, M. (2002) *Authentic happiness: Using the new positive psychology to realize your potential for lasting fulfilment*, New York, NY: Free Press.

Seligman, M. and Peterson, C. (2003) 'Positive clinical psychology', in L. G. Aspinwall and U. M. Staudinger (eds) *A psychology of human strengths*, Washington, DC: American Psychological Association, pp 305-17.

Standing, G. (2011) *The precariat: The new dangerous class*, London: Bloomsbury.

Stiglitz, J. E., Sen, A. and Fitoussi, J.-P. (2009) *Report by the Commission on the Measurement of Economic Performance and Social Progress*, www. stiglitz-sen-fitoussi.fr.

Taylor-Gooby, P. and Stoker, G. (2011) 'The Coalition programme: a new vision for Britain or politics as usual?', *The Political Quarterly*, 82(1), 4-15.

Thaler, R. and Sunstein, C. (2009) *Nudge: Improving decisions about health, wealth and happiness*, London: Penguin Books.

Tomlinson, M. (2016), 'Risking peace in the "war against the poor"? Social exclusion and the legacies of the Northern Ireland conflict', *Critical Social Policy*, 36(1), 104-123.

Tomlinson, M. and Kelly, G. (2013) 'Is everybody happy? The politics and measurement of national well-being', *Policy & Politics*, 41(2), 139-57.

Ward, S. J. and King, L. A. (2016) 'Poor but happy? Income, happiness, and experienced and expected meaning in life', *Social Psychological and Personality Science*, DOI: 10.1177/1948550615627865.

Part 4:
Bringing it together

THIRTEEN

The multidimensional analysis of social exclusion

Nick Bailey, Eldin Fahmy and Jonathan Bradshaw

Introduction

Previous chapters in this volume explore different dimensions of poverty and social exclusion in the UK, while the companion volume (Dermott and Main, 2017) presents evidence on the poverty and social exclusion experienced by different social groups or in different locations. Although many of these contributions also examine how disadvantage in one area relates to disadvantage in others, they essentially focus on one or two aspects of exclusion at a time. This chapter seeks to bring these analyses together by presenting an overarching multidimensional analysis of social exclusion, exploring in more depth the relationships between the dimensions of exclusion. As noted in the Introduction, there are many ways in which this task could have been approached. Rather than selecting just one, this chapter explores complementary approaches using a range of statistical techniques. By doing so, we hope the results provide a more holistic understanding of how different domains of exclusion relate to each other and of the different forms which social exclusion may take.

The chapter is organised into a number of sections. The first provides an introduction to the concept of social exclusion, while the second describes levels of exclusion using the main indicators available in the PSE-UK 2012 survey and, where available, how these have changed since 1999. The chapter then discusses two different approaches to constructing broader measures of exclusion for each domain or groups of domains, in order to facilitate the multidimensional analysis which follows. The results of this multidimensional analysis are then presented, exploring the relationships between domains, and the variations in the forms of exclusion across different social groups, including between poor and non-poor groups. Lastly, the chapter considers the wider significance of these findings for policies to promote social inclusion and well-being in the UK.

The concept of social exclusion

As noted in the Introduction, the concept of social exclusion emerged into UK discourses on poverty and living standards from France in the early 1990s (Bradshaw, 2004). Early advocates, including Room (1995), argued that it expanded on income- and expenditure-based measures of poverty by adopting a more dynamic, multidimensional perspective which emphasised the structural processes underpinning disadvantage. Despite fundamental differences in views on its causes (and appropriate policy responses), some consensus is evident in its conceptualisation in academic and policy research. First, in contrast to the narrower focus upon material resources in poverty research, social exclusion is said to refer to a process of being 'shut out' from, or denied access to, social, economic, cultural, and political systems (Walker and Walker, 1997), and to an enforced inability to participate in widely accepted social norms which can arise from a variety of sources (Gordon et al, 2000; Burchardt et al, 1999, 2002; Duffy, 1995; Room, 1995). Second, social exclusion is typically viewed as a dynamic process rather than as a static condition (Silver, 1994; Madanipour et al, 1998; Room, 1995). Third, social exclusion is a relational concept, and not simply a material state, characterised by powerlessness, denial of rights, diminished citizenship and disrespect (Room, 1995; Walker and Walker, 1997; Lister, 2004).

Initially the concept was greeted with some scepticism within the academic research community, not least because of concerns that it might be used to divert policy attention away from the maldistribution of incomes and material resources. Various commentators have also noted the way in which the concept has been adapted selectively to the changing environments of policy making in ways which reflect different understandings of its antecedents and causation, and hence of appropriate policy responses (for example, Byrne, 1999; Levitas, 1998; Silver, 1994).

Whilst the language of social exclusion has informed European policy debates in this area since at least the 1980s, most recently in the proposed European Pillar on Social Rights in 2016,[1] the UK government was the first national administration to explicitly focus on tackling social exclusion, with the establishment in 1997 of the Social Exclusion Unit by then Prime Minister Tony Blair. Here, social exclusion was defined as:

> A combination of linked problems such as unemployment, low skills, poor housing, family breakdown, high crime

rates that lead people or places to be excluded from the mainstream. (SEU, 2004)

As Levitas (1998) cogently argues, New Labour's adoption of the term reflected a shift away from the redistributive impetus of social democratic politics towards a 'social integrationist' emphasis on inclusion through paid work and an uneasy accommodation with neo-liberal economic orthodoxy. Writing in a similar vein, Fairclough (2000) emphasises the way New Labour's language of social exclusion disguised a discursive shift away from an emphasis on the structural drivers of multiple disadvantage towards an individualised, deficit model focused on the characteristics of the excluded themselves.

These are valid and important criticisms of the use of the concept of exclusion, but they do not constitute grounds to reject the concept in its entirety. First, social exclusion responds to the documented inadequacies of income-based poverty measures, which fail to represent the range of material and social resources envisaged by Townsend (1979) in his classic definition of poverty (see the Introduction in this volume). Second, it illuminates not only the material conditions associated with multiple disadvantage but also the unequal social and political relationships and processes that accompany these conditions and help to sustain them. In doing so, the concept addresses the relational agenda associated with lack of voice, denial of rights, social stigma, disrespect and misrecognition that are central to the lived experience of poverty (Lister, 2002, 2007). Viewed as an enforced exclusion from customary living standards, lifestyles, systems and opportunities, social exclusion describes diverse processes of marginalisation which extend far beyond poverty as material insufficiency. Whilst constrained material resources are undoubtedly a key driver of exclusion (a contention we examine empirically below), the concept encompasses a wider range of exclusionary processes including social discrimination, fear of violence, social isolation, geographical peripherality, and lack of access to services. Whilst these are often associated with poverty, they are clearly distinct phenomena. Moreover, in addressing this agenda, the concept of social exclusion responds to wider concerns about the limitations of distributional politics in addressing problems of misrecognition centred on gender, ethnicity, disability, and sexual orientation (Fraser, 1995; Honneth and Fraser, 2003).

From definition to measurement

The Bristol Social Exclusion Matrix (B-SEM)

Whilst social exclusion has been an influential concept, its operationalisation and measurement remain challenging. The abstract character of social exclusion has often limited its utility as a framework for empirical measurement (Levitas et al, 2007). There are many examples of studies which have compiled data on different domains of exclusion using a diverse range of sources (for example, the Joseph Rowntree Foundation's *Monitoring poverty and social exclusion* series of reports). While valuable for tracking social developments over time and holding policy makers to account, this approach does not facilitate investigation of how the various domains of exclusion overlap at the individual level, nor understanding of the different forms that exclusion can take. The main barrier to such work has been the lack of household survey data with sufficient breadth of coverage, as Levitas et al's (2007) review showed.

In the UK, some studies have been conducted using the British Household Panel Survey (BHPS). Drawing upon BHPS data for 1991-95, Burchardt et al (1999, 2002) construct measures on five key dimensions of exclusion: consumption, savings, work, political engagement and social activity. They go on to chart their prevalence and dynamics over this period. Barnes (2005) also uses BHPS data, capturing exclusion on financial situation, material possessions, housing and neighbourhood circumstances, social relations, and physical and mental health. He excludes labour market status from his set of domains since one of his primary purposes is to explore the relationships between paid work and exclusion. Taylor et al (2004) also use BHPS data to investigate multiple disadvantage over the 1991-2001 period. Beyond the BHPS, the 1999 PSE survey was the first to set out to operationalise and measure social exclusion in the UK, although the coverage it provides is similar to that possible using the BHPS. Drawing upon these data, Levitas (2006) examines vulnerability to exclusion across four dimensions: adequate income, labour market, local services and social relations.

These early attempts at survey measurement were often relatively crude because of the limitations of existing surveys and insufficient empirical validation. As the Introduction notes, one of the main aims of the PSE-UK 2012 study was to improve on this situation by operationalising a much richer measure of social exclusion. Drawing on a review of existing studies in this area, Levitas et al (2007: 9) offer a useful working definition:

> Social exclusion is a complex and multi-dimensional process. It involves the lack or denial of resources, rights, goods and services, and the inability to participate in the normal relationships and activities, available to the majority of people in a society, whether in economic, social, cultural or political arenas. It affects both the quality of life of individuals and the equity and cohesion of society as a whole.

Levitas et al (2007) then propose an operational measurement framework, the B-SEM, and it is this framework which informed the development of the PSE-UK survey. The B-SEM was constructed as a heuristic device to assess the scope for secondary analysis of social exclusion. It was subsequently adopted by the UK Cabinet Office as a framework for secondary survey analyses of social exclusion across the life course (for example, Cusworth et al, 2009; Fahmy et al, 2009; Oroyemi et al, 2009). It comprises three key themes and ten domains of exclusion (as illustrated in Figure 0.1 in the Introduction[2]).

Indicators of exclusion

Table 13.1 presents prevalence estimates for selected social exclusion indicators across each of the B-SEM domains for the UK private household population in 2012. In selecting indicators, we draw inspiration from Townsend's (1979) seminal relative deprivation theory, conceptualising social exclusion as exclusion from activities, lifestyles and opportunities which are customary, or are at least widely encouraged, in the UK today. While Townsend's relative deprivation theory focuses on the exclusionary effects of insufficient command over resources (principally income), the indicators presented below reflect a wider range of social processes which result in the effective exclusion of people from social norms and lifestyles, including social isolation, poor access to services, labour market exclusion, lack of political voice, poor health, poor housing, and harassment and discrimination. As these are indicators rather than measures, we are not suggesting that each can be used to identify the socially excluded in a direct sense. Rather, we suggest they are likely to be associated with exclusion. The prevalence rates vary from 58 per cent who took no action about local problem or national issue (excluding voting) and

Table 13.1: Social exclusion domains and indicators, UK

	Domain	Indicator	%
A. RESOURCES	A1: Material and economic resources	Less than 60% PSE-equivalised median household income AHC	25.2
		Income less than 60% threshold in PSE and Family Resource Survey	18.4
		Has (well) below average living standards	12.7
		Cannot afford 3+ social or material necessities	34.0
		Genuinely feels poor 'all the time'	8.7
		Income a little or a lot below that needed to avoid poverty	25.0
		Has been often/mostly poor across lifetime	10.1
		In arrears on any bills in last year	23.1
		Falling behind with bills	21.6
		Had to borrow money from friends, family or other	22.3
		Cannot afford unanticipated, necessary expense of £500	36.8
		Not a home owner	33.7
	A2: Access to services	Lacks adequate access to 3+ local services	21.4
	A3: Social resources	Low social support (scores less than 15)	15.5
		Less than monthly contact with friends	5.6
		Less than monthly contact with relatives	6.3
		Speaks to less than 3 friends monthly	24.4
		Speaks to less than 3 relatives monthly	29.8
		Not satisfied with personal relationships	16.8
B. PARTICIPATION	B1: Economic participation	Not in employment	40.6
		No working-age adults in household in paid work	19.1
		Unemployed more than 12 months in last 5 years	8.0
		Not satisfied with current job (in employment only)	14.2
	B2: Social participation	Does not participate in 6+ common social activities	45.8
	B3: Cultural participation, education and skills	Does not use any listed social and cultural facilities	19.6
		Completed full-time education at age 16 or less	52.2
		Limited language skills (non-native English speakers)	2.6
	B4: Political and civic participation	Not member of any group or organisation	43.4
		Took no action about local or national issue (excl. voting)	57.6
		Did not vote in most recent UK general election	42.0
		Low efficacy: disagrees with all three statements	12.1

(continued)

Table 13.1: Social exclusion domains and indicators, UK (continued)

	Domain	Indicator	%
C. QUALITY OF LIFE	C1: Health and well-being	'(Very) bad' or 'fair' general health	27.2
		Limiting longstanding illness	22.3
		Poor mental health (GHQ greater than 3 on 0-4 scale)	28.7
		Low life satisfaction (less than 6 on 0-10 scale)	20.0
	C2: Housing and local environment	Multiple problems with accommodation	25.3
		Experiencing 3+ neighbourhood problems	24.1
		Home not in 'good' state of repair	31.2
		Dissatisfied with accommodation	11.1
		Neighbourhood dissatisfaction	14.0
	C3: Crime and social harm	Experienced harassment or discrimination for any reason	15.3
		Has criminal record	5.1

Notes: Data for UK adults. AHC = after housing costs.

52 per cent who completed full-time education at or before age 16, to 3 per cent with limited language skills, and 5 per cent of respondents who have a criminal record.

For many of these indicators, it is possible to examine change over the 1999–2012 period, at least for the British sample. Table 13.2 shows the percentage of adults in Britain identified by each of the 27 indicators available for both 1999 and 2012 surveys. While changes in question wording limit comparability for some items, the data show a general picture of worsening exclusion. On resources, the proportion in low-income households remained stable (the first indicator) and the rise in deprivation was not significant but the prevalence of subjective poverty and, especially, financial insecurity (in arrears on bills, having to borrow, lacking home ownership) all increased significantly over this period, as did problems of access to services. On participation, exclusion from economic participation appears broadly stable over this period, but exclusion from social, cultural and civic participation became more widespread on at least one indicator. Quality of life also worsened in relation to mental health problems, as well as problems with poor housing. Across the set of 27 indicators, eleven showed rising exclusion but only one showed significant improvement (social contact with relatives).

Table 13.2: Social exclusion in Britain, 1999 and 2012

Domain	Description	% 1999	% 2012	Change	Significance
	Less than 60% of PSE-equivalised median household income AHC	24.9	25.1	0.2	
	Cannot afford 3+ social and material necessities	31.0	34.0	3.0	
	Genuinely feels poor 'all the time'	6.7	8.7	2.0	
	Income little or lot below that needed to avoid poverty	19.6	24.8	5.2	*
A1: Material and economic resources	Has been often/mostly poor across lifetime	8.7	10.2	1.5	
	In arrears on any bills in last year	13.7	23.1	9.4	*
	Had to borrow money from friends, family or other source	11.1	22.2	11.1	*
	Not a home owner	23.6	33.8	10.2	*
A2: Access to services	Lacks adequate access to 3+ local services	12.6	18.1	5.5	*
	Low social support (scores less than 15)	15.9	15.5	-0.4	
	Less than monthly contact with friends[1]	7.5	5.6	-1.9	
A3: Social resources	Less than monthly contact with relatives[1]	8.3	6.4	-1.9	
	Speaks to less than 3 friends monthly[1]	21.7	24.5	2.8	
	Speaks to less than 3 relatives monthly[1]	36.2	30.0	-6.2	*
B1: Economic participation	Not in employment	43.6	40.5	-3.1	
	No working-age adults in household in paid work	16.7	19.0	2.3	
B2: Social participation	Does not participate in 6+ common social activities	34.1	45.6	11.5	*
B3: Cultural participation, education and skills	Does not use any listed social and cultural facilities	15.9	19.6	3.7	*
	Completed full-time education at age 16 or less	52.6	52.3	-0.3	
B4: Political & civic participation	Not member of any group or organisation	44.2	43.2	-1.0	
	Did not vote in most recent UK general election	27.6	41.7	14.1	*

(continued)

Table 13.2: Social exclusion in Britain, 1999 and 2012 (continued)

Domain	Description	% 1999	% 2012	Change	Significance
C1: Health and well-being	Limiting longstanding illness[1]	23.7	22.3	-1.4	
	Poor mental health (GHQ greater than 3 on 0-4 scale)	18.3	28.8	10.5	*
	Multiple problems with accommodation	17.5	25.5	8.0	*
C2: Housing and local environment	Home not in 'good' state of repair	30.7	31.4	0.7	
	Dissatisfied with accommodation	7.8	11.2	3.4	*
	Neighbourhood dissatisfaction	14.1	14.2	0.1	

Notes: (1) indicates minor changes in question wording between PSE 1999 and PSE-UK 2012 surveys. AHC = after housing costs. No comparable indicators for 'C3: Crime and social harm' domain. Significance p<0.01.

Domains and dimensions of exclusion

Theory-driven approach

Two approaches have been adopted to producing summary measures of the domains or dimensions of exclusion. In the first, we take a more theory-driven approach, constructing measures for each of the domains which emerged in the literature review for the B-SEM. We construct an overall B-SEM index as well as scores for each domain, using the 42 items in Table 13.1. For each item, we have chosen a threshold to indicate 'exclusion' so each is a binary measure. We therefore count the number of items on which people are excluded. Our measure reflects prevailing norms, lifestyles and opportunities by weighting the items by their inverse sample prevalence prior to aggregating; in other words, we regard an item as indicating a greater degree of exclusion when relatively few people are in the excluded category. Thus, indicators with a very low prevalence in the sample (for example, criminal record, limited language skills) are weighted more highly than indicators denoting more widespread forms of exclusion (for example, not voting). The overall B-SEM index has a continuous normal distribution.

We then select threshold values for the overall B-SEM index and B-SEM domain scores to facilitate comparisons between domains or between population subgroups (for example, by age, gender). We establish a threshold value for the overall index on statistical grounds at one standard deviation above the sample mean, identifying 17 per cent of households as socially excluded. Whilst this is an arbitrary threshold, it allows us to 'anchor' subsequent descriptive analysis by specifying threshold values for each domain which identify a similar proportion of respondents as excluded.[3]

Empirical approach

Our second approach is to use exploratory factor analysis (EFA) to identify the different dimensions of exclusion empirically. Where the first approach imposes the B-SEM domain structure on the data by constructing scores for each domain, this approach allows the grouping of indicators to emerge from the data to a greater extent, although we still start with a set of measures which try to capture the various aspects identified by the B-SEM. In addition, where the first approach builds scores from binary indicators of exclusion, this approach starts with continuous scores which try to reflect degrees of advantage or disadvantage across the spectrum, avoiding the use of thresholds.

We construct 18 scores for every adult, drawing on multiple indicators in each case (see the Appendix to this chapter for details). In brief, we first break domains down into multiple sub-domains where the data suggest this is appropriate. For example, the 'Housing and local environment' domain was covered by 29 questions, but these appeared to represent six different sub-domains which were more or less independent. We constructed some domain or sub-domain scores from questions which were only available for specific groups within the population: older people (questions on access to services for this group); working-age adults (questions on employment status and quality of paid work); and families (questions on services for this group and problems with schools or education). For reasons of space, these are not discussed here (see Appendix to this chapter and Bailey and Bramley (2017) for more details).

Using the 18 scores available for all adults, EFA was undertaken to group domains and sub-domains together where appropriate, identifying a smaller number of broader dimensions of exclusion. We did numerous analyses, including additional scores as well as exploring results for various sub-groups (older people, working-age adults, families), and we tested various specifications for the factor solutions (see chapter Appendix for summary). While there is some variation in the number of factors which emerge and in the composition of each, there is also a great deal of stability in underlying patterns. Five factors emerge in almost all the models with a consistent core of components, covering six of the domains of the B-SEM. Each adult is given a factor score for each dimension (mean zero, standard deviation one), with positive scores reflecting higher levels of inclusion (for example, more economic resources or more political participation).

The following shows the descriptive label given to each dimension and summarises the main sub-domains on which each loaded (that is, the sub-domain scores which matter most for the overall factor score) in order of importance:

1. **economic resources and housing (A1/B2/C2):** economic resources; social activity; (low) housing problems; (low) unpaid childcare;
2. **political, civic and cultural participation (B4/B3/A4):** political/civic/voluntary activity; cultural activity; educational qualifications; political efficacy;

3. **family and social resources (A3):** contact with family; social support; contact with friends;
4. **neighbourhood environment (C2):** (low) neighbourhood dissatisfaction/social problems; (low) neighbourhood problems – physical/litter; (low) neighbourhood noise/pollution;
5. **health and well-being (C1):** well-being; (low) limiting health/disability.

It is notable how some of these dimensions cross not only domains within the B–SEM but also the broader groupings. The first factor, for example, combines domains from all three of the B–SEM groupings of resources, participation and quality of life. Neighbourhood environment was also closely related to this group (and in some versions of the factor analysis, combined with this factor).

It is also evident that some B–SEM domains do not feature at all (or only very weakly) in these dimensions. Access to services (A2) is absent, reflecting the fact that variations in that measure are not closely related to variations in any of our other exclusion measures. As Chapter 4 shows, access to services is not strongly related to factors such as income or deprivation, in part because of the conscious efforts of policy to ensure a fair distribution of these. In other cases, such as crime and social harm (C3), the absence may reflect limitations of measurement, with very few people recording any instances of harms on our set of indicators. The omission of economic participation (B1) reflects the fact that this is available only for working-age adults: we wanted to use a set of scores covering all adults.

Profiles of social exclusion in the UK

We can use these two approaches to look at variations in forms of social exclusion across the population. Using the first approach, Table 13.3 shows the proportions excluded on each domain. These results reveal that the social patterning of exclusion varies according to the domain in question. This is most obvious in relation to demographic differences. For example, older respondents (aged 65+) are at greater risk of exclusion from cultural participation, education and skills and political and civic participation, as well as exclusion on the grounds of health and well-being. However, they are less vulnerable than younger respondents to exclusion on the basis of material and economic resources or social resources, poor housing and local environments, or crime and social harm. Lone parents and single working-age adults show high levels of exclusion across a range of domains.

In general, groups identified by socio-economic status (for example, occupational class, worklessness, or housing tenure) show more consistent relationships with exclusion than those defined by demographic differences (for example, of age, gender, family type, and ethnicity). For example, social renters and, to a slightly lesser extent, private renters have above average levels of exclusion on almost every single domain – the exception being access to services. Those in routine occupations are above average on six out of nine domains. The economically disadvantaged are consistently and significantly more vulnerable to nearly all forms of disadvantage covered by the B-SEM domains. One partial exception here are those identified as small employers or own account works, that is the self-employed. This group has below average levels of exclusion in terms of material or economic resources (A1) but is above average on four of the other domains, covering three of the four participation domains as well as housing and living environment.

For comparison, Table 13.4 shows the factor scores for the five dimensions obtained using the second approach, with broadly similar results. Looking at variations by age, for example, we see some dimensions where younger adults have greater risks of exclusion, most notably in relation to economic resources and housing but also neighbourhood environment. By contrast, older people have greater exclusion risks in relation to civic and cultural participation, while the middle aged are more excluded in relation to family and social resources. Health and well-being as measured in this approach are not as clearly related to age. Gender differences do emerge more clearly, with women's greater risks of economic exclusion and men's greater risks of exclusion through weak family and social resources more evident.

With household type, there is a general sense of a gradient from pensioners (single or couple) who face the lowest exclusion risks through to lone parents and single adults of working age who face the highest risks, as the previous approach also identified. Couples, with or without children, are somewhere in between. This is particularly stark in relation to the economic resources and housing dimension and the neighbourhood environment dimension, but also social resources. There are further domains where lone parents and single adults share greater risks of exclusion with pensioners, all being worse than the couple households: health and well-being, and political and civic participation, notably.

With markers of socio-economic status, we see a similar picture to the previous approach. Those in higher status occupations enjoy far lower risks of exclusion not just on the economic resources and

Table 13.3: The prevalence of social exclusion by B-SEM domain and selected respondent characteristics

		A1: Material and economic resources	A2: Access to services	A3: Social resources	B1: Economic participation	B2: Social participation	B3: Cultural participation, etc.	B4: Political and civic participation	C1: Health and well-being	C2: Housing and local environment	C3: Crime and social harm
					Proportion excluded on domain:						
All		17	18	18	15	17	22	24	16	18	19
Age group	18-29	25	16	17	21	16	18	28	10	29	31
	30-44	22	16	19	12	19	15	21	12	22	21
	45-64	15	19	21	19	17	26	19	19	15	18
	65+	5	19	15	7	17	29	23	22	8	8
Sex	Male	17	17	20	12	15	20	16	15	20	21
	Female	19	17	17	13	19	19	19	17	20	17
Family type	Pensioner couple	3	19	10	13	13	25	20	19	7	7
	Pensioner single	9	17	22	7	24	35	28	27	11	9
	Couple and 1+ child	18	16	18	7	19	9	12	11	23	18
	Couple	8	19	15	11	11	26	18	11	14	17
	Lone parent and 1+ child	50	18	25	17	34	14	17	26	37	27
	Single	24	17	25	28	18	27	23	21	23	31
Employment status	Employed	13	16	17	0	12	20	20	8	18	18
	Unemployed	55	16	28	75	37	22	42	23	29	34
	Inactive	23	19	20	37	22	25	27	29	20	19

(continued)

Work intensity										
All working-age adults in work	11	15	17	0	11	17	14	8	17	19
1+ working-age adult in work	16	17	16	4	16	17	16	12	22	16
No working-age adults in work	41	19	28	69	30	24	24	34	31	34
All adults over retirement age	4	21	14	1	16	27	22	22	8	7
Ethnicity										
White British	17	18	18	13	17	20	16	17	20	18
Mixed	23	18	28	8	27	6	12	22	24	35
Asian	16	13	15	12	19	20	23	13	16	21
Black	44	14	26	13	25	18	17	14	33	30
Other	18	13	23	11	13	23	25	11	21	21
Occupational class										
Employers; higher managerial/professional	3	14	18	0	4	17	8	5	7	17
Lower managerial/professional	7	14	16	0	8	15	10	6	17	17
Intermediate	10	17	15	0	12	22	18	7	18	22
Small employers/own account	14	18	16	0	20	23	32	10	21	19
Lower supervisory and technical	14	20	16	0	16	23	24	7	23	18
Semi-routine	23	17	17	0	16	17	29	11	21	16
Routine	28	18	19	0	24	28	38	10	24	17
Settlement type										
Urban areas	20	13	19	13	18	20	18	16	22	20
Rural/sparsely populated areas	10	32	18	12	14	19	14	16	14	15
Housing tenure										
Owner occupier	4	17	15	7	11	18	13	11	12	14
Social renter	52	17	26	26	34	25	28	32	35	28
Private renter	37	16	29	19	28	20	24	17	36	31
Other	5	51	6	14	15	12	11	27	17	14

Notes: Underlining shows values above average for population as a whole, i.e. greater than the value in 'All' row at top of table. Breakdown by occupational class is only for those 18-79. Economic participation refers to labour market engagement (workless households). Respondents with occupational class data are, by definition, not living in workless households.

Table 13.4: Social exclusion factor scores by selected respondent characteristics

		Economic resources and housing (A1/B2/C2)	Civic/cultural participation (B4/B3/A4)	Family and social resources (A3)	Neighbourhood environment (C2)	Health and well-being (C1)
All	All	0.00	0.00	0.00	0.00	0.00
Age	18-29	-0.46	-0.01	0.03	-0.25	0
	30-44	-0.33	0.06	-0.08	-0.12	0.04
	45-64	0.17	0.03	-0.04	0.07	-0.04
	65+	0.52	-0.11	0.15	0.24	0
Sex	Male	0.06	0.03	-0.11	0	0
	Female	-0.06	-0.02	0.1	0	0
Household type	Pensioner couple	0.51	-0.02	0.2	0.22	0.12
	Pensioner single	0.46	-0.23	0.08	0.26	-0.17
	Couple and 1+ child	-0.5	0.11	0.01	-0.2	0.16
	Couple	0.21	0.04	-0.05	0.01	0.06
	Lone parent and 1+ child	-1.02	-0.29	-0.06	-0.34	-0.38
	Single	-0.19	-0.2	-0.37	-0.11	-0.51
	Other	0.14	0.16	0.04	0.09	0.1
Employment status (working age only)	Employed	-0.04	0.12	-0.03	-0.01	0.18
	Unemployed	-0.86	-0.36	-0.08	-0.45	-0.57
	Inactive	-0.42	-0.13	-0.12	-0.23	-0.49

(continued)

Household work intensity	0	-0.82	-0.58	-0.28	-0.42	-1.04
	<0.4	-0.7	-0.1	-0.16	-0.63	-0.4
	0.4 to 0.8	-0.2	0.07	0.03	-0.02	0.15
	0.8 to 0.99	-0.02	0.18	-0.15	-0.04	0.14
	1.0	0.07	0.11	-0.09	0	0.17
	Pensioner household	0.49	-0.09	0.16	0.24	0.02
Ethnic group	White	0.02	0	0.02	0	0.01
	Asian/Asian British	-0.06	0.03	-0.08	0.01	-0.02
	Black/Black British	-0.61	-0.08	-0.3	-0.17	-0.27
	Other	-0.39	0.19	-0.37	-0.17	-0.09
Occupational class	Employers and higher managerial/professional	0.27	0.5	-0.11	0.12	0.38
	Lower managerial/professional	0.09	0.43	-0.05	0.03	0.32
	Intermediate	0.03	0.08	0.04	-0.02	0.19
	Small employers/own account	-0.12	-0.13	-0.02	0.04	0.05
	Lower supervisory/technical	-0.14	-0.15	0	-0.08	0.2
	Semi-routine	-0.26	-0.23	0.09	-0.09	0.04
	Routine	-0.27	-0.41	-0.05	0.03	-0.04
Urban-rural (4 cat, UK)	Large urban	-0.05	0.01	-0.04	-0.09	-0.03
	Other urban	-0.04	-0.09	-0.01	-0.03	-0.04
	Small town	0.13	0.04	0.11	0.24	0.05
	Village, rural	0.19	0.15	0.08	0.25	0.2
Tenure	Owner occupier	0.26	0.16	0.07	0.11	0.2
	Social rented	-0.63	-0.46	-0.13	-0.28	-0.58
	Private rented	-0.49	-0.12	-0.23	-0.17	-0.17

Notes: Breakdown by employment status is for working-age only, and by occupational class is for 18-79 only.

housing, and related neighbourhood domains but also on civic and cultural participation, and on health and well-being, although they do not have advantages in relation to family and social resources. The greatest levels of exclusion are for renters, especially social renters, and for those in routine and semi-routine occupations while the high levels of exclusion in more urban centres are also apparent, although it is in other urban areas that civic and cultural exclusion is greatest.

Relationships between domains of exclusion

Table 13.5 shows the pattern of association between the ten B-SEM domains. For each domain, it shows the risk of exclusion across the other nine domains for 'excluded' respondents relative to 'non-excluded' respondents (that is, the relative risk ratio). The domains have been sorted by their association with material and economic resources (A1). The strongest relationships are between the domains of material resources, economic and social participation, housing and local environment, and health and well-being. These emerge as closely related in the factor analysis approach with several of these domains combined into a single dimensions there.

At the other extreme, the domain of access to services is barely associated with any of the others. It not only has the lowest association with material and economic resources but also shows very little relationship with any of the other domains. This reinforces the idea that it has a very different and particular set of drivers, primarily rural location. This is of course well recognised in the literature on rural disadvantage, as Chapter 10 in the companion volume shows (Bailey and Gannon 2017). The domain of cultural participation, education and skills also has relatively weak associations. It has most positive relationships with social participation, health and well-being, and political and civic participation. Again, several of these domains get combined in the factor analysis approach.

For comparison, Table 13.6 shows the correlations between the social exclusion dimensions produced using factor analysis. Since these factors are already groups of domains in some cases, this shows relationships at an even broader level. The strongest associations are between economic resources and neighbourhood, and between health and well-being and civic and cultural participation. In other respects, the dimensions appear relatively independent, with very little association between neighbourhood environment and civic or cultural participation, and rather weak associations between family and social resources and both economic resources and housing, and civic and cultural participation.

Table 13.5: Relationships between domains of social exclusion, relative risk ratios

	A1: Material and economic resources	B2: Social participation	C2: Housing and local environment	C1: Health and well-being	B1: Economic participation	C3: Crime and social harm	B4: Political and civic participation	A3: Social resources	B3: Cultural participation, etc.	A2: Access to services
A1: Material and economic resources	..	1.76	1.59	1.41	1.37	1.31	1.23	1.22	1.08	1.06
B2: Social participation	1.79	..	1.32	1.43	1.23	1.17	1.38	1.33	1.20	1.06
C2: Housing and local environment	1.51	1.31	..	1.16	1.10	1.23	1.03	1.16	[1.00]	1.05
C1: Health and well-being	1.49	1.47	1.19	..	1.34	1.27	1.17	1.37	1.21	1.10
B1: Economic participation	1.58	1.24	1.16	1.34	..	1.28	1.29	1.18	1.09	1.03
C3: Crime and social harm	1.29	1.15	1.22	1.22	1.23	..	0.96	1.21	[0.99]	1.04
B4: Political and civic participation	1.24	1.25	1.04	1.11	1.18	0.97	..	1.09	1.28	0.98
A3: Social resources	1.21	1.31	1.16	1.30	1.16	1.21	1.12	..	1.11	1.05
B3: Cultural participation, etc.	1.07	1.15	[1.00]	1.15	1.05	[0.99]	1.24	1.09	..	1.07
A2: Access to services	1.06	1.06	1.06	1.09	1.02	1.04	0.98	1.05	1.08	..
Mean number of exclusions	3.6	4.1	3	4.1	3.8	3.4	3.2	3.6	2.8	2.3

Notes: [] indicates 95% CI spans 0. Estimates show the relative risk (by column) for each B-SEM domain (by rows). For example, for respondents excluded on material and economic resources (A1), they are 76% more likely (1: 1.76) to experience exclusion on social participation (B2). Since these are *relative* risk estimates, their distribution is not symmetrical.

Table 13.6: Relationships between dimensions of exclusion, factor score correlations

	Economic resources and housing	Neighbourhood environment	Health and well-being	Civic and cultural participation	Family and social resources
Economic resources and housing	1	0.52	0.38	0.22	0.18
Neighbourhood environment		1	0.27	0.07	0.25
Health and well-being			1	0.52	0.45
Civic and cultural participation				1	0.18
Family and social resources					1

Relationships between exclusion and poverty

The previous section has shown how lack of material resources is associated with many but not all domains of exclusion. To make the relationships with clearer, we explore here the relationships with various measures of poverty. Poverty is often measured using income poverty measures and indicators of deprivation, and these are of course both components of the B-SEM domain representing material and economic resources described above. We examine four measures of poverty (see the Introduction for details):

- **relative low income:** respondents living in households with incomes less than 60% per cent equivalised median after housing costs;
- **deprivation:** respondents unable to afford three or more consensually-defined social and material necessities;
- **PSE poverty:** respondents classified as poor on both income and deprivation measures;
- **subjective poverty:** respondents reporting incomes 'a little' or 'a lot below' that needed to avoid poverty.

Table 13.7 shows the proportion of PSE adult respondents who were excluded on each domain by poverty status on each of our four measures. Not surprisingly, the greatest differences are for levels of

Table 13.7: Levels of exclusion on domains by poverty status

Poverty status		A1: Material and economic resources	A2: Access to services	A3: Social resources	B1: Economic participation	B2: Social participation	B3: Cultural participation, etc.	B4: Political and civic participation	C1: Health and well-being	C2: Housing and local environment	C3: Crime and social harm
					Proportion excluded on domain:						
Low income AHC	No	13	19	25	19	18	17	17	23	24	16
	Yes	75	21	40	52	45	29	32	39	45	26
	Diff	62	2	15	33	27	12	15	16	21	10
Deprivation	No	2	16	21	14	9	21	15	15	17	13
	Yes	61	22	38	43	41	22	28	40	43	30
	Diff	59	6	17	29	32	1	13	25	26	17
PSE poor	No	8	18	24	14	14	20	17	19	19	15
	Yes	75	21	39	57	47	24	31	43	49	31
	Diff	67	3	15	43	33	4	14	24	30	16
Subjective poverty	No	9	16	25	18	14	20	16	17	24	16
	Yes	75	25	38	49	47	23	32	48	43	30
	Diff	66	9	13	31	33	3	16	31	19	14

Notes: Figures show the proportion excluded on each domain using the thresholds for each noted above. AHC = after housing costs.

exclusion on the material and economic resources domain, whichever measure of poverty is used. For example, of those PSE-deprived (lacking three or more necessities), 61 per cent were excluded on this domain compared with just 2 per cent of those not deprived. Poverty also has strong relationships with both economic and social participation, as well as the quality of life domains. There are much weaker relationships with other domains, including services exclusion, cultural participation and social resources.

Table 13.8 presents a similar analysis using the factor analysis approach, showing average scores for each of the five dimensions by poverty status; lower scores indicate a higher degree of exclusion. As previously, the poor experience greater levels of exclusion whichever poverty measure we use and whichever dimension of exclusion we examine. but the strength of the relationships varies considerably. The gap between poor and non-poor is greatest in relation to the economic resources and housing dimension, although differences in health and well-being are also substantial. Differences are least in relation to family and social resources.

Table 13.8: Levels of exclusion on dimensions by poverty status

Poverty status		Economic resources and housing	Civic and cultural participation	Family and social resources	Neighbourhood environment	Health and well-being
	No	0.18	0.12	0.03	0.08	0.16
Low income AHC	Yes	−0.67	−0.44	−0.12	−0.31	−0.59
	Diff	*−0.85*	*−0.56*	*−0.15*	*−0.39*	*−0.75*
	No	0.43	0.21	0.08	0.18	0.3
Deprivation	Yes	−0.9	−0.44	−0.16	−0.38	−0.63
	Diff	*−1.33*	*−0.65*	*−0.24*	*−0.56*	*−0.93*
	No	0.3	0.14	0.05	0.13	0.21
PSE poor	Yes	−1.07	−0.52	−0.19	−0.46	−0.77
	Diff	*−1.37*	*−0.66*	*−0.24*	*−0.59*	*−0.98*
	No	0.38	0.2	0.09	0.17	0.29
Subjective poverty	Yes	−0.78	−0.41	−0.18	−0.34	−0.59
	Diff	*−1.16*	*−0.61*	*−0.27*	*−0.51*	*−0.88*

Notes: Figures show the mean factor score for each group on each dimension. Factors scores have mean zero and standard deviation one. Negative scores indicate greater exclusion. AHC = after housing costs.

Conclusion

As a concept, social exclusion appears to be less salient in the late 2010s than it was in the 2000s, at least in UK and European public and social policy discourses. The UK Social Exclusion Unit was downgraded and subsequently dissolved well before the end of the Labour government in 2010. In the European Union, social exclusion has become associated with the 2020 Poverty and Social Exclusion strategy, which has narrowed the target to evaluating progress in relation to three indicators – the at-risk-of-poverty measure (low income), material deprivation (lacking three or more items) and low household work intensity.

However, whilst the term is less visible in policy discussions or documents, the concept remains highly germane, not least to contemporary debates about quality of life, well-being, life satisfaction and happiness. A growing body of UK evidence on the connections between subjective and societal well-being, quality of life, and life satisfaction now exists (for example, ONS, 2016; NEF, 2009; Donovan and Halpern, 2002). This also reflects wider international interest in the empirical measurement of these concepts (Kahnemann and Krueger, 2006; Diener and Suh, 1997) and in their policy applications (for example, Eurostat, 2015; OECD, 2011; Layard, 2011; Stiglitz et al, 2009). This 'well-being' agenda has become increasingly prominent in policy rhetoric, including in right-leaning UK policy circles, because of the UK National Well-being Programme launched in 2010 and then Prime Minister Cameron's avowed commitment to 'measuring our progress as a country not just by our standard of living but by our quality of life' (Cameron, 2010).

At the same time, social exclusion remains critically relevant in understanding the unequal distribution of life opportunities and prospects that informs the current (2015-2017) government's new Life Chances Strategy and the wider suite of (non-statutory) indicators of life chances the government intends to develop. In January 2016, the then Prime Minister's speech setting out the principles for this strategy repeated his pledge of an 'all-out assault on poverty' and talked of a 'more social approach' (Cameron, 2016). As with well-being, many of the key concerns prompting action on life chances and social mobility overlap with the social exclusion agenda, for example, in relation to the priorities underpinning the Life Chances Strategy: family life and the early years; improving the education system, including expanding National Citizen Service; promoting opportunity for everyone, including through work experience, mentoring, community arts, and urban regeneration; and helping people in crisis (for example, addiction, poor mental health).

What then can these data tell us then about the nature of the challenges facing government in acting to promote social well-being, quality of life, and greater opportunities for all? First, although we have only a limited range of comparable indicators in the 1999 and 2012 PSE surveys, they suggest that the prevalence of different aspects of social exclusion in Britain have mostly either remained constant or have increased, sometimes significantly, over this period. Financial insecurity and financial hardship have become much more widespread, due to the recession and ensuing unequal growth, combined with austerity. Compared with 1999, social, cultural and political participation seem to have diminished, and mental health and housing problems also appear to have become more widespread. As with poverty, vulnerability to social exclusion remains strongly socially patterned, although the risks vary across domains.

Second, poverty remains strongly associated with almost all aspects of social exclusion. This is most evident for social resources, social participation and quality of life measures. Indeed, the association with material resources may be stronger in 2012 than in 1999 because it is no longer the case, as it was in the 1999 PSE study, that lack of social support is more prevalent among the non-poor.

Third, these data begin to shed some light on the dimensional structure of social exclusion. In addition to constrained material circumstances, limited social resources (networks, contact, support), economic and social non-participation, and poor health and well-being seem especially central to the experience of social exclusion in Britain. Despite the evidence of overlaps between poverty and exclusion, we believe there is still a strong case for considering other dimensions of social exclusion in poverty studies. Income poverty and deprivation do not give the whole picture. This chapter has shown that there are many people who are not poor or deprived yet who experience exclusion on other one or more domains.

Social exclusion thus describes a range of interconnected but discrete processes including material impoverishment, as well as social isolation, discrimination, poor heath and lack of voice, which limit people's capacity to fully participate in society in the ways envisaged within Townsend's classic definition of deprivation (Townsend, 1979). As such, we believe that the concept of social exclusion can enrich our understanding of the processes driving the effective marginalisation of substantial numbers of people from contemporary norms of social, cultural, economic and political participation in the UK, and the opportunities and lifestyles to which they give rise. Critics have rightly been sceptical about the ways in which the concept of social exclusion has often been misapplied in policy making to obscure the persistence of material inequalities and the maldistribution of resources that underpins it. Whilst these are valid criticisms, they do not amount in our view amount to a case for abandoning the study of social exclusion in its entirety, but rather should serve as an impetus to future research in this area.

Notes

[1] Communication from the Commission to the European Parliament, the Council, the European Economic and Social Committee and the Committee of the Regions, *Launching a consultation on a European Pillar of Social Rights*, Strasbourg, COM(2016) 127 final.

[2] In this chapter, we revert back to the original version of the B-SEM produced by Levitas et al (2007). As the Introduction notes, this underwent some revision in the development of the PSE-UK survey.

[3] Threshold values (percentage excluded on B-SEM domain) are as follows: A1: Material and economic resources 1.50 (17.4%); A2: Access to services 0.36 (17.1%); A3: Social resources 0.45 (16.5%); B1: Economic participation 0.41 (12.4%); B2: Social participation 2.53 (17.5%); B3: Cultural participation, education & skills 1.65 (19.6%); B4: Political & civic participation 1.12 (17.0%); C1: Health & well-being 0.50 (14.9%); C2: Housing & local environment 0.57 (19.5%); C3: Crime & social harm 0.05 (15.3%).

References

Bailey, N. and Bramley, G. (2017), 'Introduction', in G. Bramley, and N. Bailey (eds) *Poverty and social exclusion in the UK: volume 2 – the dimensions of disadvantage*, Bristol: Policy Press.

Bailey, N. and Gannon, M. (2017) 'More similarities than differences: poverty and social exclusion in rural and urban populations', in E. Dermott and G. Main (eds) *Poverty and social exclusion in the UK: volume 1 – the nature and extent of the problem*, Bristol: Policy Press, pp 219-238.

Barnes, M. (2005) *Social exclusion in Great Britain: An empirical investigation and comparison with the EU*, Aldershot: Ashgate.

Bradshaw, J. (2004) 'How has the notion of social exclusion developed in the European discourse?', *The Economic and Labour Relations Review*, 14(2), 168-86.

Burchardt, T., Le Grand, J. and Piachaud, D. (1999), 'Social exclusion in Britain, 1991-1995', *Social Policy and Administration*, 33(3), 227-44.

Burchardt, T., Le Grand, J. and Piachaud, D. (2002) 'Degrees of exclusion: developing a dynamic, multidimensional measure', in J. Hills et al (eds) *Understanding social exclusion*, Oxford: OUP.

Byrne, D. (1999) *Social exclusion*, Buckingham: OUP.

Cameron, D. (2010) 'PM speech on wellbeing', a transcript of a speech given by the Prime Minister on wellbeing on 25 November 2010, London: Cabinet Office.

Cameron, D. (2016) 'Prime Minister's speech on life chances', 11 January 2016, https://www.gov.uk/government/speeches/prime-ministers-speech-on-life-chances.

Cusworth, L., Bradshaw, J., Coles, B., Keung, A. and Chzhen, Y. (2009) *Understanding social exclusion across the life course: Youth and young adulthood*, London: Social Exclusion Task Force, Cabinet Office.

Dermott, E. and Main, G. (2017) *Poverty and social exclusion in the UK: volume 1 – the nature and extent of the problem*, Bristol: Policy Press.

Diener E. and Suh, E. (1997) 'Measuring quality of life: economic, social and subjective indicators', *Social Indicators Research*, 40: 189-216.

Donovan R. and Halpern D. (2002) *Life satisfaction: The state of knowledge and implications for government policy*, London: Cabinet Office Strategy Unit.

Duffy, K. (2005), *Social exclusion and human dignity in Europe*, Strasbourg: Council of Europe.

Eurostat (2015), *Quality of life indicators*, Online publication, ISSN 2443-8219, http://ec.europa.eu/eurostat/statistics-explained/index.php/Quality_of_life_indicators.

Fahmy, E., Gordon, D. and Patsios, D. (2009) *Understanding social exclusion across the life course: Working age adults without dependent children*, London: Cabinet Office.

Fairclough, N. (2000) *New Labour, new language*, London: Routledge.

Fraser, N. (1995) 'From redistribution to recognition? Dilemmas of justice in a 'post-socialist' age', *New Left Review*, 212: 68-93.

Gordon, D. et al (2000) *Poverty and social exclusion in Britain*, York: Joseph Rowntree Foundation.

Honneth, A. and Fraser, N. (2003) *Redistribution or recognition? A political-philosophical exchange*, London: Verso.

Kahneman, D. and Krueger, A. (2006) 'Developments in the measurement of subjective well-being', *Journal of Economic Perspectives*, 20(1): 3-24.

Layard, R. (2011) *Happiness: Lessons from a new science* (2nd edn), London: Penguin.

Levitas, R. (1998) *The inclusive society: Social exclusion and New Labour*, Basingstoke: Macmillan.

Levitas, R. (2006) 'The concept and measurement of social exclusion', in Gordon et al (eds) *Poverty and social exclusion in Britain*, Bristol: Policy Press.

Levitas R., Pantazis C., Fahmy E., Gordon D., Lloyd E. and Patsios D. (2007) *The multi-dimensional analysis of social exclusion*, Bristol: University of Bristol.

Lister, R. (2002) 'A politics of recognition and respect: involving people with experience of poverty in decision making that affects their lives', *Social Policy and Society*, 1(1): 37-46.

Lister, R. (2004) *Poverty*, Cambridge: Polity Press.

Lister, R. (2007) 'From object to subject: including marginalised citizens in policy making', *Policy and Politics*, 35(3): 437-55.

Madanipour, A., Cars G. and Allen, J. (1998) *Social exclusion in European cities*, London: Jessica Kingsley.

NEF (New Economics Foundation) (2009) *National accounts of well-being*, London: New Economics Foundation.

OECD (2011) *Compendium of well-being indicators*, Paris: OECD.

ONS (Office for National Statistics) (2016) *Measuring national well-being: Life in the UK, 2016*, London: ONS.

Oroyemi, P., Damioli, G., Barnes, M. and Crosier, T. (2009) *Understanding the risks of social exclusion across the life course: Families with children*, London: Social Exclusion Task Force, UK Cabinet Office.

Room, G. (1995) *Beyond the threshold: The measurement and analysis of social exclusion*, Bristol: Policy Press.

SEU (Social Exclusion Unit) (2004) *Breaking the cycle: Taking stock of progress and priorities for the future. A report by the Social Exclusion Unit September 2004*, London: Office of the Deputy Prime Minister.

Silver, H. (1994) 'Social exclusion and social solidarity: three paradigms', *International Labour Review*, 133(5-6).

Silver, H. (2007) *The process of social exclusion: The dynamics of an evolving concept*, Chronic Poverty Research Centre, Rhode Island, USA: Brown University.

Stiglitz J., Sen A. and Fitoussi J.-P. (2009) *Report of the Commission on Economic Performance and Social Progress*, http://www.stiglitz-sen-fitoussi.fr/en/index.htm.

Taylor, M., Berthoud R. and Jenkins S. (2004) *Low income and multiple disadvantage 1991-2001. Analysis of the British Household Panel Survey*, London: Social Exclusion Unit/Office of the Deputy Prime Minister.

Townsend, P. (1979) *Poverty in the United Kingdom*, London: Allen Lane and Penguin Books.

Walker, A. and Walker, C. (1997) 'Poverty and social exclusion in Europe', in A. Walker and C. Walker (eds) *Britain divided*, London: Child Poverty Action Group.

Appendix: Factor analysis for multidimensional social exclusion

With this approach, the aim was to combine measures to capture levels of inclusion or exclusion in relation to each domain of the B-SEM as fully as possible, and then to use these scores to explore the multidimensional nature of exclusion. The approach had two stages, described much more fully in Bailey and Bramley (2017). In the first, exploratory factor analysis and other techniques were used to identify questions which could be grouped together to provide fewer and more continuous measures for each domain or sub-domain. At times, factor analysis was used to confirm that a group of questions reflected a single latent variable or factor, but the questions were then combined using simple averages because they were all measured on the same scale (for example, for 'A3: Social Support', we used the average of scores on seven questions on this topic). At other times, factor analysis was also used to produce the combined score (for example, for 'A1: Economic Resources').

We did not assume that the questions in the survey which had been designed to capture a particular domain did indeed form a single, coherent group. Rather we sought to check whether this was the case using exploratory factor analyses. Where these suggested multiple factors were present, we split the domain into sub-domains. For example, analysis of the questions in the survey designed to capture the 'C2: Living Environment' domain from the B-SEM suggested multiple different factors, for both housing and neighbourhood elements.

In the second stage, factor analysis was used on the set of domain and sub-domain scores to explore whether the domains of the B-SEM could be reduced to a smaller set of factors. This is an inherently subjective approach. Results are affected by choices made about the specification of the factor solution, for example. We conducted some sensitivity testing using different specifications, but ultimately used a specification which permitted factors to correlate ('oblimin'). There was also an iterative process of refining the domain and sub-domain scores in the first stage after examination of initial results from the second stage suggested problems with multi-collinearity.

Some variables are measures for all individuals but others only for the household. In the latter case, these are attributed to all members of the household. Some variables are measured only for those of working age or in paid work or only for older people, so models which include these must be restricted to sub-groups of the population. These restricted measures do not therefore form part of the final model reported in the chapter although they were used in exploratory analyses.

Three domain scores emerge as having very little relationship with the others and hence only weakly correlated with any of the factors emerging in the results. These were: 'A2: Access to services', 'C3: Criminal record' and 'C3: Fear of Crime'. There were dropped from the final model. The final model was based on a set of 18 domain and sub-domain measures available for all individuals.

Table A13.1: Sub-domain scores and indicators for factor analysis

Domains/sub-domains	Components/questions
A1 Economic resources	*Factors score from:*
	Income (log) [equivalised, AHC]
	Income 1yr ago (log) [equivalised, AHC]
	Adult deprivation [lacking PSE adult/household necessities]
	Debt: mortgage/rent arrears etc
	Debt: credit arrears etc
	Debt: money lender etc
	Subjective poverty [average from three questions]
	Luxuries [count of seven luxury items]
	Quality of items [average across seven items]
A3 Social support	Average from seven questions on social support (perceived)
A3 Contact with family	Combine ordinal qns on (i) frequency and (ii) number of contacts
A3 Contact with friends	Combine ordinal qns on (i) frequency and (ii) number of contacts
A4 Education	Highest qual (patched from hhld if missing)
B1 Participation in unpaid childcare	Banded hours on childcare
B2 Participation in social activity	Count of activities done or not wanted (excl. necessities items)
B3 Participation in cultural activity	Count of cultural activities from seven qns
B4 Participation in civic, political or voluntary activity	Factor score from:
	Civic participation [no. memberships of organisations]
	Political participation [no. of political actions taken]
	Volunteering [no. of hours volunteering]

(continued)

Domains/sub-domains	Components/questions
B4 Political efficacy	Average from three qns on sense of political efficacy
C1 Well-being	*Factor score from:*
	– Well-being: day-to-day [one qn]
	– Well-being: community [one qn]
	– Well-being: life [one qn]
	– Shame [two qns]
	– Mental health [GHQ12]
C1 Limiting health problems or disability	*Factor score from:*
	General health [one qn]
	Health/disab limiting [poor health/disability and limiting]
C2 Housing dissat/space prob	Overall satisfaction
C2 Housing repair prob	Disrepair qn and five qns on problems with dwelling conditions
C2 Housing heating prob	Seven qns on problems with costs of heating home
C2 Neighbourhood – dissatis/social prob	Overall satisfaction and six qns on social problems
C2 Neighbourhood – noise/pollution	Three qns on noise or pollution
C2 Neighbourhood – phys prob/litter	Five qns on physical environment, litter, etc.

Notes: An additional domain (A4: cultural resources) has been added to the B-SEM framework for this element while two domains (A2: access to services and C3: crime and social harm) are omitted from the final analysis. AHC = after housing costs.

FOURTEEN

Conclusions and emerging themes

Glen Bramley and Nick Bailey

Introduction

In this concluding section we attempt to provide some synthesis from the rich detail and insights developed across the preceding chapters. We do not attempt to simply reproduce the conclusions from each chapter. Rather, we have identified some larger themes which cut across the individual chapters and place the emergent findings from the PSE-UK 2012 study into a broader intellectual and policy context. This book presents predominantly quantitative findings from the PSE-UK survey structured thematically, mainly around the domains of social exclusion as set out in the Bristol Social Exclusion Matrix (B-SEM, see Levitas et al, 2007 and our Introduction), but with some additional themes around the measurement of living standards and wider well-being included.

In developing our narrative on the larger cross-cutting themes, we have a particular eye on the discourses about poverty, whether in popular debate, the media, academia or 'policy communities', and about associated issues of policy, including poverty-related targets and standards. The authors contributing to this volume are academics active in research on poverty and social exclusion, but also often actively contributing to these discourses and policy debates. While this volume and its companion (Dermott and Main, 2017) present the largest concentration of output and reflection from the PSE research, it should be recognised that there are other important published outputs (notably Lansley and Mack, 2015; Daly and Kelly 2015; edited collections of papers in *Critical Social Policy* (volume 36, issue 1, 2016) and *Journal of Poverty and Social Justice* (volume 22, issue 3, 2014), and the PSE website, www.poverty.ac.uk/pse-research), not to mention several TV programmes.

The centrality of poverty

The central message of this volume is that poverty is a reality, that we can measure it most effectively through the PSE's consensual deprivation approach, and that it still has very pervasive adverse effects on society which we can clearly document. Townsend's (1979) notion of poverty as the inability through lack of resources to participate in normal social activities continues to find strong public support and is reflected in the close relationship of exclusion from social activities with material poverty (as drawn out particularly by Mack in Chapter 1 and Bailey in Chapter 6). Poverty in terms of the shortfall in economic resources is the most central and important domain of social exclusion (as demonstrated by Bailey, Fahmy and Bradshaw in Chapter 13), and it is particularly strongly linked to a number of other domains including employment, housing and social activities. Prior and Manley show convincingly in Chapter 8 that both current and past poverty, particularly as measured by PSE, are strong predictors of physical and mental health problems. The fuel poverty story reported by Bramley in Chapter 9 shows particular examples of how poverty can affect people's health and quality of life. Pemberton, Pantazis and Hillyard develop in Chapter 10 a more general account of the social harms of poverty, embracing impacts through physical and mental well-being, autonomy and relationships, synthesising qualitative as well as quantitative evidence. Tomlinson and Wilson in Chapter 12 review the current vogue for focusing on well-being and 'happiness', but show clearly that the most important route to improving these psychological outcomes is through lifting people out of poverty and economic insecurity.

A more market society?

Some would argue that changes since 1979, and continuing currently, are making for a more 'marketised' society, with more goods, services and experiences subject to market mechanisms and processes. If true, this might be expected to make for a closer correlation of 'other' domains of exclusion with the core economic resources domain. One example discussed by Bramley in Chapter 9 is housing, where the rise of private renting and the decline of both social renting and home ownership may be seen as undermining Britain's traditionally distinct welfare/housing regime, which helped to insulate the poor from an inevitable experience of housing deprivations; the chapter does find however that this transition has not been complete. Another example might be the trend to 'financialisation' discussed by Bramley and Besemer in Chapter 11, with its associated growth of financial 'stress' and debt problems, even as conventional measures of financial exclusion decline. However, the findings on certain other domains, for example social networks and support (Chapter 5) and local services (Chapter 4) show that these remain distinct in their patterns and less closely related to economic resources.

Inequality

Some argue that we should frame the discussion more in terms of 'inequality' than 'poverty'; others might beg to differ. Clearly the PSE-UK study provides a wealth of evidence on inequality across different domains. Inequality in Britain rose dramatically in the 1980s and remains worse than in many developed countries (Hills, 2015), although recent trends have been less clear-cut (Introduction chapter). One aspect of concern is what has been happening to the incomes and wealth of the 'top 1 per cent', or even the 'top 0.1 per cent', with an increasing range of voices suggesting that rising inequalities at this end of the spectrum are economically, socially and politically damaging (Dabla-Norris et al, 2015; Ostry et al, 2016; Piketty, 2013; Stiglitz, 2012; Sayer 2015). However, the PSE-UK survey is probably not the best vehicle for investigating this group, not least because of the challenges of getting a representative sample of the richest households in this kind of survey. Another aspect is the bottom 1-3 per cent, the people in very severe poverty and destitution addressed by Bramley, Fitzpatrick and Sosenko in Chapter 3. They report some evidence that the incidence has increased and spread to wider groups in the population, for reasons picked up further later in this chapter.

The chapters in this collection underline that inequality is a major concern, not just in terms of income but across a whole range of domains. As Patsios, Pomati and Hillyard show in Chapter 2, there are striking inequalities in 'What we have', 'What we do' and 'Where we live'. When Tomlinson and Wilson look at subjective well-being and happiness (Chapter 12), they find that the most glaring inequality is the low levels experienced by the poor. This provides very striking support for a traditional 'utilitarian' argument for redistribution, to raise average happiness levels. Across demographic groups, the most striking story is the dramatic improvement of the situation of retirement age households in UK, a group for whom poverty – and financial stress more generally – seems to be increasingly rare (as drawn out in our own Introduction, but also the accompanying Dermott and Main volume). This group, at least the majority who are home owners, are also benefiting from the increasingly skewed distribution of wealth, because of housing price increases and the evolution of occupational pensions. Findings in relation to other dimensions of exclusion, such as Wilson, Fahmy and Bailey's work on social participation (Chapter 5), also suggest this group are doing well, at least on average.

Disadvantaged groups

If the retirement age group is the demographic which is currently most favoured, who appear to be most frequently disadvantaged, looking across the domains of poverty and social exclusion? Patsios, Pomati and Hillyard in Chapter 2 highlight the low average living standards of single working-age people and lone parents, in particular. Bailey, Fahmy and Bradshaw highlight in Chapter 13 a number of groups who feature recurrently, including: younger and single adults; lone parents; the unemployed and economically inactive; Black and other minority ethnic groups; renters, particularly in the social sector; and those in 'routine' occupations. Bailey in Chapter 6 also highlights the extent of poverty and other forms of exclusion for those in paid work. On the whole this is not a new-looking profile of 'the poor', apart from the virtual disappearance of older people from the list. The companion volume (Dermott and Main, 2017) examines the situation of different groups of people in more depth, as well as the place dimension of poverty.

Falling living standards and expectations

Most of the authors involved in this volume grew up in a context of expectations of continual improvement of living standards which post-WW2 economic growth had supported through most years for most of the population. The period leading up to and beyond the PSE-UK 2012 survey was something of an exception to that, as underlined in our Introduction, with flatlining or declining real income levels, and this is strongly confirmed by the headline findings on worsening PSE poverty discussed in Lansley and Mack (2015). Chapter 13 suggests that two-thirds of comparable deprivation or exclusion indicators worsened between 1999 and 2012. Economic growth of the UK remains rather low, and is currently uncertain owing to Brexit, and during the period leading up to 2012 there were strong rises in some elements of the cost of living which are important for lower income households, particularly energy costs and housing costs (with the shift to private renting). It is striking also that expectations had clearly fallen, as reflected in the changes in what constituted necessities as underlined by Mack in Chapter 1, whereas between 1983 and 1999 they had been rising. Cost of living pressures clearly affected groups above the poverty level, sometimes termed 'the squeezed middle', who showed more evidence of struggle as highlighted by Bramley and Besemer in Chapter 11 (where evidence of financial stress on this group is presented). Bailey argues in Chapter 6 that there is a growing issue of both 'in-work' poverty and 'exclusionary employment', and this parallels some wider societal debates about the growth of 'precarity' in the labour market and more widely (Standing, 2011). Bramley noted in Chapter 9 that some housing needs or deprivations appeared to worsen in this period, after a long period of progressive improvement, while Bramley and Besemer suggested in Chapter 4 that a range of local services were starting to worsen under the impact of austerity.

Disengagement or alienation?

The cumulative impact of all of the above could be extremely negative, not just for immediate welfare but also possibly leading to a loss of confidence in the economic (and political) system. As researchers, we see a growing gulf between the evidence on the harm caused by poverty and inequality, and the direction of travel in policy. Policy has never been 'evidence-based' in a simple or direct sense, but research and evidence seem to be losing what little traction they had on the worlds of policy and politics. We do not in this volume directly address media portrayals of poverty but accept that this is a significant issue in its own right The evidence of a decline of civic/political engagement addressed by Fahmy in Chapter 7 seems a bit ambiguous, although it is clear that the poor participate less, even when controlling for class and education, and Chapter 13 reports declining participation in political activities and groups, common social activities or use of cultural facilities.

The sense of alienation of sections of society from mainstream politics was given a significant boost by the outcome of the UK's EU Referendum in 2016, although perhaps somewhat paradoxically, the voting turnout was notably high. In subsequent reactions, including by the incoming Prime Minister, Theresa May, there has been considerable emphasis on parts of Britain which may feel 'left behind' by economic events as well as ignored by the 'metropolitan establishment' and the political elite. The regional dimension of poverty is discussed more by Tomlinson's chapter in Dermott and Main (2017).

The damaging effects of poverty

There are many reasons we should care about poverty. While representing first and foremost an affront to our sense of social justice, poverty also causes significant and lasting harm to individuals and to society (see Pemberton, Pantazis and Hillyard in Chapter 10). These harms create very substantial costs for society, not least financial costs to the public sector (Bramley et al, 2016a). The proposition that poverty and inequality impose such harms and costs is increasingly widely acknowledged, although there may be debates about the exact patterns and directions of causality and the role of other possibly confounding factors.

Within this volume, significant evidence is presented on the nature, extent and significance of such harmful and costly effects. Prior and Manley present this particularly clearly in Chapter 8 on poverty and health, by showing the scale of difference in both physical and mental ill health associated with poverty, and that these effects are robust to the inclusion of a wide range of socio-demographic controls and to the use of time-lagged measures of poverty to address issues about the direction of effects. Chapter 12 reinforces this by underlining that the strongest factor correlated with lower levels of happiness and well-being is poverty. Chapter 10 complements this by presenting arguments and evidence on the different types of social harm (for example through impacting on autonomy and relationships), including through the use of qualitative research findings linked to PSE. Chapter 5 shows that, while social networks and support can help some individuals and families to withstand economic adversity, at the same time persistent and recurrent poverty can wear down such relationships and see a progressive withdrawal of poor people from social engagement (notably social activities), thereby contributing further to risks to health and well-being. Chapter 3 shows how combinations of persistent poverty, lack or loss of supportive relationships, and the rough ends of welfare reform and administration are leading to a significant incidence of outright destitution in the UK in 2015.

Precarious lives?

Some have characterised life for rising proportions of the population in the UK, and elsewhere, as being increasingly uncertain and risky, with terms like 'precarity' being frequently used (Standing, 2011). Expressions of economic precariousness include the growing extent of marginal self-employment activities, contract and agency working including 'zero-hours contracts', and unpaid internships rather than proper paid training jobs. Lynch (2016) focuses on the stresses and strains of Britain's 'just managing' families. In a new approach to defining social class in Britain, Savage et al (2015) proposed an emergent structure in which the 'precariat' (accounting for 15 per cent of the population) occupied the bottom rung, below groups labelled 'emerging service workers' (19 per cent) and 'traditional working class' (14 per cent). After discussing the problems of stigmatisation, Savage et al go on to argue that

> ... the precariat concept is preferable to that of an underclass because Standing's term draws direct attention to the way that the vulnerability of these groups is linked to their structural location in society. It also avoids the clichéd stereotypes. The precariat are not passive, culturally disengaged or morally limited. (Savage et al, 2015: p 353)

In Chapter 6, Bailey develops the concept of 'exclusionary employment' and suggests that one third of the working population are in this category, suggesting a somewhat broader phenomenon. Clearly different definitions and thresholds produce different numbers, but perhaps the wider point is that relatively poor quality of work affects a large and possibly growing section of the UK population. It is certainly clear from PSE evidence from successive surveys that 'in-work' poverty is a growing phenomenon, and that therefore it is becoming less true that work constitutes a general route out of poverty. In addition, precarity of employment can also be linked to precarity in the housing market. The share of households in the private rented sector has increased dramatically in the last twenty years, and in most of the UK the standard private tenancy offers little security beyond six months (Chapter 9). A growing share of working households in their middle years and families are now obliged to live in such an insecure tenure, having been excluded from owner occupation by unaffordability and from social renting by its unavailability, particularly in higher demand regions. Another form of precarity stems from the growth of household debt, creating a source of stress for both poor and middle income households, as documented in Chapter 11.

Pemberton, Pantazis and Hillyard in Chapter 10 question the adequacy or appropriateness of the concept of 'risk society', and the associated emphasis on 'resilience', in some social theory and policy literature of the last two decades. It is clear that a weakness of these discourses is to not recognise that the exposure to risk is in fact strongly patterned, and that certain groups (notably the 'precariat' as defined above, and the poor more generally) are disproportionately exposed to such risks and disadvantaged in being able to counter or absorb them. Striking evidence of this inequality of risk in the case of homelessness is presented by Bramley and Fitzpatrick (2017) drawing on PSE and other data. While it is true in a general sense that some individuals and families may display more resilience than others in overcoming hardship or specific adverse events/harms, resilience can be weakened by a range of factors, such as a lack of social support networks or a previous stressing of these networks (Chapter 5), prolonged experience of poverty or repeated bouts of severe poverty (Chapter 3), or episodes of mental ill health confronting wholly inadequate service provision (Layard and Clark, 2014).

Social exclusion

The PSE studies have been based to a considerable degree on the premise that governments and policy communities are interested in the wider concept of 'social exclusion', a concept which overlaps with but is distinct from 'poverty'. While Bailey, Fahmy and Bradshaw question this presumption in Chapter 13, at least implicitly, we would say that the jury is perhaps still out. The specific language of social exclusion may have been used somewhat less frequently in recent years, but there is still a very live political and policy debate about both poverty and wider inequalities in life chances. The debates about how definitions of poverty and related targets may evolve over time, picked up further later in this chapter, serve to illustrate this. Having attempted to measure social exclusion in a comprehensive way through the B-SEM framework, what have we learned about the utility of this concept?

First, as already underlined (under the 'Centrality of poverty' section), this body of research confirms the view that poverty remains central to the experience of exclusion. While the strength of the associations between poverty and the different domains of exclusion may vary, Chapter 13 shows that the groups which suffer multiple forms of exclusion all have – albeit to greater or lesser extent – significant material disadvantage. Social exclusion is not an alternative focus to or substitute for poverty, but rather a reminder to look beyond the immediate material position. Second, it is also true that the 'social exclusion' perspective, when applied systematically, does expose some different clusterings of problems which are less closely associated with poverty, particularly in the areas of family and social networks and support, political and civic/cultural participation, and local services. In some instances, such as local services, we would argue that this lack of close association with other domains of exclusion is good news since it is evidence of policy success (as developed further later).

On a more pragmatic note, we would acknowledge that some aspects of social exclusion are less adequately and completely measured in the PSE-UK survey. For this reason we have found it more difficult to provide a rounded account of them in this volume. This applies particularly to education and cultural resources and participation, and perhaps also to crime and criminalisation. While the current survey has been the first to try to operationalise such a broad measure of exclusion, there is undoubtedly scope for improvement.

A less cohesive society?

A question posed by some of the issues raised in this concluding chapter might be: 'Is society becoming less cohesive?' One should always, of course, guard against naïve assumptions about the nature of British society in the past. With the exception of Northern Ireland, we have managed to avoid civil wars and revolutions over the last couple of centuries, but Britain has also been a notably class-ridden society. Perhaps the period of the Second World War and its aftermath, which saw the foundation and consolidation of the modern welfare state under consistently improving economic conditions, was a period of relatively high national consensus and cohesion (Hennessy, 1992). Conversely, the period since the 1970s has seen more economic instability and political change, including at times polarisation, major occupational changes associated with transition to a post-industrial economy in a globalised world, and greater population diversity associated with greater international migration.

The PSE-UK study is not primarily focused on questions relating to social cohesion, for example in terms of values and attitudes. Nevertheless, in the one area of attitudes which we examined explicitly, namely attitudes to what constituted essentials for living in the UK today, we found remarkable consensus across groups. In terms of changes over time, we detected some areas where change might have some bearing on social cohesion. In Chapter 4, it was shown that local public services in the information, leisure and cultural field, which are generally open to the whole population, have tended to see a reduction in usage, so that services previously used by majorities are now only used by minorities (for example, libraries). Socio-technical change, with the growth of online access to information and services, was seen as a factor behind this trend, but it could have as a consequence some loss of social cohesion. Services for children expanded in the period after 1999, so that families might have experienced more involvement in public services, such as children's centres or after school clubs, but this process will have gone somewhat into reverse during the period of austerity after 2010. In Chapter 7, some mixed evidence was presented on political and civic participation, with some evidence of decline which might be taken as another indicator of declining cohesion.

If attitudes towards poverty, including views about its causes and the role of individual agency, are a guide to social cohesion, then we can probably say from evidence from other sources (particularly the British Social Attitudes Surveys) that attitudes to welfare have hardened over time (although there is some tendency for this to relate to the economic cycle). This seems to be particularly true for views about unemployment benefits, and possibly more generally for benefits to working-age households. Overall, the proportion *disagreeing* with the statement that the government should spend more money on welfare benefits rose from 15 per cent in 1989 to 44 per cent in 2009, before dropping back to 31 per cent in 2015 (NatCen 2016).

A behavioural agenda

The way that public attitudes to welfare and poverty fluctuate over time is associated with beliefs or assumptions about behaviour and about the choices which people make. If you believe that whether people are working or not is more a matter of choice than opportunity, and that there are not structural barriers of geography and discrimination which make it much more difficult for some people to find work, then you are more likely to favour welfare policies which impose conditions and create incentives for working-age people to actively seek work. The behavioural agenda may be seen as entailing a continuum from the more subtle, psychological approaches of the 'nudge' school towards the more crude and coercive world of job-seeker benefit sanctions.

However, it has long been recognised that people have both more understanding of and more sympathy, or empathy, for people more similar to themselves in terms of experience (Culyer, 1983). Thus the generation of the 1930s who experienced mass unemployment with inadequate social protections, as well as the privations of World War 2, were much more sympathetic to the plight of unemployed people in the earlier years of the post-WW2 welfare state. By contrast, the prolonged period of falling unemployment up to 2008 may have underlain the changing attitudes mentioned in the preceding section.

It is perhaps more in the qualitative research associated with the PSE study, as well as in other contemporary studies (for example, Fitzpatrick et al, 2016), that one may gain more insight into the real and perceived nature of the choices facing people in poverty. And it should also be stressed that behavioural sciences have shown clearly how our capacity to make 'good' decisions or to put long-term benefits ahead of short-term rewards is heavily influenced by our material position and hence poverty (Behavioural Insights Team, 2016).

During the period of the PSE research, there has been a concerted and partially successful attempt to redefine poverty in the UK, retreating from the apparent consensus around the child poverty targets achieved in 2010. This attempt is closely bound up with a focus on behavioural issues. For example, in proposing a redefinition of these targets, the Centre for Social Justice (CSJ) (2012) made the following statement:

> ... our main concern is that the exclusive use of an arbitrary line to measure child poverty tells us almost nothing about how the disadvantaged live their lives. .... Yet we know from our own extensive research as well as the research of others that the key drivers of poverty are family breakdown, educational failure, economic dependency and worklessness, addiction and serious personal debt .... (Centre for Social Justice, 2012: p 4)

We would take issue with this statement, and certainly with its implications. First, you could argue that the statement is equally or even more true the other way around – that is, family breakdown, educational failure, and serious personal debt are all strongly found following and as a consequence of poverty. Clearly it is a very substantial and unwarranted assertion that the direction of causality contained in the CSJ formulation is the dominant one. Secondly, the statement insinuates that these are all examples of personal behavioural choices indicative of moral weakness and fecklessness, or possibly weakness in certain public institutions such as schools, rather than broader structural features of the economy, society and the state. Yet such assumptions are blind to the real constraints facing many people in their daily lives – women driven out of relationships by violence and abuse, schools which routinely fail to address additional educational needs, the negligible chances of a person with limited qualifications or work experience finding a decent job in many localities, or the crude and uncoordinated practices of debt collection agencies in public as well as private sectors.

It is sometimes said that extreme cases make bad law, and this may be true of the kind of response to poverty implied by the CSJ intervention. It is suggested that 'addiction' is one of the key causes of poverty, which tends to imply that this is very common and that for most people in poverty this is a factor. Yet this is simply not true. Serious addictions to drugs or alcohol are closely related to certain other social problems, particularly chronic offending, single homelessness and, to some extent, mental ill health. This cluster of 'complex needs' is a significant issue for the individuals affected and their families, friends and neighbours, and for a range of services they use, placing significant burdens on public expenditure (Bramley et al, 2015). But they are a small part of the total population affected by poverty – between 2 per cent and 5 per cent of the total number of adults in poverty in England at that time.

Positive stories

It is easy to lapse into a negative, critical stance in the light of debates such as those just mentioned. However, it is also important to highlight positive messages where these are apparent within the research. One good example is the picture presented on local and public services (Chapter 4). Insofar as some people were excluded from a number of services, the pattern of who and where was not systematically related to poverty or to the other domains of social exclusion. In other words, there is no inevitability to the potential link between deprivation and local services exclusion. It is not invariably true in Britain that if you are poor you will have no services or only poor quality services available to you – an assumption that would typically be made in some other 'advanced' countries, such as the USA. Through the combination of activities by local government (both as service provider and as planning and regeneration agency), the NHS, and other public regulation, there is generally good service provision across the board in most areas. Furthermore, although there was some evidence of retreat for some services, in the important area of children's services, the availability and quality improved markedly between 1999 and 2012.

There are other examples of positive stories on the lack of close correlation of some other domains of social exclusion with core material poverty, for example housing where Chapter 19 argued there was still a degree of insulation of housing deprivations from economic deprivation, for educational and cultural resources/participation (albeit not very thoroughly measured or analysed here) and similarly for social activities and support (Chapter 5) and civic and political engagement (Chapter 7). Some aspects of living standards have improved over time (Chapter 1), fewer people are excluded from basic financial services (Chapter 11), and people continue to feel a little bit happier year by year (Chapter 12). It is a real strength of the PSE-UK approach that it can draw attention to these positives, giving credit to policy makers and institutions where due, as well as highlighting continuing problems or challenges.

Where next?

In drawing these threads together it is incumbent on us to suggest what the most important 'take-away' lessons are for certain key questions facing UK in relation to poverty and social exclusion in 2017:

- What is the right set of poverty targets for governments to work to and for the policy community to focus on, and hence for the statistical agencies to measure?
- Is social exclusion still the key 'twin concept' to run alongside poverty and is it appropriately encapsulated by the B-SEM framework? Do other terms – inequality, social mobility, or life chances, for example – provide a better means of focusing our attention?
- How do key conclusions emerging from the PSE-UK study link up with current agendas for policies to tackle poverty, particularly the Joseph Rowntree Foundation's anti-poverty strategy, 'Solve UK poverty'? (JRF, 2016a, b)

Poverty targets

It was a significant advance for Britain to place legislation on the statute book specifically on poverty through the 2010 Child Poverty Act. This established a framework of targets to provide a benchmark for progress towards the goal, first established as a government target by Prime Minister Tony Blair in 2001, to first halve and then eliminate child poverty over 10 and 20 years respectively. The key targets were the four measures of: relative low income; absolute low income against a fixed base year; combined low income and material deprivation; and persistent poverty. The third of these drew on the approached developed in the earlier PSE studies. At the same time, the EU was developing a parallel set of targets and measurement tools utilising the EU-SILC datasets (Guio et al, 2016). These also drew on the PSE approach, incorporating a measure of material deprivation into the EU's headline poverty reduction targets (EU 2010).

Despite cross-party support for the 2010 Act, the change of government later that year set in train a process to question the basis of the targets, as briefly described in Chapter 1. Particularly influential through its links with Iain Duncan Smith, then Secretary of State for Work and Pensions, was the Centre for Social Justice (CSJ, 2012), which argued that these measures of child poverty were inadequate, placing too much emphasis on income while neglecting what CSJ saw as 'the main drivers of poverty', which it listed as 'family breakdown, educational failure, economic dependency and worklessness, addiction and serious personal debt'. It proposed a recasting of targets and indicators to place more emphasis on the latter factors rather than the former.

It should be clear from much of the content of this volume that the present authors reject the thrust of this critique. We have already commented above, under the 'behavioural agenda' heading, on the inadequacy of the CSJ approach. More fundamentally, it is simply logically wrong to sidestep the definition of poverty and talk about causes, without being clear about what is the phenomenon that these are causing. The CSJ then compounds this error by pushing a tendentious list of alleged causes without giving consideration to the full range of present and past causes of poverty. Poverty is fundamentally about the lack of material resources to enable human well-being, thriving and participation in society, yet the CSJ intervention and some of the subsequent policy responses represent an attempt to airbrush the main source of material resources, income, out of the picture.

The most important conclusion of the present study, reviewing the findings across all the chapters in this volume, is that material poverty remains central to most aspects of social exclusion in Britain today. This conclusion is reinforced by many other studies which exploit the growing richness of longitudinal data, to show the longlasting and often cumulative effects of poverty in childhood and younger adulthood on later life chances, whether in terms of education and skills, earning power, health, or wider participation in many aspects of life. Although PSE is fundamentally a cross-sectional survey, key questions on past experiences of poverty show a strong relationship with contemporary outcomes in this respect (see especially Chapter 8).

Notwithstanding the critical reaction of the wider policy community, as well as many academics, the post-2015 Conservative government legislated in the Welfare Reform and Work Act 2016 to abolish the Child Poverty Act and its associated targets. The only formal targets set were in relation to children in workless families and educational attainment. After a prolonged campaign, the government agreed to commit in law to regularly publishing data on the number of children in poverty under the old targets, but it is clear this represents a major downgrading in their status. The government duty to publish a child poverty strategy was also removed by this legislation. A previous Child Poverty Commission was reconstituted as the Social Mobility and Child Poverty Commission in 2012, while under the 2016 Act this was renamed once more as the 'Social Mobility Commission', a further attempt to airbrush poverty out of the picture (CPAG, 2016).

It should also be emphasised that the UK/England policy agenda here has increasingly diverged from that pursued in the devolved administrations of Scotland, Wales and Northern Ireland. Broadly, these countries continue to focus on child poverty and to promote a range of strategies and key outcome targets that give significant emphasis to poverty as well as wider life chances.

It seems likely that the debate about poverty measurement will continue to run. Following intensive criticism of the Child Poverty Act measures from some members of government, an independent Social Metrics Commission has been established to try to identify new measures which can command long-term cross-party support. In their Interim Report (Social Metrics Commission, 2016), the Commission argued that these measures needed to meet a number of criteria, including being scientifically credible as well as having support across the political spectrum. Given the views expressed by some in government about the existing well-established poverty measures, it remains to be seen whether the Commission can identify any new indicators which will satisfy both criteria.

Whither social exclusion?

We have touched at various points in this book on the origins, development and interpretation of the concept of social exclusion. The PSE-UK study was a serious attempt at measuring all aspects of exclusion in a systematic way within one household survey instrument, providing a unique opportunity to better understand the interrelationships between as well as the distinctiveness of particular domains of exclusion. This and the companion volume are our best attempt to put this picture together in one place and to provide a rich account of the meanings and realities of social exclusion, albeit one resting mainly on quantitative data. What can we conclude from the exercise as a whole?

First, we would claim to have been, in the main, successful in generating and analysing an appropriate set of measures which provide a balanced picture of multidimensional social exclusion in the UK today. This picture enables us to say much more confidently how important economic resources, or material deprivation, are in the broader picture, re-emphasising the centrality of poverty and the validity of the original Townsend conceptualisation from 50 years ago (Townsend, 1979). In this volume in particular, we focus on the nature of the different dimensions, including how they are best measured and how they may be changing over time as well as how they interrelate with one another.

Are the B-SEM domains the correct ones for structuring analysis and commentary in the future? From a statistical point of view, Chapter 13 suggests they can be grouped together to a considerable degree, although the picture of closeness of association depends on the measures and techniques used to some extent. Using the approach of categorising people as excluded or not on each domain, most domains appear to be positively associated with each other but in many case the overlaps look quite modest. Using the factor analysis approach based on continuous scales of more or less exclusion, the domains of the B-SEM appear to collapse to perhaps five composite dimensions, with one or two domains (notably access to services) not closely correlated with any others. These five comprise: economic resources (with social activities and housing); political/civic/cultural participation; family and social resources; neighbourhood environment; and health and well-being. This suggests there may be a degree of duplication or redundancy in the present conceptual framework, and scope for a realignment of the current set of domains.

In terms of policy discourse, social exclusion has perhaps gone out of fashion since 1999, but the underlying issues remain essentially similar. One can discuss 'life chances' or 'outcomes' and still be essentially discussing the same issues. However, the discussion may now place a stronger emphasis on the dynamics of change, on the legacy of experiences at an earlier stage for opportunities in the present, and on barriers to change or factors which facilitate change. This parallels a change in the analytical landscape, with (as earlier noted) more emphasis on longitudinal datasets and data linkage as enhancements to conventional cross-sectional household survey methods. It is claimed that such developments offer significant opportunities for quantitative social sciences to gain a greater handle on issues of causation. While this focus on micro- and longitudinal data might be seen as putting a greater emphasis on a questionable 'behavioural agenda', and downplaying broader structural explanations, this is not necessarily the case. It may serve to provide a stronger demonstration of the longer-term, cumulative and geographically linked negative influences of material poverty on life chances and outcomes. These issues can be seen illustrated and discussed in a number of chapters in this volume (for example, Chapters 8 and 12).

Policy strategies

It has not been the purpose of this book to develop, review or critique policies which bear directly or indirectly on poverty and social exclusion, although inevitably particular policies do come into the picture. Our main purpose has been to provide an evidence-based assessment of the state of poverty and social exclusion in the contemporary UK, and to explore the nature of the different dimensions of exclusion and how they interrelate. However, governments follow strategies, implicitly or explicitly, even though the disjointed incrementalism of typical policy making as well as the impact of 'events' often mean that the actual operative policies do not represent a clearly coherent strategy. Other bodies – including think tanks, pressure groups and charities, as well as academics – also put forward their ideas for policy strategies, whether comprehensive or sectoral.

A particularly interesting contemporary example of this is the Joseph Rowntree Foundation, a charity which specialises in policy-oriented research and is active in the fields of poverty, place-making/housing and social policy. It has recently launched an anti-poverty strategy under the headline 'Solve UK poverty' (JRF, 2016a,b), based on a four-year programme of research and policy development. One of the present authors contributed to this background research, including: the study of 'Destitution in the UK' reported in Chapter 3; a study 'Counting the cost of poverty' (Bramley et al, 2016a), which showed how much it costs the public finances to leave poverty unsolved; and a study entitled 'What would make a difference?', which modelled the longer term impacts of a wide range of policy and contextual scenarios on outcomes in terms of a range of poverty and inequality measures (Bramley et al, 2016b).

This latter study suggested that it would be difficult to eliminate relative low-income poverty, but that substantial progress could be made in reducing 'combined poverty' (relative low income combined with material deprivation) and severe poverty or the depth of poverty (poverty gap shortfall against Minimum Income Standard) by around half to two-thirds. This could be done through a concerted strategy of different measures, which could still be relatively fiscally neutral, while also greatly improving housing affordability and access. Among the measures highlighted as offering some of the best potential were improved childcare packages, closing the gender pay gap, implementing the Full Living Wage and positive indexation of this in future, and convergence of regional growth rates, as well as restoring cuts in Universal Credit.

To go further it would probably be necessary to widen the agenda into a broader counter-inequality strategy, taking up some of the ideas canvassed by the late Tony Atkinson (2015) in his recent volume. These include such concepts as modifying the nature and emphasis of technological change and innovation, labour market policies and social partnership, national savings products, and possible universal child and 'participation' income. As these and other ideas are expanded and explored, we anticipate that the research reflected in this volume will play its part in influencing the evolving agenda, while the PSE data itself, and other datasets whose design and content has been influenced by PSE, will play a key role in building the evidence base for more effective policies.

References

Atkinson, A. (2015) *Inequality: What can be done?*, Cambridge, MA: Harvard University Press.

Beatty, T. and Fothergill, S. (2016) *The uneven impact of welfare reform: The financial losses to places and people, Report of Research for Joseph Rowntree Foundation and Oxfam*, Sheffield: Centre for Regional Economic and Social Research.

Behavioural Insights Team (2016) *The behavioural insights team: Update report 2015–16*, www.behavioural insights.co.uk

Bramley, G. and Fitzpatrick, S. (2017) 'Homelessness in the UK – who is most at risk?', *Housing Studies*, July.

Bramley, G., Hirsch, D., Littlewood, M. and Watkins, D. (2016a) *Counting the cost of UK poverty*, York: Joseph Rowntree Foundation, https://www.jrf.org.uk/report/counting-cost-uk-poverty.

Bramley, G., with Leishman, C., Cosgrove, P. and Watkins, D. (2016b) *What would make a difference? Modelling policy scenarios for tackling poverty in the UK*, https://pureapps2.hw.ac.uk/portal/files/10844984/Bramley_WhatWouldMakeaDifference_Report.pdf.

Bramley, G., Fitzpatrick, S., with Edwards, J., Ford, D., Johnsen, S., Sosenko, F. and Watkins, D. (2015) *Hard edges: Mapping severe and multiple disadvantage: England*, London: Lankelly Chase Foundation, www.lankellychase.org.uk.

Centre for Social Justice (CSJ) (2012) 'Rethinking child poverty', *CSJ Policy Paper*, http://www.centreforsocialjustice.org.uk/core/wp-content/uploads/2016/08/CSJ_Child_Poverty_secondversion.pdf.

CPAG (Child Poverty Action Group) (2016) 'Child poverty promise and Child Poverty Act', *Policy Briefing*, http://www.cpag.org.uk/content/child-poverty-promise-and-child-poverty-act.

Crossley, S. (2016) 'The trouble with the Troubled Families Programme – repeating the failed attempts of the past', *LSE British Politics and Policy* blog, http://blogs.lse.ac.uk/politicsandpolicy/the-trouble-with-the-troubled-families-programme-repeating-the-failed-attempts-of-the-past/.

Culyer, A. J. (1983) 'Economics without economic man', *Social Policy and Administration*, 17, 188-203.

Dabla-Norris, E., Kochhar, K., Ricka, F., Supaphiphat, N. and Tsounta, E. (2015) 'Causes and consequences of income inequality: a global perspective', *International Monetary Fund Staff Discussion Note SDN/15/15*, IMF, https://www.imf.org/external/pubs/ft/sdn/2015/sdn1513.pdf.

Daly, M. and Kelly, G. (2015) *Families and poverty: Everyday life on a low income*, Bristol: Policy Press.

DCLG (Department of Communities and Local Government) (2016) *National evaluation of the Troubled Families Programme: Final synthesis report*, London: DCLG.

Dermott, E. and Main, G. (2017) *Poverty and social exclusion in the UK – Vol 1, the extent and nature of the problem*, Bristol: Policy Press.

European Commission (EC) (2010) *Europe 2020: A European strategy for smart, sustainable and inclusive growth. COM(2010) 2020 final*, Brussels: EC.

Fitzpatrick, S., Bramley, G., Sosenko, F., Blenkinsopp, J., Johnsen, S., Littlewood, M., Netto, G. and Watts, B. (2016) *Destitution in the UK: Final report*, York: Joseph Rowntree Foundation.

Guio, A.-C., Marlier, E., Gordon, D., Fahmy, E., Nandy, S. and Pomati, M. (2016) 'Improving the measurement of material deprivation at the European Union level', *Journal of European Social Policy*, 26(3): 219-333.

Hastings, A., Bailey, N., Bramley, G., Gannon, M. and Watkins, D. (2015) *The cost of the cuts: Their impact on local government and poorer communities*, York: Joseph Rowntree Foundation.

Hennessy, P. (1992) *Never again: Britain 1945–51*, London: Cape.

Hills, J. (2015) *Good times, bad times: The welfare myth of Them and Us*, Bristol: Policy Press.

JRF (Joseph Rowntree Foundation) (2016a) *Solve UK poverty*, https://www.jrf.org.uk/solve-uk-poverty.

JRF (2016b) *UK Poverty: Causes, Costs and Solutions* #solveukpoverty, York: Joseph Rowntree Foundation, www.jrf.org.uk

Lansley, S. and Mack, J. (2015) *Breadline Britain: The rise of mass poverty*, London: OneWorld.

Layard, R. and Clark, D. (2014) *Thrive: The power of psychological therapy*, London: Penguin.

Levitas, R., Pantazis, C., Fahmy, E., Gordon, D., Lloyd, E. and Patsios, D. (2007) *The multi-dimensional analysis of social exclusion*, Bristol: University of Bristol.

Lynch, D. (2016) 'Hanging on: the stresses and strains of Britain's "just managing" families', *Briefing*, Resolution Foundation, http://www.resolutionfoundation.org/wp-content/uploads/2016/09/Hanging-On.pdf.

NatCen (National Centre for Social Research) (2016) *British Social Attitudes: Chapter Summary: Welfare*, http://www.bsa.natcen.ac.uk/latest-report/british-social-attitudes-33/welfare.aspx.

Ostry, J., Loungani, P. and Furcedi, D. (2016) 'Neoliberalism oversold?' *Finance and Development*, June, 38-41.

Picketty, T. (2013) *Capital in the twenty-first century*, Cambridge, MA: Belknap Press.

Portes, J. (2016) 'Troubled families – anatomy of a policy disaster', blog, http://notthetreasuryview.blogspot.co.uk/2016/10/troubled-families-anatomy-of-policy.html. Posted 16 October 2016.

Savage, M., Cunningham, N., Devine, F., Friedman, S., Laurison, D., McKenzie, L., Miles, A., Snee, H. and Wakeling, P. (2015) *Social class in the 21st Century*, London: Penguin Random House.

Sayer, A. (2015) *Why we can't afford the rich*, Bristol: Policy Press.

Social Metrics Commission (2016) Interim report, London: SMC.

Standing, G. (2011) *The precariat: The new dangerous class*, London: Bloomsbury.

Stiglitz, J. (2012) *The price of inequality*, London: Penguin.

Townsend, P. (1979) *Poverty in the United Kingdom*, Harmondsworth: Penguin.

Index

References to tables and figures are in *italics*

A

Abel-Smith, B. 27–8
Abramsky, S. 261
absolute poverty 45, *46*
access to local services *see* local services
alienation 347
arrears
  and destitution *103*, 104, 107
  and fuel poverty 235–6
  and housing *229*
  and health 277
  and social exclusion 280–1
  trends 254, *254*, 268, 272–7, *273*,
   276–7
  see also financial exclusion
at-risk-of-poverty (AROP) measures
  10–11
Atkinson, A. 360
austerity 46, 47–8, 96, 127–9, 204, 247,
  258
autonomy harms 248, 253–6, *254–5*, 263

B

B-SEM *see* Bristol Social Exclusion
  Matrix (B-SEM)
Bailey, N. 139, 160, 162, 163, 170, 338
banking services 269, 270, 271–2, *273*,
  278–9, 282–3
Barnes, M. 314
Barnett, P.A. 140
Beatty, T. 251
Beck, U. 246
behavioural agenda 352–4
Belfield, C. 250, 275–6
Besemer, K. 121, 139
borrowing money
  policy responses 269–70, 271
  and social exclusion 280–2
  and social networks 274, 281–2
  trends 254, 268, 272–8, *237–4*, *276–8*
  see also financial exclusion
Boyson, Rhodes 31
Bramley, G. 111, 121, 230, 233–4, 338
Brand, C. 60–1, *86–9*
Breadline Britain 29–32, 36, 42, 59, 217,
  219
Bristol Social Exclusion Matrix (B-SEM)
  2, 15–17, *16*, 60, 61, 162, 314–15,
  316–19

British Household Panel Survey (BHPS)
  97, 110, 314
Burchardt, T. 314

C

capabilities approach to deprivation 36,
  60
Carnegie Trust 305
Centre for Social Justice 48, 353, 356
Chamberlain, E. 293–4
Chase, E. 258
Child Poverty Act 2010 48, 49, *296*,
  355–6, 357
Child Poverty Strategy 271, 357
children
  child poverty 48–9, 271, 355–7
  child poverty measurement 48–9
  local services for 117–19, *118*, 120, *124*
  and necessities 4, *9*, *34*, *38*
choice discourse 247, 263
citizenship *see* civic and political
  engagement
civic and political engagement 179–96
  concept of 181–3
  determinants of 192–5, *194*
  impact of poverty on 187–96, *188–9*,
   191, *194*
  importance of 180
  indicators of *184*, 185–6
  and mental health 217–18, *218*
  and multidimensional analysis of social
   exclusion 311–35
  and political efficacy *184*, 185–6,
   190–2, *191*
  UN International Covenant on Civil
   and Political Rights 195
  understanding 182–7, *184*
civic voluntarism model 182, 185, 190,
  192
Coalition government (2010–15) 5,
  47–50, 247, 258, 271, 292
cohesiveness of society 351–2
Conservative government/party (2015)
  35, 49, 247, 292, 333, 356–7
  Thatcher years 31
Cribb, J. 250

D

Daly, M. 290
Davies, W. 291, 305

debt
  and destitution *103*, 103–4, 107
  and fuel poverty 235–6
  and health 277
  and housing *229*
  increasing 47
  linked to financial exclusion 268
  policy response to 269–71
  and social exclusion 280–1
  and social harm 254, 255
  trends 272–7, *273–4*, *276–7*
  see also financial exclusion
deprivation
  capabilities approach to 36
  deprivation index 28–9
  measuring 11–12
  trends 42–7, *43–6*
  wider views of 36–9
  see also living standards in UK
deprivation index 28–9
destitution
  defined 91, 97–8
  impact of 106
  levels of 98–102, *100*, *102*, 110–11
  measuring 97–8, 101, 110–11
  national and local estimates 100–2, *102*,
    110–11
  people affected by 99–100, *100*
  routes into *103*, 103–4, 107–8
  sources of support *105*, 105–6, 107
disadvantaged groups 346
disengagement 347
Dolan, P. 291

E

Edin, K. 255
Egerton, M. 140
employment 159–77
  defining exclusionary 161–3
  exclusionary occupations 164–5, *167*
  and health and well-being 168–70,
    169–70, 174–5, 210, 216–17
  importance of 159
  insecure 47, 159–60
  labour market progression 163, 164,
    176
  and living environment 173–5, *174*
  and mental health 216–17
  and multidimensional analysis of social
    exclusion 311–35
  and other dimensions of exclusion
    168–75, *169–70*, *172*, *174–5*
  risk of exclusionary employment
    163–7, *166–7*, 176
  and social participation and networks
    169, 171–3, *172*, 174–5
  and welfare systems 160
  workplace injury/illness *169*, 170, *170*,
    251, *252*

F

Fairclough, N. 313
financial exclusion 267–84
  banking services 269, 270, 271–2, *273*,
    278–9, 282–3
  concept of 267–8
  debt 47, *103*, 103–4, 107, *229*, 235–6,
    254–5, 268–71, 273–7, *273*, *274*,
    276–7
  and financial capability 283
  financial harm 253–4, *254*, 255
  and multidimensional analysis of social
    exclusion 311–35
  policy responses to 269–71, 283–4
  and social exclusion 280–1
  and social networks 281–2
  and societal trends 282–4
  subjective assessments of financial stress
    277–80, *278*, *280*
  trends in 271–3, *273*
financial harm 253–4, *254*, 255
financial stress, subjective assessment of
    277–80, *278*, *280*
fuel poverty 235–8, *237*, 251

G

Galbraith, J.K. 36
Gordon, D. 11, 78, 207
Gotlib, I.H. 140

H

Hall, P. 186
harm *see* social harm
Harrington, M. 181
Harrison, E. 262–3
health 203–19
  cause and effect of poverty 204
  and employment 168–70, *169–70*, 210,
    216–17
  and fuel poverty 236
  general health 205–11, *206*, *208–9*
  and inequalities 203–4
  and life satisfaction score 293
  and living environment 210–11, 217,
    251
  mental health 211–18
  and multidimensional analysis of social
    exclusion 311–35
  and past poverty 207, 209, *209*, 215
  and poverty 205–9, *208–9*, 212–15,
    213–14, 251
  and social exclusion 209–11, 215–18,
    218
  and social harm 248, 250–2, *252*
  and social participation 140–1, 153
  stress 253–6
  see also well-being
health selection hypothesis 204
Hick, R. 36, 37
home insurance 272, *273*

Households Below Average Incomes
39–40
housing 225–38
affordability of 226–8, *227*
and economic resources 71–2, *72*
and exclusionary employment *169*,
173–5, *174*
fuel poverty 235–8, *237*, 251
and health 210–11, 217, 251
home insurance 272, *273*
importance of 225
and mental health 217
and multidimensional analysis of social
exclusion 311–35
needs over time *230*, 230–2, *232*
owner occupation 228, 231–2, *232*,
325, *327*, 346
private renting 153, *169*, 173, *174*,
226–8, 231, *232*, 240, 278, *303*, *325*,
327, 349
and social participation 72–4, *73*
social renting 231–2, *232*, *233*, 278,
303, *325*, *327*
specific deprivations 228–32, *228–30*,
232
and welfare systems 233–4
see also neighbourhood
Human Rights Act 1998 181

I

income-based poverty measures 10–11,
39–42, *40*
inequality 345–6, 360
insurance 272, *273*

J

Joseph Rowntree Foundation 355, 359

K

Kohl, J. 69

L

labour market
deregulation of 159–60
and exclusionary employment 164–5,
167
progression in 163, *164*, 176
see also employment
Laflamme, L. 251–2
Lansley, S. 1, 3, 8, 10, 31, 42, 45, *46*, 47
Layard, R. 290
Leggett, W. 263
Levitas, R. 2, 14, 15, 16, 37, 313,
314–15
Lewis, J. 294
Li, Y. 186
Liddell, C. 251
life chances 333
lifestyle choice discourse 247, 263
Lister, R. 181, 256

living environment *see* housing;
neighbourhood
living standards in UK 57–80
architecture of the framework 60–5,
63–4, *86–9*
and different measures of poverty 74–8,
75–7
falling 346–7
key findings from framework 65–78,
66, *68–70*, *72–3*, *75–7*
measuring 60–5, *63–4*
methodology 62, 65
new conceptualisation of 58–60
objective vs subjective indicators 65–78
potential use of analytical tool 71–4,
72–3
and welfare typologies 69–71, *69–70*
'what we have' 65–8, *66*, *68*, 74–8,
75–7
local services 113–29
attitude to 114–15, *115*
and austerity 128–9
constraints 120–4, *124*, 127–8
geographical aspects 122–4, *124*, 128
importance of 113
and multidimensional analysis of social
exclusion 311–35
and social exclusion 125–7, *126*, 128
trends in usage and adequacy 36–7,
116–19, *116*, *118*
usage of *119*, 119–20, 127–8
Low, N. 180
Luthar, S. 246
Lynch, D. 349

M

Mack, J. 1, 3, 6, 8, 10, 22, 31, 42, 45,
46, 47
marketisation 344–5
Matthews, P. 139
measures of poverty *see* poverty measures
mental health
and civic and political engagement
217–18, *218*
and past poverty 215
and poverty 212–15, *213–14*
and social exclusion 215–18, *218*
and social harm 248, 250–2, *252*
and social participation 217–18, *218*
and stress 253–6
see also health; social harm
migrants, destitution *103*, 104, 105, *105*,
106
Minimum Income Standard (MIS) 41–2
misrecognition 256–60, *258*
Morris, C. 251
Mullan, K. 140

N

necessities
change over time 42–7, *43–6*

changing attitudes to 31–6, *32–4*, 42–3
and children 4, *9*, *34*, *38*
criticisms of approach 36–8
as deprivation measure 11–12
development of the concept 29–31
and public opinion 3, 6–10, *7–9*, 22–3,
   30–6, *32–4*, 41
and social activities 37–9, *38–9*, *45*
neighbourhood
   and access to local services 122–3, *124*
   and economic resources 71–2, *72*
   and exclusionary employment *169*,
      173–5, *174*
   satisfaction with 238–9, *239*
   and social participation 72–4, *73*
   see also housing; local services
New Labour 4–5, 31, 41, 48, 246,
   269–70, 292, 312–13
nudge theory 263

O

Offer, S. 139
Office of National Statistics (ONS) 61–2,
   292–3, 294, 295
othering 256
owner occupation 228, 231–2, *232*, *325*,
   327, 346

P

Pantazis, C. 207
Parry, G. 183
Payne, S. 216
Pemberton, S. 248
Piachaud, D. 28–9
policy strategies 359–60
   political engagement *see* civic and
      political engagement
poverty
   absolute 45, *46*
   centrality of 344
   damaging effects of 348
   defined 5–6
   policy strategies 359–60
   relationship with social exclusion
      330–2, *331–2*
   relative 1, 5–6, 29, 35, 45, *46*
   target setting 355–7
Poverty and Social Exclusion UK (PSE-
   UK) Survey
   context for 4–5
   history of 3–4
   importance of 1–3
   methodology of 22–3
   and poverty measures 5–17
   see also poverty studies
Poverty in the UK survey 28
poverty measures
   deprivation measures 11–12, *12*, 28–9
   deprivation trends 42–7, *43–6*
   destitution 97–8, 101, 110–11
   income-based 10–11, 39–42, *40*

lessons learnt 49
and living standards 10–14, *12–14*, 23
and measuring social exclusion 14–17,
   16, 37
PSE poverty measure 12–13, *13*
severe poverty 93–5
subjective poverty measures 13–14, *14*
survey methodology 22–3
see also living standards in UK;
   necessities
poverty studies 27–51
   and changing political backdrop 47–50
   and deprivation trends 42–7, *43–6*
   and income-based measures 39–42, *40*
   lessons learnt 49–51
   and necessities 29–37, 41, 42–7
   re-emergence of 27–9
   and wider views of deprivation 36–9
   see also Poverty and Social Exclusion UK
      (PSE-UK) Survey
powerlessness 253–6
precariat 348–50
private renting 153, *169*, 173, *174*,
   226–8, 231, *232*, 240, *278*, *303*, *325*,
   327, 349
PSE poverty measure 12–13, *13*
PSE-UK *see* Poverty and Social Exclusion
   UK (PSE-UK) Survey
public services *see* local services
public spending 5

Q

Quality of Life policy group 292

R

reciprocity 139
relational harms 248, 260–2, *261*
relative poverty 1, 5–6, 29, 35, 45, *46*
resilience discourse 246, 262–3
risk discourse 246, 262
Room, G. 312
rural areas 122, 238, *239*, *325*, *327*

S

Savage, M. 349
Schaeffer, L. 255
Scott, K. 291
self-employment 165
self-esteem 256–60
Sen, A. 29, 36, 60
Sennett, R. 259
services, access to *see* local services
severe poverty
   defined 91, 109–10
   growing concern of 92
   measuring 93–5
   survey evidence of 95–7, *96*
shame 139, *143*, 144, *147*, *151*, 258–60
social activities *see* social participation and
   support
social cohesion 351–2

social exclusion
  challenges facing government 334
  concept of 2, 14–15, 333–5, 350–1,
    357–9
  current policy 333–4
  domains and dimensions of 320–31,
    324–7, 329–32, 338–9, 340–1
  factor analysis 338–9, *340–1*
  indicators of 315–19, *316–19*
  measuring 14–17, *16*, 37, 314–19,
    316–19, 338–9, *340–1*, 358–9
  multidimensional analysis 311–35
  profiles of 322–8, *324–7*
  relationships between domains 328–30,
    329–30
  relationships with poverty 330–2,
    331–2, 350–1
social harm 245–63
  autonomy harms 248, 253–6, *254–5*,
    263
  choice discourse 247, 263
  concept of 248
  financial harm 253–4, *254, 255*
  injuries 251–2, *252*
  measuring 248–50
  methodology 249–50
  misrecognition 256–60, *258*
  and physical and mental well-being
    248, 250–2, *252*
  relational harms 248, 260–2, *261*
  resilience discourse 246, 262–3
  risk discourse 246, 262
  see also health; well-being
social participation and support 137–53
  constraints 142–4, *143*, 146–9, *146–7*,
    152–3
  and exclusionary employment *169*,
    171–3, *172*, 174–5
  and financial exclusion 281–2
  and health and well-being 140–1
  importance of 137–41, 152–3
  levels of participation 37–9, *38–9, 45*,
    145–9, 146–7
  and living environment 72–4, *73*
  and mental health 217–18, *218*
  and multidimensional analysis of social
    exclusion 311–35
  reciprocity 139
  and relational harms 260–2, *261*
  satisfaction with 149–52, *151*
  and social networks 141–5, *143*,
    149–52, *151, 169*, 171–3, *172*, 174–5,
    281–2
social renting 231–2, *232*, 233, *278, 303*,
  325, 327
social wage 113
Standing, G. 263
stigmatisation 59, 139, 144, 256–60
stress 253–6
subjective poverty measures 13–14, *14*

T
Taylor, C. 256
Taylor, E. 180
Taylor, M. 314
Titmuss, R. 50
Townsend, P. 3, 5–6, 27–9, 59, 138, 315,
  344

U
UK-LS *see* living standards in UK
UN International Covenant on Civil and
  Political Rights 195
Understanding Society survey 95, 109,
  230
unemployment 160, 210, 216–17
United Kingdom Living Standards index
  (UK-LS) *see* living standards in UK

V
Veenhoven, R. 71
Veit-Wilson, J. 61, 73
Verba, S. 182, 185, 190, 192
violence 252, *252*

W
Wacquant, L. 260
Walker, R. 258
Ward, S. 181–2
Welfare Reform and Work Act 2016
  271, 356–7
welfare typologies 69–71, *69–70*
well-being 289–306
  challenging contemporary framing of
    305–6
  Coalition government (2010–15) 48
  concept of 48, 290–2
  and exclusionary employment 168–70,
    169–70, 174–5
  inequality 293
  measuring 48, 60–2, 78–9, *86–8*,
    292–5
  and mental health 211–18
  and multidimensional analysis of social
    exclusion 311–35
  and poverty 295–300, *296–9*
  and social harm 248, 250–2, *252*
  and social participation 140–1, 153
  social profile of low satisfaction 300–5,
    301–3
  and welfare typologies 69–71, *69–70*
  see also health
Wendt, C. 69
WHO Commission on Social
  Determinants of Health 204
Wilkinson, R. 252
workplace injury/illness *169*, 170, *170*,
  251, *252*

Z
Zapf, W. 69, *69*, 71